In Search of Pedagogy
Volume II

In the **World Library of Educationalists,** international experts themselves compile career-long collections of what they judge to be their finest pieces – extracts from books, key articles, salient research findings, major theoretical and practical contributions – so the world can read them in a single manageable volume. Readers will be able to follow themes and strands of the topic and see how their work contributes to the development of the field.

Jerome S. Bruner is one of the most distinguished and influential psychologists of his generation. His theories about cognitive development dominate psychology around the world today, but it is in the field of education where his influence has been especially felt. In this two volume collection, Bruner has selected and assembled his most important writing about education. Volume I spans the 20 years from 1957 to 1978. Volume II takes us from 1979 to 2006.

Each volume starts with a specially written introduction by Bruner, in which he gives us an overview of his career and contextualizes his selection of papers. The articles and chapters that follow reveal the thinking, the concepts, and the empirical research that have made Bruner one of the most respected and cited educational authorities of our time. Through chapters from his best-selling books, his autobiography, and original journal articles, the reader can follow Bruner's thinking on questions such as: How do human beings presume to educate their young, the only species on earth that does so? Do our ways of "educating" conform to what we have been learning about learning during these past centuries? How can we adapt what we know in general about the nature of learning processes to fit modern conditions such as poverty, race discrimination, and urban life?

Professor Bruner writes about these matters with the grace and passion for which he has become world famous. He discusses the scientific issues alongside the political and "administrative" ones, and draws on his research findings and his active participation in projects on improving schooling in America, the UK, and Europe. This two-volume set is the ultimate guide to Jerome Bruner's most important and influential work, and is ideal for students and academics who want to be able to follow the development of his thinking over his incredible 70-year career.

Jerome S. Bruner is a University Professor, principally teaching in the School of Law, New York University, USA.

Contributors to the series include: Richard Aldrich, Stephen J. Ball, James A. Banks, Jerome S. Bruner, John Elliott, Elliot W. Eisner, Howard Gardner, John K. Gilbert, Ivor F. Goodson, David Labaree, John White, E. C. Wragg.

World Library of Educationalists Series

In Search of Pedagogy Volume II

The selected works of Jerome S. Bruner

Jerome S. Bruner

Routledge
Taylor & Francis Group

LONDON AND NEW YORK

First published 2006
by Routledge
2 Park Square, Milton Park, Abingdon, Oxon OX14 4RN

Simultaneously published in the USA and Canada
by Routledge
270 Madison Ave, New York, NY 10016

*Routledge is an imprint of the Taylor & Francis Group,
an informa business*

© 2006 Jerome S. Bruner

Typeset in Sabon by
Newgen Imaging Systems (P) Ltd, Chennai, India
Printed and bound in Great Britain by
TJ International Ltd, Padstow, Cornwall

British Library Cataloguing in Publication Data
A catalogue record for this book is available
from the British Library

Library of Congress Cataloging in Publication Data
A catalog record for this book has been requested

ISBN10: 0–415–38675–6 (hbk)
ISBN10: 0–415–38676–4 (pbk)
ISBN10: 0–415–38682–9 (hbk set)
ISBN10: 0–415–38689–6 (pbk set)

ISBN13: 978–0–415–38675–3 (hbk)
ISBN13: 978–0–415–38676–0 (pbk)
ISBN13: 978–0–415–38682–1 (hbk set)
ISBN13: 978–0–415–38689–0 (pbk set)

CONTENTS

ACKNOWLEDGMENTS

The following chapters have been reproduced with the kind permission of the respective journals

Bruner J. S. "Psychology and the image of man." *TLS*, December 17, Times Literary Supplement, 1976.

Bruner J. S. "Learning the mother tongue." *Human Nature*, 1, 42–49, Unesco, 1978.

Bruner, J. S. and David R. Olson, "Symbols and texts as tools of intellect." *Interchange*, 8, 1–15, Oxford Wolfson College: Clarendon Press, 1978.

Bruner J. S. "The language of education." *Social Research*, 49, New York: The New School for Social Research, 1982.

Bruner J. S. "Play, thought, and language." *Peabody Journal of Education*, 60, Nashville, TN: Lawrence Erlbaum Associates Inc, 1983.

Bruner J. S. "The meaning of educational reform." *National Association of Montessori Teachers Journal* (Special Edition: Schools of Thought: Pathways to Educational Reform), 16, 29–40, Education Commission of the States, 1991.

Bruner J. S. "Science education and teachers." *Journal of Science Education and Technology*, 1, 5–12, New York: Plenum Publishing Corporation, 1992.

Bruner J. S. "Celebrating divergence: Piaget and Vygotsky." *Human Development*, 10, 1–23, Basel: S. Karger, 1997.

Bruner J. S. Education Reform: A report card. *The Bulletin*, Winter 2003. Boston, MA: American Academy of Arts and Sciences.

Bruner J. S. "A short history of psychological theories of learning." *Daedalus*, Winter 2004. American Academy of Arts and Sciences.

The following chapters have been reproduced with the kind permission of the respective publishers

Bruner, J. S. "Learning how to do things with words." In J. S. Bruner and Alison Garton (eds) *Human Growth and Development: Wolfson College Lectures*. Oxford: Clarendon Press, 1976.

Bruner, J. S. "Play as a mode of construing the real." In S. L. Katz (ed.) *Proceedings of the Yale Conference on the International Year of the Child*, New Haven, CT: Yale University Press, 1979.

Bruner, J. S. "Care away from home." In J. S. Bruner (ed.) *Under Five in Britain*, London: Grant McIntyre, 1980.

Bruner, J. S. "How mind begins." In J. S. Bruner (ed.) *In Search of Mind: Essays in Autobiography*. New York: Harper & Row, 1983.

Bruner, J. S. "Narrative and paradigmatic modes of thought." In E. Eisner (ed.) *Learning and Teaching the Ways of Knowing* (Eighty-fourth Yearbook of the National Society for the Study of Education) Chicago, IL: University of Chicago Press, 1985.

Bruner, J. S. "Life as narrative." Originally published as *Discurso de Investidura doctor "honoris causa,"*. Madrid: Madrid University, 1987.

Bruner, J. S. "Folk pedagogy." In J. S. Bruner (ed.) *The Culture of Education*. Cambridge: Blackwells, 1996.

Bruner, J. S. "What are we learning about learning in schools?" In B. S. Kogan (ed.) *Common Schools, Uncommon Futures: A Working Consensus for School Renewal*, New York: Teachers College Press, 1997.

Bruner, J. S. "Infancy and culture: a story." In S. Chaiklin, M. Hedegaard, and U. Jensen (eds), *Activity Theory and Social Practice*. Denmark: Aarhus University Press, 1999.

Bruner, J. S. "Some reflections on education research." In E. Lagemann and L. Shulman (eds) *Issues in Educational Research: Problems and Possibilities*. San Francisco, CA: Jossey Bass, 1999.

Bruner, J. S. "Culture, mind, and narrative." *Enfance*, written especially for the present volume.

INTRODUCTION

Volume II, gathers together my education-related writings from 1978 to the present – quite different times than the earlier quarter century covered in Volume I. The world had indeed changed, and so had we all. For all that, my views about education and pedagogy seem, in retrospect at least, to have grown in a rather predictable way. No conversion experiences! Perhaps the most notable change in these more recent years has been a heightened interest in *how* cultures shape mental development. For it has become more evident to me over these years that it is not only *institutional* structures that matter – be they kinship, school, or even a system of law – but, as well, a culture's ways of telling stories about "life" as it is presumably lived: its forms of narrative. I have become convinced that there are two very different modes of mental activity, the narrative and the paradigmatic, and I shall have much more to say about these presently, particularly their implications for pedagogy.

My own personal life went through some marked changes during this period as well. Having left Harvard for Oxford early in the 1970s, still in my early forties, I was challenged by the "new" cultural perspectives I encountered – not only in Britain, but on the Continent as well, for I visited often. My decade abroad, I should also mention, was not all spent within the walls of the academy. For (as in America) I soon became involved in issues of public education and its improvement. You cannot venture far into that domain, obviously, without running headlong into struggles over power and privilege, as I noted in Volume I. And the papers collected in this second volume reflect that hard fact.

I returned to America at the end of the 1970s, first to familiar Harvard where I'd spent so many years before migrating to Oxford, and then to New York, my "home town," for I am a New Yorker born and bred. While at Oxford, I continued my work on the early years of life, particularly on the onset and early development of language and its impact on mental and social activity. But Oxford changed my ways of looking at these matters. Those were the latter years of the "linguistic turn" in Oxford philosophy, and the works of John Austin, Peter Strawson, the young Rom Harre, and the brilliantly skeptical Isaiah Berlin provided rich food for thought. It was their emphasis on Speech *Acts* rather than lexico-grammatical *structure* that was most appealing, particularly the shaping influence of communicative *intentions* in shaping both language use and lexico-grammatical structure.

My own research and writing began soon to reflect this new emphasis, particularly in studies of the role of mother-child interaction in language acquisition. And it was a short step from there to studying later interpersonal influences on language development – particularly in playgroup and nursery-school settings. I soon became involved with the Preschool Playgroup Association of Great Britain (the much loved "PPA"), and in due course with the Ministry of Education in London. Much of this work is detailed in Chapter 3, which reproduces a chapter from a book written shortly after my 1980 return to America, entitled *Under Five in Britain*.

The book was a "final report" on a project started shortly after my arrival in Britain, a product of that Oxford "Preschool Research Group" mentioned in Volume I. Recall that its long-term aim was to explore ways of strengthening preschool education in Britain, hopefully by advising Margaret Thatcher's Ministry of Education. Let it be said that our advice was not always welcome there! To begin with, our efforts were neither financed nor sponsored by the Ministry. Our "angel," rather, was Britain's Social Science Research Council, and our closest collaboration was with the beloved PPA, then under the brilliant and courageous leadership of Lady Plowden. The PPA's objective was then (and always has been) to help found and then to advise *locally* controlled preschool playgroups, better to assure the support of parents, townspeople, and local authorities. The Ministry in London saw itself (and perhaps always has) as the source of *national* standards and of auxilliary finanical support.

There was, in consequence, a well-mannered stand-offishness between the two, perhaps inevitably, particularly in Anglo-American cultures where centralized and localized conception of educational policy and practice so often clash. Chapter 3 deals more broadly with one aspect of this underlying conflict: how to deal with the puzzling implications of the modern need for "care away from home" in early childhood. Indeed, by the latter 1970s, more than a third of British women were employed outside the home, part-time or full, and the numbers were increasing at a faster rate than the growth of first-class care for the children of working mothers. Much of that growth was stimulated by those locally controlled "playgroups" encouraged and advised by Britain's PPA. Some observers, nonetheless, saw this growth as a threat to Britain's "middle-class strand of child care," as Tessa Blackstone astutely put it (Chapter 3). In some deeper sense, then, it was not just *educational* reform that was in progress, but some form of *cultural* "revolution" as well. In any case, Chapter 3 explores these issues, and while its details are obviously out of date, the general problems it poses are still with us, despite the fact that preschool is now, finally, an obligatory feature of British public education.

Perhaps it was this preschool venture that turned my interest increasingly to *how* cultures go about setting limits upon and, indeed, shaping mental development. Chapters 1 and 2 offer some of the theoretical background that underlies the concerns discussed in Chapter 3. The first of them describes the required interactive character of early language learning, and the second deals with the role of play in easing the child's way into "real-world" interaction.

Chapters 4 and 5 elaborate on these issues further, the former explores how particular languages predispose their speakers toward culturally dominant ways of framing and evaluating "realities." The latter deals with how play, thought, and language interact in the development of mental capacities. Chapter 5 was originally presented as an invited address before the annual meeting of the PPA of Great Britain in 1983 and represents something of a retrospect on my playgroup work while at Oxford.

In the years that followed, my interests refocussed, as I shall relate, but before I come to that, let me offer a general comment on this work relating to preschool education – whether "head starts," playgroups, or whatever. It eventually led in the mid-1990s to an invitation to serve as consultant to the remarkable preschools of the city of Reggio Emilia in Italy. I have served in that role ever since, mostly through late Spring visits, and with the astonishing assistance of e-mail. That lively city has even made me a *cittadino honorario* so that I might feel more at home there. Alas, in the course of my work there I have scracely written a published word about Reggio Emilia and its preschools, so I have nothing to include in this volume. But meanwhile, Reggio has moved ahead in providing summer training and demonstrations for preschool teachers – teachers in the thousands.

Does one ever know whether one's writings or one's advice makes a real difference in the ways of preschools, their teachers and in the lives of young children, whether in Reggio Emilia or anywhere? I suspect that the impact is principally through "consciousness raising," helping those involved directly in preschool education become conscious of new possibilities, new ways. A half century ago, as I mentioned in Volume I, there was virtually no real research on the early beginnings of human cognition: much ideology despite the absence of empirical work. I think those early research efforts, first at Harvard and then later at Oxford, had a real effect in making parents and educators aware of the possible advantages to be gained by "starting early." Indeed, as a witty friend of mine once put it, that work (and kindred work during those decades) may even have served to remind many of the self-evident fact that children really have "minds" in need of nurturing, and that one could discover through scientific research how best to provide such nurture.

I'm struck, in this regard, by something that happened as I was writing this very Introduction. I received a first-ever "Award" from the European Early Childhood Research Association, "In recognition of significant contributions to the field of Research in Early Childhood." I was vastly flattered, of course, but set thinking as well. I've finally concluded – and this is surely not false modesty – that the main contribution of this research has been to help make the "obvious" strange and challenging again. The "obvious," of course, is the proverbial "Well begun is half done." What our early gang of "baby researchers" did, I think, was to make the world aware that "well begun" is to be determined not only by custom, but by experimentation and empirical inquiry.

Now to the realignment of my interest since those earlier Harvard and Oxford years. I sketch it briefly and in condensed form in Chapter 6, whose origin was a 1984 Invited Address to the American Psychological Association on "Narrative and paradigmatic modes of thought." I had returned from Oxford to the New School.for Social Research at the beginning of the 1980s, rather at a loss about what next. I have always had strong literary interests, and while casting about for a next emphasis in my research, I came upon two issues of *Critical Inquiry* (Fall, 1980; Summer, 1981), edited by W. J. T. Mitchell, the literary critic. Their focus was on "narrative" and it contained articles by distinguished novelists, critics, philosophers (including my much admired friend Nelson Goodman), even one by a psychoanalyst. It led me to explore further the works of such then-emerging writers as Julian Barnes, Tzvetvan Todorov, Gérard Genette, Milan Kundera, and the short-tempered Jacques Derrida. I was particularly taken by the claims of the psychoanalyst Donald Spence who viewed the psychotherapeutic process as guided by narrative patterning as well as by psychodynamics.

My reflections on this reading finally led me to conclude that "There are two irreducible modes of cognitive functioning – or more simply, two modes of thought – each meriting the status of a 'natural kind.' Each provides a way of ordering experience, of constructing reality, and the two (though amenable to complementary use) are irreducible to each other" (see Chapter 7). Rather to my surprise, that paper, "Life as narrative," seemed to catch the imagination of human scientists and educators alike. In response, I soon found myself writing on the implications of narrative thinking for educational practice, even in mathematics teaching where a narrative version of a "math problem" often serves to guide a later mathematical-paradigmatic reformulation (Chapters 8 and 9).

Indeed, David Olson, the Canadian psychologist-educator, soon joined me in an attempt to explore how narrative created "folk pedagogies" that guided how we conceive of teaching (Chapter 10). In Chapter 11, there are further after-thoughts on this topic. Shortly after, I was provided the opportunity to reflect upon how this new turn of things bore on the then two prevailing theories of child development – Piaget's and Vygostsky's. I was invited to present a keynote address to a joint conference of the admirers of these two great scholars held in Geneva in 1996. It is contained in Chapter 12 of this volume. I have also included a related paper (Chapter 13) presented at an international conference in Copenhagen in 2003 on infancy studies. I entitled it "Infancy and culture: A story," for it seeks to illustrate how theories of infancy reflect a culture's "success" amd "trouble" stories about early childhood.

The next three chapters are about how changing learning theories have affected (or failed to affect) pedagogical theory and practice (Chapters 14–16). The last of these is the most inclusive, ranging from early associationist theories to modern structuralist ones. It appeared in the Winter 2004 issue of *Daedalus*, the journal of the highly respected American Academy of Arts and Science, in a number dedicated to learning theory and education, a topic not likely to have found its way into that publication a generation earlier. Times have indeed changed.

Chapter 17, the final chapter in this volume, takes a somewhat new cultural turn. It asks why narrative, wherever it appears, always requires (as Aristotle early noted) a troubling upset in expectations – the story's *peripeteia*, to use the classic term. Without it, somehow, there is no story, as it were. I had, of course, long argued that cultures pass on their distinctive ways through their stories. But I had never fully appreciated that the *peripeteiae* of stories also contain "warnings" about very particular and local threats to these culturally valued ways. The nature and origins of these disruptions and how they are coped with by a story's protagonists, indeed, even serve to define narrative's *genres*, as with Aristotle's unforgettable description of tragedy in the *Poetics*.

I presented this paper at a 2005 conference in Toulouse on their topic of "Culture and Mind." The thoughtful French social scientist, Daniel Sperber, remarked in his comments afterwards that he understood it as signalling a "shift from Bruner 1 to Bruner 2." The former, it seemed to him, was satisfied to recognize that, indeed, "Culture with a capital C" gave shape to our thoughts. "Bruner 2" now seemed to be insisting that the *local cultural setting* of a story and its *peripeteia* were what mattered most. For it is through local settings that cultures pass on their evaluative messages, and through the depiction of threats to these local expectations that it carries its "warnings." Particular acts of bravery, as it were, become comprehensible only when we understand the countervailing local temptations to cowardice that had to be overcome. Perhaps, Sperber remarked, psychologists will now begin attending to "culture in the small," to a *culture's* inherent local dynamics, rather than dealing with it in the large "with capital letters." For as Mise van der Rohe once said of architecture, so it is with culture: the truth is in the details. Or better: in the details as well.

We psychologists, I suspect, have indeed been slack in detailing context – whether in analyzing narratives or "real life" settings. Granted we have come some way from the rapid generalities of "culture-and-personality" theories. But hardly far enough. We would do well, I think, to bear this in mind in our discussion of how schools, classrooms, and teacher-pupil relations operate. But change is in the air, as the current work of such scholars as Michael Cole, James Wertsch, and others attest. I welcome it.

One final word – a reflection on how one should conceive of and study "education." I used to play squash weekly with my late friend, Francis Keppel, then Dean of the Graduate School of Education at Harvard. Early one Fall, in the opening weeks of the new term, he remarked as we were strolling back to our offices from the squash courts, that his job was really to help his faculty "reinvent" education each year, what education *could* be. But of course, that's not a job *just* for deans of schools of education or their faculties. It's a job for all of us. Indeed, God spare us a system in which education as the exclusive domain of professional educators! Or doing justice the domain of lawyers and judges alone. Or health in the care of doctors only.

And let us give up once for all the idea that "education" is only for the "young." I teach in the post-graduate School of Law at New York University. How do you prepare law students in their twenties and early thirties to master a system of law in a way that cultivates their understanding yet makes them effective litigators before a court of law? Indeed, how can justice not only be done but also *appear* to be done? These pose pedagogical questions that are as compelling as they are ancient. I recommend two books that struggle with them. They might be of some interest beyond the law. One of them is by Anthony Amsterdam and myself: *Minding the Law* (2001). A second is my own *Making Stories: Law, Literature, and Life* (2003).

CHAPTER 1

LEARNING HOW TO DO THINGS WITH WORDS

J. S. Bruner and Alison Garton (eds), *Human Growth and Development: Wolfson College Lectures* (1976), Oxford: Clarendon Press

I have had a share of good fortune in having been in attendance at the two preceding Wolfson Lectures in the series. Both of these lectures had the effect of altering the plans I had made for my own lecture – a somewhat unsettling if exhilarating experience. But it has provided me with an opportunity to reconsider the nature of language development from the different perspectives provided by my colleagues. I shall begin, then, by setting my own task, but before going on, I would like to double back over some of the major themes from earlier lectures, better to relate to them.

What I shall be discussing is how the human infant learns to use language in a fashion that meets the requirements of social living, as a member of a culture-using species. To succeed at such living requires far more than that one speak in well-formed sentences, or that one's words and sentences meet the requirements of reference and meaning and truth-testability. To speak, rather, requires that one's utterances meet criteria of conventional appropriateness or felicity not only with respect to the context in which speech occurs, but also to the acts of those with whom one is involved in dialogue. If I say 'Italy is a boot', the sentence may be well formed, but it is quite unclear whether it is true or false, useful or useless, appropriate or inappropriate unless you know to whom it is addressed and under what circumstances. To anyone conversant with the debates in linguistics and linguistic philosophy over the last fifteen years – ever since John Austin first introduced these matters – this will all have a very common-sense and familiar ring. But I should like to probe a bit further. I would like to explore in a more systematic empirical way how communicative functions are actually realized in the life of very young children and how the nature of early interaction between mother and child provides the matrix for the acquisition of language and, indeed, gives it its distinctive structure. Once one examines the detail of early language acquisition, how the child goes from prelinguistic communication to the early mastery of language, it will come as no surprise that, later, the question 'How would you feel about a breath of fresh air?' is not interpreted as inquiring into one's naïve theory of respiratory physiology but as an invitation to go for a walk.

Now let me double back briefly. The two previous speakers, considering the development of the child, have stressed the powerful role of interaction, of skills in maintaining a connection with adults and peers. Professor Hinde's emphasis was upon the structure of a primate group and how it affected the attachment of the young macaques he was investigating. For Professor Rutter, the establishment and maintenance of social connection was proposed as the buffering factor that prevented a poor family-social background from pressuring a child into an abnormal pattern of development. My own lecture will be in the same spirit, and I shall be emphasizing, as I noted, the manner in which the child's transition from his primate background into the use of the powerful cultural tool of language depends upon the development and, indeed, the exploitation of the mother–infant bond.

Models of language acquisition

I must now intone a necrology in order to set the background. It is for LAD, Chomsky's (1962) famous Language Acquisition Device, a veritable child prodigy that, for its ten years of sway, helped produce a new way of seeing what is involved in acquiring language – and thereby dug its own grave. LAD, for those not acquainted with it, was what linguists refer to as a discovery procedure, that is to say, a means of discovering the rules by which acceptable sentences in. a language are put together. Its input was a sample of the language, however encountered; its output was the set of syntactical rules that would generate all the well-formed sentences possible in the language and none that were ill-formed. The base of this recognition or discovery programme was presumed to be the language-learner's innate grasp of the universals of language. The local language being learned, according to this view, was merely a realization in local form of the syntatic universals of language. The innate grasp of these linguistic universals of language was assumed to be independent of any knowledge of the non-linguistic world. Nor, indeed, did the recognition programme require anything more than that the learner (or discoverer) of the language be a bystander: the spoken corpus of speech flowed round and into him, and the rules came out the other end. It did not require, for example, that he should already know what the language referred to – that he should have concepts about the real world being referred to – nor that the learner should have to enter into particular kinds of dialogue with the speakers of the language. As an enthusiastic David McNeill put it in 1970, 'The facts of language acquisition could not be as they are unless the concept of a sentence is available to children at the start of their learning.'

A decent necrologist should not carp. There are some features of LAD that are plainly and baldly wrong. The child's knowledge of language is deeply dependent upon a prior mastery of concepts about the world to which language will refer. Those of you who had the good fortune to hear Dr Eve Clark's paper in this series of lectures will appreciate to what degree this point is buttressed by data. It is also clear, and will hopefully be clearer before the hour is out, how dependent language acquisition is upon the nature of the interaction that takes place between child and mother. Being a witness at the feast of language is not enough of an exposure to assure acquisition. There must be contingent interaction. But for all that, Chomsky has taught us something that is profoundly important. It is that the child is equipped with some means for generating hypotheses about language that could not simply be the result of learning by association and reinforcement what words go with what in the presence of what things. There is indeed something pre-programmed about our language-acquiring capacity. But we need not, as my good friend George Miller once put it, vacillate between an impossible theory that assumes we learn everything by association (the facts deny it and the sheer arithmetic tells us that there would be just too much to learn even in a dozen lifetimes), and, on the other hand, a magical theory that says we already know about sentences before we start. There appears to be some readiness, rather, quickly to grasp certain rules for forming sentences, once we know what the world is about to which the sentences refer. And the rules that govern these sentences are neither imitated – for often one does not find them in the speech of the adults with whom the child is in contact – nor are they to be thought of as simple reflections of the world of concepts that the child has learned for dealing with the extra-linguistic environment, though they are plainly related. So though we come to bury LAD, we must not be so foolish as to withhold all praise.

I should like to propose an alternative. I shall propose that the child communicates before he has language. He does so in order to carry out certain functions that are vital to the species. These primitive communicative acts are effected by gesture, vocalization, and the exploitation of context. There is enough that is universal about such pre-lexico-grammatical communication to suggest that a part of it is innate, and easily triggered. There is a progressive development of these primitive procedures for communicating, and typically they are replaced by less primitive ones until eventually they are replaced by standard linguistic procedures. These progressive changes and procedural leaps are massively dependent upon the interaction of the mother (a word I shall use for 'caretaker' generally with a certain statistical licence) and the child. Mothers *teach* their children to speak, however willing the children may be, and I rather take their willingness to be part of the innate preparation for language. Washoe and Sarah and the other talking chimps (Brown, 1973), viewed closely, are *not* eager pupils.

The progressive changes that occur prelinguistically seem to provide precursors or, to use the stronger word, prerequisites for mastering lexico-grammatical speech. Concerned as I shall be this evening with the growth of reference and with the emergence of communication in support of joint action, I shall sketch roughly what I think may be involved in such development.

With respect to reference, it would seem that at the start there is a strong push present in the infant to share features of the sensory world with the mother and an equally strong push for the mother to orient to the features of the world to which the child is attending. At the outset, referential activity on the part of the child is very much captive of his needs: he tends to attend to what he wants and to show signs of wanting it. He has intentions and shows them, gesturally and vocally and in appropriate contexts. Mothers invariably interpret signs of desire as intentional communicative acts, and respond appropriately. As Ainsworth and Bell (1974) have shown, the mothers who respond to their children's vocalization during the first half of the first year end up in the last quarter of that year with children who cry less and vocalize and gesture more in a communicative way. In time, the sharing of attention is extended by both parties to matters that are sensorially vivid, or surprising or even rare. Indexing procedures, gestural and vocal, emerge and change. They very rarely have the character of being signs for specific events, but, as Harrison (1972) notes, they are procedures for noting which among several candidates for attention has in fact achieved the focus of attention – reaching towards, pointing, etc. Betimes, as the child develops models of what constitutes a steady-state environment, he begins to develop means of indicating objects and events that diverge from his theory or model of that world. It is interesting that a profound change in his signalling occurs at this point. And at the end of the first year there emerges yet another distinct step: the deep hypothesis that how one vocalizes affects how another's attention can be altered, that sounds and sound patterns have semanticity. At that point, a quite new means of generating hypotheses, strongly influenced by mother's utterances, comes into being. Something more like the philosopher's reference and less like ostension emerges. We shall see more of this in a moment.

With respect to action and joint action, let me sketch briefly what is at issue. For anybody to understand action, whether he be child or adult, requires the ability to categorize a flow of events in a complex, possibly natural way. Most human action has at least the following minimal set of categorizable components: the act itself, an agent, an object, a recipient of the action, an instrument, a locus, and a time marker. Or to say it in common sense, understanding the actions of human beings involves knowing what is done to what, by whom, to whom, where, by what instrument, and in what order. It is also necessary to distinguish its start and its finish. All of that is obvious, and I even suggested that it was 'natural', a moot point. In order to communicate in a way that makes possible joint action, there must be, at very least, some way of signalling the intent to act as well as indicating when one's intentions have been fulfilled, but that is scarcely enough for regulation. There must also be a way of indicating what the action is, who is to be the agent and who the recipient, on what object is the action to be performed and with what instrument, where and when. You will immediately recognize my list as being a parallel to the classic case grammar with categories like subject, verb, object, indirect object, locative, instrumentive, plus some form of time or tense marker. There must, as well, be some primitive mood marking procedure to distinguish indicating from commanding or requesting. For full effectiveness, there must be also some way of using these cases in a rule-bound order in an utterance that permits shifting and substitutability. For now I am the agent and you the recipient, and then you become the agent and I the recipient, and sometimes you use the instrument in a particular place, and sometimes I do but in a different place. And to be effective in signalling about the course of an action, I must be able to indicate when something should start and when it should stop – and not just the action as a whole, but those parts of it that are carried by an agent or recipient, are directed to particular objects with particular instruments, etc.

By this recounting of the obvious, I hope I have convinced you of three things. The first is that the course of action is nicely matched to the structure of speech: that the two are not arbitrarily related. The second is that it takes a fair amount of early learning to master the intricacies of joint action, even without language proper. And the third is that the conventions and procedures by which we represent the aspects of action – case grammar – do not naturally arise out of our mastery of joint action in and of itself, although a knowledge of the requirements of joint action would surely provide some powerful hints to the learner about the structure of the linguistic code. And perhaps there is a fourth matter of which you may have become convinced: that for human beings to share in an action, with or without the aid of regulatory language, there must be a considerable amount of intersubjective sharing between them, a sharing of many presuppositions that buffer the co-operating parties from shocked surprise – the classic problem of 'other minds'.

Joint attention and reference

We come now to the empirical part of our inquiry. We have been studying children from roughly three months of age to about their second birthday, visiting them in their homes fortnightly, and video-recording a half-hour of ordinary play-interaction between the mother and child, often much enriched by the presence of the experimenter. This has been supplemented by occasional video-recordings made by parents of behaviour they thought we should see and had not (often very valuable indeed) and by diary records. As a preliminary, we looked at six children in this way; more latterly we have concentrated on three, and I shall mostly be telling you about two of them. The object of the exercise was to explore how communication between the pairs was established before language proper came on the scene and how, gradually, the older modes of communication were replaced by more standard language. Our effort, as you may guess from what has already been said, was to explore how language was used, how its forms were made to serve functions. I shall concentrate as noted on two uses of communication: for referring and for carrying out joint action. I choose the two because they may stem from quite different roots, the one relating to the sharing of attention, the other to the management of complementary intentions. In each of them we shall see the emergence of communicative forms that have language-like properties which, at the opportune moment, and with the help of an adult, provide a clue for the child as to how to crack the linguistic code he is encountering. Let me say, before turning to these matters, that I shall not burden you with the dates or milestones at which new forms appear in language, but only with rough indications. It is the order of emergence that matters rather than absolute dates, for some children learn quickly and some less so, with no seeming effect on later performance. Nor is it evident that all children go through precisely the same order, for the literature on the subject and our own data suggest that order is dependent on context in some degree and reflects the individual progress of the mother–infant bond.

So let me turn first to the course of reference. The deep question about reference is how one individual manages to get another to share, attend to, zero in upon a topic that is occupying him. At the start, the child can neither reach nor point towards an object that he wants or is interested in. He can of course cry or fret, he can of course look at what interests him and that, as we shall see, stands him in good stead. As for the mother, her options are almost as limited as the child's: neither her vocalizations nor her gestures are able to accomplish the end of bringing the child's attention to objects or events she wishes to single out. From the mother's side, her first and most useful basis for sharing the child's 'referent' is her power of interference backed by her inevitable theory of what the child is intending. She inevitably interprets the child's actions as related to wants and needs: he cries because he is hungry or wet, stares at something because he wants to take possession of it or, simply, is 'fascinated by it'. She is not the least disturbed by the difficulty of philosophers in establishing communicative intent, how we know that others are attempting to send a message. She simply assumes it, and indeed, Macfarlane's (1974) study of greeting rituals of mothers towards their new-borns suggests that, from the start, the maternal theory is premised on the infant's acts being purposeful and his gestures and vocalizations being attempted communications. It is not surprising, then, that in a recent study by Collis and Schaffer (1975), the mother's line of regard follows the infant's line of regard virtually all the time that the two of them are together in an undistracted situation.

But perhaps more interesting is the infant's behaviour. Dr Michael Scaife (Scaife and Bruner, 1975) working in my laboratory here at Oxford has demonstrated that infants as young as four months of age will also follow the mother's line of regard outward to the surrounding environment. Some of you who have read about infantile egocentrism may be surprised, since this indicates that the child can use another axis than his own egocentric one to guide his orientation. Scaife now reports that there are indications that such gaze-following may occur even when the child is not interacting directly with, the adult involved. If two adults, conversing with each other, now look jointly in a convergent direction, and they are within the infant's range of attention, the infant's line of regard will often converge with theirs, all of this before the infant is much over a year.

Before the child begins his reaching career, his chief focus of attention is his mother's face, eye contact leading to smiles, vocalizations, and a variety of exchange manœuvres – of which more later. Once the child begins reaching for objects, however, *en face* contact between mother and child drops drastically from about 80 per cent of contact time to roughly 15 per cent. Characteristically at this stage the child either orients to the objects he reaches for, manipulates, and mouths, *or* he orients to the mother. At 5 months, for example, he never looks to the mother when his attempts to reach or to grasp an object fail. He is possessed by the one or the other and does not alternate. At this stage, the chief communicative feature of the child's object-directed activity is his first vocalization in the event of not being able to reach or get hold of something he wants.

Note the infant's typical reach at this stage. It is an effortful gesture reeking with intention to possess the object: hand and arm fully extended, fist opening and closing, body bent forward, mouth often working, eyes fixed on the object. This gestural effort, which gives no indication of being communicatively directed towards the mother, is none the less treated by her as communicatively intended, and the mother often obtains an object the child cannot reach. The child in time comes to expect this support.

By 8 months, usually, the child reaches metamorphoses. It becomes markedly less exigent, and he begins looking towards the mother while he is in the act of reaching for an object. The gesture is changing from an instrumental reach to something more like an indicator – a semi-extended arm, hand held somewhat angled upward, fingers no longer in grasp position, body no longer stretched fully forward. His gaze shifts from object to mother and back. He can now reach-for-real and reach-to-signal.

For a few months after the appearance of indicative reaching, there is a transitional phase. Indicative reaching becomes dissociated from the intention to get an object: it may signal only and the child may not even take an indicated object that is proffered. Indicative reaching increasingly extends outward to objects more remote spatially. And, characteristically, the mother conforms to the change, interpreting reaching as interest rather than as desire, and chatting accordingly to the child's reach.

What emerges next suggests that new forms of communication emerge initially to fulfil old functions, and then bring in new functions with them. It is the pure point, and in no sense is it gesturally like a reach – forefinger extended, the infant not reaching bodily forward. Initially it is used like an indicating reach. But like most new forms, pointing explodes in usage soon after first appearance. At 13 months, for example, six pure points were observed in Richard in a half-hour's play with his mother. At 14 months/3 weeks, in a holiday setting, 29 pure points occurred in the same time, and in a three-hour observation session the next day more than a hundred were observed. The objects selected as targets were governed by the following rules: (a) objects more than a metre distant and either novel or in an unexpected context, (b) neither novel nor unexpected, but a *picture* of a familiar object, (c) neither novel nor pictured, but imaginary or hypothetical, the locus being indicated (as pointing upward to the ceiling, and saying 'bird'). Though Richard had few words, he was working on the hypothesis that his uttered sounds had semanticity. And we should note, finally, that his pointing was typically accompanied by vocalization and by looking back at the interlocutor. Needless to say, his mother interprets his pointing much as she would interpret that of an adult.

I should like to note one thing particularly about the growth of pointing over the next months. It is extended to many things, as in indicating a choice between objects, aiding request, and so on. But it is also a prime instrument in the children we have studied for exploring the relation between objects and both their loci and possessors. At $15\frac{1}{2}$ months, the turning on of a light evokes in Richard a point towards the ceiling and 'li(ght)'; later the sound of an auto in the drive produces a point towards it and 'Daddy'; a picture of a wine bottle in a book results in a point to the bare dining table, etc. Such instances are invariably shared by glancing back at the adult. I mention this point here to make clear one matter that tends to be swamped by the implicit notion that referencing or indexing is somehow associative. I would urge that however associative it may be, such indicating behaviour also serves for generating and testing hypotheses, bringing objects (even if they are hypothetical) into the realm of discourse.

Again, the mother goes readily along with the new development and begins incorporating the child's pointing and his interest in semantic or naming sounds into dialogue. Indeed, it was the Russian linguist Shvachkin (1948) who noted that the child's interest in the phonemic system of the language coincided with his interest in naming. The mother's new medium for dialogue is 'book reading', and I have no doubt that cultures without picture books find suitable substitutes.

Looking at picture books together concentrates the joint attention of mother and infant upon highly compressed foci of attention.* They are foci of attention, moreover, that by virtue of being representations rather than real things eliminate competition from virtually all other response systems – notably the reaching system. In this sense, the medium is part of the message and it is not surprising that, at the earliest stage, the mother spends hard effort in getting the child into the medium – converting the book from an object to be banged and mauled into a carrier of pictures to be looked at. The end point of that enterprise is the establishment of a dialogue pattern, and that dialogue pattern, we shall see, is crucial to the development of labelling.

There is a period of several months – from a year to about fifteen months – when the mother's strategy seems to be devoted to getting the child to look, to point, and to vocalize at the right junctures in the dialogue exchanges between them. I fully agree with Catherine Snow and Ferguson (1977) that the establishment of such turn-taking, sequenced dialogue is a prerequisite for language acquisition. In Richard's case, the dialogue is controlled by three linguistic devices used by his mother in a highly predictable way. The first is the attentional vocative *Look* or some variant, appropriately accompanied by pointing. The second is what linguists call a 'Wh.. question' and it takes the form of some such question as 'What's that, Richard?' again often with a supporting point. Interrogatives are not novel: they constitute from a third to a half of the mother's utterances during the first year, a matter to which we shall return. The third device is labelling. During this stage and the next, described later, the mother's labels are always nominals – object words or proper names, never attributes or states or actions.

The dialogue exchanges initiated by one mother while she and Richard were looking at pictures together show the following striking regularity. Where there are two or more rounds in the exchange, in eight cases out of ten, the mother says 'Look' before either asking a 'Wh.. question' or proffering a label. If there are only 'Wh.. questions' and labels in the dialogue, the former precede the latter. The almost invariant order was from a vocative through a question to a realization of the label. And each was given in an appropriate context. And so, for example, 'Wh.. questions' follow only upon the child's gesture of pointing, and never upon a vocalization. A wide range of vocalizations are accepted in this first 'dialogue establishing' stage as appropriate responses to either an attentional vocative or a 'Wh.. question', however wide they may be of the standard lexical mark. If Richard responds with a vocalization, his mother's response to him in the great majority of cases is a label. Indeed, in mother-initiated dialogues, she responds to Richard's reaction in about 75 per cent of the instances, virtually always giving him full marks for an appropriate communities intent. A small point adds a sense of the meticulousness of this process. The mother makes a rather sharp distinction between those vocalizations of the child that slot into the dialogue routine of book-reading, and those that are out of place in the exchange. The latter vocalizations and gestures are treated by the mother as procedural – 'You like this book, don't you, Richard?' or 'Yes, it's very exciting, isn't it?' – such remarks always addressed to him directly and without reference to the book.

You will be quite right if you infer that the child initially is learning as much about the rules of dialogue as he is about lexical labels. But once the dialogue routine is fully established, at about 18 months or earlier, it becomes the scaffold upon which a new routine is established. For now the mother comes more sharply to distinguish between vocalizations that are 'acceptable' and those that are not. They are now in a 'shaping stage'. Mother tightens the criterion of acceptability as soon as there emerges a sign that the child is trying to produce words. I should warn you that my last sentence includes the whole field of developmental phonology, about which I know just enough to know the depth of my ignorance. But it is not the phonologist's theories that interest us here, but the mother's. When Richard slots in a sound that she thinks too wide of the mark, she will now respond not with a label, but with the question, 'What's that, Richard?' or with a highly emphasized label.

But to put it that way may seem to give too much of a role to pure imitation. Rather, what is notable is that the child does not learn his labels by directly and immediately imitating his mother's labellings. Compare the likelihood of Richard uttering a label during the second half of his second year of life under two conditions. One is in response to the mother's just previously uttered label. The other is in response to his mother's 'What's that?' question. The latter produces four times as many labels as the former. A label for the child is something that slots into a position in a dialogue. Indeed, 65 per cent of the labels uttered by Richard during this second half of the second year were said without the mother having uttered the label in that exchange. And an interesting sidelight: Richard responds to 'Wh.. questions' almost invariably on the first time round. Where he responds with a label in response to a mother's label, it almost invariably requires at least one repetition by his mother to get him to do so. We are not, as a species, copy-cats.

One regularity during this shaping phase suggests how crucial is the role of the mother in *teaching* language and its use. She is constantly establishing linguistic distinctions between the given and the new, the familiar and unfamiliar. She is, for example, much more likely to use 'What' questions with special intonation for pictures the child already knows and can label easily. New or less familiar pictures are labelled forthwith. The result is a presuppositional structure about what one asks about and what one tells.

Perhaps a good way to put the mother's pedagogical role in perspective is to look at it as providing a stabilizing scaffold during the two phases of label learning we have been exploring, a stabilizing scaffold with respect to which the child can vary his responses as his mastery permits. And so we find, for example, that the time devoted to dialogue exchange remains constant over these months. The number of turns in an exchange remains roughly the same. The repetition rate for labelling remains the same. The probability of the mother's reciprocating the child's response remains unchanged. And once the child is in the shaping stage, the mother's rate of confirming correct utterances remains about the same. All of these are controlled by the mother. They are what the child can count on in dialogue with her.

What things change over time, on the other hand, are almost all under the child's control. For one, there is a steady increase in the number of 'book reading' exchanges initiated by the child – from 0 per cent to 40 per cent. There is a steady increase in the child's rate of responding to gestural or verbal overtures initiated by the mother. He even learns to respond to repeated, rhetorical requests, ones he has just answered, suggesting that he is even learning to conform to the arbitrariness of pedagogical exchanges!

So much then for indexing and referencing. It is a very incomplete story as I have told it, but at least it gives a sense of how related acquisition is to use, to the functions of dialogue and exchange. We turn now to communication in support of joint action.

Joint action and grammar

I want very briefly to consider three issues. The first has to do with the precursors of mood in grammar. The second follows from this, as you will see, and concerns the differentiation of joint action into its parts, a matter I have already touched on briefly. And the third has to do with starting, regulating, and stopping joint action.

With respect to mood, let me underline one point made by Catherine Snow. She says: 'One of the most ubiquitous features of...mothers' speech at even the earliest age...[is that] they constantly talked about the child's wishes, needs, and intentions...as if the mother's task was to find out something that the baby already knew...Persistent crying was referred to...as if it reflected a very well-defined sense of agency; the babies' behaviour was never described as random and only rarely as a function of physiological variables. It was seen, just as adult behaviour was seen, as intended and intentional.' And, indeed, we know from the work of Ricks (1972) that mothers *can* recognize better than chance what general state produces their baby's cry and act accordingly. Not surprising then that the opening months of an infant's life reveal a transformation in the infant's crying from what may be called a demand mode – the standard biological cry, upped when untended to a very wide sound spectrum with a heavy load of high frequency, fricative noise – to a request mode in which energy is concentrated in a fundamental frequency, with the cry stopped for moments at a time in anticipation of response. Request crying gradually achieves stylization and differentiates to match the context – hunger fretting, wet fretting, and so on. By responding to these cries, as already noted, the mother recruits the child's vocalizations from demand and request into more subtle communicative patterns later in the opening year of life (Ainsworth and Bell, 1974). In mood, then, initial crying is transformed from an exigent demand into anticipatory request, with the infant leaving slots for the mother's response.

What follows is the beginning of exchange and turn-taking, first in vocalization and, then, with the growth of manipulative skill, in the exchange of objects – forerunners of dialogue. Danial Stern (1975) has shown exquisitely how mother–infant gesturing and vocalizing become synchronized in the opening months, and our own data on the first half year also show coordinated cycles of eye-contact and calling, controlled principally by the mother, of course, but increasingly by the infant. As the months go on he increasingly initiates acts of vocal exchange.

The exchanges then are imbedded in anticipatory body games like 'Round and Round the Garden' and 'This Little Pig', in which vocal exchanges are made contingent on the progress of an interaction and various highbrow technicalities like terminal marking are being mastered in earthy but useful ways.

The next step in interaction appears to be closer to the exchange of objects than to vocalization. Alison Garton, Eileen Caudill and I were led by this to some rather detailed studies of these exchanges, on the hunch that they might serve as a base for later dialogue. You may be amused by a few details of our expedition into the primitive economics of mother–infant exchange. If a market or economy reliable enough to sustain a steady flow of goods is established, can messages then develop that will flow in the same channels? Obviously, the first step for the mother is to get the infant to enter the game of taking objects, which need not concern us though it is of considerable interest as a chapter in the child's increasing capacity to mobilize not only a motoric response but also his attention upon the task (see Bruner, 1973). We have recorded sessions where more than 50 per cent of the time went into the perfecting of this skill. The mother characteristically assumes that the child *wants* the object; what he must be helped to do is *try*. The next step is getting the child to give the object back. If we define agency as handing off, and recipiency as receiving, the child's entry into the exchange economy is steady and striking and surprising to nobody (Figure 1.1). Concurrently, another unsurprising but important transition is taking place. Now the child rather than the mother alone begins *initiating* exchange episodes (Figure 1.2). As he gets into exchange, he is less reluctant to give up an object: his possession time before

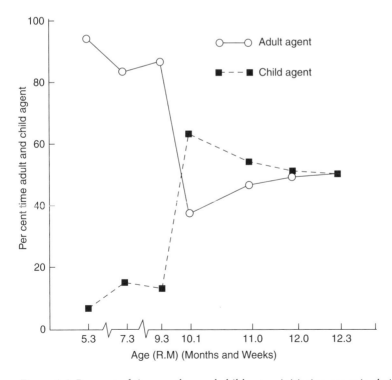

Figure 1.1 Per cent of time mother and child act as initiating agent in their exchanges.

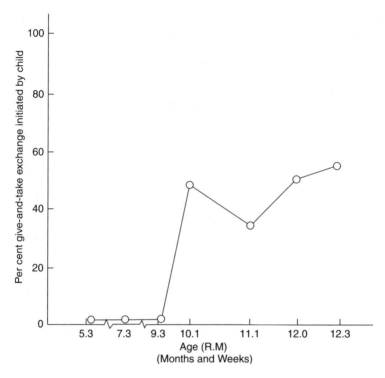

Figure 1.2 Per cent of give-and-take exchanges initiated by child at different ages.

handing off drops steadily (Figure 1.3). Indeed, by 13 months, the concept of exchange itself, rather than the joy of possession, seems to dominate his play. He is able now to enter a *round* of exchange involving two other persons and to maintain the direction of the exchange flow (Figure 1.4).

A stunning number of linguistic prerequisites is being mastered. Role shifting is one. Another is turn-taking. A third is the coordination of signalling and acting, for typical of these exchanges is that the child not only hands off the object in minimal time, but looks to the recipient's face as he does so. And should his turn be delayed, he will point, reach, vocalize, or label to get matters righted. Put in the metaphor of case grammar he is differentiating in action between agent and recipient, forming a primitive development of locus with deixis in the sense of knowing to whom the object is to be handed in multiple exchange, learning some elements of time marking in the sense of knowing who comes before and who after. And in addition to all this, the child has come not only to participate in exchanges initiated by others, but to initiate them himself.

I wish there were time and that we had the necessary data fully to describe the manner in which the child during this period learns not only how to start but how to stop the action. For it reveals much about the precursory development of negation as a linguistic form. Initially, negation amounts to no more than a resistive gesture directed towards an act directed to the child; the gesture becomes stylized and is used communicatively. In time, such proto-negation is extended to rejection of a specific object, or a specific agent carrying out an action with an object, or to a temporal misplacement (as in peekaboo) – all of these directed towards activity

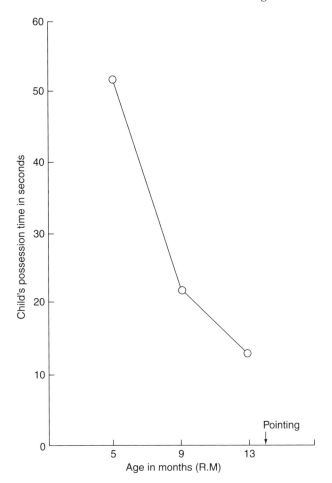

Figure 1.3 Child's possession time at different ages.

initiated by others. Eventually, by 15 months or thereabouts, the child comes to be able to apply negation to his own acts and will approach a forbidden object saying 'No, no' and/or shaking his head. The uses of negation suggest the features of the interaction that the child has singled out conceptually.

I cannot resist mentioning an interesting extension of negation that occurs after the developments just noted, around 17 months, for it suggests yet another instance of the way in which a communicative form is extended to new functions. The new functions in question are more referential than pragmatic. A transitional phase is the use of negation for some mix of unexpectedness and inappropriateness, as when Richard fails to be able to put a large object into a thin box and utters a well formed 'No'. In his record at that time, there are also instances in which the unexpected absence of an object from a container within which it was expected to be provokes a 'No'. And in the work of Bloom (1973), Greenfield and Smith (1976) and other investigators one finds instances of negation being used for disappearance of an object, self-produced as in 'all-gone' or otherwise produced,

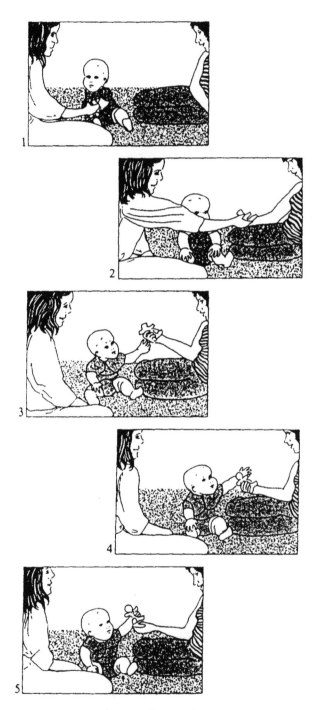

Figure 1.4 Child entering three-person exchange.

or for cessation of an event in the environment. And finally, well into the second year, negation is captured by the rules of dialogue where it can be used for dealing with the linguistic representation of an event contained in a question: 'Do you want more milk?' 'No.' There are various studies now in progress here at Oxford, on propositional negation by Roy Pea and on reference to absent or possible objects by Alison Gopnik, that will shed some light on how eventually negation takes its rightful place as an instrument in specifying truth functionality.

I hope it has been clear from this very brief account of the development of early communication as a means of regulating joint action that language does not grow solely from its own roots but is dependent upon interaction and particularly the interaction of intentions held by two consenting parties, one of them initially willing and able to give the other the benefit of the doubt.

Some unresolved issues

One last word. I have said very little indeed about the mastery of well-formedness, of grammatical speech *per se*. I am deeply cognizant of the truth of the statement that one cannot learn the rules of grammar from learning the concepts involved in managing interaction and managing joint attention. I have been tempted in the past by the hypothesis that there is something in the deployment of attention that leads naturally to the child adopting the rule that in sentences Agent comes before Action, and Action comes before Object, the near universal SVO order, but I think such assumptions about naturalness lull one into intellectual drowsiness. Rather, I would take the view that the child's knowledge of pre-linguistic communication, related as it is to a world of action and interaction, provides him with tell-tale clues for constructing and testing hypotheses about the meaning and structure of the discourse into which he quickly enters. He does, as LAD would have us believe, have a stunning capacity to infer and to generate rules, indeed to over-generalize them. His hypotheses are based in part upon his knowledge of the requirements of action and of interacting with another. His mother, the tutor, gives him every hint she can. And her hints are first-class, for she is not operating in the dark like a Turing machine. She knows from the start what it will take to speak the native language, and treats the child's efforts from the start as if he *were* a native speaker or were soon to be. Her predictions work out in 99.9 per cent of cases! There may indeed be something innate about the child's ability so swiftly to crack the linguistic code. But there is almost certainly something innate about the mother's ability to help him to do so.

Note

* The work on 'book-reading' has been done jointly with Dr Anat Ninio of The Hebrew University of Jerusalem.

References

Ainsworth, Mary D. and Bell, Sylvia M., 'Mother–infant interaction and the development of competence.' In K. Connolly and J. S. Bruner (eds), *The Growth of Competence*, London and New York: Academic Press, 1974.

Bloom, Lois, *One Word at a Time: The Use of Single Word Utterances Before Syntax*. The Hague: Mouton, 1973.

Brown, R., *A First Language: The Early Stages*. Cambridge, MA: Harvard University Press, 1973.

Bruner, J. S., 'Organisation of early skilled action.' *Child Development*, 44, 1–11, 1973.

Chomsky, N., 'Explanatory models in linguistics.' In E. Nagel, P. Suppes and A. Tarski (eds), *Logic, Methodology and the Philosophy of Science*. Stanford University Press, 1962.

Collis, G. and Schaffer, H. R., 'Synchronisation of visual attention in mother–infant pairs.' *Journal of Child Psychology and Psychiatry*, 16 (4), 315–20, 1975.

Greenfield, Patricia, M. and Smith, J. H., *The Structure of Communication in Early Language Development*. New York: Academic Press, 1976.

Harrison, B., *Meaning and Structure*. New York and London: Harper and Row, 1972.

MacFarlane, A., 'If a smile is so important.' *New Scientist*, 895, 164–6, 25 April 1974.

McNeill, D., *The Acquisition of Language: The Study of Developmental Psycholinguistics*. New York: Harper and Row, 1970.

Ricks, D. M., 'The beginnings of vocal communication in infants and autistic children.' Unpublished Doctorate of Medicine thesis, University of London, 1972.

Scaife, M. and Bruner, J. S., 'The capacity for joint visual attention in the infant.' *Nature*, 253 (5489), 265–6, 1975.

Shvachkin, N. Kh., 'The development of phonemic speech perception in early childhood.' *Izvestiya Akademii Pedagogcheskikh Nauk RSFSR*, 13, 101–32, 1948. Translated from Russian by E. Dernback and edited by D. I. Slobin, in C. A. Ferguson and D. I. Slobin (eds.), *Studies of Child Language Development*. New York: Holt, Rinehart and Winston, 91–127, 1973.

Snow, Catherine E. and Ferguson, C. A., *Talking to Children: Language Input and Acquisition*. Cambridge: Cambridge University Press, 1977.

Stern, D., Jaffe, J., Beebe, B., and Bennett, S., 'Vocalising in unison and in alternation: two modes of communication within the mother–infant dyad.' Paper presented at the Conference on Developmental Psycholinguistics and Communication Disorder, New York Academy of Sciences, New York, January 1975. (Published in *The Transactions of the New York Academy of Sciences*.)

CHAPTER 2

SYMBOLS AND TEXTS AS TOOLS OF INTELLECT

J. S. Bruner and David R. Olson, *Interchange* (1978), 8: 1–15,
Oxford Wolfson College: Clarendon Press

The child interacts with the world on many levels. He acts directly in the physical world of objects and events and in the social world of parents, siblings, and peers. On the basis of these interactions, he constructs a world of social relations, of roles and statuses, as well as of physical objects, events, and relationships. The worlds both of social relations and of physical events are shaped by the symbol system that is used to represent and interpret them. Our concern in this paper is with the impact on development of the symbol systems by which social and physical 'reality' are represented.

Much of a child's experience of both these worlds is formed and formalized through schooling. Whether for reasons of economy or effectiveness, schools have settled on teaching/learning out of the context of action and through media that are primarily symbolic and decontextualized. Schooling generally reflects a 'naive psychology' based on the general assumption that the effects of experience can be considered as knowledge, that knowledge is conscious, and that knowledge can be translated into words. Symmetrically, words can be translated into knowledge; hence, one can learn, that is, acquire knowledge, from being told. Thus teachers and texts are suitable means for transmitting such knowledge.

An auxiliary postulate of naive psychology is the belief that the difference between child and adult is the possession of knowledge. Therefore the chief mission is to impart knowledge.

These assumptions have several important and persisting effects on educational thought. First, they lend a certain blindness to the effects on learning of the *medium* of instruction as opposed to the knowledge content, a blindness that McLuhan (1964) has reminded us of. A second consequence is a deemphasis of, and a restricted conception of, the nature and development of *ability*. As the effects of experience were increasingly equated to the accumulation of knowledge, the nature of that experience was considered less and less important. Since knowledge was the test of accumulative experience, ability could be taken for granted: one had more or less ability for acquiring knowledge. Abilities were properties of the mind with which one was endowed genetically. Culture and experience were fruits of their operation rather than conditions for their development. The result of this type of interpretation was to downgrade the task of cultivating abilities in students, except for those abilities that led to the accumulation of decontextualized knowledge.

Critics have, of course, long attacked overemphasis upon the acquisition of knowledge. For Dewey (1916) experience was twofold – 'trying' and 'undergoing' – the former requiring some activity and a recognition of the consequences that ensued. Such twofold experience, wisely deployed, would result, Dewey argued, in the natural and integrated development of knowledge, skills, and thinking. Schooling, he argued, attempts to develop the three independently of each other and with little regard for the experience of which they are products. No surprise, then, that schools frequently failed to achieve any of them. Dewey's revised conception of the relationship between experience and knowledge reappears in the current attempts at education reform, which emphasize the role of process instead of content, or more specifically of activity, participation, and experience instead of the acquisition of factual information (Bruner, 1960; *Living and Learning*, 1968). The contemporary critic and Dewey alike would attack the assumption that knowledge is acquired independently of the means of instruction and independently of the intended uses to which knowledge is to be put.

Most educational reform has been opposed to 'accumulative' schooling where learning is divorced from action, carried principally by a formal text accompanied by the recitation method designed to 'cover a subject' – with reformers ranging over time from Rousseau to Comenius to Montessori to Piaget to Bruner to Illich. But it is hard to do as one preaches. Comenius, for example, is best known for introducing pictures into children's textbooks and was the author of over 100 texts for children. While, as Piaget (1957) acknowledges, Comenius as a theorist advocated active intellectual processing, his practical innovations succeeding in doing the exact opposite – namely, making education more passive, verbal, and text-bound.

But may it not be that emphasis upon knowledge conveyed by text creates its own distinctive set of skills, skills related to translating experience into symbol systems and translating symbolic descriptions into vicarious experience? Perhaps the fervour of reformers from Comenius to Piaget has obscured the fact that the modern school may have been unwittingly creating a new type of intellectual competence while claiming something quite different in response to the critics' attack. They may have been doing so because there is no alternative once text becomes the dominant medium for transmitting knowledge. That skill may be nothing less than verbal intelligence.

Knowledge and activity

To see this clearly requires that we go back and examine the relation of knowledge to human activity. Living systems have an integrity of their own; they have commerce with the environment on their own terms, selecting from the environment and building representations of that environment as required for survival and fulfilment. A picture of physical reality is constructed by selective mediation. It is a point that is explicit and central to Piaget's (1971) conception of adaptive behaviour in general and of intelligence in particular: objects and events are not passively recorded but rather acted upon and perceived in terms of action performed.

What does this imply about the nature and consequence of experience? As we have said, we have a picture of reality that is biased by or coded in terms of our actions on it; knowledge is always mediated or specified through some form of human activity. Any knowledge acquired through any such activity, however, has two facets: information about the *world* and information about the *activity* used in gaining knowledge. In an aphorism: from sitting on chairs one learns both about 'chairs' and about 'sitting.' This distinction is reflected in ordinary language in the terms *knowledge* and *skill*. There are, therefore, two types of invariants that are specified through experience. The set of features that are more or less invariant across different activities may be considered as the structural or invariant features of *objects* and *events*. Similarly the set of operations or constituent acts held invariant when performed across different objects and events may be considered as the structural basis of the activities themselves – what we call *skills* and *abilities*. It is our hypothesis that 'knowledge' reflects the invariants in the natural and social environment, while 'skills' or 'abilities' reflect the structure of the medium or per-formatory domain in which various activities are carried out. Obviously, major value must be attributed to both facets of experience. More important to our pre-sent concern, 'gaining knowledge from text' also cultivates special (if sometimes distorted) abilities, and we shall return to these later.

Consider more specifically how knowledge and skills are related in practice. The performance of any act may be considered a sequence of decision points, each involving a set of alternatives. These decision points are specified jointly by the intention motivating the act and the structure of the medium or environment in which the act occurs. An effective performance requires that the actor have knowl-edge available that permits him to choose between these alternatives. In making choices, he must 'analyse the task' in the sense of keeping in mind not only the end state he is seeking but also where he is with respect to that end state. He must assess the means while keeping the end criteria in mind. It is a universal routine – in love, in war, in writing a paragraph or solving an equation, or, indeed, in managing to get hold of objects during the initial phases of infant mastery of reaching.

From this point of view, mastery depends on both the acquisition of knowledge required for choosing between alternatives and the acquisition of skills or proce-dures for utilizing that knowledge in attaining some goal. The most obvious way to acquire such knowledge is through active attempts to achieve various goals in a variety of domains, that is, by learning through one's own direct contingent experience. In virtually all accounts of learning, the consequence of an act (that is, the reinforcement) is postulated as the major source of both skill and knowledge.

Knowledge and symbolic activity

But there are other ways to acquire knowledge. From seeing a person struggle with a load, one can make some estimate of its weight. That is, one can experience vicar-iously or mediately. Psychological studies have repeatedly shown that learning can occur when neither of the primary conditions for learning through contingent expe-rience – self-initiated action or direct knowledge of its results – is fulfilled, through modelling or observational learning (Bandura, 1969; Herbert & Harsh, 1944).

A second alternative to learning directly is through symbolically coded information transmitted through the textual media, such as the spoken or printed word, film, or diagram. Vygotsky (1962) and Bruner (1966) have emphasized the manner in which language provides a highly specialized means for teaching and learn-ing with minimal reference either to the normal context or to the forms of action to which such knowledge would normally be tied. Language thus provides a major means for acquiring knowledge without regard for its usefulness in a particular line of action. Instruction through language splits knowledge from practical action.

There are, then, three modes of experiencing which map onto the three forms of representation discussed earlier by Bruner (1966) as enactive, iconic, and symbolic: the first related to knowledge from direct action, the second to imitation of and observation of models, and the third to knowledge specified in a symbol system. These three models of experience probably map onto evolutionary development (Bruner, 1972). While all animals learn from contingent experience, primates are distinctive in their capacity for learning by observation – there is an enormous amount of observation of adult behaviour by the young with incorporation of what has been learned into a pattern of play. The human species is, of course, marked by its capacity to extract knowledge from coded experience-in-text.

We have, as already noted, three principal means of interacting with and constructing the world: by acting upon it, by observing it, and by learning by being told or reading about it. We have conjectured elsewhere (Olson & Bruner, 1974; Olson, 1976) that while these different forms of experience converge and overlap representationally in terms of the knowledge they convey, they *diverge* as to the skills they demand and develop.

Consider, then, the nature of mental skills associated with gaining knowledge through text. What are the special skills involved in extracting this knowledge? How do they differ from those involved in learning from direct action or from observation?

What of direct action? The skills remain implicit, rendered invisible by our habitual focus on the concrete course and outcome of the activity. As we examine a rock by turning it over in our hand, we are aware of the fact that we acquire knowledge about the rock, but the skilled manipulation that gives rise to the observational knowledge of the rock is 'transparent', unnoticed. Or our attention is upon the ball when we kick it, not on the act of kicking, though we learn about kicking. Similarly, if we examine the general skills that make up our cognitive or intellectual abilities, we see that they possess the same property. There is an explicit focus on state or object, while process remains implicit or tacit. Yet verbal, numerical, and spatial abilities, we suggest, reflect skills achieved in attending to words, numbers, and displays in space.

It is this consideration, perhaps, that led Piaget to insist that the initial structure of any knowledge must be thought of as growing in some major way out of the 'internalization of activity'. Overt activities – rotating an object in space, lining up objects to form a straight line, ordering objects serially – come to be internalized or carried out mentally. For the very young child an object is a constituent of a form of action. In time an increasingly economical representation of these action/object schemas develops. An object manipulated for various ends comes eventually to be represented as a single object. The child develops structures of the whole that come to stand for the objects, their relations, and their logical properties.

But operations specified by Piaget are largely those appropriate to the manipulation of real objects in the physical environment. His basic premise is that their internalization not only produces the groundwork for logic but assures that logic will be appropriate to the structure of the world one experiences. But internalized activity related to the physical environment does not begin to describe the range of activities of the human mind. And such activity certainly does not give a picture of the skills involved in extracting knowledge or vicarious experience from 'text'.

Specifically, this account bypasses how we learn to cope with the cultural or symbolic environment. 'Learning from the culture', like learning from physical activities, involves the act of extracting information to decide among alternatives; it also involves skilled procedures and it results, finally, in a biased knowledge of reality. Sentences, for example, because they are always *about* something, either elaborate upon or are assimilated to the general structures of knowledge developed by other forms of experience. But the skills involved in using sentences are unique to that particular mode of expression and communication. The skillful use of any symbol system involves the mastery of both its structure and its rules for transformation. Once mastered, these skills may be considered to be forms of 'intelligence', primarily because the range of their applicability is virtually open. But as we shall see, it is a specialized form of intelligence.

Symbols: the tools of the intellect

Our argument is that an important part of intellectual activity is the direct consequence of our learning to reflect consciously upon the structures implicit in our native language, a form of reflection made possible to a large extent by the invention of writing.

Before we examine this hypothesis, we must characterize the role of symbols in human cognition generally. The far limit of the range of applicability of symbols is seen in the arts, which may be viewed as the boldest attempt to test the combinatorial limits of a symbol system. Play has much the same function (Bruner, 1972). Such expanded symbol systems are then applied to nature, if appropriate, for theoretical and practical ends. In this way our use of symbol systems, like our practical activities, results in a version of 'reality' appropriate to that activity. There is no one fixed objective reality to 'copy' or to 'imitate' by means of our symbol systems, but only a construction of that reality in terms of the kinds of practical and symbolic activities in which we engage. Thus, Nelson Goodman (1968, p. 6) is led to say that 'the world is as many ways as it can be truly described.' Similarly, Cézanne pointed out that the artist does not copy the world in his medium but instead re-creates it in terms of the structure of that medium.

Man in culture, like the artist, is in continual search for ways of applying symbol systems to ordinary experience. The translation of experience into any one symbol system will make the knowledge more suitable for some tasks than for others, and each such system will possess distinctive possibilities for generating valid representations. A historical account of the intellectual roots of the Industrial Revolution may be of a different medium but not necessarily of greater validity than Yeats's famous epigram:

> Locke sank into a swoon;
> The garden died;
> God took the spinning jenny
> Out of his side.

Yet a scientific and technological culture such as ours has put a premium on translation into a few symbol systems – ordinary language as specialized in the arts and the sciences; logical and mathematical statements; and spatial systems such as maps, models, graphs, and geometry. We will confine our attention to a few of these.

We would argue that it is not only scholars, poets, and scientists who seek constantly to cast experience into symbolic codes. Our conjecture is that there is a form of metaprocessing that involves the constant reorganization of what we know into the categories provided by symbol systems. It is a matter of 'going over one's past experiences to see what they yield' (Dewey, 1916), both for the purpose of facilitating the communication that is required for the survival of the culture and for the purpose of rendering one's own personal experience comprehensible. This form of metaprocessing, of re-presenting knowledge in various symbolic forms, comes into play in many circumstances – in failed communication, in our inability to interpret what we encounter, when we run into interpersonal conflict, when we run into difficulties in attempting to carry out an action or solve a problem. In particular, it is systematically recruited in formal schooling in learning rules, formulae, definitions, algorithms, and the like. It is involved in all translations of specific experience into general accounts. It can occur in any mode, but it is best represented by the poet's or essayist's search for the appropriate phrase or the summarizing aphorism and by the scientist's search for the most general mathematical statement.

It is this re-presentation of knowledge in various symbolic forms that is responsible for the radical economization of the experience of the tribe or nation in a few great myths and, more generally, for the world view implicit in one's native language. It should not, however, be assumed that this is simply an issue of translation. It more generally requires that the creator have more information available than was required for the ordinary direct experience of that event. This greater demand can easily be seen when one attempts to draw a map of a territory that one knows quite well or when one tries to give a description or make a drawing of a friend's appearance. One looks at or otherwise experiences an event somewhat differently when dealing with it for different purposes; that is no less true when those activities are different symbolic activities than when they are different physical activities. It follows that in drawing an object, one requires somewhat different information about it than one does for manipulating or describing it. In this sense, media of expression and communication are *exploratory devices* – a point of immense importance to an understanding of the child's acquisition of knowledge.

Finally, recording knowledge into symbolic forms, as we have seen, organizes knowledge into a form that is particularly appropriate for educational purposes. Since it is often difficult for the child (or the adult, for that matter) to see causal linkages between events widely separated in time, he is greatly aided by a symbolic account of those events. Such accounts, whether in the form of an abstract equation, a principle, a noiseless exemplar, or an appropriate model, have the effect of 'time-binding' and 'culture-binding' and thereby surpassing ordinary individual experience. The same accounts that render experience comprehensible render it instructable.

The very success of textlike symbolic representations may blind us to their limitations. As one kind of summary of experience, they are plainly powerful. But to substitute text for either experience or observation is plainly absurd. It is not just that summary texts can be memorized with no understanding. That is a conspicuous failure we can guard against. Rather, even at best, with reflection on text, the nature of the act of knowing is different, as well as the data on which knowledge is based. Indeed, textual acquaintance with knowledge may even interfere with direct experience. Aphorisms, formulae, vocabulary items, may serve as educational markers that trap experience into excessive assimilation. The 'cure' is usually thought to be a judicious mix of lecture, practical experience in the lab or life, and appropriate observation. And this often has a good effect in exacting cognitive conflict and consequent reflection. But we know precious little, theoretically or pedagogically, about the distinctive properties of the knowledge acquired through action, observation, or text, or about the distinctive patterns of skill for which those forms of knowledge are appropriate. Further, we have neither a good theory nor a good practical procedure for relating the knowledge acquired by means of action, observation, and text to the new problems and situations confronted in out-of-school contexts. This is the problem of transfer and, it seems to us, is a major area of neglect, not only in education but in the behavioural sciences generally.

We shall, in what follows, consider the distinctive properties of the knowledge and skills that are recruited and developed in learning from one symbolic form – namely, studying and producing *written* texts.

From meanings to definitions

Children are fluent speakers of a natural language. By school age, they have mastered the major phonological, morphological, and syntactic properties of their language. The meanings in their language, however, appear to change with development and with schooling. Recall the famous description of child language given by Vygotsky (1962):

> The word, to the child, is an integral part of the object it denotes. Such a conception seems to be characteristic of primitive linguistic consciousness. We all know the old story about the rustic who said he wasn't surprised that savants with all their instruments could figure out the size of the stars and their course – what baffled him was how they found out their names. Simple experiments show that pre-school children 'explain' the names of objects by their attributes. According to them, an animal is called a 'cow' because it has horns, 'cow' because its horns are still small, 'dog' because it is small and has no horns; an object is called 'car' because it is not an animal. When asked whether one could interchange the names of objects, for instance, call a cow 'ink' and ink 'cow', children will answer no, 'because ink is used for writing and the cow gives milk.' An exchange of names would mean an exchange of characteristic features, so inseparable is the connection between them in the child's mind. . . . We can see how difficult it is for children to separate the name of an object from its attributes, which cling to the name when it is transferred, like possessions following their owner.
>
> (pp. 128–129)

Not only are words and objects poorly differentiated; the preschool child has little awareness of his own knowledge of words. When asked 'What is the word for this?' while a shoe is pointed at, for example the child will simply look puzzled. If the question is reformulated as 'What is this?' the child will reply, 'A shoe'. The child's attention is focused upon the objects designated by the words, not the words themselves. Interestingly Lord (1971) in his study of oral poets in Yugoslavia found they had little conception of a word: 'When asked what a word is he will reply that he does not know, or he will give a sound group which may vary in length from what we call a word to an entire line of poetry or even an entire song' (p. 25).

When asked for the meanings of words he is using, a child will often list functions or the salient properties of the object named. An apple is 'to eat' or 'something round and red'. Yet by the age of 7 or 8 children have begun to see not only the relation between words and things but also the relation between the words themselves (e.g., opposites) and to give definitions by relating words to other words in the lexicon. An apple (to one child) became 'a domesticated fruit'. This transition from words/things to words/words coincides with the well-known shift in word associations called the syntagmatic-paradigmatic shift. Young children given one word and asked to state another pick a word which could complete a known action (e.g., horse-ride; house-play; car-drive), while older, school-age children given the same word respond in terms of their structural relation to other words in the lexicon (e.g., horse-cow; dog-animal; car-truck).

With development and perhaps only with development in a literate culture, the language comes to be an autonomous domain in which 'meaning' in the dictionary sense can be established. As de Laguna (1927, p. 91) insisted, child language is initially context dependent – 'to understand what baby is saying it is necessary to see what baby is doing' – while adult language moves towards internal, decontextualized, and formalized meaning. In Grice's (1967) terms, speakers of a written language and particularly readers of written text come to see that words and sentences have a meaning *per se*, the sentence meaning, which may be somewhat different from the speaker's meaning, what a speaker means by that word or sentence on any particular occasion. 'All men are equal' written by Thomas Jefferson would have the same sentence meaning but a different speaker's meaning from the identical sentence if written by Erica Jong. This development, we suggest, is one of the unintended consequences of literacy.

The Greeks believed their provision of definitions such as 'a circle is a locus of points equidistant from a fixed point' was an intellectual achievement beyond common sense. They transcended conventional 'meaning' and achieved formal definition. Decontextualized meaning is not quite formal definition, but it is a step on the way. Speaking a written language, as Greenfield (1972) puts it, imposes some of the same 'decontextualizing' effect achieved by definition. Studies of the cognitive processes of unschooled subjects show how this works. Luria (1971) and more recently Scribner and Cole (1973) asked both literate and non-literate farmers 'Which pictures belong together?' showing them a set of four pictures – saw, axe, shovel, piece of wood. The more literate collectivized farmers clustered them in terms of the 'abstract' category, tools. Traditional peasant farmers, on the other hand, clustered them on the basis of concrete, practical actions – 'it is necessary to fell the tree, then to cut it up, and the shovel does not relate to that, it is just needed in the garden' (p. 268). The fact that we take the first answer as indicative of higher degree of intelligence reflects the bias of our-view of intelligence. Our suggestion, rather, is that these indicate different forms of intelligence, the former reflecting something about the nature of the medium called a written language.

Why it is that meanings tend towards definitions under the impact of literacy requires a brief look at the nature of definitions. The primary feature of a definition is the use of an existential copula 'is a'; 'A rabbit is an animal'; and it may well be that in text, in literate usage generally, copulas become more crucial. Have lock (1973), for example, has argued that one of the chief activities of the post-Homeric *writers* (recall that Homer was a preliterate, oral poet) was the construction of 'a program of principles' to replace the 'panorama of happenings' of the Homeric epics. To illustrate, in an oral culture the 'concept' of courage is described in the temporally ordered narrative accounts of the deeds of the gods, whereas for the literate classical Greeks it is defined in the non-temporal, logical principle 'Courage consists in a rational understanding of what is to be feared.' Homeric Greeks rarely used definitions or existential verbs. Their emergence coincided with the development of the phonetic alphabet, and their use seems endemic to setting forth and reflecting on written statements. Here is how Havelock states his case:

> The syntax of memorised rhythmic speech is therefore not friendly to that type of statement which says 'The angles of a triangle are equal to two right angles' or 'Courage consists in a rational understanding of what is to be feared or not feared.' It is not friendly precisely to that kind of statement which the Socratic dialectic was later to demand, a statement which prefers its subject to be a concept rather than a person, and its verb to be an 'is' verb rather than a 'doing' verb. Neither principles nor laws nor formulas are amenable to a syntax which is orally memorisable. But persons and events that act or happen are amenable. If a thing always is so, or is meant to be so (or not so), it is not

a living (or dead) man or woman, and it is not to be discovered in action or situation. It is not a 'happening'. Orally memorised verse is couched in the contingent: it deals in a panorama of happenings, not a programme of principles.'

(p. 51)

Greenfield (1972) in her studies of the Wolof of West Africa also reported an absence of copula verbs, what we have called existential verbs of being, among those without schooling. While both the schooled and the unschooled used some superordinate terms for grouping sets of objects, the descriptions of the groupings by the schooled Wolf contained the copula – 'These *are* red' – while those of the unschooled omitted it. Interestingly, too, some studies of non-standard dialects of English also report a tendency to omit the copula (Bailey, 1968; Bereiter & Engleman, 1966; Labov, 1970; Stewart, 1966), a finding suggesting that 'standard' English has a particular bias towards a written language. By the same token, the copula appears later than other verbs in the language acquisition of English-speaking children. The evidence then suggests that devices such as the copula 'is' are particularly useful in literate contexts, useful in an attempt to define terms more formally, without reference to extra-linguistic context.

Not surprising, then, that in our literate culture intelligence is usually characterized as involving 'abstraction' and 'rationality' rather than practical wit. Thus, for a good test score, a word is defined in terms of other, preferably superordinate terms (a pen is a 'writing instrument') rather than by pointing to an exemplar; an apple and a peach alike are 'fruit,' not 'to eat' or 'round.'

Definitions to propositions

The articulation and explication of meanings in the form of definitions is merely one symptom of literate usage. There may be other linguistic forms symptomatic of 'speaking a literate language.' The main point we wish to make is not about grammatical forms but about what they are symptoms of – the literate process of decomposing meanings into categories, categories into intersects of defining properties, etc. It is this analytic, combinatorial mode that is the overspill of literate usage into the thought processes. And if 'abstraction' exploits the orderliness of the lexical system of categories, 'rationality' consists of tidying up and exploiting the logical relations among propositions. $A > B > C, \therefore A > C$ somehow implies that if you prefer steak to goulash and lobster to steak, you should prefer lobster to goulash. IQ tests in literate societies were built on such logical problems. Yet there is ample evidence (Cole *et al.*, 1971; Wason & Johnson-Laird, 1972) to show that ordinary reasoning is, in most instances, formally inadequate. Conclusions as often follow from personal beliefs and empirical knowledge as from the explicit premises. Yet we honour the rational drawing of conclusions as the ideal to be aspired to and correct such delightful appeals to concrete experience as the one reported by Luria (1971) for Central Asian peasants:

Question: All the bears in Pinsk are white;
             Ivan saw a bear in Pinsk.
             What colour was the bear?
Answer: Ask Ivan, I've never been to Pinsk.

It is only when, as in literate usage, we require that one stick exclusively to the text that we think our Central Asian peasant quaint.

Nor do we wish to imply the opposite – that following an explicit logical argument is merely a form of snobbery. It is an important tool in the formation and criticism of arguments. If the argument is explicit, it is more vulnerable to criticism precisely by those logical rules. Thus they are critical to some forms of thought and to disciplined inquiry.

Writing and text

Thus far we have considered how literacy alters the language usage and subtly affects the cognitive processes of those learning the language. What of the practice of *writing* itself as an expressive and as a communicative device? How may it affect the writer and its eventual reader? May it not serve as a means of expanding, reordering, and even 'discovering' reality? It has been argued (Ricoeur, 1971) that written communication is not simply a reflection of reality, but rather a means of enlarging reality: 'Text frees itself from the limits of ostensive reference. For us the world is the ensemble of references opened up by texts' (p. 11). Poetry since the eighteenth century has been described precisely in these terms (Hamilton, 1963; Ong, 1971).

Can this play a role in the development of intellectual competence? Inhelder and Piaget (1958) describe the stage of formal operations in just such terms – the possibility of separating the experienced from the possible. They say:

> Finally, in formal thought there is a reversal in the direction of thinking between *reality* and *possibility* in the Subjects' method of approach. Possibility no longer appears merely as an extension of an empirical situation or of actions actually performed. Instead it is *reality* that is now secondary to *possibility*. Henceforth, they conceive of the given facts as that sector of a set of possible transformations that has actually come about; for they are neither explained nor even regarded as facts until the Subject undertakes verifying procedures that pertain to the entire set of hypotheses compatible with a given situation. In other words, formal thinking is essentially hypothetico-deductive. By this we mean that the deduction no longer *refers to perceived realities but to hypothetical statements*, i.e. it refers to propositions which are formulations of hypotheses which postulate facts or events independently of whether or not they actually occur. . . . The most distinctive property of formal thought is this reversal of direction between *reality* and *possibility*; instead of deriving a rudimentary theory from the empirical data as is done in concrete inferences, formal thought begins with a theoretical synthesis implying that certain relations are necessary and thus proceeds in the opposite direction.
>
> (p. 251)

Progressively, aided by the decontextualized atmosphere of school, the literate child comes to manage statements as propositions with entailments – to recognize that a statement may be true not because it is empirically plausible, or has been experienced, but simply because it is entailed by another proposition to which he has already assented. If not all achieve this skill, as already noted, at least it is held up as an ideal, and text itself provides the opportunity for reflecting upon what is in the text, without regard for extralinguistic considerations. It is as when Hecataeus began criticizing the historical accuracy of the Homeric poems after they had been written down. He became aware of the inconsistencies that were apparently overlooked in their oral transmission. So he could proclaim: 'The stories the Greeks tell are many and in my opinion ridiculous' (Goody & Watt, 1963: p. 322).

When text becomes autonomous from speech, the construction of reality can proceed on two planes – a plane of intralinguistic logic, and a plane of ordinary experience. Ordinary experience can then be shaped more readily by a logically derived pattern of expectancies. Experience, so to speak, can be pitted against logic. If they do not match, we pause, extract new logical implications, or reexamine experience. In this way we more readily create possible or hypothetical worlds, of which the world as experienced is merely one. This is a power that probably does not rely exclusively upon experience of dealing in autonomous text, but the procedures that we learn for dealing with such text powerfully predispose us in that direction. We honour it as the prototype technique of science; but its main impetus, if not its origin, derives from the habit of reflecting on textualized statements and their entailments.[1]

There are probably three reasons why language and symbols generally have been undervalued in accounts of the functioning cognition. One is the repeated failure of the Whorfian hypothesis to generate verifiable predictions about particular languages. Aside from a flurry of studies in how codability of inputs affects memory, there has been a lack of specific hypotheses about quantifiable, discrete effects of language. This general objection fades as we become clearer about the acquisition of language and the manner in which acquisition itself depends upon mapping language onto knowledge of the world, much of it invariant across cultures. If the child's language did not map directly onto that knowledge, he would have no means of breaking the linguistic code (Bruner, 1975; Macnamara, 1972). Hence, it is unreasonable to expect that the acquisition of language might markedly affect a child's or adult's cognition in a simple, semantic way by segmenting the world differently. It may, however, still direct his attention, permit cooperative efforts, permit rehearsal, and the like, none of which are likely to have immediately evident, dramatic cognitive consequences.

A second reason for undervaluation, as Scribner and Cole (1973) have recently pointed out, and as anthropologists have proclaimed under the banner of cultural universals, is that constituent cognitive operations seem universal across all cultures though they may be patterned differently to meet the demands placed on them by different cultures. To expect the presence of an operation, or even its hypertrophy, in a particular culture or linguistic community requires that we understand the cultural or linguistic demands which tend to bring it into prominence or lead to its specialization. Each culture has invented its own set of techniques for utilizing basic cognitive resources. These devices and their effects become more apparent in the cognitive processes that develop in school-age and older children in any literate culture, for it is at this point that specialized demands are made upon the young in a strict way. School, specializing in literate and numerate techniques, begins to shape the more general modes of thought to which we have been referring. Schools do not create them; they specialize them and equip them with new technique.

The third source of undervaluation of the role in thought of symbol systems has recently come to the fore in the writings of Havelock, Goody and Watt, McLuhan, and Popper. It appears that we aimed too low. While the acquisition of a spoken language is universal and mapped onto 'ordinary' contextualized experience, the acquisition of a *written* language is *not* universal, and its historical consequences are only now becoming apparent in the form to which we have alluded. The differences Whorf sought may lie not so much between various language communities as between oral and written forms of language!

Having insisted that the language of explicit, written textual statements provides an intellectual tool of great power, generality, and cultural significance, we may ask when and under what circumstances this tool conies into use to produce the changes in thought we have been discussing. Is the potential for using this tool present in the language of children, in their capacity for handling concepts? Or, so to speak, must this potential be created? We would opt for the former alternative on the basis of evidence on the differences and similarities between the 'uneducated' and the 'educated' mind or between the 'savage' and the 'civilized' mind (Levi-Strauss, 1962).

The growth of literate competence

We may take the position that 'early' patterns are replaced by later ones or that new powers of mind are added to the old with more experience in working with decontextualized written materials. Rather than a replacement theory or an addition theory, we would prefer a specialization theory. Logical, explicit, definitional, written text does not so much *add* new functions to language or thought as it specializes some functions present in early language while presumably inhibiting certain others. These are precisely the functions required for verbal definition, for analysis of propositional structure and entailment, for argumentation from text, for criticizing theories, and for fitting together the 'possible' and the 'real' in the manner discussed earlier. These functions are present to some degree in the language of children before they learn to read and write, for even a child's language possesses some semantic depth; Hutten-locher (1974), for example, has shown that children's representations of cats and horses are related conceptually in a superordinate long before they know such a word as *animal*. But it is trafficking in text that will eventually specialize this form, of grouping and make it a 'professional deformation' for the text-dependent literate.

For the young child, language serves many functions concurrently and in extricably, as Austin (1962) and Searle (1969) point out. With the specialization of language in the form of explicit written prose as an instrument of formal schooling, the language is specialized to serve one or two functions with increased priority. Language is used now for the achievement of precision of reference without particular regard to who it is that is being addressed. It is this functional specialization that is fostered by schooling and by means of written prose text. If language thereby becomes socially less accommodating, that too is part of the price of shifting from our undifferentiated oral language where the discourse is highly sensitive to the feelings and status of the interlocutor.

This specialization is precisely what Horton (1967) and Gellner (1973) see as the source of the differences between the 'scientific' mind of Western man and the 'primitive' mind of traditional man. As long as language remains un-specialized for literate use, as in the case of the 'unlearned' (whether child or traditional adult), it remains capable of performing many functions at once – stating facts, binding one socially to the hearer, and so on. Language, Gellner urges, is an all-purpose tool in such cases. But in Horton's words: 'People come to see that if ideas and language are to be used as efficient tools of explanation and prediction, they must not be allowed to be tools of anything else' (p. 164). And it is the specialization of language in service of logical argument under the impact of writing that serves those *analytic* functions characteristic of the scholar's intellect, the conventional verbal intelligence.

So, if we strike a balance sheet, we can say that 'speaking a written language' or 'thinking textually' hugely increases one's tendencies to be analytic – to generate ideas of the possible to match against the actualities of experience. But what we have said implies that the cost of this power may be aridity. Other functions of language become subordinated to the textual one, and we risk what Iris Murdoch once called 'the dangers of dryness'. One can only contend (as each of us has contended on different occasions – Bruner, 1975; Olson, 1977) that there are other evocative and metaphoric languages that provide a discipline that protects against such dangers. But whatever functions of language become specialized, that specialization inevitably lures the speaker from the multiplicity of functions embedded in ordinary all-purpose discourse. While it is perhaps this dilemma that puts some off educating *any* special function, that option may no longer be open in a specialized society.

Notes

A version of this paper will appear in G. Steiner (Ed.), *The Psychology of the 20th Century*, Volume VII: *Piaget's Developmental and Cognitive Psychology within an Extended Context* (Zurich: Kindler, forthcoming). We are grateful to Catherine Cragg for her editorial assistance.

1 See Popper's account of World 3 knowledge. According to Popper (1972: pp. 158–164) 'the third world (part of which is human language) is the product of men, just as honey is the product of bees, or spiders' webs of spiders' (p. 159). As examples, Popper cites number theory or any other theory which is supported by a chain of arguments and by documentary evidence. Such theories are objective in the sense that they are essentially permanent across individuals and generations: Newton's theories did not die with Newton. More important, they are explicit; each step in the construction is logically dependent on the preceding step such that the reader not only understands but, if the theory is properly constructed, must agree with the conclusion.

References

Austin, J. L. *How to do things with words*. J. O. Urmson (Ed.). New York: Oxford University Press, 1962.

Bailey, B. L. Language and learning styles of minority group children in the United States. Paper read to the American Educational Research Association, Chicago, 1968.

Bandura, A. *Principles of behavior modification*. New York: Holt, Rinehart and Winston, 1969.

Bereiter, C. and Engelman, S. *Teaching disadvantaged children in the preschool*. Englewood Cliffs, NJ: Prentice-Hall, 1966.

Bruner, J. S. *The process of education*. New York: Macmillan, 1960.

Bruner, J. S. On cognitive growth. In J. S. Bruner, P. M. Greenfield, and R. Olver (Eds), *Studies in cognitive growth*. New York: John Wiley and Sons, 1966.

Bruner, J. S. Nature and uses of immaturity. *American Psychologist*, 1972, 27, 687–708.

Bruner, J. S. From communication to language – A psychological perspective. *Cognition*, 1974/75, 3, 225–287.

Cole, M., Gay, J., Glick, J., and Sharp, D. *The cultural context of learning and thinking*. New York: Basic Books, 1971.

de Laguna, G. *Speech: Its function and development*. College Park, MD: McGrath Company, 1970. (Reprint of 1927 edition.)

Dewey, J. *Democracy and education*. New York: Macmillan, 1916.

Gellner, E. The savage and modern mind. In R. Horton and R. Finnegan (Eds), *Modes of thought*. London: Faber and Faber, 1973.

Goodman, N. *Languages of art: An approach to a theory of symbols*. Indianapolis: Bobbs-Merrill, 1968.

Goody, J. and Watt, I. The consequences of literacy. *Comparative studies in society and history*, 1963, 5, 304–345.

Greenfield, P. Oral or written language: The consequences for cognitive development in Africa, the United States and England. *Language and speech*, 1972, 169–178.

Grice, H. P. *Logic and conversation*. The William James Lectures, 1967 (mimeo).

Hamilton, K. G. *The two harmonies: Poetry and prose in the 17th century*. Oxford: Clarendon Press, 1963.

Havelock, E. *Preface to Plato*. New York: Grosset and Dunlap, 1967.

Havelock, E. Prologue to Greek literacy. *Lectures in memory of Louise Taft Semple, second series, 1966–1971*. Cincinnati: University of Oklahoma Press for the University of Cincinnati Press, 1973.

Herbert, J. J. and Harsh, C. M. Observational learning by categorizing. *Journal of Comparative Psychology*, 1944, 37, 81–95.

Horton, R. African traditional thought and Western science. In B. R. Wilson (Ed.), *Rationality*. Oxford: Blackwell, 1970. Original printing (Africa) 1967.

Huttenlocher, J. The origins of language comprehension. In R. Solso (Ed.), *Theories in cognitive psychology: The Loyola Symposium*. Potomac, Md.: Lawrence Erlbaum Association, 1974.

Inhelder, B. and Piaget, J. *The growth of logical thinking*. New York: Basic Books, 1958.

Labov, W. The logic of non-standard English. In F. Williams (Ed.), *Language and poverty: Perspectives on a theme*. Chicago: Markham Publishing Company, 1970.

Levi-Strauss, C. *The savage mind*. London: Weidenfeld and Nicolson, 1966. (First French edition, 1962.)

Living and learning. Report of the Provincial Committee on Aims and Objectives of Education in the Schools of Ontario. Toronto: Ontario Department of Education, 1968.

Lord, A. *The singer of tales*. New York: Atheneum, 1971.

Luria, A. R. Towards the problem of the historical nature of psychological processes. *International Journal of Psychology*, 1971, 6, 259–272.

Macnamara, J. The cognitive basis of language learning in infants. *Psychological Review*, 1972, 79, 1–13.

McLuhan, M. *Understanding media: The extension of man*. New York: McGraw-Hill, 1964.

Olson, D. R. Towards a theory of instructional means. *Educational Psychologist*, 1976, 12(1), 14–35.

Olson, D. R. From utterance to text: The bias of language in speech and writing. *Harvard Educational Review*, 1977, 47, 257–281.

Olson, D. R. and Bruner, J. S. Learning through experience and learning through media. In D. R. Olson (Ed.), *Media and symbols: The forms of expression, communication and education*. 73rd Yearbook of the NSSE. Chicago, IL: University of Chicago Press, 1974.

Ong, W. *Rhetoric, romance and technology: Studies in the interaction of expression and culture*. Ithaca: Cornell University Press, 1971.

Piaget, J. *John Amos Comenius: Selections*. Paris: UNESCO, 1957.

Piaget, J. *Biology and knowledge*. Chicago, IL: University of Chicago Press, 1971.

Popper, K. *Objective knowledge: An evolutionary approach*. Oxford: Clarendon Press, 1972.

Ricoeur, P. Metaphor and the main problem of hermeneutics. University of Toronto, 1971 (mimeo).

Scribner, S. and Cole, M. Cognitive consequences of formal and informal education. *Science*, 1973, 182, 553–559.

Searle, J. R. *Speech acts: An essay in the philosophy of language*. Cambridge: Cambridge University Press, 1969.

Stewart, W. Social dialect. In *Research Planning Conference on Language and Development in Disadvantaged Children*. New York: Yeshiva University, 1966.

Vygotsky, L. S. *Thought and language*. Cambridge, MA: MIT Press, 1962.

Wason, P. C. and Johnson-Laird, P. N. *The psychology of reasoning*. London: B. T. Batsford Limited, 1972.

CHAPTER 3

PSYCHOLOGY AND THE IMAGE OF MAN

TLS (1976), December 17, Times Literary Supplement

One sometimes agrees to deliver a lecture on a set theme, only to discover that the theme is not quite what one had expected. Having agreed to deliver a Herbert Spencer Lecture in Oxford on how psychology had affected common sense about man or had itself been affected by that common sense – thinking then that it would make an amusing summer interlude of historical writing – I soon discovered it would not go so easily. For once I had started on the inevitable first notes, it was plain to me that I was not embarked at all on a summer of intellectual history but on a much thornier enterprise, partly philosophical, partly psychological, and only trivially historical – trivial in the sense that it was no surprise that, in the later nineteenth century, psychology had modelled itself on those successful natural-science neighbours in whose district it had decided to build its mansion, and had suffered the consequences thereafter.

I can recall my early dark thoughts. Little question, to begin with, that the most powerful impact on common sense had come from Freud. Yet Freud was, and is, peripheral to and grossly atypical of academic psychology, so much so, indeed, that apart from providing cautionary methodological tales with which to warn the unwary undergraduate, his work is not even covered in the Oxford syllabus. Or take it another way: has psychology affected issues of public concern on which it could reasonably be expected to have a bearing, say economics? Here, surely, is a powerful mode of thought and of policy-making that treats psychological matters like risk, preference, delayed gratification in saving and investment. It even proposes notions like utility through which the values and probabilities of outcomes are assumed to combine to determine choice. Yet though economics had, in the lifetime of official psychology, been through the revolutions of Marshall, of Keynes, of Schumpeter, and of Morgenstern and van Neumann, there is not a trace of any influence exerted by psychologists. A minor exception, perhaps, is in the application of psychology to industrial relations – a not altogether successful venture at that, and one also sufficiently peripheral to psychology to be ignored (perhaps deservedly) in the syllabus of most university departments.

And finally, since I do not wish to make too much of my initial gloomy thoughts, let me remark on the strange fact that, in recent years, the most conspicuous public voice of psychology has been motivated by the assertion that scientific psychology shows that the human enterprise is altogether wrongly conceived that it would be better managed by human engineers than by law, and that when ordinary people acted human they were muddled by notions like choice, freedom, dignity, intention, expectations, goals, and the like. B. F. Skinner, in *his* Herbert

Spencer lecture two years ago, implied indeed that human affairs so conceived could be shown to be 'wrong' in much the same way as Copernicus had shown that the heliocentric universe was 'wrong'.

My winter of discontent did indeed lead me to explore the impact of psychology on common sense – and vice versa – but it led me also to look more deeply into what might be called the interface between 'expert psychology' on the one side and the common-sense views of man on the other. I was drawn to a disturbing conclusion on the matter of why experimental or academic psychology had not had more of an impact on the broad cultural conception of the nature of man or why, perhaps, its contribution had been negatively reductionist. It was not that psychology had not yet found out enough, was not empirically advanced enough to enter the debate with authority. Rather, it was the stronger conclusion that psychology had initially defined its task in such a way that it could *never* have had much of a direct impact, given the nature of its concepts of explanation. Its initial concerns, its theoretical orientation, its style of research were not fitted to the kinds of processes or patterns that shape human affairs as they occur in human affairs as they occur in human societies: symbolic systems like language, conceptual structures in terms of which human beings carve up and interpret the world around them, and the cultural constraints imposed by human institutions were not within its terms of reference. These systems include everyday concepts like purpose, mind, responsibility, loyalty, even Cabinet responsibility – transmitted concepts that serve as the basis for human institutions like the law and economic exchange, institutions which, so to speak, provide a buffer against individual variation.

The founding contract of academic psychology was such that, in the main, these matters were ruled out as belonging elsewhere, or, more accurately, as nothing but second-order phenomena to be derived from first principles. The larger edifice of human affairs, it was felt, would be elucidated by the stones that comprised it. We had, I believe, painted ourselves into a very tight little corner where we had much control and certainty – like lower computer specialists who insist that their task is to describe the hardware and the machine language and not the properties of the programs they comprise – and the price we may have had to pay had we followed on this way would have been perpetual and justifiable modesty.

There are historical reasons why this was so, stemming from our early childhood of envy among the natural sciences and our attempts to emulate (or, better, simulate) their successes, and I shall consider these in a moment. It seems to me that I have not exaggerated. Indeed, I am sure that there are still psychologists of the highest intelligence and good will who would insist today that the course upon which we originally embarked is a sound one for psychology, but after forty years of participating in the enterprise with mounting contrary conviction, I would be less than candid if I did not call it as I saw it. Indeed, I am encouraged to air my conclusions because I think that winds of change are blowing and that one can already sense the new course on which we are embarking.

All of this is *not* to say, please note, that psychology has not got on with it. For it certainly has. But our modest successes, have all been, in a special way, *in vitro*, treating chunks of behaviour out of the controlling contexts in which they ordinarily occur, even though the contexts have a massive influence over the chunks. The more rigorously isolated from context and the more tightly controlled the conditions of experiment, the more precise and the more modest the results have been. The justification, of course, has been that this is the traditional way to proceed in a line of inquiry called 'the natural sciences', refining one's investigative procedure to a paradigm or model that is presumed to elucidate phenomena in real life. This brave and bold approach doubtless worked in physics, where the connection between controlled experiment and nature had become clear. For reasons that will concern us in a moment, it is not plain that such a programme is yet suitable to psychology or will ever be. The disturbing symptom in our discipline has been its steady loss of conceptual unity. It increasingly consists of a collection of topics-cum-procedures, between which it is ever more difficult to discern workable conceptual connections. Each topic develops its paradigm and its literature, even its own heroes. Each topic has a way of digging itself into an isolated trench, with less and less connection even with the neighbouring trenches, the end of the digging being reached not through success but boredom. Again, let me insist that this is not to say that some of the topics have not been of the greatest interest – the study of human perception, being a conspicuous case of one topical success after another. But perception, on the other hand, is studied *in vitro*, and efforts to relate perception to motivation or to learning or to social behaviour each begin as a new topic-cum-procedure.

Let me move on to a more detailed diagnosis of our historical difficulties, better to come to terms with what I think is needed to rescue psychology from its past and perhaps to assure it a place in the general debate on the nature of man.

Psychology paid its price of admission to the natural sciences in the nineteenth century by a tacit agreement to ban both mind and purpose from its armamentarium of explanatory concepts. A decent nineteenth-century natural science had no truck with either mentalism or teleology. And, indeed, given the ghost-in-the-machine use of such concepts in that period, neither of them deserved a place. To anybody conversant with the history of psychology over the past century, it is surely plain that such an initial taboo could not be sustained, save in the form of an ideological preface. Mentalistic concepts were there all along – in Titchener's method of structural introspection, in concepts like 'imagery' and even in the hallowed doctrine of threshold and just-noticeable-difference. And intentionality was surely an implicit premise in theories of attention, with notions like 'set' being used heuristically to deal with self-directed intentions to behave in a certain way. Indeed, we preferred to conceive of these as mental-*like* phenomena or purposive-*like* behaviours, as in Tolman's purposive behaviourism. Even the period of radical behaviourism, ushered in by J. B. Watson and now perhaps flickering to a close in the polemics of Professor Skinner, was, we should remember, accompanied by a rise of the phenomenological theories of Gestalt psychologists who, you will recall, insisted upon a distinction between man's physical or geographical environment and the effective phenomenal or behavioural environment that mediated between a world of physics and the world of experience as it affected man's conduct.

Three concerns of post-war psychology further hastened the trend away from radical behaviourism: the emergence of so-called 'cognitive psychology', with massive reliance on concepts like hypothesis, strategies, expectations. Cognitive psychology soon found common cause with artificial intelligence, whose heuristic spirit was not in the least constrained by a fixation on the nineteenth century. The third hastening trend has been the arousal of interest among psychologists in the nature and use of language and other man-made rule systems.

In spite of all this, much of psychology has remained true (perhaps because there is something compelling about infantile fixation) to its early vow. We are still embarrassed by concepts that smack of mind or mentalism, still embarrassed by the possibility that purpose and intention will suck us back into the swamp of teleology. Mentalism and teleology are still four-letter words in psychology. And here is where the difficulty arises, I think, but in a rather surprising way.

For while we have become increasingly free of our ancient phobias about mind and purpose – most of us now being willing to treat them at least in the 'as if' spirit of a heuristic – we have not altogether freed ourselves of the positivistic bias that goes with the older style of 'hard-nosed' research. Let me explain more fully what I mean by this. The contrast that is relevant, I think, is between what can be called a structural approach and a point-by-point sequential approach.

Let me use as a typical example the notion of a stimulus and a response, the two of them being defined independently of each other. A light comes on or a buzzer sounds and an organism responds to *it*, the response again being an *it*. Stimuli and responses are then, in some sense, said to be connected or related, or the occurrence of a response *after* the appearance of a stimulus is said to change in probability by virtue of some condition either in the stimulus presentation beforehand or in the consequences that follow the pairing, what is often called a reinforcement. Stimuli and responses have a kind of thing or event status, and each can be operationally defined – the former, as a nonsense syllable or a light flash or what not; the latter, the response, of course, being an observable event like a button press or a verbal response.

Perhaps the first sign that all was not well in this positivistic heaven came as an offshoot of the theory of information, when it was shown that the nature of a stimulus could not be defined merely in centimetres, grams, and seconds, but also depended upon the ensemble of alternative stimuli that might have occurred, how many bits of information were transmitted, or more succinctly, what was the uncertainty in the event. Well, that could also be dealt with by a sleight of hand in which the set of permissible stimuli to be presented was controlled by the experimenter, and probability of occurrence could then be stated as another property of the stimulus – so that to c, g, and s could be added p. But suppose, now, the set of alternatives were not independent of each other but, rather, were part of a structure, a structure whose existence was in the head or mind of the subject, like his language and its rules. How are we to interpret the comprehension of a sentence?

Take an example: *May we come in?* Is it a stimulus? Well, not *really*. The sentence itself appears, rather, to be a complex function which seems to be mapping a context into a proposition that 'carries' a certain meaning. The elements are more like triggers than stimuli. 'May' signals a speech act requesting permission and recognizes that the addressee (s) is on his own turf as defined by some code. 'We' signals that one should consider contexts involving at least three participants in which at least one is the addressee, etc. 'Come' indicates that the speaker and his companions want to move towards the addressee or to where he will be when they all get there, and contrasts with 'go'; it involves spatial deixis. 'In' signals that the destination is enclosed, container-like – a room, a house, a pub, a sauna.

In order to translate such a sentence into a proposition one would need to know, not only how the addresser and addressee organize their worlds, but also to have some hypotheses about where they might be or even what they are *doing*. The sentence might have been uttered by a dentist on behalf of himself and his nurse, the two poised with drill, addressing a patient open-mouthed on the chair! One could make no sense of such a sentence without taking into account the congnitive structures in terms of which the world is organized by the participants and, indeed, how language maps into those structures. The notion of a self-contained stimulus (or response) fades as, indeed, does a simple sequential account of the order of processing between input and final output. And what is the output?

Most of what humans respond to in the so-called real world has this property: without a structural description of the cognitive organization in the minds of the participants in an action, one cannot even locate, still less define the stimulus. Indeed, we have long been warned about this difficulty, even before our linguistic colleagues forced us to confront it. Was it not Sir Frederic Bartlett who argued so persuasively the impossibility of a theory of memory based on the storage and retrieval of such isolated elements as nonsense syllables? I think I have made clear enough what I intend by structure for us to go on to the next point.

It is another heritage of psychology's early alliance with nineteenth-century natural sciences that it cut itself off from considering the possibility that mental structures derive from what anthropologists call 'culture': a society's set of theories, values, ways of acting and thinking, and respecting. Hoping to keep its biological base, to remain with the *Naturwissenschaften* rather than suffer the denigration of being a *Geisteswissenschaft*, psychology chose to avoid questions of how human beings were able to operate with such complex rule systems as kinship, economic exchange, and the law, and did so in a most extraordinary way. It could keep its attention focused inside the individual skin (rather than upon the culture) by invoking a response system: call it a tendency to conform to social norms. Men had a tendency to conform, and in conformity-demanding situations normal distributions of response were transformed into J-curves. At least, two differentiable types of situations were thereby recognized, although the statistical criterion thus provided was not really used very searchingly. But then, it is not a very searching analysis of the rules of chess, or courtship, or investment to say simply that people conform to them. As Roger Barker has been fond of pointing out, the best predictor of human behaviour is a specification of where the person is: in post-offices, we *do* behave post-office.

The effects of these three historical habits that have so dogged psychology – its anti-mentalism, its tendency towards positivism of the old school, and its refusal to consider in detail how a culture patterns human action – put psychology in a curious light. It has come, in some inevitable way, to stand as a champion of reductionism, often against its will and its spirit. Partly this is because the three historical deformations *are* reductionist in their very nature: if you think responses are all and mind is a nonsense, if you do not take into account the structural complexity of what it is that men respond to, and if you take man to be a creature of biology tempered by a certain amount of learning, then it is a very dim picture indeed that one offers in the debate about man's nature.

But there is also something in the nature of the research we do as a result of our positivist tradition which tempts the reader of our results into reductionism. It stems from our built-in fascination with the methodology of one or at most three independent variables at a time and our delight in finding experimental situations where such small numbers of variables do account for a large part of the variance. I would offer as an example in my own field of developmental studies the extremely catastrophic experimental situations used by Harlow and his associates to demonstrate the enormous importance of terry-cloth clinging in the young rhesus monkey's attachment to a mother surrogate. Doubtless, when all else fails, terry cloth will do. But compare Harlow's results with the subtleties that have emerged from studying infant-mother interactions *in situ* reported this year by the ethologist Robert Hinde in his Wolfson Lecture!

You might think that, having said all that, I would now don sackcloth and ashes, resign my Watts Professorship in the University of Oxford and slink away to do penance, or perhaps battle. Not in the slightest! As I have already hinted, all is not lost. Consider my Oxford microcosm. Professor Weiskrantz is busily at work studying how certain brain lesions produce a state of 'blind-sight', as he calls it, in which his patients manage to be able to supply correct answers to questions about visual events they have been presented with of which they claim to have no direct awareness. He would not blench if you congratulated him on his interesting work on the neurology of consciousness. My own work is shot through with reference to the role of intention in early language acquisition – intention as exhibited by the child and as perceived by the mother. And my distinguished colleague Dr Broadbent is studying business games the better to understand how businessmen, civil servants, and politicians come to policy decisions. He would not stoop, I assure you, to the low-level nonsense of the leader-writer on *The Times* who found nothing more enlightening to say about the Government's efforts to get hold of the sterling exchange crisis than that it was acting like Pavlov's dog, now hitting the lending rate button, now the import control lever, and so on.

The three of us, I suspect, are straws in the wind, and I would like to say why I think so by examining briefly how psychology is coping with mind and intention, how we are faring in efforts to get hold of the structural contexts that determine the underlying significance of 'stimuli', so-called, and how finally I see hope for psychology joining forces with the sciences of culture, even perhaps including economics. Having done that, I would like to pay a tribute to Freud, an appreciation of why he caught and transformed our thinking about man. Perhaps we can then assess what it takes to affect common sense.

Mind, intention, and culture

Let me look first at 'mind' and 'purpose' to see how these might be faring – whether psychology is addressing anything to common sense aside from spirited tracts about the non-existence of both of these in the style of the village atheist. To locate ourselves, we shall need some analysis first.

I shall begin with the commonsense distinction between 'intended' or purposeful behaviour in contrast to 'caused' behaviour. We say of *intended* action that it is carried out 'for the sake of' achieving an end in mind, in contrast to 'caused' behaviour which is understood to be contingently related to a set of antecedent conditions. Typically, the *cause* of a behaviour is determined by a method in which we control a set of antecedent conditions, defined independently of the consequent behaviour that the antecedents may be found to produce. When a relation is found between the antecedent and consequent, we invoke a contingent link between the two, usually in the form of a 'mechanism' or 'hypothetical construct'. That in any case, is the surface structure of what we do. In fact, there is much that is implicit in our selection of both the antecedent conditions, the consequent behaviour, and the intervening contingent construct. For example, if it should be the case, as it most certain would be, that the incidence of diarrhoea in infants is highly correlated with the antecedent softness of asphalt highways, we would immediately recognize that this is an 'empty correlation' and we would look for a more sensible link between antecedent and consequent, like the temperature limits for the culturing of a relevant bacillus. 'Theories' are what provide the causal glue between antecedents and consequents, but only certain kinds of theories.

Where the analysis of intended action is concerned, the principal objection is, of course, that to invoke intention as explanation is circular, that it explains nothing. Such explanations cannot help in the search for antecedents. But is the use of intention limited in this way? Antecedents and consequents must obviously be defined independently lest one become involved in the dizzy enterprise against which Hume warned us of defining the antecedent by the consequent, and vice versa. 'Why did he attend Congregation?' 'Because he wanted to'. 'How do you know he wanted to?' 'Because he did'. Plainly, explanation of the antecedent *why* of behaviour gets nowhere by this route.

But now let me pose two questions about explanation by cause and description by intention. The first is a question of distinguishability, the second of consequentialness. I shall be crude, I am not a philosopher. But psychologists trying to get their house in order must use philosophical analysis and, therefore, you will hear overtones (probably out of tune) of G. E. M. Anscombe, Quine, John Searle, Charles Taylor, and Rom Harré. If Wittgenstein was right, that the philosopher's task is to help the fly out of the bottle, I can only hope there will be a Wittgenstein in the wings.

I begin with the well-known example of two utterances that are both distinguishable and differ widely in their consequences: one is, 'I am going to take a walk', and the other, 'I am going to be sick'. The first implies that something is under my control as an agent. The latter implies a prediction made on the basis of antecedent sensations, and agency is not implied. In the first utterance a non-contingent link is implied between intention and action. If a contingent link were intended, I would have said something like 'The chances are I am going to take a walk', which would be an appropriate reply to the question, 'What do you think you will be doing next Sunday morning?' Now, the category distinction between actions implying intention and behaviours that do not is made all the time in all languages, all cultures, and is irresistible. I am ignoring for the moment whether, in Professor Skinner's curious sense, it is pre-Copernican or 'wrong' as a description, for that at present is irrelevant. The distinction is made and it is a compelling feature of man's experience.

As Mrs Anscombe is at pains to point out, the *consequences* of the distinction are serious. Failure to do what one said one would do is, in the case of intentional actions, interpretable as lying (though extenuating circumstances are recognized). Failure in the second case is interpretable only as a mistake, unless one reinterprets the statement to be an intentional effort to deceive, but then it is relocated in the first category. At this point, very different consequences in terms of the behaviour of *others* towards the speaker can be expected. Different Gricean cooperative principles apply. Mistakes are expected; lies are not. The first produce disappointment, the second indignation.

Now we may note that both lying and mistake-making are also amenable to analysis by antecedents: the liar may more likely be the child of a broken home; the mistake-maker may have undergone permissive schooling. But that is not the issue. The issue, rather, is whether the act in question was experienced as a lie or a mistake, whether something is or is not intentional. If the latter, if an intention is carried out, no further questions need be asked.

For it is taken as axiomatic by human beings that what we do is congruent with what we intend to do. Only the exceptions require analysis. When intention is not carried out contingency is not permitted as extenuating. Intention and execution are assumed to be structurally linked. Extenuating circumstances for an unfulfilled intention are either changed intention – 'I decided not to go for a walk when I heard that lions were loose in the park', or alien forces – 'I was locked into my room'. There is no objective test available for determining whether a 'real' intention exists in the person who proclaims it. Intentions are inferred or attributed on the basis of conventional contexts and their recognition conditions depend upon what, in contemporary philosophical jargon, is known as 'uptake'. To describe an intention and the action on behalf of it is to give a structural description of an event as it is interpreted by the participants.

It is much as with a speech act. The intention implied in a speech act does not *cause* the procedures that are used in its execution, whether syntactic or semantic. But as Searle properly notes, the role of these in the meaning of the sentence cannot be analysed without attributing an intent to the act: to inform, to warn, to praise, etc. If one says, 'Would you be so kind as to pass the salt?' the constituents are to be understood in terms of a request that is made contrastive to a command, and not to be understood in terms of what it appears to be on the surface: a question about the limits of the addressee's compassion. The effort is to define the structure of a set of constituents in an act. And that is what we do when we assign an act to an intention structure.

The argument, thus far, is simply that human beings can and irresistibly *do* distinguish certain acts of their fellow men as intentional, that we see others as having something in mind and as behaving on behalf of what they have in mind. Our response towards them and their acts is sharply affected by whether we categorize it as intentional. The argument extends beyond that. It would be a vain enterprise to explain or even to discuss the *causes* of any human behaviour without taking into account whether or not intention had been attributed. At least where social or transactional behaviour is concerned, even the causal chain between antecedent and consequent must contain an account of how the participants categorized each other's acts.

What all this suggests, at the very least, is that we adopt 'the perception of intention' and 'the perception of mindfulness' as topics for research. We could at least find out what 'cues' lead us to 'see' certain behaviours as intentional acts or as leading to the inference that somebody or some thing is in possession of a 'mind'. Let it be said immediately that there is a flourishing 'topic' in psychology that deals with just this issue, called 'attribution theory'. People do distinguish between action caused by circumstances and action caused by intent and with devastating consequences for their evaluation of what they have observed. To illustrate, when they themselves are involved in a situation, they are much more likely to see their own behaviour as a result of circumstances. When they observe others, they see the action as produced by intention (when it is conventional or expected) or by quirkly dispositional traits steering intention (when the behaviour is unconventional or unexpected).

'Actors attribute to situations what observers attribute to actors' appears to be one conclusion. But the general conclusion from this work is that 'Behaviour belongs to the person; the "field" acts on everyone.' Yet, the research has not really found the so-called cues by which the inference of intent is made. For, in fact, there are no simple cues in the conventional sense. What is involved is a structural inference, based on a constellation of events. In this sense, it is precisely as in linguistics. What is the cue by which we recognize a dependent clause or an imbedding? It is not marked by parentheses or tree diagrams, but inferred from the understanding of the rules of a sentence.

Stimulus and the anticipated input

I commented on the fact that the inference of intent was at once ubiquitous, universal, and irresistible. And indeed, one could go on to explore the biological roots of such perceptions. Heider and Simmel long ago produced an animated film involving the movement of squares, triangles, and circles which is compelling seen as animate figures involved in a scenario of intent, much as Michotte has a like film for inanimate causality. There is little question that intention movements in lower organisms trip off appropriate, goal-linked behaviour in their conspecifics, and Menzel (1974) has recently shown the manner in which young chimpanzees use the direction of locomotion of a better informed animal to guide their own search for a hidden reward object. Indeed, the past two decades of research in neuro-physiology suggest that there is a feed-forward mechanism in neural functioning by which, to put it metaphorically, an about-to-occur action is transmitted by an efference copy of that action around the nervous system. As von Holst and Mittelstaedt put it nearly thirty years ago, input stimuli do not impinge upon a neutral organism, but are processed by a comparator against anticipated input – the monkey knows when his hand is being shaken by a stick and when he is shaking the stick.

The perceptual processing of the organism that yields inferences of intent seems not to be all that illusory as an account of what is going on in the nervous system. Not only is there good reason to believe that human behaviour is in fact organized into acts carried out 'for the sake' of achieving certain ends, but also the receptive human nervous system is ready to perceive behaviour as so structured, indeed, perhaps, *too* ready. It should follow, then, that any description of human behaviour must take into account this powerful if loose programme of perceptual processing if it is to predict how human beings are going to behave in an environment containing other human beings. It must do so in the same spirit as the linguist who takes into account the fact that human beings process strings of words as sentences or the student of perception who takes into account the fact that human perceivers organize input into figure ground configurations.

But I must reiterate that societies prescribe rules and codes based on the kinds of perceptions and inferences we have been discussing. People starve to death biologically for these codes, turn away from sexual attractions, go to war, etc. All of these domains are more or less tightly regulated by systems of roles, of rules, of exchange, etc. Increasingly, anthropologists are developing formal procedures for describing such rule systems. Increasingly, psychologists are becoming interested in how such rule systems are acquired, and it is certainly not by the conventional linking of stimuli and responses.

The implication of all that I have said is certainly not just that we consider psychological phenomena at different 'levels', this one molecular, a next one molar, still another yet more molar, *ad infinitum*. It is more revolutionary than that, I think. The conclusion is that a reaction to any feature of an environment is, to use Chomsky's phrase, most likely to be 'structure dependent'. By structure dependency he means, and I mean, that the significance of any feature is determined by its position in a structure. The position of a piece on a chess-board, the function of a word in a sentence, a particular facial expression, the colour or placement of a light, these cannot be interpreted without reference to the person's internalized rules of chess or language, the conventions he holds concerning human interaction, the traffic rules in force in his mind. To set out with even so innocently positivistic an objective as studying, say, the threshold for recognizing different colours is a surprisingly empty exercise without a notion of how colours are contextualized in the task. Some years ago, for example, Postman and I showed that the recognition threshold for the colour red varied in exposure time by a full order of magnitude depending upon whether red was conventionally expected in that setting or not.

What then is the status of experiments that strip expectancy down to a level, say, of chromatic equiprobability? It is said that by so doing one obtains a 'neutral' situation which permits one to explore the basic 'colour discrimination' mechanism.

What is basic in this context? Well, it turns out to be the case under fairly simple conditions that the recognizability of colours to which one has been previously exposed is a function of their linguistic codability – roughly the number of elements in the linguistic description required to differentiate them from other colours in the array presented. Are not linguistic codability and expectancy as basic to a theory of colour perception and colour recognition as the spectral composition of the input?

It would seem to me – and this is very much in the spirit of the late Egon Brunswik – that the task of psychology as an experimental discipline is to investigate representative settings in which phenomena are contextualized in order to come anywhere near approximating what might be called a systematic description of ordinary behaviour. If it cannot do this, it cannot achieve generality. But far worse than that. It risks ending up peddling paradigms designed more for narrow nicety than for descriptive or explanatory power, as in theories of learning where attentional factors are minimized to a point approaching zero, and where, it would seem, context and materials are designed for achieving maximum experimental control rather than representativeness.

My emphasis on structure sensitivity in 'natural' situations leads me to look for leads in linguistics. For I admire linguistics not only for its willingness to look at natural, ordinary behaviour – speaking or comprehending ordinary speech – but for its aim of describing the banal and the ordinary systematically. If I ask a linguist about sentences, he will not insist that we confine our discussion to the movements of lips, tongue, and glottis. If I ask him about reading, he will not go on about cross-modal matching. Chomsky, in his recent *Reflections on Language*, has an interesting point to make. He begins with what he chooses to call 'science making', the manner in which people ordinarily put knowledge together. In some domains, this human capacity appears to be extraordinarily powerful, as in the creating of physical sciences and mathematics, in other domains rather feeble, as in matters involving people exercising their will.

Science making, whether lay-modest or grand, depends upon a human capacity to make structure-sensitive distinctions and to do so easily, immediately, and with a minimum of prior tuition on the point at issue. There is, as always with Chomsky, an insistence that the capacity involved is innate, by which he means that certain capacities are species specific, including the human capacity to organize knowledge in a human way – with which I find no quarrel. One of these natural capacities is, of course, the faculty to proceed with astonishing speed and facility into the uses of language. He then goes on to say:

> Alongside the language faculty and interacting with it in the most intimate way is the faculty of mind that we might call 'common sense understanding', a system of beliefs, expectations, and knowledge, concerning the nature and behaviour of objects, their place in a system of 'natural kinds', the organization of these categories, and the properties that determine the categorization of objects and the analysis of events. A general 'innateness hypothesis' will also include principles that bear on the place and role of people in a social world, the nature and conditions of work, the structure of human action, will and choice, and so on. These systems may be unconscious for the most part and even beyond the reach of conscious introspection.

The starting point for Chomsky, then, would be to examine the natural ways, or better, the ecological representative ways, to use Brunswik's term, in which people look at and account for objects involved in events and how they look at and account for people and their actions.

As I read Chomsky, he is proposing that we begin our inquiry into the nature of human functioning with a structural description of ordinary knowing, to set as our goal the elucidation of those structures as we find them. It is the ordinariness of the enterprise that appeals to me. For it is just such ordinariness that has so often been lost from psychology in its efforts to deal positivistically with isolated variables. It is what has led us in the past to get stuck in little trenches labelled 'serial position curve' when the intent was to study memory. This is changing. It is not that we had to build upon the dreary, pioneering studies of Ebbinghaus on the rote learning of a nonsense syllables, but to escape, to run away from our adoptive home. The study of memory like much else in psychology is beginning again to concern itself with what people ordinarily do when they remember, even with what they do to save themselves from having to remember. The study of cognition in general, with its new emphasis on natural categories, is making striking progress. Developmental psychology, as it moves away from a total reliance on narrow, single-variable experiments, is moving nicely, thanks in large part to the impetus given by Piaget and Vygotsky. The psychology of language and communication, the micro-analysis of social psychology, all of these as they become more paradigmatic of the ordinary begin to have a broader impact within and beyond psychology. But what I also see, and I am deeply impressed by it, is the extent to which comparable structural descriptions in anthropology, sociology, linguistics, and artificial intelligence begin to make possible for us a more fruitful exchange.

The 'exemplary' case of Sigmund Freud

Now, finally, why Freud had such an impact on common sense. I think there are three crucial points to make. Before I do so, however, let me put in perspective one possible impediment to a proper appreciation. It has to do with his emphasis on sexuality, particularly his insistence that it was not only ubiquitous but had its origins in infancy. Undoubtedly this insistence (and particularly its oversimplification in the hands of both admirers and detractors) did seize the imagination of educated and uneducated alike. But had that been all, his views would have created a *frisson de scandale* much as Havelock Ellis's had done, and would soon have been converted to smut. His power in public discussion had rather to do, I think, with these things: his attention to and reinterpretation of the ordinary (the psychopathology of everyday life, as he chose to call it), his deeply puzzling examination of this relation between the intended and the unintended, and finally his interpretation of the nature or meaning of 'significance'. A word about these.

For Freud, the ordinary conduct of everyday life was the starting point. Neurosis was not a blemish nor a disease, but a continuation of ordinary living. The ordinary, for Freud, was as much in need of interpretation as the extraordinary. One did what one intended to do, yes, but there was a hidden reason, a latent content as well as a manifest one. Intention, in Mrs Anscombe's sense cited earlier, was reopened for examination. The Freudian slip became a tool for reinterpreting the ordinary.

But then, if the ordinary is not what it seems, what is it? Here is where Freud's literary genius took charge. Beneath the ordinary is a drama. Each of us is a cast of characters, acting out a script. Looked at carefully, our reactions to the world could be seen as an enactment of the script. It is in terms of these scripts that the surface of experience has systematic meaning or significance. Freud's scripts may have been culture-bound projections of *fin-de-siècle* Vienna. But for him they served as the cognitive systems in terms of which the symbolic significance of events could be understood. One of the scripts or codes was, of course, the epic struggle of the ego, the superego, and the id – the ego as free agent trying to strike compromises between the priggish, societal demands of the superego on the one hand and the hedonistic, lusting, pleasure-principled id on the other. Indeed, he even tried his hand at a theory of perception in his essay on the 'magic writing-pad' to account for the motivated way in which perceptual selectivity operated, balancing between a near-hallucinatory programme in the service of drive and prohibition, and a reality-orientated one serving the sturdy little ego, almost like a judas eye through the middle of a distorting mirror. And as if these coding principles were not enough, Freud reinvented cultural forms like the Oedipal drama with its principles of categorization such that to the experiencer, every older man was a father, every older woman a mother, every ingratiation a denied parricide or a maternal seduction.

The ordinary, in a word, was to be understood as explicable in terms of its symbolic coded value; coded values were to be understood in terms of the way in which the world was organized in secret thought below the surface; the response of society and of the self – whether indignation or anxiety or guilt – was to be understood in terms of the sharing of these codes. Memory, perception, action, motivation were all to be seen as structure-sensitive constituents of this overall operation. The system may have been plainly wrong in content and detail, may indeed (as we know from a decade or two of principally American experimental research to tame it) have been totally unamenable to test by controlled experiment of the kind representing the older positivism. But surely it represented a modern ideal and, in an abstract way, constituted the kind of explanation that we speak of as structurally systematic. Various writers have pointed out its similarities in this abstract sense to the theoretical programmes of Chomsky, de Saussure, and Piaget – all of them based on the analysis of surface phenomena derived from underlying structures through the interposition of transformation rules – in Freud's case, dream work and the distortions of ego defence mechanisms were the principal transformations. Perhaps, as intellectual historians, we should take seriously the fact that this type of formulation has had so powerful an impact on common sense, on interpretations of the ordinary. The details of the Freudian drama have by now receded, but the approach in its formal character has become part of educated common sense.

Please do not misinterpret. I am not proposing that only those theories which have a general cultural impact be taken seriously. God save all counter-intuitive ideas! My claim, rather, is that educated human beings, given their intrinsic 'science-making' or theory-making capacities, know how to do things and know that they do them. A theory of human behaviour that fails to make contact with man's conceptions of his world and his way of knowing, that sets these aside as epiphenomena, will neither be an adequate theory of human behaviour nor will it prevail in common sense. Physics had to make the world of nature, as experienced, comprehensible to man. The task of the psychologist is more difficult. For in making man comprehensible to himself, we start with man's knowledge of himself, his intricate sense of what he is like. Unless we begin from a better systematic description of that, we will fail. I doubt that we will, although our first century has not, I fear been very impressive.

Note

This is the text of Professor Bruner's Herbert Spencer Lecture, given in Oxford on October 29, 1976.

CHAPTER 4

LEARNING THE MOTHER TONGUE

Human Nature (1978), 1: 42–49, Unesco

Learning a native language is an accomplishment within the grasp of any toddler, yet discovering how children do it has eluded generations of philosophers. St Augustine believed it was simple. Recollecting his own childhood, he said, "When they named any thing, and as they spoke turned towards it, I saw and remembered that they called what they would point out by the name they uttered.... And thus by constantly hearing words, as they occurred in various sentences, I collected gradually for what they stood; and having broken in my mouth to these signs, I thereby gave utterance to my will." But a look at children as they actually acquire language shows that St Augustine was wrong and that other attempts to explain the feat err as badly in the opposite direction. What is more, as we try to understand how children learn their own language, we get an inkling of why it is so difficult for adults to learn a second language.

Thirty years ago, psychologies of learning held sway; language acquisition was explained using principles and methods that had little to do with language. Most started with nonsense syllables or random materials that were as far as researchers could get from the structure of language that permits the generation of rich and limitless statements, speculations, and poetry. Like G. K. Chesterton's drunk, they looked for the lost coin where the light was. And in the light of early learning theories, children appeared to acquire language by associating words with agents and objects and actions, by imitating their elders, and by a mysterious force called reinforcement. It was the old and tired Augustinian story dressed up in the language of behaviorism.

Learning theory led to a readiness, even a recklessness, to be rid of an inadequate account, one that could explain the growth of vocabulary but not how a four-year-old abstracts basic language rules and effortlessly combines old words to make an infinite string of new sentences. The stage was set for linguist Noam Chomsky's theory of LAD, the Language Acquisition Device, and for the Chomskyan revolution.

According to this view, language was not learned; it was recognized by virtue of an innate recognition routine through which children, when exposed to their local language, could abstract or extract its universal grammatical principles. Whatever the input of that local language, however degenerate, the output of LAD was the grammar of the language, a competence to generate all possible grammatical sentences and none (or very few) that were not. It was an extreme view, so extreme that it did not even consider meaning. In a stroke it freed a generation of psycholinguists from the dogma of association, imitation, and reinforcement and turned their attention to the problem of rule learning. By declaring learning theory dead, it opened the way for a new account. George Miller of The Rockefeller University put it well: We had two theories of language learning – one of them, empiricist associationism, is impossible; the other, nativism, is miraculous. The void between the impossible and the miraculous remained to be filled.

Both explanations begin too late – when children say their first words. Long before children acquire language, they know something about their world. Before they can make verbal distinctions in speech, they have sorted the conceptual universe into useful categories and classes and can make distinctions about actions and agents and objects. As Roger Brown of Harvard University has written, "The concept...is there beforehand, waiting for the word to come along that names it." But the mystery of how children penetrate the communication system and learn to represent in language what they already know about the real world has not been solved. Although there is a well-packaged semantic content waiting, what children learn about language is not the same as what they know about the world. Yet the void begins to fill as soon as we recognize that children are not flying blind, that semantically speaking they have some target toward which language-learning efforts are directed: saying something or understanding something about events in a world that is already known.

If a child is in fact communicating, he has some end in mind – requesting something or indicating something or establishing some sort of personal relationship. The function of a communication has to be considered. As philosopher John Austin argued, an utterance cannot be analyzed out of its context of use, and its use must include the intention of the speaker and its interpretation in the light of conventional standards by the person addressed. A speaker may make a request in several ways: by using the conventional question form, by making a declarative statement, or by issuing a command.

Roger Brown observed young Adam from age two until he was four and found that his middle-class mother made requests using a question form: "Why don't you play with your ball now?" Once Adam came to appreciate what I shall call genuine *why* questions (i.e., "Why are you playing with your ball?"), he typically answered these – and these only – with the well-known "Because." There is no instance, either before or after he began to comprehend the genuine causal question, of his ever confusing a sham and a real *why* question.

Not only does conceptual knowledge precede true language, but so too does function. Children know, albeit in limited form, what they are trying to accomplish by communicating before they begin to use language to implement their efforts. Their initial gestures and vocalizations become increasingly stylized and conventional.

It has become plain in the last several years that Chomsky's original bold claim that any sample of language encountered by an infant was enough for the LAD to dig down to the grammatical rules simply is false. Language is not encountered willy-nilly by the child; it is instead encountered in a highly orderly interaction with the mother, who takes a crucial role in arranging the linguistic encounters of the child. What has emerged is a theory of mother-infant interaction in language acquisition – called the fine-tuning theory – that sees language mastery as involving the mother as much as it does the child. According to this theory, if the LAD exists, it hovers somewhere in the air between mother and child.

So today we have a new perspective that begins to grant a place to knowledge of the world, to knowledge of the function of communication, and to the hearer's interpretation of the speaker's intent. The new picture of language learning recognizes that the process depends on highly constrained and onesided transactions between the child and the adult teacher. Language acquisition requires joint problem solving by mother and infant, and her response to her child's language is close tuned in a way that can be specified.

The child's entry into language is an entry into dialogue, and the dialogue is at first-necessarily nonverbal and requires both members of the pair to interpret the communication and its intent. Their relationship is in the form of roles, and each "speech" is determined by a move of either partner. Initial control of the dialogue depends on the mother's interpretation, which is guided by a continually updated understanding of her child's competence.

Consider an infant learning to label objects. Anat Ninio and I observed Richard in his home every two weeks from his eighth month until he was two years old, video-taping his actions so that we could study them later. In this instance he and his mother are "reading" the pictures in a book. Before this kind of learning begins, certain things already have been established. Richard has learned about pointing as a pure indicating act, marking unusual or unexpected objects rather than things wanted immediately. He has also learned to understand that sounds refer in some singular way to objects or events. Richard and his mother, moreover, have long since established well-regulated turn-taking routines, which probably were developing as early as his third or fourth month. And finally, Richard has learned that books are to be looked at, not eaten or torn; that objects depicted are to be responded to in a particular way and with sounds in a pattern of dialogue.

For the mother's part, she (like all mothers we have observed) drastically limits her speech and maintains a steady regularity. In her dialogues with Richard she uses four types of speech in a strikingly fixed order. First, to get his attention, she says "Look." Second, with a distinctly rising inflection, she asks "What's that?" Third, she gives the picture a label, "It's an X." And finally in response to his actions, she says "That's right."

In each case, a single verbal token accounts for from nearly half to more than 90 percent of the instances. The way Richard's mother uses the four speech constituents is closely linked to what her son says or does. When she varies her response, it is with good reason. If Richard responds, his mother replies, and if he initiates a cycle by pointing and vocalizing, then she responds even more often.

Her fine tuning is fine indeed. For example, if after her query Richard labels the picture, she will virtually always skip the label and jump to the response, "Yes." Like the other mothers we have studied, she is following ordinary polite rules for adult dialogue.

As Roger Brown has described the baby talk of adults, it appears to be an imitative version of how babies talk. Brown says, "Babies already talk like babies, so what is the earthly use of parents doing the same? Surely it is a parent's job to teach the adult language." He resolves the dilemma by noting, "What I think adults are chiefly trying to do, when they use [baby talk] with children, is to communicate, to understand and to be understood, to keep two minds focussed on the same topic." Although I agree with Brown, I would like to point out that the content and intonation of the talk is baby talk, but the dialogue pattern is adult.

To ensure that two minds are indeed focused on a common topic, the mother develops a technique for showing her baby what feature a label refers to by making 90 percent of her labels refer to whole objects. Since half of the remainder of her speech is made up of proper names that also stand for the whole, she seems to create few difficulties, supposing that the child also responds to whole objects and not to their features.

The mother's (often quite unconscious) approach is exquisitely tuned. When the child responds to her "Look!" by looking, she follows immediately with a query. When the child responds to the query with a gesture or a smile, she supplies a label. But as soon as the child shows the ability to vocalize in a way that might indicate a label, she raises the ante. She withholds the label and repeats the query until the child vocalizes, then she gives the label.

Later, when the child has learned to respond with shorter vocalizations that correspond to words, she no longer accepts an indifferent vocalization. When the child begins producing a recognizable, constant label for an object, she holds out for it. Finally, the child produces appropriate words at the appropriate place in the dialogue. Even then the mother remains tuned to the developing pattern, helping her child recognize labels and make them increasingly accurate. For example, she develops two ways of asking "What's that?" One, with a falling intonation, inquires about those words for which she believes her child already knows the label; the other, with a rising intonation, marks words that are new.

Even in the simple labeling game, mother and child are well into making the distinction between the given and the new. It is of more than passing interest that the old or established labels are the ones around which the mother will shortly be elaborating comments and questions for new information:

Mother (with falling intonation):   What's that?
Child: Fishy.
Mother: Yes, and see him swimming?

After the mother assumes her child has acquired a particular label, she generally drops the attention-getting "Look!" when they turn to the routine. In these petty particulars of language, the mother gives useful cues about the structure of their native tongue. She provides cues based not simply on her knowledge of the language but also on her continually changing knowledge of the child's ability to grasp particular distinctions, forms, or rules. The child is sensitized to certain constraints in the structure of their dialogue and does not seem to be directly imitating her. I say this because there is not much difference in the likelihood of a child's repeating a label after hearing it, whether the mother has imitated the child's label, simply said "Yes," or only laughed approvingly. In each case the child repeats the label about half the time, about the same rate as with *no* reply from the mother. Moreover, the child is eight times more likely to produce a label in response to "What's that?" than to the mother's uttering the label.

I do not mean to claim that children cannot or do not use imitation in acquiring language. Language must be partly based on imitation, but though the child may be imitating another, language learning involves solving problems by communicating in a dialogue. The child seems to be trying to get through to the mother just as hard as she is trying to reach her child.

Dialogue occurs in a context. When children first learn to communicate, it is always in highly concrete situations, as when mother or child calls attention to an object, asking for the aid or participation of the other. Formally conceived, the format of communication involves an intention, a set of procedures, and a goal. It presupposes shared knowledge of the world and a shared script by which mother and child can carry out reciprocal activity in that world. Formats obviously have utility for the child. They provide a simple, predictable bit of the world in which and about which to communicate. But they also have an important function for the mother in the mutual task of speech acquisition.

When a mother uses baby talk, her intonation broadens, her speech slows, and her grammar becomes less complex. In addition, baby talk virtually always starts with the here and now, with the format in which the two are operating. It permits the mother to tune her talk to the child's capabilities. She need not infer the child's general competence for language, but instead judges the child's performance on a specific task at a specific time (see Table 4.1).

Table 4.1 As children's requests change with increasing sophistication (center), their mothers switch from establishing the sincerity of a request to identifying the object wanted (top). The sharp increase in replies having to do with who will get or control an action ("agency") reflects a demand for sharing and a difference in wishes (bottom)

	Age in months				
			More than 15		
	10–12	13–14	15–16	17–18	20–24
Mother's questions when children request nearby objects *Type of question*					
About intention ("Do you want it?") (%)	93	90	42		
About referent ("Do you want the x?") (%)	7	10	58		
Number of questions (%)	27	29	12		
Forms of early requests *Request for*					
Near and visible object (%)	100	74	43	22	11
Distant or invisible object (%)	0	16	24	8	24
Shared activity (%)	0	10	14	23	36
Supportive action (%)	0	0	19	47	29
Minutes of recording	150	120	120	120	150
Number of requests/10 minutes	1.5	1.6	1.8	4.3	2.3
Adult responses to children's requests *Type of response*					
Pronomical question					
Open question (who, what, which) (%)	78	55	36	8	1
Closed question (yes, no) (%)	3	10	18	30	22
Comment/Question (yes, no) (%)	6	27	36	25	36
Comment/Question on agency (%)	8	2	0	20	28
"Language lesson" (%)	6	6	9	14	4
Request for reason (%)	0	0	0	3	5
Other (%)	0	0	1	0	4
Number of utterances	36	51	22	116	100

A second major function of speech is requesting something of another person. Carolyn Roy and I have been studying its development during the first two years of life. Requesting requires an indication that you want *something* and *what* it is you want. In the earliest procedures used by children it is difficult to separate the two. First the child vocalizes with a characteristic intonation pattern while reaching eagerly for the desired nearby object – which is most often held by the mother. As in virtually all early exchanges, it is the mother's task to interpret, and she works at it in a surprisingly subtle way. During our analyses of Richard when he was from 10 to 24 months old and Jonathan when he was 11 to 18 months old, we noticed that their mothers frequently seemed to be teasing them or withholding obviously desired objects. Closer inspection indicated that it was not teasing at all. They were trying to establish whether the infants really wanted what they were reaching for, urging them to make their intentions clearer.

When the two children requested nearby objects, the mothers were more likely to ask "Do you really want it?" than "Do you want the X?" The mother's first step is pragmatic, to establish the sincerity of the child's request.

Children make three types of requests, reflecting increasing sophistication in matters that have nothing to do with language. The first kind that emerges is directed at obtaining nearby, visible objects; this later expands to include distant or absent objects where the contextual understanding of words like "you, me," "this, that," and "here, there" is crucial. The second kind of request is directed at obtaining support for an action that is already in progress, and the third kind is used to persuade the mother to share some activity or experience.

When children first begin to request objects, they typically direct their attention and their reach, opening and closing their fists, accompanied by a characteristic intonation pattern. As this request expands, between 10 and 15 months, an observer immediately notes two changes. In reaching for distant objects, a child no longer looks solely at the desired object, but shifts his glance back and forth between the object and his mother. His call pattern also changes. It becomes more prolonged, or its rise; fall is repeated, and it is more insistent. Almost all of Richard's and Jonathan's requests for absent objects were for food, drink, or a book to be read, each having its habitual place. Each request involved the child's gesturing toward the place.

When consistent word forms appeared, they were initially idiosyncratic labels for objects, gradually becoming standard nouns that indicated the desired objects. The children also began initiating and ending their requests with rules. The development of this pattern is paced by the child's knowledge, which shared with the mother, of where things are located and of her willingness to fetch them if properly asked. Once the child begins requesting distant and absent objects, the mother has an opportunity to require that the desired object be specified. Sincerity ceases to be at issue, though two other conditions are imposed: control of agency (who is actually to obtain the requested object, with emphasis on the child's increasing independence) and control of "share" (whether the child has had enough).

Requests for joint activity contrast with object requests. I think they can be called precursors to invitation. They amount to the child asking the adult to share in an activity or an experience – to look out of the window into the garden together, to play Ride-a-cockhorse, to read together. They are the most playlike form of request, and in consequence they generate a considerable amount of language of considerable complexity. It is in this format that the issues of agency and share (or turn) emerge and produce important linguistic changes.

Joint activity requires what I call joint role enactment, and it takes three forms: one in which the adult is agent and the child recipient or experiencer (as in early book reading); another in which there is turn taking with the possibility of exchanging roles (as in peekaboo); and a third in which roles run parallel (as in looking around the garden together). Most of what falls into these categories is quite ritualized and predictable. There tend to be rounds and turns, and no specific outcome is required. The activity itself is rewarding. In this setting the child first deals with share and turn by adopting such forms of linguistic marking as *more* and *again*. These appear during joint role enactment and migrate rapidly into formats involving requests for distant objects.

It is also in joint role enactment that the baby's first consistent words appear and, beginning at 18 months, word combinations begin to explode. *More X* (with a noun) appears, and also combinations like *down slide, brrm brrm boo knee, Mummy ride*, and *Mummy read*. Indeed it is in these settings that full-blown ingratiatives appear in appropriate positions, such as prefacing a request with *nice Mummy*.

Characteristically, less than 5 percent of the mother's responses to a child's requests before he is 17 months old have to do with agency (or who is going to do, get, or control something). After 17 months, that figure rises to over 25 percent. At that juncture the mothers we studied began to demand that their children adhere more strictly to turn taking and role respecting. The demand can be made most easily when they are doing something together, for that is where the conditions for sharing are most clearly defined and least likely, since playful, to overstrain the child's capacity to wait for a turn. But the sharp increase in agency as a topic in their dialogue reflects as well the emergence of a difference in their wishes.

The mother may want the child to execute the act requested of her, and the child may have views contrary to his mother's about agency. In some instances this leads to little battles of will. In addition, the child's requests for support more often lead to negotiation between the pair than is the case when the clarity of the roles in their joint activity makes acceptance and refusal easier. A recurrent trend in development during the child's first year is the shifting of agency in all manner of exchanges from mother to infant. Even at 9 to 12 months, Richard gradually began taking the lead in give-and-take games.

The same pattern holds in book reading, where Richard's transition was again quite rapid. Role shifting is very much part of the child's sense of script, and I believe it is typical of the kind of "real world" experience that makes it so astonishingly easy for children to master soon afterwards the deictic shifts, those contextual changes in the meaning of words that are essential to understanding the language. At about this time the child learns that I am *I* when I speak, but *you* when referred to by another, and so too with *you*; and eventually the child comes to understand the associated spatial words, *here* and *there, this* and *that, come* and *go*.

The prelinguistic communicative framework established in their dialogue by mother and child provides the setting for the child's acquisition of this language function. His problem solving in acquiring the deictic function is a *social* task: to find the procedure that will produce results, just as his prelinguistic communicative effort produced results, and the results needed can be interpreted in relation to role interactions.

For a number of years an emphasis on egocentrism in the young child has tended to blunt our awareness of the sensitivity of children to roles, of their capacity to manage role shift and role transformation. Although there is little doubt that it is more difficult for a young child to take the view of others than it will be

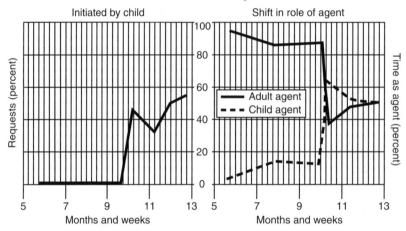

Figure 4.1 Toward the end of the first year the child gradually begins taking the lead in give-and-take games. Through such joint activity a child learns about sharing and taking turns.

for him later, this aspect of development has been greatly exaggerated. In familiar and sufficiently simple situations the child is quite capable of taking another's view. In 1975 Michael Scaife and I discovered that babies in their first year shifted their glance to follow an adult's line of regard, and in 1976 Andrew Meltzoff found in our laboratory that babies only a few weeks old appeared to have a built-in mechanism for mimicking an adult's expression, since they obviously could not see their own faces. More recently, Marilyn Shatz has shown that quite young children are indeed able to "take another's position" when giving instructions, provided the task is simple enough.

According to Katherine Nelson and Janice Gruendel at Yale University, what seems to be egocentrism is often a matter of the child not being able to coordinate his own scripts with those of the questioner, although he is scrupulously following turn taking (which is definitely not egocentric). They found that when "egocentric" four-year-olds do manage to find a joint script, they produce dialogues like the following. Two children are sitting next to each other talking into toy telephones:

Gay: Hi.
Dan: Hi.
Gay: How are you?
Dan: Fine.
Gay: Who am I speaking to?
Dan: Daniel. This is your Daddy. I need to speak to you.
Gay: All right.
Dan: When I come home tonight we're gonna have...peanut butter and jelly sandwich...uh...at dinner time.
Gay: Uhmmm. Where're we going at dinner time?
Dan: Nowhere, but we're just gonna have dinner at 11 o'clock.
Gay: Well, I made a plan of going out tonight.
Dan: Well, that's what we're gonna do.

Gay: We're going out.
Dan: The plan, it's gonna be, that's gonna be, we're going to McDonald's.
Gay: Yeah, we're going to McDonald's. And ah, ah, ah, what they have for dinner tonight is hamburger.
Dan: Hamburger is coming. O.K., well, goodbye.
Gay: Bye.

The child takes into account his or her partner's point of view, phrases his turns properly, and says things that are relevant to the script they are working on jointly. That is surely not egocentrism. But even managing the deictic function of language provides evidence that children realize there are viewpoints other than their own.

The last type of request, the request for supportive action, has a very special property. It is tightly bound to the nature of the action in which the child is involved. To ask others for help in support of their own actions, children need at least two forms of knowledge. One of them represents the course of action and involves a goal and a set of means for getting to it. The second requirement is some grasp of what has been called the arguments of action: who does it, with what instrument, at what place, to whom, on what object, etc. Once children have mastered these, they have a rudimentary understanding of the concepts that will later be encountered in case grammar.

The degree to which a child comes to understand the structure of tasks is the degree to which his requests for support in carrying them out become more differentiated. These requests do not appear with any marked frequency until he is 17 or 18 months old and consist of bringing the "work" or the "action" or the entire task to an adult: A music box needs rewinding, or two objects have to be put together. In time a child is able to do better than that. He may bring a tool to an adult or direct the adult's hand or pat the goal (the chair on which he wants up). He is selecting and highlighting relevant features of the action, though not in a fashion that depends on what the adult is doing. Finally, at about the age of two, with the development of adequate words to refer to particular aspects of the action, the child enters a new phase: the requests action by guiding it successively. The pacemaker of the verbal output is progress in the task itself.

Let me give an instance of this successive guidance system. Richard, it transpires, wishes to persuade his mother to get a toy telephone from the cupboard; she is seated (and very pregnant). Successively, he voices the following requests:

Mummy, Mummy; Mummy come... Up, up... Cupboard... Up cupboard, up cupboard; up cupboard... Get up, get up. Cupboard, cupboard... Cupboard-up; cupboard-up, cupboard-up... Telephone... Mummy... get out telephone.

His mother objects and asks him what it is he wants after each of the first two requests. She is trying to get him to set forth his request in some "readable" order before she starts to respond – to give a reason in terms of the goal of the action. Richard, meanwhile, achieves something approaching a request in sentence form by organizing his successive utterances in a fashion that seems to be guided by his conception of the needed steps in the action. The initial grammar of the long string of task-related requests is, then, a kind of temporal grammar based on an understanding not only of the actions required, but also of the order in which these actions must be executed. This bit of child language is an interpersonal-script based on a young child's knowledge of what is needed to reach the goal in the real world; it is the matrix in which language develops.

In looking closely at two of the four major communicative functions (indicating and requesting), we discovered a great deal of negotiating by the mother about pragmatic aspects of communication: not about truth-falsity and not about well-formedness, but about whether requests were sincere, whose turn it was, whether it should be done independently or not, whether reasons were clear or justified.

There is, of course, more to communication than indicating and requesting. Another major function of speech is affiliation, the forming of a basis for social exchange. This involves matters as diverse as learning to acknowledge presence, to take turns, and to enter what has been called the "cooperative principle" underlying all speech acts.

The final function is the use of communication for generating possible worlds, and it has little to do with asking for help or indicating things in the real world or, indeed, with maintaining social connection. The early utterances of the children we have studied show one clear-cut characteristic: Most of the talking by mother and by child is *not* about hard-nosed reality. It is about games, about imaginary things, about seemingly useless make-believe. What is involved in the generation of possible worlds is quite useful for both conceptual and communicative development – role playing, referring to nonpresent events, combining elements to exploit their variability, etc.

Had we gone on to look at the other two functions, affiliative activity during which mother and child learn the rules for interacting and the sort of play in which possible worlds are created, the case for mother–infant interaction would have been as strong. There is an enormous amount of teaching involved in transmitting the language, though very little of it has to do with language lessons proper. It has to do with making intentions clear, as speaker and as actor, and with overcoming difficulties in getting done in the real world what we want done by the mediation of communicating. And this is why learning a second language is so difficult. The moment we teach language as an explicit set of rules for generating well-formed strings out of context, the enterprise seems to go badly wrong. The rule in natural language learning is that language is learned in order to interact with someone about something the two of you share.

Where does that leave the problem of language acquisition? Well, to my way of thinking it brings it back into the sphere of problem solving – the problem being how to make our intentions known to others, how to communicate what we have in consciousness, what we want done in our behalf, how we wish to relate to others, and what in this or other worlds is possible.

Children still have to learn to use their native lexicons and to do so grammatically. They learn this in use, in order to get things done with words, and not as if they were ferreting out the disembodied rules of grammar. I think we have learned to look at language acquisition not as a solo flight by the child in search of rules, but as a transaction involving an active language learner and an equally active language teacher That new insight will go a long way toward filling the gap between the impossible and the miraculous.

References

Clark, Herbert, and Eve Clark. *Psychology and Language: An Introduction to Psycholinguistics*. Harcourt Brace Jovanovich, New York, 1977.

De Villiers, Jill G., and Peter A. de Villiers. *Language Acquisition*. Harvard University Press, Cambridge, MA, 1978.

Miller, George, A. *Spontaneous Apprentices: Children and Language*. The Seabury Press, New York, 1977.

Snow, Catherine, E., and Charles, A. Ferguson, eds. *Talking to Children*. Cambridge University Press, Cambridge, 1977.

CHAPTER 5

PLAY AS A MODE OF CONSTRUING THE REAL

S. L. Katz (ed.), *Proceedings of the Yale conference on the International Year of the Child* (1979), New Haven, CT: Yale University Press

It was given me as my part of this symposium to discuss the relation between play and learning, and I shall try to perform my duty briefly. Not that there is any lack of material on the subject, for there is a good supply at hand; nor is it that I distrust the artificiality of the research on which our knowledge is based, though that does give me pause. It is not easy to understand what adult-designed experiments mean to children. Rather, I want to save time to talk about a closely related practical matter: how we institutionalize play activity for children in preschools and comparable institutions. I am fresh from a three-year study of British preschool provision. And I helped edit a jumbo Penguin on play a few years ago, to which I can refer you for the state of the art on play research.

Let me start by sketching a few propositions about play as a human activity. The first thing about it is that engagement in play involves reduction of the consequences of error or failure. In some difficult to describe way, it is activity that is not for keeps – though I am fully aware of the manner in which certain rule-governed social play, notably team games and competitions, create their own world of consequences. Another way of saying this is that play is not for extrinsic but for intrinsic rewards – that it is autotelic. Much early play, moreover, has the property that means-end relations in pursuit of goals are loosened or disengaged. We may vary our means without excessive attachment to results, indeed unless we can do so, the play gets boring. Watch even an infant stacking blocks or nesting cups and you will be struck by the patterned variability. A third feature of play is that it is carried out in a constrained and more or less scripted possible world – constrained and scripted in the sense that play defines what is autonomously within the domain and what are the ways of proceeding within that domain. You will recall the celebrated example from Sully of the twin sisters, one of whom says to the other, "Let's play Sisters" and the game is all about equal shares of everything, an interesting possible world quite unlike the real world the two little girls inhabit. This feature is usually recognized by the use of such words for play as "fictive" or "simulative." The latter .of these two terms suggests, moreover, that play in some way is an imitation of life, that it is specular, a mirror on reality. And so it may often be, though more often in the eyes of the analytic beholder than of the participant. Further, it is said of play that it externalizes our inner life upon the environment whilst other, contrasting activities (like learning, for example) internalize the environment into our inner life, what Professor Piaget distinguishes as the difference between assimilating the world to the mind in contrast to accommodating the mind to the world. Finally, play involves challenge and obstacles. It is no fun without.

To assure ready reference backward later, let me give each of these features of play a tag. The first feature I shall call the *irreality* of play. The second, its uncoupling of means and ends, let us call the *flexibility* of play. The contained possible world in which it operates marks the *autonomy* of play. Its mirroring of reality is the *specularity* of play. We may use the term *externalization* to talk of play's route from the inside out. And finally, *challenge*. Irreality, flexibility, autonomy, specularity, externalization, and challenge. And, let me add *pleasure*, would that it could be defined! But do not be deterred by indefinability, for if you are, then you may be in the wrong conference!

Before I try to sketch the consequences of play for learning and problem solving, we need a moment's thought on the uses to which play is put, for though the participants play for pleasure, others urge them to play with other purposes in mind. The principal use to which play is put is, of course, socializing the child to the ways of the society. This is a surprisingly boring topic. For example, the sharing society of the Tengu we learn, introduces its children to group games that are concluded by achieving a tie score. Our children more likely play zero-sum games or winner-take-all. It is boring, alas, because the bare statement of such facts makes it seem that our children are vigorous and competitive, and then we are forced to explain why they spend hours passively watching the tube. There probably is a way in which play serves a socialization function, but it is not clear what it is. Why is early language so much richer in playful situations involving, say pretending, than in the more functional and mundane activities of the child's life? Language is certainly a major instrument of socialization.

It is also said that play has a projective, displacement, or working-through function, over and beyond its pleasure – that it is *therapeutic*. Children should play to work out their problems, according to this view. A curious assertion, it *is* noted in the literature that the most disturbed children are often the very ones who play least, or play least creatively (a word I promise not to use again). Zestful, lively children play most and most complexly, and malnutrition cuts down play drastically. The argument is made that the disturbed child would be helped by playing. And so he should play, for that is his right. But there is very little evidence that persuasively demonstrates that the play will have a therapeutic effect if the root source of the disturbance remains unaltered. Yet one must be careful: twenty minutes of play per day with peer monkeys went a long way toward rescuing Harlow's macaques raised on a terry-cloth mother surrogate.

Finally, there is the classic, evolutionary view that play has the function, and indeed can be used to equip the child with the skills he will need as an adult member of the tribe, that his career in play is a "run-up" to the serious business of life. It is pretty tall talk, that, and doubtless it has some truth in it. Children who are early exploratory in play are more curious actively at school later, though a correlation is not a cause (Hutt and Bhavnani, 1972). But when play is shaped from the outside to have *too* evident a relation to later life, it becomes so consequential that it ceases to engage the to-be-taught players. (I should have included in my original list that play is voluntary, but that would have been too much like assuring you that Moby Dick, after all, was a whale.)

Our little excursion into the extrinsic uses of play leaves us with the sense that the purposeful exploitation of play, whether for socialization, therapy, or preparation for life, does not lend itself to the engineering spirit! Arranging the play of children for high-minded ends may, in fact, have the effect of doing them out of a fair amount of childhood. I take this little excursion so that in the sections following, we may resist the drawing of immediate blueprints based on extant knowledge of what play can do to help children develop.

Now to our first task: assessing the role of play on learning and problem-solving. (I have used the two terms interchangeably up to here not by chance, but because most of the learning we are interested in is really problem-solving: mobilizing means to achieve an end under the control of an intention. Hereafter, in order to disguise my pedantry, I shall just use the term problem-solving.) I want to take as my text an experiment by Sylva, Bruner, & Genova (1976) – their work, my lab. The work was done with preschoolers from 3 to 5 years of age. The children had an interesting little task – getting a good chunk of colored chalk out of a transparent box for their very own without getting out of a chair. This necessitated their clamping together two sticks for reaching it, the needed tool materials being at hand. If they didn't succeed after a bit, they were given graded hints ranging from "Have you used everything you can think of that might help you?" to "I will hold these two sticks together here. Can you clamp them together tightly with this clamp?" There were three groups of children. One group had a period of play with sticks and clamps outside the experimental situation, including a brief initial demonstration of how a clamp can be tightened on a *single* stick. A second group was given a demonstration of how sticks could be joined together with a clamp. A third group got no treatment, save the demonstration of a clamp being tightened to a single stick. The two control groups were "yoked" to the play group, so that time of exposure could be equalized. Let me quickly run through the results. Children who have initial play, and children who observe the principle before the task, have far more spontaneous solutions without the aid of hints than the "no treatment" group. Now, the remaining play children make much better use of hints than either of the other groups. Interestingly enough, the children who play first are much more likely to be goal-directed and opt out less than the other children. The players, moreover, are strikingly more likely to begin with simpler solutions than the children who observed the correct principle to start with. They worked their way up from there, and far more of them showed a steady process toward more complex means of solving the task. Interestingly, more of those who observed the solution principle in advance solved the problem without hints on the very first try, but many more of the playful ones saw it through to solution hintlessly after a first wrong start.

What was it that helped the "play children?" Well, for one thing, the group that saw the task as an extension of play were less easily frustrated. They gave up less readily, learned from their own errors, had the confidence to start simply and get a feel for the situation, and changed their solution techniques much more often and more flexibly. Indeed, knowing the principle in advance may have prevented correct solution when there were setbacks in attempting to apply it – although the children saw the demonstration of the correct principle before being introduced to the task and were not told that it was the only way. They did not generate hypotheses with anywhere near the gusto or frequency of their playing mates. And besides, the initial play seemed to have given the playful children a better sense of the varying serial orders in which assemblies could be made, a pretty useful piece of knowledge.

Like all experiments, this one is an odd little microcosm, a world of its own. But perhaps it illustrates a few points considered in the beginning. It was evident in this little world that the children who took the experiment in the spirit of play felt less "on the spot," carried on as if they had less to lose. They generated more hypotheses about how to proceed and gave up wrong ones more readily, stuck to the goal more and gave up less easily, treated their failures not as daunting or humiliating but as informative. In down-to-earth terms, they were happier problem-solvers. We were somber enough experimenters to have forgotten to count instances of laughter in the several groups, but it was our impression after the fact that the play group laughed more – which would probably have delighted Huizinga. One other thing I must mention. The "players" showed more involvement with the materials and how to get them together, and more interest and sensitivity as well to hints from the experimenter when these were offered. They were "with" the problem and not running away.

So let me now go through our list of features of play. Plainly, the separation of the task from the realities of "pride and prejudice" helped the playing children escape the ordinary frustrations. They were measurably more flexible in generating test solutions and were not stuck so hard with their errors. The task was indeed treated as autonomous and they stuck to it as such without relating it to how the rest of life was going for them. And they were plainly getting more pleasure than their more extrinsically motivated mates. But there is an odd conflict between what we called the mirroring of reality and the inside-to-outside direction of the activity. The playing children were attracted by the task and its demands. There was not much projecting of fantasy. Perhaps it was the wrong kind of task for that. A fantasy task might have yielded more externalizations of inner feelings from the play group than from the others. It is hard to know. The only point I would make is that for realistic tasks, a playful attitude may in fact have the effect of producing more realistic behavior. Play is not only a prod to fantasy, and that will be worth reconsidering before we are done.

Let me now shift away from the little world of experimentation to the large world in which children perform the incredible feat of learning their native language. This is not the occasion for a summary of what is involved in bringing off this achievement, save I should note that it involves not only cracking the syntactical code of a particular language and the network of meanings that are carried by that code, but also learning how to get things done with words, how to carry out one's intentions while taking into account the presuppositions and perspectives of one's interlocutors by systematically marking such distinctions as the opposition of given and new, salient and subsidiary and the like – not to mention mastering the adjacency rules of conversation and the arts of topic maintenance. To those of us who spend a good part of our working lives analyzing the talk of children, all of this does indeed seem an incredible feat, made the more poignant by our own difficulties in trying to understand the rules and, as they are called, the maxims that they follow. And at that, I have failed to mention the child's swift mastery of the sound system of his native language which even shows up in his late babbling before he has entered upon lexico-grammatical speech. Well, it would seem like serious business – learning how to bring another's attention to what *you* are attending to, learning to get others to help, learning to pose possibilities, and learning to do this in a manner to meet what are called sincerity and felicity conditions. In fact, a great deal of the acquisition of language takes place not under the duress of striving for real goals, but in playful situations. As George Miller put it in his delightful book on language acquisition – appropriately titled *Spontaneous Apprentices* – the growing edge of language is found in playful, pretending, "useless" activity. It is in these relatively inconsequential, yet structured situations that one finds the earliest occurrences of such grammatical marvels as conditionals, imbeddings, anaphora and ellipsis, topicalization, and the like. You may respond by pointing out, quite rightly, that indeed, most of the child's early life is spent in play, and I would agree. But if you analyze your speech corpus and separate out the "serious" times (when the child could really *use* some more language to get what he badly wants) from the less serious times, you will find that it is not in the furnace of necessity but in play that the most daring linguistic hypotheses are generated. And that should give us pause, for by all odds the most complex intellectual feat brought off by the young child is his mastery of his native tongue. And I beg you to desist from concluding that it is because language is innate. However much that may be, the case forms of Hungarian are not innate, nor the ergative particles of Kaluli, nor the aspect markings of Portugese verbs, nor the odd rules for the accusative and genitive in Russian not to mention its deleted copula in contrast to our overworked one.

Those of you who are outsiders to developmental linguistics will perhaps be amused to learn that in the last decade the mother has come back into the picture as a factor in language acquisition! There is currently in vogue a view of the mother's role called the "fine-tuning theory" that underlines the extent to which the mother responds to the growing competence of the child by raising the complexity of her speech to match his and also by providing rather self-contained action formats in which the two of them come to share procedures and presuppositions. There is an enormous amount of language tuition that is inadvertent rather than in the form of explicit language "teaching," the object of which is more to help the child get on with his enterprises in play, than to impart to him the rules of how to speak – which in any case, most of us do not understand in an explicit way, fortunately for the child. It is very puzzling that the mother carries on her talk in "baby talk," the so-called BT register of shortened sentences, exaggerated stress marking, idealized phrase marking, etc., close to the child's level. What good is it to the child learner to have the mother talking to him in language that he already understands, Roger Brown has asked. The answer is probably that the rule for learning anything is to keep at it, and whatever keeps the two of them in conversation will do that and provide the child with the chance to entertain and try but new hypotheses. It is also, doubtless inadvertently, an excellent way of assuring that the child will not fail, that language is an autonomous sphere in which you can try out combinations with no danger to either pride or outcome. So the child becomes a spontaneous apprentice indeed – often to the point of distraction. And we know from Nelson's important work that if the mother makes an issue of a word and corrects too bluntly, the likely effect is that the word will temporarily drop out of the child's lexicon.

Bear in mind what the child is working with in mastering language, and what he seems to like about what he is doing. He is working with something as far from finger-paint, sand, clay, or a water-table as you could possibly imagine. It is as far from those things as a formal minuet is from leaping about in exuberant joy. Both of those, minuets and exuberant leaps, are joys to perform, the latter naturally and the former with a little opportunity for practice. And the lesson of language acquisition is surely that the child appears to be getting great pleasure in practicing the non-dangerous but infinitely structured game of language. There is a stunning study by Ruth Weir of her son's language after he had been put in his crib for the night with the lights out. It is full of metalinguistic play, as the great linguist Roman Jakobson says in his introduction to Weir's book – permissible and systematically impermissible word orders and sound sequences which the child thinks are very funny, as children do in their word play with each other. There is an enormous fund of playful zest in language learning, enough so that the linguist Karl Bühler even thought it useful to give it the name *Funktionslust*, pleasure in exercising the linguistic function solely for its own sake. If that stands, I want to add to it my list of Lusts as well – Monopolylust, Cowboy-and-Indianlust, Hide-and-Seeklust, etc.

Now I may turn at last to what concerns me most about play and its use in the preschool. You will have suspected by now that I take the view that play is an *approach* to anything you may care to undertake and not a thing – a process, not a product. Erik Erikson told me that the subjects in the longitudinal growth study at California whom he revisited when they were well launched into grown-up life could be distinguished most strikingly as those who sharply separated work and play in their lives and those who had let the two (rather like the child mastering language) remain fused. The latter, he felt, had led the more interesting lives.

There is a curious ideology that grew up during the last generation in nursery schools and playgroups in Britain. Its main lines were that there were certain *activities* that were *really* play and that these were best unconstrained by structured properties in the material or activities played with. I have already mentioned sand, clay, finger-paint, and water. I can add to this approved list, spontaneous interaction in contrast to structured games governed by rules. There were probably two premises that underlay this choice of the instruments of play. One was the view already explored – that play should be from the inside-out and that it projected inner tensions on the world possibly in some releasing if not therapeutic way. The other (and it has to do with the banning of formulated games with rules) was that adults should stay off children's backs, and that traditional games were imposed by adults rather than created by the child himself.

Now let me turn to our study in Britain, that part of it having to do with nursery schools and playgroups which was directed by Kathy Sylva. Many hours of close observation were made of children in these schools and groups, using what is known as the "target child" observation technique in which an individual child is observed in the group setting for a half hour at a time. Observations on his play and other activities including language and other social interactions are made every thirty seconds. It is an extremely interesting technique for it permits one to see the flow of a child's activity over a considerable period, how long he stays committed to what kinds of activities, under what circumstances, and with whom. It certainly provided eye-opening material for our study of the state of preschool provision in Britian, a project undertaken for the Social Science Research Council of Great Britain.

Before I say a word further about the results, and lest what I say be taken as critical, I must report to you that as far as the part-time care of children in Britain (i.e., the under-fives of nonworking mothers, it was found to be in excellent shape and with some rather unique features. The most striking of these is the development of the voluntary sector, the playgroup movement, mostly under the auspices of the nationwide Preschool Playgroup Association – the PPA as it is known locally far and wide. It is run by parents, parents who are offered training if they wish to lead or help lead groups, run on a shoestring in church halls and other handy-andy sites. It was founded through a letter by one Belle Tutaev who wrote to The *Guardian's* correspondence columns in 1962 asking whether there were any other parents who would like to team up with her to start a group to work on their own on a rota basis. Today, seventeen years later, there are thousands of such groups organized locally all over England, Scotland, Wales, and Northern Ireland (and in the Republic of Ireland as well) with over a half million children enrolled. More than that, it has created a sense of a community of parents and given a practical voice to the Woman's Movement (the young marrieds, of course) that is incomparable. My British friends and colleagues, past masters at doing things rather quietly and low key, think it is totally unremarkable. I, an American unsocialized by nearly a decade of living among them, think it is one of the most extraordinary achievements in behalf of children anywhere in the Western World! And it is more so in the light of a sorry performance on the part of successive Governments in supporting preschool education in spite of splendid White Papers. The total annual outlay of Government funds on these playgroups is less than two million pounds, less than five pounds per child per year! It is a sign of the liveliness of the PPA that they have taken our observational research instrument, the Target Child Schedule, and are using it as one of their techniques of training parents who aspire to help lead playgroups. Now let me return to the matter at hand. Please excuse the flag waving!

Obviously, like good social scientists, we put our observations on the computer. We can therefore easily compute such useful measures as the average length of different play bouts and the amount of higher-level elaboration that different activities undergo under different circumstances in the course of play, where "high level" simply means the extent to which new materials and procedures are incorporated into the play in progress. The first thing that I want to report is that in terms of length of play bout and higher order elaboration of play, the leading activities are ones that have an intrinsic structure in them that can be used, varied, and reworked. These include constructional activities with, how shall I say, hard materials; small scale toys and such presumably school oriented activities as form blocks, number games, letter boards, and the like. The category also includes pretend play, and I will want to say a word more about that in a moment. Sand, clay, finger-paints, and the water-table trail well behind. A second point has to do with adults. The presence of an adult nearby increases length of play bouts and elaboration of play, the simple accessible presence where something can be fleetingly shown by the child to the adult in a fashion quite familiar to those who have worked with three-to-fives. The adult, besides, seems to have a buffering effect. But let it be said that an adult intent upon pushing her own program can also *disrupt* children at play. In another of our studies, Dr David Wood of Nottingham has shown that a minimum amount of training in which a teacher wears a recording device and records her interactions with the children, then goes over the recording with a member of the research team, something that she decides she wants to do without urging, can drastically reduce these managerial intrusions. Adult presence, by the way, also increases the incidence of children talking to each other.

Interestingly enough, two is indeed company. The longest play bouts and the most elaborated ones are most likely to occur when a *pair* of children (or a child and an adult) are playing together. And this is enhanced, particularly in the elaboration of pretend play, when the pair are able to construct some private locale in which to operate – a great favorite often being a blanket draped over two chairs! It is not all funny: such privacy is part of the technology for cultivating the young mind.

Now we come to the temptation of control. What do we do about this to improve the quality of nurseries and playgroups? (By the way, I am not saying that the only thing that matters in the life of a child is prolonged, concentrated play at a high level, though it is interesting that when a child has a share in such he is less likely to be a wanderer or "flitter." Rather, the point I would make is that a good share of it is desirable.) Well, for one thing, we would do well to get away from the notion that if a task is itself structurally demanding it does not allow the child to express himself playfully. The characteristics of the tasks that compel the child's prolonged attention and his elaborative activity are ones that have a means-end structure that can be varied, and feedback that the child can use without somebody first having to interpret it to him. It is as true for language as for other activities. A four-year-old girl says to another in a play, about, "Shall I keep your tea warm while you answer the phone," and the other replies, illustrating Goffman's back-to-back ellipsis, "I won't be a moment."

We can certainly get away from our soft-material biases, but I doubt deeply whether much would be served by incorporating a directive about it in Orders of the Days for Nursery Teachers and play-leaders: get them on structured tasks in pairs, etc. I think, rather, that we do far better to interpret the lesson as underlining the *right* of children to play and to construe the meaning of play in a deep sense. That sense, as I have been struggling to say, is an *approach* toward *doing* things, *whatever* has to be done. I think that is the way, in Erikson's sense, we keep play from becoming a separate activity apart from life, to be indulged in on Sundays and after retirement.

Let me end on an ideological note. I have been struck by the degree of grim conviction with which people view play – whether psychoanalysts, games mistresses in provincial schools, pedagogues with a message, Her Majesty's Inspectorate, whatever. Play *is* serious business, I know. But might it not be better to observe a bit more again what children *do* and to expose our convictions to our observations? I strongly recommend that over a period of weeks we observe a single child a few times for a halfhour at a time, and brood over what we see. We will, I think, have less of a theory and more of a pragmatic ruefullness about the impact of what we do in the name of proper practice. In Britain, for example, where most nursery teachers and play-leaders are well trained and eager to help children, it surprised all of us, that a child converses with an adult (conversation defined as a three-turn exchange) on average only once every nine minutes, which is anything but prolific. And at that, it is more likely to be about managerial matters than about an activity into the heart of which the teacher can enter. Is that good enough? (This can be improved by the David Wood technique mentioned earlier.) Or to take another example, prolonged and elaborated play is more likely to be ended by distraction than by having reached its own climax. Have we done enough imaginatively to achieve what the great Yale architect Serge Chermayeff called "privacy baffles," ways of dividing spaces in such a way that pairs at play can be more readily protected from being run down – low partitions and walls or whatever, or even more chairs and more blankets to go over them?

I do not mean to end on a diminuendo of small detail, nor do I think that is what my examples are about. Rather, I am suggesting that instead of trying to engineer children's *play* (which ends up tight and overformulated) we think about *shaping environments in which children can more fully and fairly play*. It will involve not grand theories but cool heads to consider how adults can better help; where buffers might go, what might better be in the cupboard of toys and games, and how to be courteous in the presence of those at play.

I hope I have convinced you that the evidence suggests that a little playfulness is a powerful aid to learning and problem-solving – though it is by no means clear how it does so in detail in different forms of activity, and what effect this has in shaping the approach of the later adult to the tasks he will encounter in "real life." Let us for the moment take all that for granted as a reasonable and viable hypothesis, and keep at our research until we know better and in more detail what is involved. The real question, viewed institutionally, is how to *help* children play. It is almost, always related in anecdotal accounts of great scientific laboratories like Bohr's in Copenhagen or Lord Rutherford's at the Cavendish in Cambridge, that they were very playful and even jolly places. Even James Watson's account of the cracking of the secret of the double helix reads a bit like *Tom Brown's Schooldays*. Grim labs riven with insecurity do not, I think, produce good science. *The New Yorker* under Ross was a little like the mad hatter's tea party. I grant that it is hard to know whether great work produces playfulness or the other way round. Certainly, playfulness by itself produces only playfulness. But I think it is worth taking seriously Erikson's hunch that a streak of play in life makes the play better and life better. If that is so, why not start early?

CHAPTER 6

CARE AWAY FROM HOME

Under Five in Britain (1980), London: Grant McIntyre

In this chapter, we concern ourselves with the kinds of preschool care available in Britain, with the need for such care, with the amount and cost of care that is available, and with how these matters compare with expectations.

The kinds of care available

There are four major forms of care away from home available for under-fives, each with variants. Since there is a good deal of confusion about differences between them (even among the parents of under-fives), let me define each as officially understood, noting exceptions as we go. I will also try to give a sense of the clientele for each type of care arrangement. 'At home' arrangements – the baby-sitter who comes to the child's home and the live-in 'nanny' or *au pair* girl – are not included.

Consider first the part-time sector – institutions or groups that take children for part of the day and cannot, therefore, serve the needs of the working mother engaged in full-time employment.

The *playgroup* is, at minimum a group of six children aged three to five looked after by some though rarely all the mothers of the children in attendance. No matter how big the premises, a group rarely enrolls more than 24 children per session, chance and minor ailments then bringing the size to about 20. Typically, a session lasts for three hours, and if a playgroup has more than one in a day, separate groups of children and adults are in each. As the historian of the playgroup movement, Brenda Crowe (1973) puts it, 'all that can be taken for granted is that the premises and the playgroup leaders have been passed by the Social Services Department; that the ratio of adults to children has been fixed officially and, in some areas, that the groups have not been allowed to start unless the playgroup leader is "suitably qualified"'. In fact, the powers of the specialist workers in Social Services Departments is such that they can waive these requirements if they think it sensible to do so. They rarely do.

Playgroups were originally conceived as a form of 'do-it-yourself' nursery school and came into being in their modern form when in 1960 the Ministry of Education denied preferment in state nursery schools to the young children of school teachers. One of those thus deprived advertised in the *Guardian* for other parents who might be interested in setting up a cooperative group. From these informal arrangements has grown an enormous playgroup movement in Britain. As we shall see in more detail in the following chapters, the curriculum is not easily described and tends to focus more on play than on instruction.

From the start playgroups were set up to fulfil a variety of local needs, from combating the anonymity and isolation of high-rise flats, to encouraging hospitalized children, to 'mixing' in racially varied neighbourhoods. Whilst there are interesting experiments along these lines, the principal form of playgroup is a group of 'normal' children from a surrounding area come to play under supervision; it *is* rather middle-class in orientation, and is volunteer in structure. The biggest by far of the associations joining playgroups into a movement is the Pre-school Playgroups Association. It actively encourages its mothers to take a part in the operation of the group and, if they become decidedly involved in leading a group, to receive training in one of the courses organized by PPA tutors or by the local College of Further Education. The encouragement is subtle, ranging from the establishment of rotas to help in supervising the group, from facilitating children's participation in various group outings to help in various money-raising fêtes. A mother can, if interested, even go on after being a 'helper', if she chooses and has the talent, to do a tutor's course. There is a tacit understanding (in the PPA, if not among other groups, such as the Save the Children Fund) that volunteer mothers will shift to other matters when their own children outgrow the playgroup, and it is taken as a matter of faith that 'preschool parents' will go on to take an active part in parent-teachers associations later. In this sense, it is also a participatory movement for mothers. But it would be a mistake to overemphasize the central role of the PPA. It is highly decentralized and the local playgroup, while it may pay national dues, is most often highly autonomous and self-governing.

Some playgroups are in parents' houses but they mostly assemble in church halls or other public halls, often rent free, but sometimes for payment (at least in 1977) amounting to £1 to £2 an hour. They usually operate from 9.00 to 12.00 a.m., the afternoon being a less preferred time for a second group. Playgroup leaders who have qualified in a PPA course may get some pay after their group has been in being for a year or two, usually £1 or £2 for a three-hour session. Not all leaders take groups five days a week, nor do most children under four go each morning. The overwhelming majority of children are three and four, the occasional younger child or older one having slipped in for some special reason. The cost per child per three-hour session averages out to about 50p and some few pay nothing if need can be established.

Playgroups are run by what might be called qualified amateurs. The ambivalence of the movement towards professionalism is suggested by two quotations from Brenda Crowe (1973). Of leadership, she says (in her role as National Adviser to the PPA):

> It does not always follow that because a playgroup leader is an NNEB (Nursery Nurses Education Board) certificate holder, SRN (State Registered Nurse), Infant or Junior Teacher, or the holder of a degree, she is automatically better at working with three and four year olds and their mothers than someone untrained. Some good playgroups are run by mothers, or others, who had no training for anything after leaving school, or who had an apparently irrelevant training. However, it is already clear that *whether or not* playgroup leaders were previously qualified, they would be helped by a specially designed Playgroup Course.

And by the same token, PPA does not see itself as in the business of educating young children, but of simply providing a good opportunity for them to play with other children under supervision. Mrs Crowe, for example, contrasts 'good' playgroups with 'uncontrolled' ones at one extreme and 'rigid' ones at the other. Of the latter she says,

> These are more difficult to explain and understand, for the children often appear to be happy.... But play and child development are so little understood by many parents that they have no such clear idea of what constitutes being happy doing the 'right' thing, or happy doing the 'wrong' thing in a playgroup. In a rigid playgroup, the children's activities are often controlled in groups, and even timed by the clock...

As an association, PPA is trying to break out of what Tessa Blackstone (1971) calls the 'middle-class strand of child care', organizing mother and toddler groups, even considering all-day care on the semi-volunteer PPA pattern. That numerically it is a success story is attested to by the fact that since Belle Tutaev's letter to the *Guardian* in 1960 it had reached a half million children by 1977. The level of support for the playgroup movement varies considerably from region to region. Local support through County Education Departments varies widely, and amounts to some subsidization and support services in authorities like Cheshire and Inner London. In terms of grants given nationally to PPA from DHSS and DES, it has never exceeded a half million pounds in any year – somewhat less than £1 per child registered. Whether one regards these grants as generous or a pittance, it is the case that the chief source of energy and talent within the playgroup movement is volunteer, and such fees as it pays playleaders and supervisors are minimal. It has turned its voluntary status into a form of pride in accomplishment not unlike, say, the Royal National Lifeboat Institution where the pride is in the doing. Certainly the leaders, tutors, and regional advisers of the PPA generate an *esprit de corps* not unlike lifeboatmen!

Yet it would be wrong to give the impression that *all* playgroups have a strong participation by the parents of children in attendance, or even that *most* playgroups are directly run by parent committees. In most instances, notably in the case of PPA, some parents (a minority) are actively involved and interested. The remainder help in various ways for a day or so each half-term. But it is usually made clear in such playgroups that if mothers wish to help more, they will be welcome and, indeed, could receive training to do more. The 'boundary' between the volunteer playgroup and the parent is, so to speak, permeable and not defined by strict qualifications and professionalism. The boundary is somewhat less permeable in the case of playgroups run by such organizations as the Save the Children Fund, where the object is to provide a service. In the twelve thousand or so PPA groups, it would be fair to say that there is at least an implicit invitation to parents to take a hand in the operation, and in a later chapter on Oxfordshire we shall examine some of the ways in which this works out.

An obvious limitation of the playgroup as an institution is its part-time operation which makes it unsuitable for the care of children whose mothers work. In a large housing estate in Inner London, 'Parkview' (Andrews, 1979) there is a playgroup with 25 places; only four are taken up by residents of the estate. Other estate mothers with under-fives go off to work and must make other arrangements.

Nursery schools. If the playgroups are the lively newcomers on the preschool scene, nursery schools are the senior service. They combine long traditions such as the kindergarten designed to stimulate the children of the more liberated middle-class, and the 'welfare' nursery school aimed at raising the working-class child from the conditions of the slum – Froebel, Pestalozzi, and Susan Isaacs on one side of 'self-realization'; Margaret and Rachel McMillan, Maria Montessori and Samuel Wilderspin on the side of 'help for the slum child'. There was never any question about the educational aims of the welfare nursery: it was frankly dedicated to improving the intellectual and practical and social skills of the slum child. In its middle-class version, there was likewise no question, until the advent of 'depth psychology', that the objective of the kindergarten was educational. The 'slum' school's educational objective was mixed with 'moral rescue', in which spirit Nancy Astor wrote her famous letter to *The Times* (of 18 August 1951) to say that it cost as much to send a boy to an 'approved school' for delinquents as it did to Eton. 'The problem of nursery school' she said 'should be gone into from a commonsense point of view.'

Perhaps Blackstone (1971) is correct in seeing the convergence of the middle-class and working-class strands in the emergence of the 'developmental' idea – the idea that the preschool is neither to *give* an elementary education nor to *prepare* for one, but to help *develop* the 'natural child'. Saving the would-be delinquent from the ravages of his broken home or the middle-class child from excessive adult pressure – these now could be seen in a common perspective.

All of which provides a good introduction to the nursery school in contemporary Britain. For in general it tends to be strongly concerned with creativity and expression, and has been until recently very resistant to seeing its function as 'pretraining for school'. The shortage of places for rising-fives in infant schools and the new emphasis upon the importance of early linguistic and intellectual skills has begun to change that. But there is much expressed concern for the individuality and expressiveness of each child. The children in attendance are three to five and in Oxfordshire they average around 40 per school. A nursery school, typically, will have two or more teachers and an NNEB qualified nurse. Teachers are almost invariably trained in nursery education at a college of education or polytechnic, or as infant-school teachers specializing in 'young primary children', and are employed full-time. Their working day usually starts before the starting hour of 9.00 a.m. and extends an hour beyond closing time around 3.00 or 3.30 p.m. Teachers also report spending a fair amount of time talking with parents about children's (and parents') problems, and their calling may often be emotionally demanding. Not all observational studies of nurseries agree on this point, however, and Barbara Tizard reports that such 'consultation' is rather rare. Nursery teachers are among the lowest paid in the teaching profession. Nursery schools are state schools and there are no fees for attendance (though there are also some few private nursery schools that charge up to £1,000 or more per year for a four-year-old.)

The nursery schools of a county, as State institutions, typically have a working contact with and get support from the Advisory Service of the Local Education Authority, and the liveliness of the exchange depends upon the interest of the Local Education Authority and the keenness of the nursery teachers.

As with playgroups, nursery schools do not provide a solution for the working mother. At Tower Hamlets in 1979, for example, there was a long waiting list for places in the day nursery, but vacancies in nursery school places.

It is not easy to characterize *nursery classes*, save by contrast with nursery schools. Nursery schools are free standing and not part of other institutions. Nursery classes, also for the three to fives, are usually physically and administratively part of the Infant Primary schools. Like nursery schools, they are State schools, charging no fees to those enrolled. In Oxfordshire, there is an average of 30 children per nursery class. Unlike the nursery school, directed by a Head Teacher who is likely to be very clearly in charge, nursery classes are in the charge of the Head of the Infant and

Primary School and taught by teachers trained usually in the teaching of lower primary school classes. The curriculum varies, and in later chapters we shall encounter some of the differences as met in Oxfordshire. Like nursery schools, nursery classes have access to the advisory and training opportunities provided by the County Education Department. Perhaps it could be said of nursery classes that they are more school-like than nursery school, but it is not strikingly so.

Specialist child workers in a county's Social Services often place problem children in nursery schools and classes but this is always with the consent of the Head. It may become a source of some tension and dissatisfaction when the number of such children becomes large enough to be felt by teachers to be disruptive.

Nursery teachers (from nursery schools and classes) are joined together in the British Association for Early Childhood Education (BAECE), which has county branches. Very few belong to the more politically active NUT. The world of nursery school teachers is middle-class, joined by a personal network, based on tacit assumptions about childhood and its cultivation. Perhaps the sharpest contrast between the playgroup and the nursery school is in parental participation, which is usually much less in the latter than the former.

Consider now the services available for children who need to be looked after for a longer part of the day than covered by nursery schools or classes or playgroups.

Childminders. Technically, a childminder is any person who looks after other people's children between the ages of zero and five, and does so for monetary reward. A mother (or father) typically brings the child to the minder's before work in the morning and picks him up again at the end of the working day – which will vary of course with parents' hours of-employment. There is very wide variation in what the child will do at the childminder's. In some instances, he will do little other than tag along as a spectator member of the household. There have been instances of children remaining idle and passive through the day with really nothing to do. Other childminders take the children in their care for excursions or, indeed, take them to a playgroup for a morning session. It is very difficult to generalize about the national picture. Obviously the care will vary with the facilities, outlook, and background of the minder.

The typical minder is herself a mother looking after her own as well as others' children. In Oxfordshire, for example, the 480 registered minders each were authorized to look after two children besides their own under-fives. The minder typically does her own housework while minding her charges. What is unique about the service is that a working mother can leave her child when she needs to in the morning, and pick him up when she is free again at the end of the day.

Minders may or may not be registered with the local authorities. It is uncertain how many minders there are in Britain, for not only are many unregistered, but there is also a fairly rapid turnover among the registered minders, who may or may not stay long at the job after registering. A minder must, in registering, have her premises approved as suitable, and there are safety and space standards applied by local social service departments. In most counties and boroughs in Britain, there is no particular incentive for a minder to register: she receives little benefit in opportunities for insurance rates, and only very rarely in terms of support services. Sanctions are not applied against the unregistered minder. The major benefit for the minder is being on a social worker's list who may then pass her name on to mothers in search of a minder's services. Some training schemes have now been organized for minders by local authorities and two London boroughs are experimenting with schemes to pay minders on a regular basis, collecting fees directly from parents. These plans are meant as incentives to improve the facility of minding and to encourage registration.

The historical roots of childminding go back over a century. Childminding was originally associated with the expansion of the great Lancashire spinning mills in the nineteenth century, but its social history has not been closely examined. As we shall see later in the chapter, there is a continuing shortage of state *maintained* full-time places for the care of the young children of working mothers. There has, accordingly, been a steady increase in demand for minders, who have provided the accordion pleat to accommodate a growing need.

Full-day nurseries. A day nursery is a well-housed, professionally staffed 'home away from home' where children can be left by a parent before work and picked up at the end of the day. The activities almost always include conventional nursery school or playgroup activities with clay, paints, water, and the like for older children, and the nursery routine with cots available for the children for naps and rest. The children play far more in group settings than they do at home, but aside from that it is difficult to characterize the atmosphere of day nurseries, for they vary as widely as views of caring for children in groups vary. They also vary widely in size, most caring for between 20 and 40 children, with staffs varying widely from two or three to eight or nine. Some take children as young as eight months, but more usually they begin at age two or even three.

There are full State maintained day nurseries, plus those run by charitable or community organizations, and also some run by commercial organizations. Some full-day nurseries have also been set up by women working at such institutions as universities, colleges, and hospitals. Some few have been established as crèches by factories with large numbers of women employees. Maintained day nurseries used to be run (as was all day care) by Local Authority health departments up to 1970, since when they have come under the jurisdiction of local Social Services Departments. A study of Lambeth, Manchester, and Leicester reports that social service workers there regard provision of day care as 'preventative social work, and not as a service provided for all in need' (Community Relations Council, 1975, p. 14). And this view prevails in other boroughs and counties. Priority for the places in day nurseries is usually given to children 'at risk' – those whose parents have marital or psychiatric problems or who are at risk in other ways. Priority is also provided for children of single-parent families. Day nurseries are not envisaged as a service for the children of working mothers. Such children are admitted mainly to 'keep the balance'. As already noted, places in nurseries are in short supply. Getting an ordinary child a place at a day nursery usually means a long wait on the list. In Lambeth, for example, where the provision of places in maintained day nurseries exceeded fourfold the DHSS guideline of 8 per 1,000, the borough could provide for only half of its *priority* children.

Mixed models. There has been a move in recent years to set up combined centres that locate a full-day nursery and a part-day nursery school in the same premises, and as of mid-1979 there were about two dozen of these in England. They enrich the day of the nursery child, although they create certain staff tensions between nursery nurses on the day nursery side and teachers on the school side, who operate on different pay scales and holidays, and have somewhat conflicting views of their roles. There is considerable interest in such a model from the point of view of providing a more comprehensive service, but the costs are of course high.

Yet another model that is emerging is the extended day playgroup in which parent participation is more prominent. There has been some discussion of such extended day playgroups in the PPA, although no policy decision has been taken about them. We will encounter one in a later chapter when London day nurseries are under discussion.

Again, childminding and day nurseries have occasionally been used in alternative ways. In Edinburgh, for example, application for a place in a State day nursery may be accepted and the child temporarily or indefinitely assigned to a minder paid for by Social Services in the event that no day nursery places are available. Social workers report that such assignment often leads to dissatisfaction in the parent who feels her child is getting 'second best'.

The need for care away from home

How much need is there for various kinds of preschool provision in Britain? Can it be sensibly assessed when there is so wide a divergence of views about what constitutes 'need'? The topic, alas, lends itself to polarization. The humane view is that every family has the right to as much 'reasonable' care as they deem necessary. But 'reasonable' is not easy to define. Does it include the right of mothers to work while their children are young? Should it take into account the nature of the setting – city versus country? Who shall bear the costs? In times of rapid and uncertain social change, occurring in the midst of economic stringency, little is served by dogmatism on such issues. The facts of modern family life in Great Britain raise all manner of problems for which we have no ready-made answers. We might properly begin by considering some of the factors that have increased demand for preschool provision. Among them are (a) the number of women working, (b) the increase in single-parent families, (c) the scattering of the extended family and the attendant pressures on the nuclear family, (d) the new status of women, (e) the stress and isolation of urban family living, (f) the changing philosophies of childhood, and (g) the reappraisal of the influence of infancy and childhood.

Take first the issue of mothers at work. The increase in Britain's labour force in the last quarter century is made up almost entirely by the entry of women into employment. In 1951, there were 15.6 million men employed in Britain. In 1976 that figure was 15.9 million. In 1951, there were 7.0 million women at work, in 1976 10.0 million. The male labour force has increased by 2 per cent in a quarter of a century, the female by 43 per cent (CSO *Social Trends*, 1977, Table 5.2). If we now ask who are these women who have swelled the British labour force the answer, unequivocally, is that they are married women. The figures are striking. In 1951 there were 4.3 million unmarried women at work, since which time that number has declined steadily until it had reached 3.2 million in 1976 – a net loss of 26 per cent. The number of married women employed in 1951 was 2.7 million and that has risen steadily since to 6.7 million in 1976, an increase in the married female labour force of 148 per cent! If we probe still further into which sector of the female married population has contributed most to the work force, it turns out to be married women with children, and if we take the 1960s as the period to examine, we find that in that decade, the percentage increase in employment for mothers of the under-fives was the highest of all – 63 per cent in the decade. What produced the change, of course, was the earlier age of marriage and, with it, the earlier age at which women began bearing children. But whatever the cause, the fact is that Britain over the last decade and a half has witnessed a huge increase in the number of married women at work who have small children.

More specifically, there were 19 per cent of mothers of under-fives in the labour force in 1971 – part- and full-time (*Census 1971: Summary Tables*, 1 Per Cent

Sample, table 37). This adds up to about 590,000 women. By 1974 the figure had increased to 26 per cent, some 900,000 young mothers at work, of whom about 185,000 were working full-time (Bone, 1977). The authoritative Report of the Central Policy Review Staff of the Cabinet Office, issued in 1978 (*Services for Young Children with Working Mothers*) estimated that there were 900,000 young children in Britain with working mothers: 700,000 whose mothers worked less than 30 hours a week, 200,000 with full-time working mothers. By international standards, the figure is not high. Swedish figures indicate more than half of mothers with children under five at work. In any case, high or not, there is a very large number of children in Britain today who, because their mothers are at work, need care away from home for part or all of the working day.

What leads women to work? It is obviously some mix of necessity and choice. Poor immigrant women with children under five work because they have to make ends meet. In Leicester in 1971, 85 per cent of 'coloured' mothers of under-fives were at work, 71 per cent in Manchester, 44 per cent in Bradford, and so forth (Relations Community Council, 1975, p. 9). And when in 1974 a cross section of mothers of under-fives was asked whether they preferred to work, more than half who were in families with an unemployed head and living on less than £20 a week said they did. The comparable figure for mothers in families earning more than £60 a week was 20 per cent – a sharp reduction by contrast, but still a considerable figure (Bone, 1977). For mothers of the under-fives in general (leaving out those who were single-parents and the sole support of their families), virtually three in ten want to work. Of the single-parent mothers, the figure is close to three quarters.

It would be a serious error to interpret the increase in women at work as the result entirely of economic pressures. Indeed, at the lower end of the scale, the pressures are ferocious and the figures cited for coloured immigrant women can only be interpreted in that light. But many young mothers wish to work, and the reasons often lie beyond economics.

One predisposing factor is the condition of life in modern urban society: anonymous, technical, and mobile. The extended family of traditional society no longer provides a supporting net, and its successor, the modern nuclear family, often isolates mother and child from close relationships with others. A sense of helplessness develops. A major conclusion of last year's Report of the Carnegie, Commission of Children (Kenniston, 1977) surely cannot be true only of the United States. It says:

> If parents are frustrated, it is no wonder: for although they have the responsibility for their children's lives, they hardly ever have the voice, the authority, or the power to make others listen to them.

In Britain a recent Government survey (Bone, 1977) indicates that about one third of parents of preschool children have been unable to find the out-of-home help they feel they need in raising their young. Whereas the traditional extended family included aunts, uncles, and grandparents who might share in child care, the result of displacement into an urban area is to cut off effective links with close kin (Stacey, 1960). The urban setting provides little by way of community. A recently completed survey of a high-density inner-London housing estate included interviews with the tenants. The most pronounced dissatisfaction was found among the parents of young children, regardless of playground facilities nearby or the height of their flat. The same study indicates that in this London housing estate, neighbourliness is 'casual and involuntary' and there is very little visiting. Those who are most disorganized by such circumstances of living are unable even to take advantage of playgroups and other facilities laid on for parents with small children (Shinman, 1975). Not very surprising, then, that there is a considerable incidence of disturbance that has aroused the concern of psychiatrists. A study by Brown (1978) estimates that 25 per cent the mothers of children the mothers of children under five are at one time or another on tranquillizers for depression and allied disorders. A comparable epidemiological study in Oxfordshire yields a very similar figure (Skegg, Doll and Perry, 1977). The conclusion that seems to emerge from all this is that many young mothers are eager to find some means of getting either relief from the chores of child care by part-time arrangements – playgroups or nursery schools – or by taking jobs that bring them into contact with other adults for a good portion of the day.

There is one special psychological spinoff that affects *urban* family life. The city is a dangerous place for children – however exciting it may be. Mothers in cities feel less capable of coping with their children and their problems than they do in the village or rural setting. Perhaps the most comprehensive study to date on this problem is by Graves (1969). She compared rural and urban Spanish, Americans around Denver, Colorado, rural and urban Buganda, and around Entebbe and Kampala in Uganda. Her interviews reveal that urban mothers come to believe more than their rural sisters that their preschool children cannot understand, cannot be taught ideas or skills by them, cannot be depended upon. The city mother rates her preschool child less independent, less self-reliant, and less helpful with family matters than does the country or village mother. It is not inconceivable, although we cannot know, that the irritability and frustration of urban mothers both produces the behaviour in children of which mothers complain and produces the perception of them as less capable and worthy. The urban environment seems both to restrict the child and harass the mother.

There have also been ideological changes that have affected the definition of family responsibility. The historian Edward Shorter (1976) argues that the trend in family life from the nineteenth to the twentieth century is from 'community obligations' to 'self-fulfilment', from 'allegiance' to 'sanctioned egoism'. He writes:

> Market capitalism was at the root of the revolution in sentiment.... The logic of the market-place positively demands individualism: the system will succeed only if each participant ruthlessly pursues his self-interest, buying cheap, selling dear, and enhancing his own interests at the cost of his competitors.... Thus, the free market engraves upon all who are caught up in it the attitude: 'Look out for number one.'

Shorter sees the isolated nuclear family not just as a result of the geography of industrial urbanization, but as a psychological matter as well. In the mid-nineteenth century, the 'liberated woman' was concerned to nurture the family, free of the pressure of work. Prosperity and the new technology turned women inward to their families – created a *more* nuclear family. But with the evolving of market capitalism, Shorter proposes, the nuclear family became the battlefield of a new civil war with women finally looking for outlets *outside* the family in order to fulfil *their* aspirations for individuality. What is certainly evident is that some very fundamental changes have been and are in process and they are altering the pattern of modern family life. Whether 'market capitalism' is the root cause must remain moot, for the changes in progress seem to be as profound in Britain as in America, in Holland as in Hungary, in Egypt as in Japan. And how much such socio-cultural factors interact with the Pill as an instrument in family planning, under the control of the woman, is very difficult to assess. It is said to reduce the size of families. Does voluntary choice also affect commitment to families already in being? Divorce is strikingly on the increase. In the United States, divorce affects more than one marriage in three, and Britain is moving towards that figure. In absolute terms, there has been an increase in divorces made final from 29,000 in 1951 to 79,000 in 1971 to 120,000 in 1975 – a quadrupling in a quarter of a century. Indeed, from the point of view of families with children under five, divorces have increased from 18,000 in 1970 to 33,400 in 1975. This partly reflects changes in the laws governing divorce, but those changes themselves reflect the altered situation.

A recent survey by Harmon (1977) in the United States noted that the number of children under six living with single parents had jumped 'by a staggering 54 per cent' between 1960 and 1973, 'such that by 1974 over 15 per cent of all under-six children were living in one parent circumstances'. While in 1974 in the United States 62 per cent of single mothers worked, the figure for all married mothers was only 40 per cent. But more striking still, the children of single mothers were far less fortunate economically. They *had* to work.

> . . . . while 8.7 per cent of children living in families headed by men were doing so at income levels lower than the officially determined poverty level, 51.5 per cent of those children in single-mother-headed families were in that condition.

The figures for Britain are comparable. In 1971, 3 per cent of two-parent families were on supplementary benefits, but 46 per cent of the fatherless families (Finer Report, 1974).

While more than half the nation's 24,000 maintained day-nursery places were filled by children from one-parent families, the provision of places was so meagre, however, that only five in one hundred children under five in one-parent families were looked after. This figure is far below any standard figure on need formulated in the White Papers of the sixties and seventies. It is ironic that in the ten-year development plans submitted to the Department of Health in 1962, only five local health authorities had plans to expand their day nurseries – and this at the start of a decade in which the British divorce rate was to treble and the female labour force to increase dramatically (Blackstone, 1971).

Nor has it been easy for the single-parent mother to wend her way through the bureaucracy to obtain help for reimbursing childminders and baby-sitters while she works. A case was *sub judice* before the Inland Revenue Special Commissioners in 1978 in which a divorced working mother who was the single source of support of her two children was appealing her right to deduct expenses for childminders and baby-sitter, as 'necessarily' as well as 'wholly and exclusively' for the performance of her job. A previous ruling, Halstead v. Condon, had found that it was not deductible. The ruling has been sustained.

Less tangible changes are affecting the demand for preschool care – ones that do not lend themselves to close statistical analyses, but which are nonetheless important. Two of these are particularly important: the changing status of women and the changing conception of childhood, both products of the last quarter century.

The first is the 'women's movement'. It has affected not only sexual politics but, the politics domesticity. Women insist more upon autonomy. They are plainly not as prepared to be isolated as much as before while bringing up small children. And as the role of physical strength in work is replaced by technical qualifications, job opportunities become available to them. So women have been doing better in 'men's' subjects and their performance in Britain on O and A levels has improved faster than their male fellow students'. As young mothers, they are often more qualified to get jobs than their mothers would have been. Being 'just a housewife' has even become a phrase of slight opprobrium.

Changing conceptions of childhood have also affected the demand for preschool provision. There has been increasing emphasis in recent years on the importance of an *early* start for the child in the preschool. It is now generally accepted in the community that the early years matter in later development to a degree not before envisaged – matter socially, emotionally, and intellectually. The roots of this belief are nourished both by new research and old historical movements.

There is, to begin with, an increasing conviction that children very early in life should get used to other children and learn to get on with them. In Turner's recent study of playgroups in Ulster (1977), this was g given as the principal reason for sending children to playgroups and it is a reason usually near the top of the list for sending children to nursery schools or playgroups. It may well be a reflection of the anonymity of urban society, of the absence of cousins and easily accessible neighbours where the isolated nuclear family has succeeded the more connected extended one. What before happened naturally must now be arranged. It may be an accompaniment of the 'other orientated' society of which Riesman (1950) wrote so persuasively two decades ago. The insistence that the preschool child 'learn to get on with his peers', whatever its origins, has certainly increased demand for preschool provision.

Doubtless too, the widespread (and principally middle-class) belief that the family by itself can generate a scenario that may stifle the child's spontaneous growth contributes a share to the demand for early preschooling. Freud and common sense 'depth psychology' have probably popularized the idea that for some part of the day it is good to 'get the adult off the child's back'. The fact of the more isolated nuclear family must surely have reinforced this belief. It took me rather by surprise to see how many brochures of nursery schools in Greater London commented on the importance of allowing the child to be free part of the day from 'adult pressures'. Interestingly, it was not until the studies of Brown and Harris (1978) on depression among young mothers that there was much public talk about the importance of 'getting the child off the mother's back'.

A new reason for preschool experience came on the scene in the 1960s. Research in America had shown that an early drab environment depressed intellectual growth. This was very quickly generalized in popular accounts to a concept of 'cultural deprivation' and projects were mounted in America and in Britain to 'compensate' for such initial deprivation. Indeed, there was a period in the mid-1960s when the more intellectual Sunday press in America and Britain produced a spate of articles on the importance of early stimulation in general. That publicity may have added to the demand for more preschool facilities.

In summary then, the demand for preschool care has increase not only for hard economic reasons, but for subtle and psychological ones as well. It is difficult to know on the basis of what has been said how much need there is for that kind of care. This is particularly true of the relation between full-day care and part-day care. It is sometimes predicted that there will be a decline in economic activity over the coming decade in Britain, in which case there may well be a sharp decline in female employment. But this is anything but certain. It is highly unlikely that there will be a decline either in the number of single-parent families where the mother must work or in the inflation fuelled economic squeeze that leads married mothers to go out to work to supplement family income. Where part-day care is concerned, all of the indicators point to a continuing increase in demand – and certainly the mushrooming of the playgroup movement speaks to that absolute issue. True, the decline in the birth rate will reduce the size of the under-five population. But the proportion of children in that population whose parents will be wanting preschool provisions for their children will doubtless rise.

The provision of care: promise and performance

The history of child care in Britain since the war is a curious counterpoint of unfulfilled official declarations of intent, and voluntary response filling gaps left by inaction. In 1978, Britain had one of the poorest child care records in Western Europe in the maintained sector, and arguably the best record in the world in the do-it-yourself care of the under-fives.

First with respect to implied promises. Contemporary targets go back at least to the Plowden Report of early 1967 and were reiterated in Mrs Thatcher's 1972 White Paper, *Education: a Framework for Expansion.* The latter acknowledges the targets of the former in the following passage (paragraphs 16–17, pages 4–5):

> The Plowden Council estimated that provision for 90 per cent of four-year-olds and 50 per cent of three-year olds would be adequate to meet the demand. The action the Government now propose will give effect to these recommendations. Their aim is that, within the next ten years, nursery education should become available without charge, within the limits of demand estimated by Plowden, to those children of three and four whose parents wish them to benefit from it.

The actual recommendations of Plowden are contained in Table 6.1, drawn from the Report (table 10, page 128, vol. 1).

The cost (in 1975 money) of the projected plan would have been roughly as follows. The White Paper recommended that 'most' of the expansion should take the form of added nursery classes, without specifying what the fraction should be. We may take the ratio of 2 to 1, nursery classes to nursery school as an appropriate guess. This would mean the provision of 500,000 full-time nursery class places and 245,700 nursery school places. On average for that year, a full-time nursery school place cost £482 per annum, a place in a nursery class £305. The total cost by this

Table 6.1 Nursery education: number of full-time equivalent places needed (where part-time defined as half-time)

Age	Time	Percentage of group	Full-time equivalent places needed	
			1975	*1979*
3–4	Full	15	132,900	137,400
3–4	Part	35	155,050	160,300
4–5	Full	15	130,800	136,650
4–5	Part	75	327,000	341,625
		Total	745,750	775,975

Table 6.2 Actual provision of nursery school and class places

	Time	Nursery schools	Nursery classes	Total
Threes	Full	6,023	12,398	18,421
	Part	20,398	47,629	68,027
Fours	Full	8,062	137,096	145,158
	Part	12,808	61,181	73,989
Rising fives	Full	588	171,188	171,776
	Part	622	7,193	7,815
Total children		48,501	436,685	485,186
Total full places		31,587	378,683	410,270

reckoning would have been £272 million per year. This does not include money for building costs, and the decline in the birth rate might have provided much of the space needed. However reached it is a great deal of money for part-day preschool provision.

In fact, of course, the provision of care has fallen far short of those figures. A fair estimate from the Association of County Councils is the following (ACC, 1977).

In 1975, then, there were only 55 per cent of the children envisaged in the Plowden quotas actually in attendance in nursery schools or classes. In a word, half the under-fives in Britain were without a place in maintained preschools. And among the under-fours, the figure is more like one in ten of those envisaged by Plowden. What took up the shortfall between promise and performance?

The answer is playgroups. As we have already noted, the playgroup movement begins in the early 1960s. By 1970, the number of children catered for was 170,000. By 1977, to put it in the bare language of *Social Trends* (CSO, 1977).

> The Preschool Playgroups Association estimate for England and Wales a membership of approximately 11,000 groups in April 1977, and the number of children on register was over 400,000. In Scotland, at 31 March 1976, there were approximately 1,800 playgroups catering for about 49,500 children.

Close to half a million children.

Since playgroups and nursery school serve the same set of family needs – provision of part-time care – we should examine their relative costs and performance. Costs certainly are quite different: the cost per child in nursery school is £475 per year at 1975–6 prices. The comparable cost for a child at a playgroup is, using the same 1975–6 base, £140. The difference undoubtedly reflects the costs of professionalism and the savings from volunteer helpers as well as shorter hours in the playgroup. Nursery schools and classes are conducted by qualified professionals in the ordinary sense of that word: people with diplomas from sanctioned courses, and other formal qualifications. They operate in costly premises. The non-volunteers who go through the training scheme of the PPA receive a small stipend. The moot question is, then, which can Britain afford and what in the long run are the benefits to be derived from the one form, or the other. The PPA, being designed to attract mothers into helping as a matter both of principle and economic expediency, may have a spin-off in community building and the creation of a sense of self-sufficiency. Although many preschool professionals would reject the idea of comparing the 'performance' of the two forms, one careful study indicates that playgroups do as well in encouraging language skills, social-emotional growth, and general intellectual development (Turner, 1977). The improvements found in that study were comparable to those found in earlier studies of nursery schools. But one study, in Ulster, however carefully done, does not decide the issue. The real question, I think, is which form of preschool can best do what, and how much each can be improved – issues to be revisited in later chapters.

British women in voluntary association have by their own efforts, then, gone a way towards making up the shortfall between the implied promises of the 1972 White Paper and the need for care. Roughly half of those envisaged by the Plowden and Thatcher reports were attending nursery schools and classes, in 1975. Those quotas may have been low. A report by Bone (1977) reports that a third of the parents of under-fives feel they are not able to find the preschool provision for their children that they believe they need. The record gives no cause for complacency when compared with Britain's EEC partners. France, with perhaps the most generous system of child allowances in Europe, does far better than Britain at providing care away from home: 25 per cent of two-year-olds, 70 per cent of three-year-olds, and virtually all fours attend state financed preschool facilities. Many of them open from 8 a.m. to 6.30 p.m. to cater for working mothers.

Turn to full-day care. The British maintained system deals meagrely with the working mother and her problems as we already know. The bare facts are these. In 1978, there were 200,000 full-time working mothers with children under five (CPRS, 1978). Fewer than a fifth of their children were provided for by maintained nurseries or crèches. The number of places has changed little since 1961 as the following figures show (*Social Trends*, CSO, 1977, table 3.5).

1961	22,000
1973	24,000
1974	25,000
1975	26,000

This covers a period when, as we know, the number of women in the labour force increased by a couple of million and the number at work full-time by tens of thousands. And since many places are assigned to children whose families are in difficulty, the figures do not really speak directly to the issue of full-time working women.

No surprise then that most of those who wish to or must work avail themselves of other means. The most available means is childminding. One cannot determine the number of childminders in Britain and the number of places they provide. An unknown number do not register. Some indication of the growth of minding can be got from the lists of those who do register. In 1961, minders provided places for an estimated 14,000 children. By 1973 that figure had risen to 92,000, since when, with increased unemployment and declining births it has fallen to 85,000 in 1976 (*Social Trends*, CSO, table 3.5). The OPCS sample survey of 1974 indicates that about three per cent of children under five are cared for some of the time by childminders. About one child in ten who is getting away-from-home care is going to a childminder (Bone, 1977, table 2.7). There is, by the way, little difference in this proportion as one moves up and down the social-class scale. Childminders, we may note, are preferred principally for the care of younger children. A third of mothers wanting care for their children during the first year prefer them, but the figure drops to two in a hundred by the time their children reach four.

Putting the matter in gross summary terms where full-day care is concerned, the figures for 1976 were roughly 30,500 children in day nurseries, and 90,000 with minders, accounting for only 120,500 of the 200,000 under-fives whose mothers were full-time members of the labour force (CPRS, 1978). As with playgroups and nursery schools and classes, so too in full day care the private, more improvised arrangement has outstripped the official, statutory one as far as numbers are concerned. We cannot even account for where many of the children go when their mothers work!

What can be said about the comparative costs and merits of day nurseries and childminders? No surprise that the cost of a day nursery is strikingly higher than the cost of a minder: approximately £1,000 per child per year for a day nursery place, and £280 with a minder – both at 1975–6 prices. Day nurseries may simply be too expensive in their present form for the public purse unless they can be shown to provide a unique service. How good are day nurseries? How good is childminding? Can they be made better? We shall turn to those issues in later chapters.

The conclusion that has suggested itself to many observers of the British preschool scene is reinforced by our closer analysis of trends and figures: the principal provision for the under-fives in Britain is informal or voluntary, dependent upon the efforts and labours of non-professionals, housed either in private dwellings or structures designed for uses other than the care of children away from home. Britain may be on its way towards becoming a socialist state in other respects but in the crucial respect of child care it is from it. Neither in times of plenty (the 1960s) nor most certainly in times of scarcity (post-1974) has there been any indication of major support for preschool care from the State – in spite of high levels promise from governments of the day, Labour and Conservative alike. But throughout this period of 'benign neglect' there has been ceaseless activity in the forging of voluntary organizations to look after part-time care, or of private initiative in providing full-day care. For all the effort, it should be repeated that, as a government survey shows (Bone, 1977), a third of the mothers of under-fives in Britain are still unable to find the help they feel they need outside the home in raising their children.

References

Andrews, C. L. (1979) *Tenants and Town Hall*. Department of the Environment Social Research Division. Housing Development Directorate. London: HMSO.

Blackstone, T. (1971) *A Fair Start*. London: Allen Lane.

Bone, M. (1977) *Preschool Children and the Need for Day Care*. London: Office of Population Censuses and Surveys.

Brown, G. W. and Harris, T. O. (1978) *Social Origins of Depression*. New York: Free Press.

Community Relations Council (1975) *Who Minds?* London: CRC.

Crowe, B. (1973) *The Playgroup Movement*. London: Allen & Unwin.

Finer Report (1974) Report of the Committee on One-Parent Families. London: HMSO.

Graves, N. B. (1969) *City Country, and Childbearing in Three Cultures*. Denver, Colorado: University of Colorado Institute of Behavioral Sciences.

Harmon, D. (1977) A survey of policies for early childhood. Paper presented at the Aspen Institute for Humanistic Studies, November 1977.

Shinman, S. (1975) Parental response to preschool provision. Brunei University (Mimeo).

Shorter, E. (1976) *The Making of the Modern Family*. New York: Basic Books; London: Collins Fontana.

Skegg, D. C. G., Doll, R., and Perry, J. (1977) The use of medicine in general practice. *British Medical Journal*, 1977; 1, 1561–1563.

Turner, I. F. (1977) Preschool playgroups research and evaluation project. Final Report submitted to the Government of Northern Ireland Social Services Department; Queen's University of Belfast, Department of Psychology.

CHAPTER 7

THE LANGUAGE OF EDUCATION*

Social Research (1982), 49, New York: The New School for Social Research

We are living through bewildering times where the conduct of education is concerned. There are deep problems that stem from many origins – principally from a changing society whose future shape we cannot foresee and for which it is difficult to prepare a new generation.

My topic, the language of education, may seem remote from the bewildering problems that rapid and turbulent changes in our society have produced. But I shall try to convince you before I am done that it is not really so, that it is not so much scholarly fiddling while Rome burns to offer a lecture on the language of education. For at the heart of any social change one often finds fundamental changes in regard to our conceptions of knowledge and thought and learning, changes whose fulfillment are impeded and distorted by the way in which we use language in talking about the world and the mental activities of human beings trying to cope with the world. I beg your leave, then, to consider some of these problems in the hope that in doing so we may uncover some vexing issues of immediate and practical concern.

Language and social reality

I shall begin with the premise that the very medium of exchange in which education is conducted – language – can never be neutral, that it imposes a point of view not only about the world to which it refers but toward the use of mind in respect of this world. Language necessarily imposes a perspective in which things are viewed and a stance toward what we view. It is not just, in the shopworn phrase, that the medium is the message. The message itself may create the reality that the message embodies and predispose those who hear it to think about it in a particular mode. If I had to choose a motto for what I have to say, it would be one from Francis Bacon, one already used by a psychologist, Vygotsky, whose writings have greatly influenced my own thinking. In Bacon's Latin, the motto is: *Nec manus nisi intellectus sibi permissus multam valent; instrumentis et auxilibus res perficitur*, or, in my free translation: Neither mind nor hand alone can accomplish much without the aids and tools that perfect them. And principal among those aids and tools is language and the canons of its use.

Let me begin my account with a central proposition. It is that most of our encounters with the world are not, so to speak, direct encounters. We do not even learn our naive physics by operating solo and directly on the world of nature. It is even at the moment of encounter already a highly symbolic world that is a product of human culture. The "immediate" experiences that we have are assigned to categories and relationships that are products of human cultural history. Direct experiences, so called, are assigned for interpretation to ideas about cause and consequence, and the world that emerges for us is a conceptual world. When we are puzzled about what we encounter, we renegotiate its meaning in a manner that is concordant with what those around us believe – or in any case within the limits of the symbolic world that we have acquired through language.

If this regimen characterizes our understanding of the physical and biological world, how much truer is it of the social world in which we live. For, in fact, the "realities" of society and of social life are themselves most often products of linguistic use as represented in such speech acts as promising, abjuring, deceiving, legitimizing, etc. Indeed, if one takes the view (as many students of social philosophy now do) that a culture itself comprises an ambiguous text that is constantly in need of interpretation by those who participate in it, then the constitutive role of language in creating social reality becomes even more central. If it is the case that, for example, ideas like the "New Federalism" or "market socialism" are ways of talking about and interpreting social obligations and priorities in human needs, then the social reality of such concepts comes into existence by acts of talking and interpreting. To give them a spurious existence as "realities" or "facts" or even "blueprints" is to violate the sense of the negotiatory process that creates them and that characterizes their entire nature.

So if one asks the question about where is the meaning of social concepts – in the world, in the meaner's head, or in interpersonal negotiation – one is compelled to answer that it is the last of these. In this view, meaning is not (as Davidson would have it, for example[1]) the sum of true propositions that can be posed about an ongoing event, nor is it the semantic nesting of propositions in somebody's head. Rather, it is what we can agree upon or at least accept as a working basis for seeking agreement about the concept at hand.

So if one is arguing about social "realities" like democracy or equity or even gross national product, the reality is not in the thing, not in the head, but in the act of arguing and negotiating about the meaning of such concepts. Social realities are not bricks that we trip over or bruise ourselves on when we kick at them, but the meanings that we achieve by the sharing of human cognitions.

Negotiating culture

A negotiatory or "hermeneutic" or transactional view of the kind I am setting forth carries with it some profound implications for the conduct of education and, by implication, for the language of education. Let me try to state some of these in general terms and then to echo them in terms of rather specific and practical matters concerned with schools and teaching.

The most general implication is that a culture as such is constantly in process of being created and recreated as it is interpreted and renegotiated by its members. To summarize it as a set of more-or-less-fixed rules that members internalize and apply to specific situations is at best a convenience for visiting anthropologists. It is like characterizing a language solely in terms of its syntax and of its semantics as derived from an analysis of its lexicon. That is indeed a *possible* characterization of a language, but it is one that fails completely to acknowledge how the language is used to get things done in the world. It does not specify how saying things imposes perspectives on scenes (to use Fillmore's phrase for characterizing the functions to which grammar is put[2]), nor does it provide us with any insight into such pragmatic matters as the signaling of stance toward what one is referring to or about the fulfillment of the so-called felicity conditions that we must meet (or violate in some principled way) in making our intentions public by saying something. When we request or indicate or promise or threaten by the use of language, we do so with regard to a loose contract (a set of "maxims," Grice calls them[3]) about preparing the ground, about meeting requirements of sincerity and relevance, about offering an attitude, and so on.

The most generative aspect of language is *not* its grammar (although we know from a generation of research on transformational generative grammar how generative grammar must be) but its possible pragmatic range of use. Or as Dell Hymes once put it, it is possible to know how to construct well-formed sentences and to use the lexicon in an appropriate referential way and still be a linguistic *idiot savant*. You would still not know that the expression "Would you be so kind as to pass the salt?" is a request honoring the voluntary agency of the interlocutor and not a simple question about his limits of compassion. And so it is with the conduct of that human enterprise that we characterize as a culture. There are underlying constraints – as in the grammar of a language – but there is enormous scope for operating within and for using those constraints in getting things done, especially in getting meanings established.

In this view, a culture is as much a *forum* for negotiating and renegotiating meaning and for explicating action as it is a set of rules or specifications for action. Indeed, there is no culture in the world that does not maintain specialized institutions or occasions for intensifying this "forum-like" feature. Story-telling, theater, the forms of science and protoscience, even jurisprudence are all techniques for "hyping" this function – ways of exploring possible worlds out of the context of immediate need. It is the forum aspect of a culture that gives its participants a role in constantly making and remaking the culture – their *active* role as participants rather than as performing spectators who play out their canonical roles according to rule when the appropriate cues occur.

Perhaps there have been societies, at least for certain periods of time, that were "classically" traditional and in which one "derived" one's actions from a set of more-or-less-fixed rules. I recall reading with the pleasure one has, almost, in watching formal ballet, Granet's celebrated account of the classic Chinese family.[4] The roles and obligations were as clearly and closely specified as the traditional Bolshoi choreography. But then I had the good fortune to become acquainted at the same time with John Fairbank's account of the extraordinary ease with which, in Chinese warlord politics, legitimacy and loyalty passed to the victor in the local politics of force, by whatever ghastliness victory had been won.[5] I find myself concluding that "equilibrium" accounts of cultures are useful principally to guide the writing of older-style enthnographies or as political instruments for use by those in power to subjugate psychologically those who must be ruled.

It follows from the view of culture as "culture-making" that I have proposed that induction into the culture through education, if it is to prepare the young for life as lived, should also partake of the spirit of a forum, of negotiation, of the recreating of meaning. But this conclusion runs counter to traditions of pedagogy that derive from another time, another interpretation of culture, another conception of authority – one that looked at the process of education as a *transmission* of knowledge and values by those who knew more to those who knew less and knew it, so to speak, less expertly. And at another level, it also rested on some presuppositions about the young as underprovided not only epistemically but deontically as well – lacking in a sense of value propositions and a sense of the society. The young were not only underequipped with knowledge about the world, which needed to be imparted to them, but also were "lacking" in values. Their deficit has been variously accounted for psychologically, most of the secular theories being quite as compelling in their way as the earlier divine theories of Original Sin. In our time, for example, we have had theories of primary process based on the axiom that immaturity rested on an incapacity to delay gratification. Or, on the cognitive side, we have had the doctrine of egocentrism, which posited a lack of capacity to see the world from any perspective other than the one in which the child occupied the position of central planet around which all else revolved.

I do not wish to argue against any of these characterizations of the child, whether driven by Original Sin, by primary process, or by egocentrism. Let us assume that, in one degree or another, they are all "true." The point. I want to make is not about their "truth" but about their force as ideas shaping educational practice. All of them imply that there should be something rooted out, replaced, or "compensated." The pedagogy that resulted was some view of teaching as surgery, suppression, replacement, deficit-filling, or some mix of them all. When "learning theory" emerged in this century, there was added to the list a further "method," reinforcement: reward and punishment could become the levers of a new technology for accomplishing these ends.

Obviously there have been other voices, and in this last generation they have swelled to a new and powerful chorus. But they have been, in the main, focused on the learning child and his needs as an autonomous learner – an extraordinarily important emphasis. Freud's was among them, particularly his emphasis upon the autonomy of ego functioning and the achievement of freedom from excessive or conflicted drives. And surely Page must be counted a major force in his emphasis on learning as invention.[6] But Piaget conceived of the child as flying solo, trying to make sense of the world on his own by forming representations of it that somehow 'fit' both the hubbub of experience and the formal properties of his own logical processes. What we lack, in the main, is a reasoned theory of how the negotiation of meaning as socially arrived at is to be interpreted as a pedagogical axiom. But there are also some rich sources of theory and research that have begun to be available on this issue, stemming from the work of Vygotsky as in Michael Cole's work, and from the tradition of Schutz as represented by the so-called ethnomethodologists like Garfinkel and, more latterly, Mehan.[7] We shall come to this work presently, but let me first see whether I can clear some ground.

Marking stance

To do so requires a detour into what may be called the functions of language. Perhaps Michael Halliday[8] provides us with the most complete catalogue of functions, although catalogues tend to mislead by their need for creating boundaries between categories. Halliday divides his functions into two superordinate classes – pragmatic and mathetic. In the former are such functions as the instrumental, regulatory, instrumental, and personal, and to the mathetic he assigns the heuristic, imaginative, and informative functions. We need not unpack these in detail but note only that the class of pragmatic functions are concerned with orienting oneself toward others and using the tool of language to obtain the ends one seeks through affecting the actions and attitudes of others toward oneself and toward the world. The ensemble of mathetic functions serves a different order of function. The heuristic is the means for gaining information and correction from others; the imaginative function is the means whereby we create possible worlds and go beyond the immediately referential. The informative function is constructed on a base of intersubjective presupposition: that somebody has knowledge that I do not possess or that, I have knowledge they do not possess, and that such imbalance can be dealt with by an act of talking or "telling." There is perhaps one function, one originally celebrated by C. S. Pence and elaborated by Roman Jakobson, that needs adding to Halliday's list – what the latter calls the metalinguistic function, turning around on one's use of language to examine or explicate it, as in the analytic mode of philosophers or linguists who look at expressions as if they were, so to speak, opaque objects to he examined in their own right rather than transparent windows through which we look out upon the world.

I mention these functions here because they provide us with useful tools for examining the language of education. Halliday remarks that it is the genius of natural, lexicogrammatical language that it permits the fulfilling of all of these functions simultaneously, indeed that it *requires* that we do so, even if we use the option of ritualizing some of the functions at a kind of "conventional zero," but even that linguistic decision carries significance, as in the contrast between the two locutions, "I'm sorry to have to tell you that your mother has just died" and simply "Your mother has just died." What one says, fails to say, or how one says it all carry what Grice[9] calls "implicatures" about the referent, about the speech act being performed, about one's own posture toward what is being said. Together, these constitute what Feldman[10] has called *stance*. The language is virtually infinitely rich in devices at all levels for marking stance – grammatically, lexically, by discourse devices. Included in a very implicit manner in this marking of stance is the perspective-on-a-scene that Fillmore[11] sees as the deep function of grammar itself.

Let me give an example of stance-marking in teacher talk, one drawn from Feldman's work. She chose as an indicating stance-marker the use of modal auxiliaries in teachers' talk to students and in their talk to each other in the staff room, distinguishing between expressions that contained modals of uncertainly and probabilism (like *might, could*, etc.) and expressions not so marked. Modals expressing a stance of uncertainty or doubt in teacher talk to teachers far outnumbered their occurrence in teacher talk to students. The world that the teacher was presenting to her students was a far more settled, far less negotiatory world than the one she was offering to her colleagues.

Stance-marking in the speech of others is what we are tuned to – the full range of functions and the devices we use for their realization. I recall a teacher, her name was Miss Orcutt, who made the statement in class, "It is a very puzzling thing not that water turns to ice at 32 degrees Fahrenheit, but that it should change from a liquid into a solid." She then went on to give us an intuitive account of Brownian movement and of molecules, expressing a sense of wonder that matched, indeed bettered, the sense of wonder that I felt at that age (around ten) about everything I turned my mind to, including at the far reach such matters as light from extinguished stars still traveling toward us though their sources had been snuffed out. In effect, she was inviting me to extend *my* world of wonder to encompass *hers*. It was not just that she was *informing* me. She was, rather, negotiating the world of wonder and possibility. Molecules, solids, liquids, movement were not facts; they were to be used in pondering and imagining. Miss Orcutt was the rarity. No wonder I developed a massive crush on her! She was a human event, not a transmission device. It is not that my other teachers did not mark their stances. It was only that their stances were so off-puttingly and barrenly informative. What was there to think about, even of Ethan Allen, except that he was what he was, a foxy mountain man. My chums and I fixed *our* stance toward him alright: we incorporated him in our backyard play, created a Ticonderoga that had the schools beat a mile, and to this day I remember that battle on 10 May 1775! I was wounded, of course.

Each fact we encounter comes wrapped in stance-marking. But now take the next step. Some stance-markings are invitations to the use of thought, reflection, elaboration, fantasy. Let me put the matter in more formal terms. As John Searle[12] puts it, expressions can be differentiated into an underlying proposition and an operation upon it. The operation is a mode of understanding or treating the proposition – an illocutionary force, an assignment to context, a perspective for interpretation. This is true at any age. To the extent that knowledge, the materials of education, is indeed chosen for its amenableness to imaginative transformation and is presented in a light to invite it, to that extent it becomes a part of what earlier I called "culture making." The child, in effect, becomes a party to the negotiatory process by which facts are created and interpreted. He becomes at once an agent of knowledge-making as well as a recipient of knowledge transmission.

Let me digress for a moment. Some years ago I wrote some very insistent articles about the importance of discovery learning – learning on one's own or, as Piaget put it later (and I think better), learning by inventing. What I am proposing here is an extension of that idea, or better, a completion. My model of the child in those days was very much in the tradition of the solo child mastering the world by representing it to himself in his own terms. In the intervening years, in large measure moved by the problem of the alienated child who by accident of birth feels no stake in the culture, I have come increasingly to recognize that most learning in most settings is a communal activity, a sharing of the culture. It is not just that the child must make his knowledge his own, but that he must make it his own in a community of those who share his sense of belonging to a culture. It is this that leads me to emphasize not only discovery and invention but the importance of negotiating and sharing – in a word, of joint culture-creating as an object of schooling and as an appropriate run-up into becoming a member of the adult society in which he is to live out his life.

Now, much of the process of education consists of being able in some way to distance oneself from what one knows by being able to reflect on one's own knowledge. In most contemporary theories of cognitive development – whether Piagetian or inspired by theories of information processing – this has been taken to mean the achievement of more abstract knowledge by the achievement of formal operations or the use of more abstract symbolic systems. And it is doubtless true that in many spheres of knowledge, as in the sciences, one does indeed climb to "intellectually higher ground" (to use Vygotsky's phrase) by this route. One does indeed come to see arithmetic as a special case when one reaches the more abstract domain of algebra. But I think it is perilous to look at intellectual growth exclusively in this manner, for one will surely distort the meaning of intellectual maturity if one uses such a model exclusively. It is not that I now "understand" *Othello* more abstractly than I did at fifteen when I first encountered that dark play. It is not even that I know more about pride, envy, and jealousy than I did then. Nor am I even sure that I understand better the furies that drive Iago to scheme the destruction of his boss and what kind of driven innocence kept the Moor from recognizing the destruction toward which his jealousy of Desdemona was leading him. Rather, it is that I have come to recognize in the play a theme, a plight, something nonadventitious about the human condition. I do not think that my interest in theater and literature has made me more *abstract*. Instead, they have joined me to the possible worlds that provide the landscape for thinking about the human condition, the human condition as it exists in the culture in which we live. They have provided me with the counterpart of those paradigms that characterize science. Perhaps it would be better to call them syntagmas, "a regular or orderly collection of doctrines," in the words of my Oxford dictionary. The regularity or orderliness comes from reflection, an act far more easily initialed in company than in isolation. For as I shall eventually wish to argue, the genesis of much of our thought is in dialogue which then becomes interior.

I do not for a minute believe that one can teach mathematics or physics without transmitting a sense of stance toward nature and toward the use of mind. One cannot avoid committing oneself, given the nature of natural language, to a stance as to whether something is, say, a "fact" or the "consequence of a conjecture." The idea that any *humanistic* subject can be taught without revealing one's stance toward matters of human pith and substance involved is of course a nonsense. It is equally true that if one does not choose, as a vehicle for teaching this form of "human distancing," something that touches the bone in some way (however one characterizes the psychological processes involved), one creates another nonsense. For what is needed is a basis for discussing not simply the content of what is before one but the possible stances one might take toward it.

I think it follows from what I have said that the language of education, if it is to be an invitation to reflection and culture-creating, cannot be the so-called "uncontaminated" language of fact and "objectivity." It must express stance and must invite counterstance and in the process leave place for reflection, for metacognition. It is this that permits one to reach higher ground, this process of objectifying in language or image what one has thought and then turning around upon it and reconsidering it.

Reflective intervention

I must tell an anecdote. A couple of years ago when I was invited to give some lectures at the University of Texas, a group of students in the honors school asked whether I would meet with them in one of their seminars. It was a very lively seminar indeed. Halfway through, a young woman (she looked sixteen, but I have reached an age where I am becoming inaccurate about such things) said she wanted to ask me a question. She said she had just read my *Process of Education* in which I had said any subject could be taught to any child at any age in some form that was honest. I thought, "Here comes the question about calculus in the first grade." But not at all. No, her question was, "How do *you* know what's honest?" I had never thought of that question before; it stunned me. She had something in mind alright. Was I prepared to be honest and open in treating the child's ideas about the subject, was our *transaction* going to be honest?

This brings me to my next topic. When we talk about the process of distancing oneself from one's thoughts, reflecting better to gain perspectives, does this not imply something about the knower? Are we not in some way talking about the forming of Self? It is a topic that makes me acutely uncomfortable. I have always tried to avoid concepts like that, and where I have been forced to the wall I have shinnied my way out by talking about "executive routines" and recursive loops and utterance-repair strategies. But I think I am forced to it in a new way now. In some inescapable way, reflection implies a reflecting agent, metacognition requires a "master routine" that knows how and when to break away from straight processing to corrective processing procedure. Indeed, culture-creating of the negotiatory kind I have been discussing involves an active participant. How shall we deal with Self?

I am by long persuasion a constructivist, and just as I believe that we construct or constitute the world, I believe too that Self is a construction, a result of action and symbolization. This is not the place for me to go into detail on the concept of Self, but I would at least like to align myself with a school of thought, better to make clear my biases on the subject. Like Clifford Geertz and Michelle Rosaldo[13] I think of "Self" as a text about how one is situated with respect to others and toward the world – a canonical text about powers and skills and dispositions that changes as one's situation changes from young to old, from one kind of task to another, etc. The interpreting of this text *in situ* by an individual is his sense of self in that situation. It is composed of expectations, feelings of esteem and power, etc. It is a-view forged principally by cognitively oriented anthropologists as a means of characterizing difference in conceptions of Self in different societies: to account, for example, for the passive, ritually bound image of Self among the Balinese in contrast, say, to the more "anger" driven image of self that characterizes the young headhunting Ilongot. The reader is referred to Rosaldo's recent volume as a representative treatment of the topic.

One of the most powerful ways of controlling and shaping participants in a society is through canonical images of selfhood. It is accomplished in subtle ways – even to the nature of the toys we give children to play with. Let me give you Roland Barthes' description of how French toys create consumers of French culture rather than creators of new cultural forms. Its wittiness, of course, provides a classic instance of distancing.

> French toys: one could not find a better illustration of the fact that the adult Frenchman sees the child as another self. All the toys that one commonly sees are a microcosm of the adult world; they are all reduced copies of human objects, as if in the eyes of the public the child was, all told, nothing but a smaller man, a homunculus to whom must he supplied objects of his own size.
>
> Invented forms are very rare: a few sets of blocks, which appeal to the spirit of do-it-yourself, are the only ones which offer dynamic forms. As for the others, French toys *always mean something*, and this something is always entirely socialized, constituted by the myths or techniques of adult life: the Army, Broadcasting, the Post Office, Medicine (miniature instrument-cases, operating theaters for dolls), School, Hair Styling (driers for permanent waving), the Air Force (parachutists), Transport (trains, Vedettes, Citroens, Vespas, petrol stations), Science (Martian toys).
>
> The fact that the French *literally* prefigure the world of adult functions obviously cannot but prepare the child to accept them all, by constituting for him, even before he can think about it, the alibi of a Nature that has at all times created soldiers, postmen, and Vespas. Toys here reveal the list of things that the adult does not find at all unusual: war, bureaucracy, ugliness, Martians, etc. It is not so much in fact the imitation that is the sign of an abdication as it is its literalness. French toys are like a Jivaro head, in which one recognizes, shrunk to the size of an apple, the wrinkles and hair of an adult. There exist, for instance, dolls which urinate; they have an esophagus, one gives them a bottle and they wet their nappies; soon, no doubt, milk will turn to water in their stomachs. This is meant to prepare the little girl for the causality of house-keeping, to "condition" her to her future role as mother. However, faced with this world of faithful and complicated objects, the child can only identify himself as owner, as user, never as creator; he does not invent the world he uses it; there are prepared for him actions without adventure,

without wonder, without joy. He is turned into a little stay-at-home householder who does not even have to invent the mainsprings of adult causality; they are supplied to him ready-made; he has only to help himself, he is never allowed to discover anything from start to finish. The merest set of blocks, provided it is not too refined, implies a very different learning of the world: then the child does not in any way create meaningful objects, it matters little to him whether they have an adult name: the actions he performs are not those of a user but of a demiurge. He creates forms which walk, which roll, he creates life, not property: objects now act by themselves, they are no longer an inert and complicated material in the palm of his hand. But such toys are rather rare: French toys are usually based on imitation, they are meant to produce children who are users, not creators.[14]

What Barthes might then have mentioned is that French culture becomes an aspect of French selfhood. Once furnished with its canonical images and formulae for reckoning, the young Frenchman or Frenchwoman becomes a seasoned operator of the system and a seasoned deployer of self. What better exemplification of the process than the production of writers like Barthes, masters of polished self-mockery?

The research of Michael Cole, Sylvia Scribner, and their colleagues[15] on cross-cultural aspects of cognition illustrate the same general point in a more systematic way – the extent to which, for example, the indigenous mode of approaching knowledge is to take it from authority in contrast to a more European version of generating it onself, autonomously, once one has acquired the constituents from the society. As Cole and his colleagues point out, the introduction of a mode of schooling where you "figure out things for yourself" not only changes one's conception of oneself and one's own role but in fact undermines the position of authority that exists not only within the culture but in the very modes of address that one uses in discourse with others.

If we relate this now to the issue to which we have been addressing ourselves – the conduct of schooling and the language in which it is carried out – one sees that there is an immediate application that follows from the "two-faced" nature of language, that it serves the double function of being both a medium of communication and a medium for representing the world about which it is communicating. *How* one *talks* comes eventually to be how one *represents* what one talks about. The stance and the negotiation over stance, by the same token, become features of the world toward which one is taking stances. And in time, as one develops a sense of one's self, the same pattern works its way into the manner in which we interpret that "text" which is our reading of ourselves. Just as Barthes' little Frenchman becomes a consumer and user of French modes of thinking and doing, so the little American comes to reflect the ways in which knowledge is gained and reflected upon, and the little American self comes to reflect the set of stances that one can actively (or passively) take toward knowledge.

If he fails to develop any sense of what I shall call reflective intervention in the knowledge he encounters, the young person will be operating continually from the outside in – knowledge controls and guides him. If he succeeds in doing so, he controls and selects knowledge as needed. If he develops a sense of self that is premised on his ability to penetrate knowledge for his own uses and can share and negotiate the results of his penetrations, then he becomes a member of the culture-creating community.

Exchange and negotiation

Earlier in this paper I mentioned two lines of inquiry that shed some light on the processes we have been discussing. One was Vygotsky; the other a little volume by Hugh Mehan called *Learning Lessons*. Let me say a word about each and then conclude. It is to Vygotsky that we owe a special debt for elucidating some of the major relations between language, thought, and socialization. His basic view was that conceptual learning was a collaborative enterprise involving an adult who enters into dialogue with the child in a fashion that provides the child with hints and props that allow him to begin a new climb, guiding the child in next steps even before the child is capable of recognizing their significance. Interestingly enough, the adult does this by virtue of his conscious awareness of connections that the child does not yet see. In a sense, the adult can be thought of as providing a loan of consciousness to the child until the child develops his own, so to speak. Vygotsky speaks of a "Zone of Potential Development," the child's ability to recognize the value of hints and props even before he is conscious of their full significance. It is much the same style as the one in which, through question and hint and "control of degrees of freedom," Socrates guides the slaveboy through geometry in the *Meno* – a kind of negotiation in which the abler frames the questions, the less able replies and gains in insight. It is a procedure, by the way, that works as well in Cambridge, Massachusetts, as in classic Athens, as we know from the promising research of Collins and his colleagues on Socratic tutoring programs.[16]

Mehan's work interests me because he illustrates the extent to which this process of exchange and negotiation – this culture-creating – is a feature of classroom routines and procedures. It is not simply that the individual learner works his solo way through the lesson but that the lesson itself is an exercise in collectivity, one that depends powerfully upon the attunement of the teacher to the expressions and intents of members of a classroom.

I suppose I can sum up the message this way. Language not only transmits, it creates or constitutes knowledge or "reality." Part of that reality is the stance that the language implies toward knowledge and reflection, and the generalized set of stances one negotiates creates in time a sense of one's self. Reflection and "distancing" are crucial aspects of achieving a sense of the range of possible stances – a metacognitive step of huge import. The language of education is the language of culture-creating, not of knowledge-consuming or knowledge-acquisition alone. In a time when our educational establishment has produced alienation from the process of education, nothing could be more practical than to look afresh in the light of modern ideas in linguistics and the philosophy of language at the consequences of our present school talk and at its possible transformations.

Notes

* This essay was given as the Bode Lecture at Ohio State University in the spring of 1982.
1 D. Davidson, "Mental Events," in Lawrence Foster and J. W. Swanson, eds, *Experience and Theory* (Amherst, MA: University of Massachusetts Press, 1970).
2 C. J. Fillmore, "The Case for Case Reopened," in Peter Cole and Jerry L. Morgan, eds, *Speech Acts* (New York: Academic Press, 1975).
3 H. P. Grice, "Logic and Conversation," in P. Cole and J. L. Morgan, eds, *Syntax and Semantics, Vol 3: Speech Acts.* (New York: Academic Press, 1975).
4 Marcel Granet, *Chinese Civilization* (London: Methuen, 1930).
5 John K. Fairbank, *The United States and China*, 4th edn (Cambridge: Harvard University Press, 1979).

6 Jean Piaget, *To Understand Is to Invent: The Future of Education* (New York: Grossman, 1973).

7 I. S. Vygotsky, *Thought and Language* (Cambridge: MIT Press, 1962) and *Mind in Society* (Cambridge: Harvard University Press, 1978): Michael Cole and Barbara Means, *Comparative Studies of How People Think: An Introduction* (Cambridge: Harvard University Press, 1981): Michael Cole and Sylvia Scribner, *Culture and Thought: A Psychological Introduction* (New York: Wiley, 1974): H. Garfinkel, "Studies of the Routine Grounds of Everyday Activities," in David Sudnow, ed., *Studies in Social Interaction* (New York: Free Press, 1972): Hugh Mehan, *Learning Lessons: Social Organization in the Classroom* (Cambridge: Harvard University Press, 1979).

8 M. A. K. Halliday, *Learning How to Mean* (London: Edward Arnold, 1975).

9 Grice, "Logic and Conversation." (see note 3)

10 Carol Feldman, "Pragmatic Features of Natural Language," *Papers from the Tenth Regional Meeting* (Chicago, IL: Chicago Linguistic Society, 1974), pp. 151–161.

11 Fillmore, "The Case for Case Reopened." (see note 2)

12 John R. Searle, *Speech Acts: An Essay in the Philosophy of Language* (London: Cambridge University Press, 1969).

13 Clifford Geertz, *The Interpretation of Cultures: Selected Essays* (New York: Basic Books, 1973): Michelle Z. Rosaldo, *Knowledge and Passion* (New York: Cambridge University Press, 1980).

14 Roland Batthes, *Mythologies* (New York: Hill & Wang, 1972).

15 Cole and Means, *Comparative Studies of How People Think*: Cole and Scribner, *Culture and Thought*.

16 A. Collins, *Socratic Teaching Programs*, memorandum (Bolt: Baranek & Newman, 1981).

CHAPTER 8

PLAY, THOUGHT, AND LANGUAGE

Peabody Journal of Education (1983), 60, Nashville: Lawrence Erlbaum Associates Inc

I am thoroughly convinced that there is a very special place for a constantly renewing dialogue between those who spend time asking questions about children and those who work more practically with them on a day-to-day basis in play groups, nurseries, and the like. I think that there has been a remarkably rapid progress among biologists, psychologists, and linguists in establishing findings about human growth in children that is highly relevant to the way in which we conduct our education and our play activities before that. We are living in a period in which many practical and theoretical interests concerning childhood are converging. It is a privilege to be a participant in that convergence. We have a special opportunity, it seems to me, for exchanging our ideas back and forth between research and practice.

My subject is the interrelationship of play, language, and thought. I shall try to be brief about it. Not that there is a lack of research on the subject to be reported, because a great deal has been accomplished. But rather, I want to leave room at the end to talk about the practical implications of this subject: how to organize the play activity of children in playgroups in order to help our children realize their potential and live more richly.

* * * *

Let me begin by setting forth in outline what I think to be the fundamental functions of play in activity of children:

Let me note first that to play implies a reduction in the seriousness of the consequences of errors and of setbacks. In a profound way, play is activity that is without frustrating consequences for the child even though it is a serious activity. It is, in a word, an activity that is for itself and not for others. It is, in consequence, a superb medium for exploration. Play provides a courage all its own.

Second, the activity of playing is characterized by a very loose linkage between means and ends. It is not that children don't pursue ends and employ means to get them in their play, but that they often change their goals enroute to suit new means or change the means to suit new goals. Nor is it that they do so only because they have run into blocks, but out of the sheer jubilation of good spirits. It provides not only medium for exploration, but also for invention.

Closely related to the previous point, it is characteristic of play that Children are not excessively attached to results. They vary what they are up to and allow their fantasies to make substitutions for them. If this variation is not possible, the child very quickly becomes bored with his activity. Watch an infant piling wood bricks and you will be struck by the diversity and the combinatorial richness of how he plays. It is an unparaleled opportunity for ringing changes on the commonplace.

Third, in spite of its richness, play is very rarely random or by chance. On the contrary, it seems to follow something like a scenario. Recall the famous example of Sully's little twin sisters, the one saying to the other "Let's play twin sisters." And then they proceed to play a game in which the general object is to share everything with absolute equality, quite contrary to the way in which things go in ordinary life. Yet in some interesting way, this scenario of total equality is a kind of idealized imitation of life. Sometimes these scenarios are harder to discern than at other times, but it is always worth looking carefully to see what in a normal sense play is about. It is often, in Joyce's words, an epiphany of the ordinary, an idealization, a pure dilemma.

Fourth, it is said that play is a projection of interior life onto the world in opposition to learning through which we interiorize the external world and make it part of ourselves. In play we transform the world according to our desires, while in learning we transform ourselves better to conform to the structure of the world. This is an extremely important activity for growth, and we will come back to it later. It gives a special power to play that is heady and, sometimes, a little frightening.

Finally, and it can really go without saying, play gives pleasure – great pleasure. Even the obstacles that we set up in play in order to surmount them give us pleasure in doing so. Indeed, the obstacles seem necessary, for without them the child quickly becomes bored. In this sense, I think we would have to agree that play has about it something of the quality of problem solving, but in a most joyous fashion. But let me be clear. Unless we bear in mind that play is a source of pleasure, we are really missing the point of what it's about.

Let me now say a word about the uses to which play is *put*, though I have just said that play is free and seemingly for itself. For it is the case that (though it is self-prompted) we often use play to achieve other ends we may have in mind. We do this necessarily but at our own peril.

Take first the way in which play is structured in order to instruct our children, however subtly, in the values of our culture. Take competition and competitiveness as a case in point. We often encourage competition in play, indeed use play to instruct our children how to compete well, and from a very early age. Let us even grant that Waterloo was won on the playing fields of Eton. But the children of the Tengu in New Guinea play games in their society that do not terminate in one party winning, but only when the two sides have achieved equality. This emphasis on equality, you will not be surprised to find out, is also very characteristic of the adult society. Does this differential emphasis on the element of competition in play serve to make our society and Tengu society as different as they are? No, that would be going a bit too far. But nevertheless, the way the competitive element is handled in childhood play is a big factor in predisposing children in particular societies to take the competitive stance that they do as adults. There is no question that the games of childhood reflect some of the ideals that exist in the adult society and that play is a kind of socialization in preparation for taking your place in the adult society. We would all agree that it is important to be conscious about how much competitiveness we encourage in the play of children, lest we create so much of it that something of the freedom of play is lost. It is one thing to *use* play as an agent of socialization in some spontaneous way. But exploiting it is somehow a different matter.

We also have it in the back of our minds, when we encourage various *kinds* of play in childhood, that the activity will serve some therapeutic function for the child. Perhaps that puts it too strongly, but it is better to overstate it than to sweep it aside. Plainly, play with other children does have an important therapeutic role or, in any case, an important role in helping children to take their place more easily in the stressful social activities of later life. We know from research on isolated monkeys raised in the laboratory, that if they have twenty minutes of play with other monkeys they will not (like total isolates) lose their capacity to interact with other animals nor will they, like those others, show a decrement in intelligence. Twenty minutes a day of free play is all that is needed to save the sanity of these poor animals.

But to organize play mainly with the view toward fostering mental health in children is also to risk losing something very important. Again there is a danger of "taking the action away from the child." We may thank God and evolution that it is difficult to exclusively take the action away from children in order to organize their play in the interest of their mental health. I do not think we know enough to play the role of great engineers to the young in their or any other domain.

And then there is play as a means of improving the intellect. Yes, of course, but...we will come back to this matter, but the same strictures about great engineering will be found to be true again. There is everything to be said, indeed, for letting the child loose in a decent setting with rich materials and some good cultural models to follow. I think I can even give a practical argument for this view – that we can be quite relaxed about not pushing children through play in order to squeeze some appropriate behavior out of them. Let me tell you about an experiment.

* * * *

It is an experiment I conducted with two colleagues, Kathy Silva and Paul Genova. It can serve as a little moral for my point. We studied children between the ages of three and five. They were given an interesting little task to do. A child had to get a pretty little piece of colored chalk out of a transparent box that was placed some distance out of reach of them. The rule of the game was that they had to get the colored chalk while they remained seated in their chair some distance off. They had all sorts of things to use: some sticks, some clamps, some string. The solution to the problem consisted of making a longer stick by joining together shorter sticks with the clamps or string. If a child didn't succeed right off the bat in solving the problem, we would give him hints, and if that didn't serve, we would then give further hints until he finally got to the end. The first hints were something like "Are you thinking of some way in which you can help yourself solve the problem?" And eventually we would say things like "Have you thought about the possibility of clamping together two sticks?" Finally, all of the children solved the problem, even if we had to guide them all the way home. I can tell you that it was the sort of play that delights the children very much.

We divided the children into three groups.

The first group of children were given a period of play before facing our task, and in the course of that play they had an opportunity to fool around with the sticks, with the clamp and a string, however they might desire. In a second group we gave each child a little pedagogical demonstration explaining how you could join together two strings with a clamp, etc. And in the third group, we simply familiarized the children with the kind of material they were going to be playing with and gave them some simple demonstrations of what the material was like. By a little clever manipulation we saw to it that all of the children had roughly the same amount of exposure to the material as far as time is concerned, although, obviously, the quality of the exposure differed according to which of the three groups they were in.

Now let me tell you what happened to the children in those three different groups.

The children in that first group who had a chance to play with the materials in advance solved the problem better than the children in the other two groups. Let me call these children in the first group the "true players." Not only did they solve the problem more often, but they seemed to make better use of the suggestive hints we gave them than the other children. Besides, the "true players" had far less tendency to abandon the task enroute when they ran into trouble. They were more frustration proof. They seemed altogether better at the way in which they went about things, those "true players." They knew how to begin simply; they had far less tendency to try out complicated hypotheses; and so forth.

Why did our "true players" do so well? To begin with, they seemed far, less frustrated in carrying out the task than did the other children. They neither seemed to resent their failed efforts nor did they feel they were losing face. That was what made it possible for them to begin simply, and also what made it possible to accept hints and suggestions more readily than the other children. The "true players" saw the task as an invitation to-play around with a problem. They did not have to cope with putting a good face on their efforts or of dealing perpetually with self-esteem. They could be free and inventive.

I know this experiment is too simple-minded. But for all that, it was a little microcosm of life. Think of the hypothesis of the great Dutch historian Huizinga: that human culture emerged out of man's capacity to play, to adopt the ludic attitude. Or of those great laboratories of physics at Cambridge under Lord Rutherford or at Copenhagen under Niels Bohr – places known for their good humor, practical jokes, and funny stories. Perhaps our "true players," like those happy physicists, could benefit from those huge benefits in spirit that play grants us.

* * * *

Let us pass now from the little world of experiments with children or with playful physicists in the great laboratories. Consider now how it is that human beings accomplish the formidable task of learning how to speak their mother tongue. For I think that we will also find here that there is a considerable role for playfulness in the child's mastery of the miracle of language. Do not be confused by the aspect of language that is innate or inborn. But remember that there is a great deal of it is that also has to be mastered through try-out and experience. We have to learn all sorts of subtle things like, for example, that when somebody says "Would you be so kind as to pass the salt?" that they are not asking us about the limits of our kindness, but are making a request for the salt in a fashion that honors our voluntary role in complying. I have spent a great deal of time in these past ten years studying how children acquire the uses of their language, and I want to give you a few of my conclusions as they bear on the issues we have been discussing.

One of the first and most important conclusions is that the mother tongue is most rapidly mastered when situated in playful activity. It is often the case that the most complicated grammatical and pragmatic forms of the language appear first in play activity. Take as an example one of the first uses of the conditional in a child of three years who says to another child: "If you give me your marbles I'll give you my revolver if you're nice." It is a long time before such complicated language is used in the more tense, practical situations of ordinary life. In general it has been my experience that playful situations are the ones where one finds the first complicated predicate structures, the first instances of ellipsis, of anaphora, and so forth. There is something about play that encourages Combinatorial activity in general, including the intrinsic combinatorial activity of grammar involved in producing more complex expressions in a language. Aside from that, it matters deeply in a child's mastery of his own language that there not be too many consequences that stem from making errors. Confrontations with adults or older children who insist that the younger child say something correctly will very frequently lead to certain kinds of expressions going underground and not being tried out for some while afterward.

There is one aspect of the early acquisition of language that is extraordinarily important in nourishing language. It poses a dilemma. The kind of talk by mothers that encourages children to enter into conversation is in what is technically called the B.T. register; that is to say, Baby talk, talk that is at the level of the child, talk that the child can *already* understand. How can the child learn his language from talk that he can already understand? That is the dilemma. The solution is simple. The importance of Baby Talk is that the child gets an opportunity to try out the different ways in which he can combine the elements of the language that he already knows in order to make more complex utterances and in order to get different things done with the language that he already has in hand. The child is not simply learning *language*, but learning to *use* language as an instrument of thought and action in a combinatorial fashion. In order to be able to talk about the world in a combinatorial fashion the infant seems to have to be able to play with the world in that flexible fashion that the playful attitude promotes.

There are some celebrated studies by linguists like Ruth Weir and Katherine Nelson that have recorded the "conversations" that young children have after they've been put to bed all alone and the lights turned out. These bedtime soliloquies provide pure little experiments, in which the child is pushing language to the full limits of its combinability. In Weir's observations, her son Anthony goes through sequences like this: "Mommy hat," "Mommy blue hat," "Mommy hat blue, no, no, no." Anthony was the classic instance of a spontaneous grammatical apprentice. Or Katherine Nelson's Emmy, who would spend five minutes of talk pushing to the limits the meaning of her father's utterance before bedtime, that only little babies cry, that she is a big girl, and big girls don't cry. The number of changes that she rings on the theme are monuments to her effort, half seriously and half playfully, to arrive at some meaning of her father's imprecation.

So we are left with the interesting dilemma that it is not so much instruction either in language or in thinking that permits the child to develop his powerful combinatorial skills, but a decent opportunity to play around with language and to play around with his thinking that turns the trick.

Now I think we can turn to the practical question about whether and how we can be, and whether we should be, engineers of play in our playgroups and nursery schools. I want to use as my text a report we published on the organization and conduct of playgroups and nursery schools here in Britain during the closing years of the 1970s.

As you all very well know, there developed during the last generation a curious ideology about the nature of play and how play should be conducted in groups.

This ideology was founded on the belief that various activities were *really* play. Anything that had any structure to it, or that in any way inhibited spontaneity was not *really* play. Moreover, *real* play had to be free of all constraints from adults and be completely autonomous of their influence. True play, in a word, came entirely from the inside out. Its typical vehicles were fingerpaints, clay, water, sand, etc. I rather suspect that the basis of this ideology of play was principally therapeutic, in the sense that it was designed to take all pressure off the child, although it had a touch too of the romanticism of Jean Jacques Rousseau.

Early in our inquiry in ordinary playgroup settings we started studying what in fact really produced rich and elaborated play in children without any particular attachment to prevailing ideology. We we about our observations with the high rigor that serious experiments deserve, in order to find out something about what children really like to do, what kinds of themes and materials they like to work with, and what it is that produced richness and elaboration in their play. As some of you will recall, we made thousands of observations using the most modern techniques, and naturally and eventually, like the modern investigators we were, we eventually committed our findings to a computer to which we directed some very sharp questions. For example, we asked the computer to figure out for us the kinds of activities and the kinds of circumstances that produced the longest episodes of play and the ones that had the biggest set of elaborations on a theme. It isn't that hard to find such things out by hand, but when you have thousands of observations to sort out, the computer helps. The results were more than a little interesting.

The sequences of play that were the longest and the richest and the most elaborated were produced by materials that had a structure that could be called instrumental – that is to say, episodes that had means that led to an end. Mostly, these were activities and materials that made it possible for the child to *construct* something. They were constructions, moreover, whose progress could be appreciated by the child without instructions from or recourse to an adult. I have to tell you that water, sand, clay, and fingerpaint were not up at the top of the list of materials that produced this form of constructive and elaborative play. Such materials, though they have much worth, do not lead to the kind of combinatorial push of which we have been talking. In order to get that push you need some sort of back and forth between means and ends.

A second answer our computer gave us about what produced prolonged concentration and rich elaboration in play rather took us aback. It was the presence of an adult. I do not mean an adult "over the shoulder" of the child, trying to direct his activity, but one in the neighborhood who gave some assurance that the environment would be stable and continuous, but would also give the child reassurance and information as, if, and when the child needed it. Let the adult intervene brusquely and steal the initiative from the child, and the child's play, or the children's play would become duller. In some ways, I think, this sympathetic presence of an adult or partner is similar to the role that an adult plays in the development of language about which we have already talked.

I think you'll be glad to learn that the third secret our computer divulged we already knew pretty well, although it is sometimes denied in the official ideology of the last generation. It is that one is a wanderer, two is company, and three is a crowd. More seriously, two children playing gether can exchange ideas, can negotiate their intentions, can elaborate as needs be, and can go on for as long as necessary. One alone has difficulty sustaining play activity. And three is indeed a distracting crowd with nobody able to hold the floor long enough to carry the day.

Watch two little girls playing at a tea party under a blanket spread across the backs of two chairs. They generate a domestic scenario of astonishing subtlety and richness. Listen to them: "Would you like a cup of tea, my dear?" And the other responds: "Oh, yes, but wait just a second, the telephone is ringing." And the first continues after a pause: "I hope it was a friend of yours." and the other: "No, it was the tailor calling back." And on it goes for five minutes. It is perhaps more difficult to know why it is that children operating on their own, solo, have such trouble in maintaining concentration. I think it relates to a point that has been made by virtually every student of child development in the last half century. Thought and imagination frequently begin in the form of dialogue with a partner, and without the support of another, it quickly collapses. At least early on. The development of thought may be in large measure determined by the opportunity for dialogue, with dialogue then becoming internal and capable of running off inside one's head on its own.

Let me tell you one last finding of our study on the sources of richness in play. I must confess I was rather surprised by it. If a child is in a class or group that during some period of the day requires its children to take part in some high level intellectual activity, then the child will play in a richer and more elaborated way when he is on his own. It is as if the activity of the class playing *together* serves as a model for the spontaneous play activity of the children playing on their own.

We can ask now whether these analogous research findings about plan can help the playgroup organizer become a better engineer of the young human soul. Well, the answer will not be as simple as one would hope. There is little question that one *can* certainly improve the materials and the atmosphere in playgroups in a way to improve the concentration of the children and the richness of their play. That does not take very much doing. It is the sort of thing that we do through the Preschool Playgroups Association encouraging the construction or purchase of better material and the use of better approaches to play. But there is a more interesting matter than that. It has to do with playgroup leaders and nursery school teachers and how they improve the quality of play of children. It takes surprisingly little to bring about small miracles. We found, for example if they simply listened to a recording of themselves interacting with children – indeed, listened to it alone – they would often recognize, immediately what was right and what was wrong. They recognized, for example, the extent to which they were either underestimating or over estimating the ability of children to take and to hold the initiative in conversation, the extent to which they were dominating, holding back etc. Playgroup leaders, having listened to a tape of themselves with their children, would often say things like: "But I don't *listen* enough to find out what they're saying." Or: "I seem to be spending all of my time as a kind of fire brigade, looking after troubles rather than helping children with their projects." They knew intuitively what they should have done but circumstances often had got in their way. It does not take a massive psychoanalysis to get these teachers back on the track! For example, computer told us, to our surprise, that on the average, infants in a play group spoke to an adult only once every nine minutes, and that in the main, these exchanges were rather superficial. Some little experiment in which leaders looked at themselves teaching were promising. Play leaders found they could divide the labor so that one could be freed up to interact more. This went a long way toward increasing the quality, the I frequency, and the length of conversations that children had with them. Play leaders became interested in what could be done. Once interested, consciousness is raised and improvement almost inevitably follows.

I doubt very much whether in any of these interventions, we really become engineers of the human soul. What it amounts to is setting up situations that make rich play possible. I happen to believe that rich, elaborated, and prolonged play makes better human beings than impoverished, shallow, and shifting play. To that extent, I suppose, I am an engineer. Or perhaps, just a human being with some interesting biasses.

Let me draw some very brief conclusions to all this.

To play is not just child's play. Play, for the child and for the adult alike, is a way of using mind, or better yet, an attitude toward the use of mind. It is a test frame, a hot house for trying out ways of combining thought and language and fantasy. And by the same token, there is much that one can do to help the process of growth. But do not overheat the hot house!

We must remember that children playing are not alone and are not best alone, however much they need their periods of solitude. But as much as they need their solitude they need to combine their ideas from their own head with the ideas that their partners have in theirs. Call it negotiation or whatever you will, it is the stuff not only of play but of thought. Let not the school cultivate only the spontaneity of the individual. For human beings need negotiation in dialogue. It will furnish the child with models and with techniques for how to operate on his own.

Finally, play under the control of the player gives to the child his first and most crucial opportunity to have the courage to think, to talk, and perhaps even to be himself.

CHAPTER 9

HOW MIND BEGINS

In Search of Mind: Essays in Autobiography (1983), New York: Harper & Row

My wonder about human development was a by-product of other concerns. I was driven to think about the initial "powers" or "functions" of mind and how we got from there to adulthood. It had little to do at the start with children or with improving education. I had always been intrigued by the enigmatic artistry, the humor, and the play of children – but never professionally. I never "studied" my own children. My naive belief in the late 1950s, after completing the book on thinking (when, like others before me, I had concluded that thought was most often wordless, systematic, and above all *swift*) – my naive belief was that by studying children one could find the slower, even the primitive forms from which the lightning of thought develops.

This, of course, is utter nonsense. I suppose it is the same genre of nonsense that sent the young Lévi-Strauss off to the Mato Grosso to find "the start" of culture. But this was 1956 and I was a grown man. I knew better, really, but deep down hoped for some miracles. Human beings, whatever their age, are completed forms of what they are, just as societies are completed forms of what *they* are. Growing is becoming different, not better or faster. You may become better or faster or more fluent at accomplishing certain external feats – like mastering mathematics or history – but the accomplishment is achieved by processes that are qualitatively different, not simply quantitatively improved. I know that is not the standard view and I shall come back to it later.

I think I know why the "idea of development" did not attract my interest sooner. But there is an irony about my late start, for in fact the first piece of research that I ever did was about a developmental question. I was a junior in college, taking one of those "reading and research" courses designed by some ingenious college dean to reduce the restlessness of hyperactive undergraduates. My teacher was a biologist whose passion was *Reptilia* and he happened at that time in his career to be interested in the reproductive cycle of his favorite species. When I came along, he was reading in the endocrinology of reproduction. He set me to examining the behavior of female rats during their estrus cycle. Perhaps he thought an aspiring young psychologist should learn about rats rather than reptiles – though he did let me come along hunting for giant snapper turtles. I took to it happily and in no time was assessing how the estrus cycle expressed itself in the vaginal smears and the behavior of my litter of Wistar Institute females.

Just about then, an endocrinologist, Rountree, had published the claim that the thymus gland, always large in preadolescent mammals, was responsible for inhibiting sexual maturity. My teacher pooh-poohed it. I thought it was interesting. Indeed, it was the first *theory* of development I had ever encountered. Besides, there is something attractive about proving an unlikely theory – more so usually than just disproving an accepted one. The notion that there is a built-in "buffer" system protecting against the attainment of sexual maturity until the organism is "ready" seemed interesting. It still does.

The upshot was that I should do an experiment to test Rountree's idea. The Biology Department would get me a weekly supply of frozen calf thymus from Armour's in Chicago, which I would reduce to "thymocrescin," as Rountree's substance was called, and we would see. I was on the edge of my first experiment – doing vaginal smears, working up a measure of sexual receptivity in my female rats, fumbling around with an aqueous extract of those precious calf glands in the big centrifuge.

The experiment came out – whether for the right or wrong reasons – as I had hoped, and I published my first paper jointly with my supervisor, Dr Cunningham. I never did another experiment on development for twenty-one years. But I never thought of the work as related to "development."

The émigré psychologist William Stern arrived at Duke just about then as a refugee from Hamburg, and gave a seminar on development that I attended. I recall only one of his lectures. It was on "space and time as personal dimensions." He contrasted personal, phenomenological space and time with their abstract Newtonian counterparts, commenting on how the former developed a personalized idiosyncratic quality with growth. I was concurrently reading that fascinating book by the German biologist von Uexküll, about how each species organizes its perception of the world into a species-specific *Umwelt*. I found the general idea very appealing, very much in the spirit of Mach's *Analysis of Sensation*, which I had read shortly before.

The idea of an *Umwelt* stuck, but not as a particularly developmental idea. It came back to mind a decade later, when I read the classic Austrian study of unemployed workers in Marienthal by Paul Lazarsfeld and Maria Jahoda. That study revealed that children and their unemployed parents had suffered a constriction of their sense of future time – they planned less, thought in the shorter term, anticipated fewer landmark events. And then an anthropologist friend steered me to a new study by Meyer Fortes and his wife on the education of West African Talensee children. They argued a comparable point. The Tale people migrated with the changes of seasonal agriculture but had no fixed calendrical dates by which to mark the changes. Time was "functional." In consequence, crises about "time" and "dates" never occurred to them. Things were not "late" or "early." And their children were not expected to reach certain "stages" by certain ages. They did what they did when they did it. They were helped to a next level of accomplishment when they were ready, with neither fret nor fanfare. They too grew up without "time crises." That was more grist for the *Umwelt* view – with a developmental twist.

"Nobody" did developmental psychology at Harvard in those days before the war. And with the exception of Freud and Piaget, nobody had much of interest to say about the subject. Arnold Gesell at Yale was dismissed as merely in the business of gathering age norms, pretty prosaic work. The developmental question largely boiled down to when things got better or faster or stronger, or more controlled.

We all knew about Piaget. I cannot remember a time when I didn't! I had read him on language and thought, on moral judgment, on physical causality. I had found him fascinating, but not as a *theorist*. He was an astute observer of children and his observations were intriguing – particularly those about egocentrism. It never occurred to any of us graduate students at Harvard that he had any bearing on anything aside from the phenomena to which he addressed himself. The controversy surrounding his work was of that boring kind in which pedants complained about the small number of children he observed. That was "dust bowl empiricism." Piaget was simply a self-contained one-man show.

Freud was quite a different story. It was the anti-illusionist quality of his thought that was so attractive, as well as the "content." Hidden sexuality was still a "new," still an exciting idea. But beyond his insistence that our sexual and aggressive motives were hidden from us, were "unconscious," and masked by defenses, there was something else. It was the claim that each of us lived in a psychic reality that was discoverable by our struggle to deal with our plights. The metaphor of an "outer" reality that could never be directly known and an inner one that one "constructs" to represent it has always been a root one for me – the drama of Plato's prisoners in the cave.

Freud's substantive account of the details of human development, on the other hand, struck me as Gothic and unsubstantiated – more like the Book of Job than real. I read him as allegory. Development as a voyage through the erogenous zones, for example, seemed fixed and unreal. But even so, I liked his hypothesis that overindulgence or overdeprivation at any stage of development was likely to fixate you there.

My anthropologist roommate at Duke, Leonard Broom, laughingly told me that Freud's was a parochial, "culture-bound" view of the family – "fin de siècle." Gothic tales laid in Vienna! But again, it was not the idea of development that caught me, but the general theory. Freud as a way of thinking about the human condition.

When I first arrived at Harvard as a graduate student, and again after the war, there was a busy traffic in "culture-and-personality" theory. There were lively people involved. The torchbearer was Clyde Kluckhohn – a romantic, a restless believer in the power of culture to shape mind, but too subtle an intelligence to embrace any simple generalizations about how the two were related. In an unspecified way, culture shaped some sort of internal Freudian dynamic – not as in Vienna, but as it should operate for a Navaho or a Balinese. And the rest of the influence came through a "world view" contained in the language. Margaret Mead visited often, as dogmatic as she was clever, and always ready to attack an ordinary psychologist on grounds that he knew only Western culture. And Ruth Benedict would come: elegant, allusive, poetic. Both were allies of Kluckhohn's in what seemed as much an ideological as an anthropological quest.

There was no lack of empirical work. Johnny Whiting worked tirelessly and with a bouncy optimism on correlating culture traits with presumed "basic personality" characteristics – of which more in a moment – and tried to put the results in the churchgoing clothes of Yale learning theory laced with psychoanalysis. Alexander Leighton was also on the scene, though his principally descriptive work did not enter much into the theoretical discussions.

I think the marriage of psychoanalysis and cultural anthropology brought out the worst in both spouses. Psychoanalysis, designed for Freud's Vienna, did not improve by being exported to the exotic cultures of the world. Do "child-rearing practices," like weaning, toilet training, forms of disciplining the child, determine whether a culture "believes in" witchcraft or creates certain forms of economic exchange? Are traditional ghosts a displacement of anxieties created by early, severe weaning? Is culture just one big projection?

The particular craze for correlational studies linking child-rearing practices in preliterate societies with cultural traits coincides with the development of the famous Yale Cross Cultural Index. In it, the monographic literature of anthropology had been parceled into categories, each describing aspects of the social, religious, or economic life of the preliterate peoples of the world. It was ideal for doing correlations between this trait and that. But the file created its own Humpty-Dumpty problem: How do you get it all back together again? The typical culture/personality study, for example, might first sort preliterate cultures into those in which weaning occurred earlier and those in which it occurred later than the median age of weaning for all recorded cultures. It might then sort the same cultures into those whose folk tales or beliefs contained devouring ghosts. The hidden assumption, of course, is that "age of weaning" has the same significance in all cultures, and so too "devouring ghosts." It works well on an IBM sorting machine, but does it do justice to the cultures whose traits one has yanked out of context?

That, of course, was the issue that brought the enterprise down. Structuralism was just waiting to be born. I recall two anthropologists warning me off. I had come to know Alfred Kroeber when he was visiting at Harvard in the early 1950s. He had to climb the stairs in Emerson Hall very slowly because of a heart condition, and we first met as we chatted our way up the long stairways together. He admired Clyde Kluckhohn, but looked askance at his push to "unify everything" – culture, personality, child rearing. For Kroeber, culture was "superorganic," with laws and structures that were independent of the idiosyncratic sources of individual human behavior. He too had been fascinated by psychoanalysis, had undergone a training analysis with Brill, and even practiced for two years in San Francisco. It only reinforced his sense of the discontinuity between individual plights and the structural nature of a culture. The other "viewer with alarm" was Claude Lévi-Strauss, whom I met in 1945 at a dinner party at the home of the French consul-general in New York – a man with the appropriate name of de Saussure, a nephew of the great structural linguist of the same name. How can you say systematically how culture affects a particular personality? You may specify how individuals enter into a system of exchanges. And when you have done that, perhaps there is nothing more that needs to be specified as far as the culture is concerned. The culture has its own inherent logic.

The development of personality was a topic that never caught my full intellectual interest. Not that I am less interested than the next man in what makes people tick. Given a choice of how to spend time reading, a novel appeals to me more than a treatise on personality. What puts me off "personality theory" is its decontextualized way of dealing with motives and dispositions. It lacks a sense of place and of setting. Stephen in *A Portrait of the Artist as a Young Man* was a creature of Dublin. Dublin exists in Stephen's devouring mind, and as he walks its streets he creates "epiphanies of the ordinary" out of what he finds there, the Dublin in his own mind that forms his reality.

In those twenty-one years between my first study of development and my next one, there was very little about mind in the study of development. Mostly it was about motives and their control. The mind came into the picture almost exclusively as a generator of fantasies and as a defender of tender turf – the brave ego doing its best between the forces of the superego and the id. The two men who made the *development* of "mind" interesting to me were Jean Piaget, the postwar Piaget, and Lev Semyonovich Vygotsky. The two of them, Piaget and Vygotsky, were alike enough in general program to be equally tempting as mentors. In the end, they were sufficiently different to be in a state of perpetual conflict with each other inside my head!

Piaget, personally and in terms of his *oeuvre*, was massive. The programmatic pace of his work moved like a glacier. He absorbed, he assimilated everything into the system of his thought. It has always been a connected system of thought, with a sufficient ambiguity to permit easy assimilation to the Genevan point of view. Its objective has been to characterize the underlying logic that gives coherence to knowledge, and to do it in such a formal, abstract way that the characterization reveals the deep kinship of all forms of thought – save, perhaps, the arts. He wrote an astonishing number of books, and each bore an astonishing resemblance of continuity to the one preceding it. He was Swiss, Protestant, logical, obsessed, driven into his eighties. His passions were epistemology and logic and how they grew by the actions of the growing child on the world. The nature of that world did not concern him much, only the selective operations on it. It provided a generalized nourishment for the processes of knowing.

Vygotsky published little, and virtually nothing that appeared in English before 1960; indeed, until the late 1950s, most of what he wrote in Russian was suppressed and had been banned after the 1936 purge. Sickly and brilliant, he died of tuberculosis in his thirties. His pace was swift and his intellectual style that of an intuitionist. He was a Russian and a Jew, deeply interested in the arts and in language. He was a friend of the film-maker Eisenstein and the literary linguist Bakhtin. His objective was to explore how human society provided instruments to empower the individual mind. He was a serious intellectual Marxist, when Marxism was a starchy and dogmatic subject. This was his undoing at the time of the Stalinist purges. One reads Vygotsky for clues, for intellectual adventure, for his extraordinary evocativeness. Though I knew Piaget and never met Vygotsky, I feel I know Vygotsky better as a person.

At heart, Piaget was an epistemologist, and a genetic epistemologist at that. He was convinced that by studying the growth of mind in the child one could retrace the evolution of the sciences. The psychological machinery in his system of thought is almost scandalously scanty. It is logical machinery in the main: ways of characterizing the logic implied by the child's way of attempting to solve a problem or of explaining why he has done something one way rather than another. The child moves up through stages of growth by dint of some virtually unspecified process of "equilibrium" between assimilation and accommodation – the former a process of shaping experience to fit one's mental schemata, the latter changing one's schemata to fit experience. You can look high and low in the dozens of Piaget's books, but you will have great difficulty finding anything more concrete than this description of these two central psychological processes.

Yet he made a tremendous contribution to our understanding of the mind of the child and how it grows, and indeed to our understanding of mind in general. And I think he did it in much the same way as Claude Lévi-Strauss has made his contribution to our understanding of human culture – by insisting on its structure and connectedness, its deep rules, its derivative structures. Piaget could be completely wrong in every detail, but he would still have to be reckoned one of the great pioneers. This is not to say that he saw it all, for he certainly did not.

The world is a quiet place for Piaget's growing child. He is virtually alone in it, a world of objects that he must array in space, time, and causal relationships. He begins his journey egocentrically and must impose properties on the world that will eventually be shared with others. But others give him little help. The social reciprocity of infant and mother plays a very small role in Piaget's account of development. And language gives neither hints nor even a means of unraveling the puzzles of the world to which language applies. Piaget's child has one overwhelming problem: to bring the inner representations of mind into equilibrium with the structures of experience. Piaget's children are little intellectuals, detached from the hurly-burly of the human condition.

I made a first visit to Geneva in 1956. Piaget arranged that the two of us should have a "debate" at the Bern meetings of the Swiss Psychological Society. We trundled off to the railway station to catch the train – an hour in advance, as was his habit. The debate was to be on our notions about perception. He proposed as its title "L'homme calme et l'homme agité"! I talked about the selectivity and the role of hypotheses, he about the difference between perception and intelligence. His perceiver was indeed calm – and collected and self-sufficient. I teased him: "You know, having purposes does not necessarily make a perceiver agitated."

But I think that a commitment to structuralism is in some deep measure a commitment to a quietism that is always off-putting to a functionalist. The one studies how structural requirements determine the forms of action. The other, as in Claude Bernard's celebrated dictum, studies the manner in which function creates form. Nor is it that one is truer or righter than the other. They are two different ways of parsing nature. Yet there is something else about Piaget's view that goes beyond this point. In some quite stubborn way, he has always resisted the idea that there is a psychological reality to culture, that it exists in some "World Three," Popperian way such that it can be "internalized" or serve as a prosthesis for mind. For Piaget, knowledge is always an invention, and the forms of invention do not include taking over the stored representations of the culture and then achieving knowledge by reconstruing them. So the child who is father to the man in the Piagetian world is indeed a calm child and a lone one.

Vygotsky's world was an utterly different place, almost the world of a great Russian novel or play – Tolstoyan or Chekhovian. Growing up in it is full of achieving consciousness and voluntary control, of learning to speak and then finding out what it means, of clumsily taking over the forms and tools of the culture and then learning how to use them appropriately. I first encountered it in the late 1940s, reading a celebrated paper by him – one of the two then available in English – on thought as developing through the internalization of speech. Like all his writing, it is sketchy, evocative, and brilliant, as if written in the heat of inspiration.

Then in 1961, after his official "rehabilitation" in Russia and a great deal of backing and filling diplomatically to obtain rights, his *Thought and Language* was translated into English by my colleague Eugenia Hanfmann. She asked me to write a preface. I read with new absorption, not simply because I had to write a preface, but because I became caught up in its complex dialectic. I was discovering a new Vygotsky.

What captivated me most was his approach to the role of context in mental growth. It was the avoided topic in Piaget. Vygotsky begins with a paradox: "Consciousness and control appear only at a late stage in the development of a function, after it has been used and practiced unconsciously and spontaneously. In order to subject a function to intellectual and volitional control, we must first possess it." What then *aids* the child to gain control?

Vygotsky's sketch of an answer was incorporated in an idea with the drab name "zone of proximal development." It consists of the child's capacity to use hints, to take advantage of others' helping him organize his thought processes until he can do so on his own. By using the help of others, he gains consciousness and perspective under his own control and reaches "higher ground." "The new higher concepts transform the meaning of the lower. The adolescent who has mastered algebraic concepts has gained a vantage point from which he sees arithmetic concepts in a broader perspective."

I returned to Harvard from my visit to Geneva in the midst of a cold and unhappy winter. It was late 1956 and *A Study of Thinking* had just appeared. I had no idea how it would be received and it never crossed my mind that we were all hovering on the brink of the "cognitive revolution" in psychology. My marriage was breaking up and my two children were very much on my mind. I cope with anxieties by throwing myself into work. Searching out what to do next, I decided to work on the development of thought, how strategies develop. It was a natural follow-up.

It was then that I thought I would find those primitive processes that were slowed-down versions of thinking in adults. I would concentrate on inference, on how children learn to go beyond the information given, particularly on the difference between slow "plodders" and swift "leapers." But I could not come up with a technique that pleased me. (In an odd irony, a quarter century later, while working on *this* chapter of *this* book, I was asked to referee a masterful review article in the *Psychological Bulletin* entitled "Hypothesis theory and the development of conceptual learning." It was all about what I might have done at that time and didn't do! It reviewed work of the period on the development of problem-solving strategies in children, on how hypotheses emerge, combine, how children are tested; how they use feedback in problem solving; etc. It was the developmental follow-up of the ideas and the methods that Jackie Goodnow and I had worked out twenty years before. I guess I must have had enough of it by then.)

My research students and I decided instead to study "learning blocks." Perhaps pathologies of development would tell us what we wanted to know. The Judge Baker Guidance Center had a large case-load of "underachieving children" and they were delighted to let us take on some of them for exploratory "tutoring," while they handled the "therapy." I have always been bemused by the distinction. In any event, we "tutored," they "therapized." In fact, we spent much time and effort trying to show the children how to deal with their anxieties and how to forestall their worst crashes. I think we helped them by letting them learn what kinds of learning situations set off their fears.

That project and the work it kicked up had the good effect of letting me gather my wits, particularly letting me look at children learning and solving problems in quite ordinary settings. I needed a respite from experimental work.

Soon enough I was back to it, trying to reconcile Piagetian structuralism and Vygotskyan functionalism. I realize now that I fell into an easy trap. I used the usual Genevan "conservation" tasks as my instruments for studying development. They consist, for those not acquainted with them, of an initial display of a quantity of some substance or liquid in a container – say a standard beaker half filled with water. This beaker is then emptied into a narrower one, in which the water level is higher. The child is then asked whether there is still the same amount of water as before, or whether there is more or less. It is a task beautifully designed to land you on the flypaper of Piagetian debate.

In the Piagetian "preoperational" stage (around five or six), the child is alleged not to grasp the reversible nature of quantity – that though it *looks* like more because it is higher, it is the same because it can be poured back to its original state. The child's conceptual grasp of reversibility, when achieved, is said to be general, to characterize all logical operations – give or take a little variability in the extent to which the general idea finds expression in different media or materials.

For Piaget, development is assured so long as the child has an adequate "aliment" of active experience with the world. You simply wait. The same order of developmental stages will unfold – possibly accelerated by richer experience – though Piaget dismissed this last point as "*la question américaine.*" Could this be so? I had already seen the striking effects of too many curriculum projects to take this whole. How could one dismiss Vygotsky's "zone of proximal development" so cavalierly? Equip a child with the conceptual means of making a leap to higher ground, and he would often generalize and transfer his knowledge to new problems quite on his own. Were "stages" so monolithic after all? Did development move along with the slow and steady pace of a glacier pressed forward by a single source?

It seemed to me that there was a richer picture behind mental growth than this one. Human beings represent their knowledge of the world in three ways. One is through habit and action: knowing what to do. A second is through imagery: depiction of events and relations. Finally, we "know" things by representing them in a symbol system like language or mathematics. Making progress in the mastery of any domain most often involved using all three modes of representation – typically progressing from enactive, through iconic, to symbolic. Indeed, understanding could be deepened by using all three modes, even (and sometimes especially) when they were in conflict with each other. If some modes were easier for the child than others, then the way of helping him across the "zone of proximal development" was to start with it and then move on to others. Let him first master a problem by practical action, for example, and then move on to pictures and words. Or mask the child from cues that "fix" him in one mode, like the *height* of the water in that tall, thin glass, so that the evocative power of the act of pouring it back could enter his consciousness and reckoning.

I must confess to a complicated relation with Piaget, for it "explains" a next step in my own thinking. Particularly for younger men, he was an enormously attractive presence. There was a purity about him that was so genuine and singular in its expression that it was as if in his company one had shaken off ordinary trivia. He was almost totally devoted to the development of his ideas. To enter that world was a privilege. Besides, he was not in any sense an austere man. There was a quality of enjoyment in whatever he did – in his work, in the trencherman way he ate, in his way of joking about ideas, in his appreciation of charming women. But there was also a preemptive quality about his consciousness. To be with him was to be a part of it. It was difficult to define one's ideas without reference to his. He made many of the men around him feel like rebellious sons when their ideas diverged – rebellious, but not independent. It was not by any means that he was disrespectful of divergence. I never saw him dismissive toward an idea anybody proposed to him seriously in the spirit of exchange. He would consider that part of it that made some contact with his own mode of thought, give it a fair hearing, accept it or agree to disagree. Those parts that did not make contact, he could not hear – like the role of language in shaping thought.

I suppose it was too much of a father-son relation for me, one that generated too much ambivalence over autonomy and independence. Bärbel Inhelder, his principal assistant and one of the most perceptive women I have ever known, was the buffer between us, and it was with her that I would try to work out our differences.

I mention this because it relates to one of the turning points in the development of my own thinking in those days. Geneva psychology was founded on the idea of "stages" of development, each with its own underlying logic of operations. The part of me that was in league with Vygotsky rebelled at the "quietism" of stage theories, quietism in the sense that stages were simply something a child lived through until he had had enough *aliment* to progress to the next one.

My solution was to convert my ideas about modes of representation – enactive, iconic, and symbolic – into stages of development. Enactive representation, in effect, is storing one's knowledge in the form of habits of acting (as in riding a bike); iconic is storage in images; symbolic, by means of a symbol system like language. Rather than concentrating on the manner in which hypotheses of each type were generated and tested at *any* age, I let my ideas fall into a chronological strait-jacket: the enactive mode first, then the iconic, and finally the symbolic. The last was particularly important, for it provided the means whereby culture and cognitive growth made contact, the medium whereby the culture's tool kit could be made the child's own.

My graduate students and I plunged in. Working together with them on a research project is for me one of the joys of teaching. We had weekly seminars, at which ideas or findings were thrashed out. I went off to Africa with Patricia Greenfield to pretest procedures for comparing schooled and unschooled Wolof children. Lee Reich also studied Eskimos in Alaska. And hundreds of Cambridge children went through our procedures. The exchange with Geneva continued. Bärbel Inhelder and her assistant, Magali Bovet, came to Harvard for a year and several of us went over to Geneva occasionally for seminars. Communication did not necessarily draw us closer intellectually, but it did so personally. Given my interest in heuristics, in hypothesis formation, in the power of certain forms of experience to give a special lift to growth, it was bound to be that way. Such pre-occupations do not fit well in a stage theory premised on the general nurturance of experience.

As I drew away from Geneva, I drew closer to Moscow. It was partly intellectual, partly personal. The personal part was Alexander Romanovich Luria, a Russian uncle in the grand manner. It was with him that I could talk and correspond about Vygotsky's ideas and my variants of them. Luria had unflagging energy, intense loyalties, unquenchable enthusiasm. In the fifteen or so years that I knew him well, I do not think that two months ever went by without a letter from him, a new book or translation of his, a coffee-table volume of Rublov's icons, or the architecture of the cathedral at Rostov, whatever. He was the czar of Russian psychology, but a more benign czar would be hard to imagine!

Luria visited the United States in 1960, staying with us in Cambridge for a week. He bubbled with enthusiasm for the beauties of the Harvard Yard and took dozens of pictures of it. The "Second Signal System" was very much on his mind and it only slowly dawned on me how crucial this idea had been to him and to his friends – both politically and intellectually – in turning Russian psychology around to cognitive ideas. It had the sanctity of being formulated by Pavlov himself. Pavlov, of course, had been the idol of the environmental determinists after the Revolution, though he was no behaviorist. His First Signal System comprises stimuli that register nature directly, those to which animals become conditioned. The second system was a transformation of the first. Through it, stimuli were converted into language and made culturally relevant. Luria and his students were hard at work on experiments demonstrating how language provided children with the means for gaining power and self-control over the worlds of external stimuli and internal impulses. Later, once language became more syntactically organized, they were enabled to solve problems by converting them (or being helped to convert them) into language, on which they could then operate. One study, for example, involved the relationship between color and form. A particular shape was a "positive" stimulus when it appeared against one background color, but not when it appeared against another. This kind of relationship is a very difficult task for young children to master. If, however, the problem was presented in a form like "Airlanes can fly on sunny days, but not on cloudy days," the children would quickly recognize that an airplane silhouette was positive gainst a yellow background, but negative when against a gray one. t was a simple but powerful demonstration, a little replica of the difference between the meaningful and meaningless cards in *A study of Thinking*.

It is difficult to appreciate how politically and ideologically important the Second Signal System was to my Russian friends. Marxist dialectic requires that experience "reflect" physical reality. It also requires that it do so in a fashion reflecting the history and culture of people. Pavlov's formulation of a Second System, the rather crude afterthought of an old man, provided the occasion for rehabilitating Vygotsky without rejecting Pavlov! For Vygotsky indeed saw language as the means by which mind mediated between culture and nature. Vygotsky's views were far more genuinely Marxist.

On a visit to the Soviet Union two years later, I learned that the proposal made by Luria to rehabilitate Vygotsky (with Leontiev and Smirnov) had meant the deposition of Ivanov-Smolensky as director of the Institute of Psychology in Moscow. He had been the strict ideological Pavlovian of the years since the purge of 1936. Ivanov's Pavlovian orthodoxy could now be applauded as admirable – and condemned as old hat.

Needless to say, Luria's news about Russian research on the role of language in early development was more than welcome to me. So were his other enthusiasms. One was about the importance of selective attention or the "orienting reflex." It was very closely linked to my earlier work on the New Look in perception. The other was about the selectivity of perception as revealed in eye movements. Luria had with him in Cambridge dozens of slides of Yarbus's work on eye movements. Yarbus had found that where the eye looked (as well as what the eye saw) was a function of what question the perceiver had been asked and was attempting to answer. The track of eye movements was like the path of a detective searching out clues related to a particular hypothesis.

Luria and I became fast friends almost immediately. We were compatible temperamentally and very much in agreement about psychological matters. His curiosity ran along much more psychological lines than did Piaget's and his interest in the cultural enablement of mind led him to be far more open to links between anthropology and psychology. Besides, he created none of those father-son problems that had dogged my relations with Piaget.

Studies in Cognitive Growth, my book on stages of representation, was published in 1966 and dedicated to Piaget. The last paragraph of the Preface says:

> Many points of disagreement are...minor by comparison with the points of fundamental agreement we share with Professor Jean Piaget. This volume would have been impossible without his monumental work. His genius has founded modern developmental psychology. It gives us all deep pleasure to dedicate this book to him on his seventieth birthday and to present it to him on that occasion at the XVIIIth International Congress of Psychology in Moscow on August 9, 1966.

It was a rather stiffly formal luncheon party, the presentation. I had traveled to Moscow with Roman Jakobson, whose wit can always be counted on, and he and a dozen others joined us for toasts and birthday wishes in a small private dining room at the Ukrayina Hotel. It was plain that Piaget did not like the book much. Jakobson saved the day with witty anecdotes. The occasion had its ironic appropriateness. Dedicated to Piaget, presented in Moscow!

It is a curious book. It had a modest influence in psychology, though it was influential among educators. It got lukewarm reviews. By then, the Piaget wave had reached cresting level. The book was too close to Piagetian thought, yet too remote from central issues in his theory, to have much impact. The Vygotskyan side of it was mostly ignored, though that has changed recently. The use of cross-cultural evidence – comparisons of Western children with the Wolof of Senegal and Eskimos – gave heart to some who were more culturally oriented. And that too grew in time. Our book was really out of step with the drumbeat to which developmental psychology was then marching.

Perhaps the book was written at a bad time in my life. I was split in my interests. My work on education had become "renowned." I was being hailed as the "greatest force in education since John Dewey." There was even an article in *Harper's* magazine about me. I was on the Education Panel of the President's Science Advisory Committee and also at work putting together a new school curriculum in social studies. I should have been working more directly on the problem of how intellectual development and education could be linked.

It was 1966, ten years since *A Study of Thinking*. The new book had not got me back to the beginnings of mental life at all. This time I would do better. I would have a look at infancy, *early* infancy, and see what I could find there about how mind began. All I knew about the topic was what was to be found in the standard reference books, and there wasn't much there: mostly reflexes, autonomic functioning, sensory processes. Young infants cannot talk to you, cannot do much with their hands, cannot move about. They cry, feed, look, comfort themselves by sucking, fall asleep with prodigious speed. The best you can do is to hitch them up to rather sophisticated physiological apparatus that measure their heart rate or breathing or skin conductance and take what you find as an indicator of some internal state of mind.

That search for internal states through physiological measurement was a little like an electronic Olympics. One investigator in Holland, for example, regularly recorded fourteen simultaneous measures in his newborns. To make such measures, the infant must be put into a highly shielded environment, else the recordings will reflect a barrage of overactivation.

I am no physiologist and I am not particularly good at delicate instrumentation. But good fortune came my way. Drew Marshall arrived on the scene – a young man fresh back from Vietnam who had just barely managed to struggle his way through the requirements of school and college but who, in fact, was extraordinarily gifted in electronic gadgetry and was blessed with a very high intelligence indeed. Between us we managed to design and build the machinery we needed.

The last babies I had had any real contact with were my own two kids, and I had enjoyed, rather than studied, their infancy. I needed tuition. I "found" Berry Brazelton. I had known him before as a pediatrician and a tennis partner. He offered to give me a peripatetic "course" on what infants "were *really* like." Hard at work on his now famous Neonatal Assessment Test, he was longing for the company of somebody interested in just my kind of questions.

Saturdays we would go off to the Boston Lying-in Hospital on our own private rounds. After a while, the more venturesome young residents on the staff began tagging along. Brazelton is a clinical artist and a charismatic teacher. I paid my fees by asking him questions, "outrageous" questions he called them, that never would have occurred to a "doctor." He came to work the next year at the Center for Cognitive Studies. My luck was building.

A very clever and rather erratic young Scot had just arrived at Harvard, Tom Bower, with a fresh PhD from Cornell. As an undergraduate at Edinburgh, he had been taught by David Hume. That in itself is not remarkable. I have had four Scottish doctoral students, all at Oxford, all loathing the place. Every one of them had been imprinted on Hume. Tom was not only interested in human infancy, but interested specifically in how mind begins. We talked a great deal and exchanged notes. I learned much from him. There are psychologists who doubt some of his research findings, since several have not been replicable. I think he may have been a little carried away in interpreting his findings. But as an intelligence he is wide-ranging, reflective, ingenious both in his questions and in devising means for answering them. He was a superb companion.

There are some odd things about babies. They are, for example, highly labile in their adjustment to the world immediately around them. So we designed an experimental room that was softer, simpler, less perceptually tempting than a world fit for older children. It was a cubicle draped in soft, cream-colored drapes. The baby was put in a comfortable, semi-upright chair in which he was held securely – what soon became known as the "Harvard chair." So soft was the visual environment that there was nowhere for the infant's eye to light! Within thirty seconds, he would be in tears. We shifted to a more burly, cluttered style. The infants were immediately more content. It was a little fable for our times, to which I shall return presently.

Infants do some things very well. One of them is to suck. They suck not only to feed, of course, but to comfort themselves – two quite different patterns. It occurred to us that perhaps we should use their sucking as a means of getting them to control the environment. It was not difficult to design apparatus that would allow us to measure an infant's sucking while he made use of it to control some feature of his environment. One of my graduate students had already discovered that infants regulated the duration of their sucking bursts according to the amount of milk delivered per suck. That was surely a way of controlling the environment. What about sucking to control aspects of the world not related to feeding or self-comforting?

My research assistant was a cheerful and bright Estonian refugee, in Cambridge with a postdoctoral biologist husband. She was doing a degree at Toronto. She was going to be at Harvard for another couple of years, so there was no rush. Ilze Kalnins was never in a hurry anyway. We could get on with the job as slowly as necessary. Working with young infants *is* slow work.

We hit on a bizarre idea. We had inadvertently noticed that when infants watch pictures, they turn away when they go out of focus. (What about that "booming buzzing confusion" of infancy?) Could we get an infant to clear up a blurred picture by sucking on a pacifier connected to the focusing mechanism? What would they do when their sucking created blur? We did the study – slowly. Infants *will* speed their sucking to clear up blur at six weeks. But they also combined their sucking with their looking in an ingenious way. While sucking to clear the blur from a picture, the infant keeps his gaze averted for a second or two, and then looks back to the cleared picture. When his sucking on the pacifier drives a clear picture into blur, he keeps looking until the last bearable moment, and *then* turns away. So not only could six-week-olds suck for "arbitrary ends," but they could combine sucking quite flexibly with another activity, looking.

To me, the infant's performance seemed like skilled activity. It had an organizing intent, an anticipated end state, flexible means to be deployed, and so forth. That is the stuff of all intelligent action – that and the capacity to combine these prerequisite routines into still more powerful skills. Even that seemed within the infant's reach, judging by his ability to combine sucking and looking to such good effect. I duly went off to a meeting in Minneapolis to report our findings. (A pleasant young woman came up after my paper and said, "That was nice. But what a pity you"re leaving developmental psychology to do infant research.')

I think it was that study more than any others in the series undertaken over those years that set the course of my thinking. It seemed to me that the heart of the matter was the elaboration of intention-directed behavior. In early development, the child has a highly limited set of goals to which he directs his actions – establishing contact with others, grouping and taking possession of objects, exploring with hand and sense organs, feeding, comforting. More strikingly, he has a limited repertory of means of achieving intended objectives. But as Edward Tolman had put it forty years before, he has from the start a remarkably sensitive "means-ends readiness," a capacity to assemble means for achieving ends. He is active in doing so, a hypothesis generator from the start. It is this means-end readiness that gives a directedness to behavior, and when his behavior seems disordered or random, it comes from his inability to formulate a plan in which ends and means match. It is then that he suffers distress and frustration.

Part of the difficulty that the young child experiences is in controlling his level of arousal or activation. He is labile – becomes overaroused, frustrated, or dormant with fatigue or boredom, to degrees that he cannot control. But when his knowledge of means and ends is sufficiently developed, it is striking in what degree he can mobilize and control his state. As with our creamy research cubicle, the world activates him or fails to. There are stimulating and supportive environments, and ones that put him to sleep or bore him beyond limits.

Two other related things those studies highlighted. One was the extent to which infants are canny in combining their own actions or their knowledge of the world to form either higher-order action routines or more generalized "cognitive maps" of their world. The other is the extent to which they play. It is as if the play – usually in the form of performing a wide range of acts on a single object or a single act on a wide range of objects – has the effect of sensitizing them to the combinability of the things of the world for goal-directed action.

And finally, people. The dependence of the species on a long immaturity makes it inevitable that we be sensitive from the start upon interaction with others. It is that sensitivity that nurtures the acquisition of language.

The research gained momentum. There was a lively group of postdoctoral fellows at work with me. An irrepressible New Zealander, Colwyn Trevarthen, was at work on the fundamental distinction between "central" and "ambient" perception: focus on figural, central detail, and attention to surrounding context. He saw the two as reflecting the integration of the old optic tectum and the visual cortex proper. Perceptual development appeared to be dependent indeed on the integration of the two. Berry Brazelton was tracing the early development of mother-infant interaction, distinguishing it from the infant's reactions to inanimate objects. When Czechoslovakia was overrun, Hanus Papousek, who had directed the Mother-Infant Research Institute in Prague, joined us, working in learning and self-recognition. Alistair Mundy-Castle came from Ghana and began a series of studies on the child's capacity to figure out visual trajectories. It was a lively shop. With our own group at the Center, with Tom Bower's, with Jerry Kagan's, and with Roger Brown steadily at work on "a first language," Harvard had become, I suppose, the world center. If that was in doubt, then when MIT got added (for it too had its flowering of infancy research, led by Richard Held), Cambridge had certainly become it.

As far as the press was concerned, the thrust of this intense effort was that infants were far more competent, more active, more organized than had been thought before. Indeed, that was surely so. We had a visitor from India one day, a London-trained pediatrician. She asked to see one of our research procedures, and Ilze Kalnins demonstrated a six-week-old sucking a blurred picture into focus. The visitor watched for a while, then blurted out almost in indignation, "But babies of that age can't see!" We had accomplished *something*.

Given the political climate of the 1960s, the research was immediately and passionately taken up. Two social revolutions were in full swing; the infancy work armed both of them with compelling arguments. One was the black movement, the other women's liberation. The early "deficit" of disadvantaged children, principally black children, was already well publicized. Head Start was under way, about which I shall have more to say in the following chapter. The new research on infancy strongly suggested that those early years of "deficit" were the very ones in which children might be acquiring highly complex and presumably useful skills. The broader implications for early education were not missed either. Maya Pines did a major feature in *The New York Times Magazine*, replete with one of our children in color on its cover. John Davies did a comparable one shortly after in the London *Sunday Times*. And the "upmarket" press in Europe and America were soon editorializing on the importance of nurturing competence in early childhood not only as an aspect of preschool care but as an instrument of education generally. Daniel Patrick Moynihan had, a few years before, written a celebrated memorandum to the President on treating the failing black family with "benign neglect." In the new atmosphere, such a proposal would have been treated as genocide, which indeed it might be.

The women's movement was agitating for day care centers to support women who worked outside the home. The potential benefits of such day care was soon added to their brief. Our Center for Cognitive Studies had its own Women's Group – and a high-powered group they were. Several of the members helped establish the new University Daycare Center at Harvard. And they were very soon emulated by tens of thousands of women around the country.

To my surprise again, the practical impact of developmental research turned out to have more to do with politics than with scientific certainty. Policymakers are not that impressed by one's doubts. Under pressure, they can wait neither for the unseating of old paradigms nor for the establishment of new ones. When a small group of us had waited upon Sargent Shriver, director of the Office of Economic Opportunity in President Johnson's administration, with a plan for something like Head Start, he scoffed. "Washington in the baby business! That's all we need with our other troubles." We proposed a small pilot project, in acknowledgment of our ignorance about how to proceed with the idea. A few months later – principally following the urging of Lady Bird Johnson, so the story has it – when the idea came to be seen as a strong addition to the Great Society, the notion of a pilot project was rejected entirely. "If it's to be justified both as needed and as possible, you cannot play around with *pilot* projects," Shriver told me. Head Start was to be mounted in every state of the Union.

Where indeed were we, leaving aside all the politics of early childhood? How does one think of the beginning of mind? For one thing, the new spate of research had already made it clear that mind was not, so to speak, something from nothing. Simpleminded empiricism was surely dead. But if, in Leibnitz's terms, nothing is initially in the mind save mind itself, what were its powers? Certainly the intelligence-bearing constituents were there from the start: the component intention-driven skills and the appreciation of means-end relations. And certainly the capacity for the combining of actions was part of the initial equipment. A capacity for representing what one had encountered was surely in being from the start, as evidenced by a spate of studies on the child's sensitivity to deviations from the ordinary. The initial representational skills probably included a good deal of built-in appreciation of space, time, and even causality – if not innate, then very easily primed by experience. The child's curiosity didn't even need to be stoked up, and all the evidence suggested that even the newborn's line of regard went to the informationally rich rather than the redundant features of his visual environment. What a five-year-old looked at was much what his mother was looking at, all else being equal. But of course, all else was *not* equal. Five-year-olds don't ask the same questions about the world that grownups do, and the eye, for all its swift skills, is no better than the questions put to it by the mind.

The question then is not where or when mind begins. Mind in some operative form is there from the start, wherever "there" may be. The question, rather, is about the conditions that produce human minds that are richer, stronger, more confident.

I remarked at the start that I had not "studied" my own children while they were growing up. Not that I didn't watch them with wonder. But I could never quite bring myself to formal study with note taking, recording, or the rest.

I cannot claim any higher principle. Perhaps like Niels Bohr and his son, I was not able to know them both as parent and investigator. I felt "attachment" in a very direct and unencumbered way. When Jane and Whit were infants, I used particularly to take pleasure in giving them their baths; there was something marvelous about the abandon of their playfulness in a tub. I would somehow manage to be home if I could for that ritual. In general, I suppose, their fantasies, their constructed worlds, engaged me more than the orderly progress of their schooling or their mastery of this or that skill. Those were no problem. As it happens, they were both bright children – differently bright, and different in character. Whit was articulate and abstract, yet with a lively dramatic sense. A week before his sixth birthday I asked him what he would like to do on August 24. "Go to a foreign country." We drove from Vermont for a weekend in Canada. Jane "made" things, literally made them. When *she* was about six, we went off to shoot clay pigeons. A photographer friend was popping flashbulbs, Jane stuffing spent shotgun shells and flashbulbs into her pockets. When we got home she asked for a package of pipe cleaners. An hour later she had a small army of dolls: flashbulbs stuck into the tops of spent shotgun shells, faces painted on the flashbulbs, pipe cleaners sticking out for arms. Whit grew up to be an Arabist diplomat, Jane a painter-photographer.

I must have thought of myself as a provider of and accomplice in their possible worlds. I read to them a great deal, indeed made up not only stories but continuing sagas that ran for months at bedtime – about a talking crow and his adventures in Vermont; about his friends, including a heroic Robin Hood eagle who came to the rescue of the helpless and the harassed; about a series of indigenous or prehistoric heroes who introduced their inventions for the first time and prevailed though they were mocked ("What a silly thing to use that for, at the tip of a travois. A wheel is to spin when you pray, idiot"). As they grew older, the adventures grew more elaborate. My wife Kay was a willing and ingenious ally. We drove one summer to California via the trail of the Astorians, following the track of the historian

Francis Parkman. We pitched tent each night near a site where the wagons had stopped and read aloud from the Parkman journals. In the early 1950s, the four of us went up into the Canadian Chibougamau Reserve over a one-hundred-mile corduroy road newly opened, rented a canoe from the Cree Indian agent, and explored "north of the trees."

I don't think my impulse was ever properly "pedagogical" either. I never felt strongly that the children ought to learn this subject or that. Perhaps it was because they were good students. I did want them to have a sense that they were in a larger world; we took them with us when we went to Europe to teach at the Salzburg seminar in 1952 or, even earlier, when we went off to explore Spain and France in our Jeep station wagon. Indeed, the idea of a "wide world" even inspired some Sunday afternoon pedagogical expeditions, I must confess. We would go off to the docks of Boston harbor and see the ships berthed there. I wanted them to know we lived in a great harbor – although the rotting wharves took some explaining to observant children.

I must report one unreserved pedagogical success, although I am not sure I had any educational objectives well in mind. It was a game, Gallery Whist, that I heard about from my friend and neighbor Robert Lee Wolff, one that, so far as I know, his mother had invented. It worked like a charm. I tried it first when we took the children along for visits to the Prado in Madrid in 1955. You set points for finding certain "unusual" things in the paintings of the museum. One morning it would be any painting of Veronica wiping the face of Christ with her veil – with double points when His face was also imaged on the surface of the veil. Another time it would be a painting of the Annunciation in which the Virgin plainly looked astonished to hear that she was to be Queen of Heaven. Dwarfs in any painting made easy points in Spain. Hard points were New World scenes in Spanish paintings of the sixteenth and the seventeenth centuries. At the end of the day, points could be converted into local currency.

There were hazards to "the game." At the Prado Jane inadvertently stumbled on black Goyas. I saw this graceful eight-year-old running toward me full tilt down one of those long central corridors. "I found something really, really scary. Quick, come see." I felt a pang, but not for long. Half an hour later I found the two of them glued to Hieronymus Bosch, so totally bewitched by the horrors he depicted that they could scarcely be dragged away.

It never occurred to me to believe in "stages" of development in the Piagetian sense. There was always *some* way in which *anything* could be made clear to them, given patience, willing dialogue, and the power of metaphor. They were bright and eager children, granted, but that surely was not the point. It was a question, rather, of finding a scenario into which they could enter. I recall once trying to demonstrate to Whit the experimental method, so called, by filling two milk bottles with colored water and capping them. Did water expand when it froze? It was winter, a bitter one; one went outside the back door, the other stayed inside. In the morning, the outside one was frozen, with cap thrust up in the air. Point made. Polite boredom. That weekend, we made one of our visits to the Peabody Museum of Anthropology. One of the cases had models of a tightly swaddled Plains Indian baby. I told Whit the prevailing theory about how that produced warlikeness among the Plains Indian braves, rather like a rage reaction against being restrained. On the way home after, he asked, "Why don't they swaddle half the babies and leave the others free, to see if that theory is true?" So the idea of "experiment" rooted in that eight-year-old head, but it took a livelier scenario than expanded frozen water to bring it out into spontaneous thought.

I suppose my interest in education was kindled by watching my children go through school. I'm sure that if I and my friends had pooled resources and set up a little kibbutz (as Elting Morison suggested once), we could have done far better at educating our kids than the schools did. My son even suggests, as a grown man, that I had a hidden theory of education from the start – something like "going beyond the information given." It never struck me as a theory but as a given! There were games, it's true, involving "guessing," like what could you tell about people, say, sitting in their cars observed on a ferry, or stopping by old cellar holes, in the woods in New Hampshire and Vermont, and making up stories about what it must have been like before the families had moved West.

Subjecting the children to experiment or assessing them according to norms would have created a distance between us that did not appeal to me. I can't do that and still have good conversation. I am not that detached. They have grown up quite interesting people. We still have good conversation. If I ever knew what their IQ was (and I don't recall that I ever did), I couldn't have cared less. Nor whether or when they could conserve quantity or comprehend sentences out of context. I knew that one of them had very low frustration tolerance, the other very high. I spent a great deal of time trying to arrange life so that they could live with what they had. I have no idea whether I succeeded – whatever that may mean.

Psychologists, on the same grounds that the cobbler's children shall go unshod, are supposed not to be good parents. That is surely tabloid nonsense. They are quite as variable and ordinary as the rest. Was I as a psychologist-parent any better able to "predict, control and explain" my children than other parents were? I wonder, for example, whether it was more obvious to me than it might have been to another parent that Jane would become a professional photographer and Whitley an Arabist-diplomat. There is too much fortuity that comes from the setting and the opportunities by which they were surrounded. Control? Both children went through blazing adolescent rebellions, in an individual way. I waited. I never felt I could make a dent.

I suppose, in a way, my own feelings toward them may have been guided by some sort of compensation for my own childhood. My father had (until his final illness) been away a great deal on business. We rarely did things together even when he was home. *I* did a great deal with *my* children. My mother, as I have related, avoided any show of affection and was not one for stories and fantasy. I suspect I was rather a demonstrative father, and I delighted in fantasy and tales shared with the children. But who knows really?

Still, if you are going to study how the mind begins, you would be well advised to have some children of your own. But that is surely no reason for having children! At that, they will be more likely to save you from your follies about how mind begins than to lead you to some evident truths.

CHAPTER 10

NARRATIVE AND PARADIGMATIC MODES OF THOUGHT

E. Eisner (ed.), *Learning and Teaching the Ways of Knowing* (Eighty-fourth Yearbook of the National Society for the Study of Education) (1985), Chicago, IL: University of Chicago Press

Let me begin by setting out my argument as baldly as possible and then go on to examine its basis and its consequences. It is this. There are two irreducible modes of cognitive functioning – or more simply, two modes of thought – each meriting the status of a "natural kind." Each provides a way of ordering experience, of constructing reality, and the two (though amenable to complementary use) are irreducible to one another. Each also provides ways of organizing representation in memory and of filtering the perceptual world. Efforts to reduce one mode to the other or to ignore one at the expense of the other inevitably fail to capture the rich ways in which people "know" and describe events around them.

Each of the ways of knowing, moreover, has operating principles of its own and its own criteria of well-formedness. But they differ radically in their procedures for establishing truth. One verifies by appeal to formal verification procedures and empirical proof. The other establishes *not* truth but truth-likeness or verisimilitude. It has been claimed that the one is a refinement of or an abstraction from the other. But this must either be false or true only in the most trivial way, for in their full development, the one seeks explications that are context free and universal, and the other seeks explications that are context sensitive and particular. Moreover, there is no direct way in which a statement derived from one mode can contradict or even corroborate a statement derived from the other. As Rorty has recently put it, one mode is centered around the narrow epistemological question of how to know the truth; the other around the broader and more inclusive question of the meaning of experience.[1]

Lest all this sound like intellectual teasing, let me quickly and loosely characterize the two modes so that we can continue more precisely with the enterprise. One mode, of course, is the paradigmatic or logico-scientific one. At its most developed, it fulfills the ideal of a formal, mathematical system of description and explanation. It is based upon categorization or conceptualization and the operations by which categories are established, instantiated, idealized, and related one to the other to form a system. In terms of these relations of connection, its armamentarium includes on the formal side such ideas as conjunction and disjunction, hyperonymy and hyponymy, and presupposition, and the devices by which general propositions are extracted from statements in their particular contexts. At a gross level, the logico-scientific mode (I shall call it paradigmatic hereafter) deals in general causes, and in their establishment, and makes use by constraining principles to assure verifiable reference and to test for empirical truth. Its language is regulated by requirements of consistency and noncontradiction. Its domain is defined not only by observables to which its basic statements relate, but also by the set of possible worlds that can be logically generated and tested against observables, that is, it is driven by principled hypotheses.

We know a very great deal about the paradigmatic mode of thinking, and have developed over the millennia a powerful set of prosthetic devices for helping us carry on: logic, mathematics, sciences, and automata for operating in these fields as painlessly and swiftly as possible. We also know a fair amount about how children who are weak initially at the paradigmatic mode grow up to be fairly good at it – or good enough to get on in the literal world and a few interpretive ones as well. The imaginative application of the paradigmatic mode leads to good theory, tight analysis, logical proof, and empirical discovery guided by reasoned hypothesis.

The imaginative application of the narrative mode leads instead to good stories, gripping drama, believable historical accounts. It deals in human or human-like intention and action and the vicissitudes and consequences that mark their course. It is essentially temporal rather than timeless (as with the paradigmatic mode, however much that mode may use temporal parameters or variables in its operations). And we know much less about it.

It operates by constructing two landscapes simultaneously. One is the landscape of action, where the constituents are the arguments of action: agent, intention or goal, situation, instrument. Its other landscape is the landscape of consciousness: what those involved in the action know, think, or feel. The two landscapes are essential and distinct: it is the difference between Oedipus sharing Jocasta's bed before and after he learns from the messenger that she is his mother. Whereas truth in the paradigmatic mode is a clear matter that depends upon tests in some possible world to determine whether an explanation captures the relevant facts, the "truth" of a narrative is in principle problematic. To be sure, as Nelson Goodman constantly reminds us,[2] the "facts" against which the truth of a scientific explanation is tested are determined by the explanation or theory. But the tests to be applied to the facts are, given the condition, straightforward. Narrative accounts, on the other hand, can be lifelike and exhibit verisimilitude even when they contain demonstrable falsehoods. The property of narrative rightness remains invariant across outcomes of truth tests performed on "factual" components of the narrative. Science "progresses" in a way that storytelling and drama do not. However much Goodman may argue that science-making and narrative-making are, after all, both only examples of constructing world,[3] the fact remains that we collect treasuries of the world's stories, but do not give pride of place to disproved scientific theories or to erroneous logical derivations. There is nothing in science and logic that corresponds to narrative or poetic license. Popper proposes that falsifiability is the cornerstone of the scientific method.[4] But believability is the hallmark of well-formed narrative. When we apply criteria of falsifiability to a narrative, we replace the narrative by a paradigmatic structure. Historical films are notable for the historians they hire as consultants who are then ignored when the story requires it.

We hear increasingly from psychoanalytic theorists that human adaptation to life itself depends upon the success of the patient (or Everyman) in generating a believable narrative, one that in some robust fashion weaves in but does not necessarily mirror the historical truth.

The prosthetic devices available for guiding the creation of narrative are far more like templates than they are like generating principles. That is to say, our cultural history has provided us with standard myths, with genres, with depictions of human situations that inspire and guide variants of them. It is in this sense, of course, that Oscar Wilde could say that life imitates art. But it is also true that there are narrative and generative principles of discourse, tale-telling, and drama that are also part of any culture's tool kit, and we will explore some of them later.

As already noted, narrative is concerned with the explication of human intentions in the context of action. Surprisingly, however, literary research reveals that there are a rather limited number of narrative forms by which such contextualizing of intention in action has been depicted. This limitation suggests that the narrative mode is not as unconstrainedly imaginative as it might seem to the Romantic. For example, most narratives that create an aura of believable lifelikeness involve a recounting of an initial canonical steady state, its breach, an ensuing crisis, and a redress, with limited accompanying states of awareness in the protagonists. This has led various literary theorists to suggest that there is a highly constrained deep structure to narrative, analogous to the deep structure, say, of a grammar, and that good stories are well-formed surface realizations of this underlying structure.[5] But this is a matter for much more research.

It is often claimed that the narrative mode is implicitly deontic, that it implies criteria of value – as represented by the canonical state-breach-crisis-redress cycle in which "good" or "evil" prevails. We shall want to examine this claim more seriously later. In any case, narrative is often said to be value-laden in contrast to logic's value-freedom.

We know very little about how narrative thinking *develops* in childhood. What we *do* know, of course, is that the ability to comprehend stories develops or is present very early. This is sometimes offered as support for the deep structure argument. But childlike storytelling, with its linear ordering "reflecting" the order of occurrence of events depicted, is a far cry from the conventions of skilled narrative with its flashback, soliloquies, metaphors, and other tropes. And the childlike emphasis on event sequences, with omission of a second level of epistemic information, is as remarkable as the child's capacities to tell or comprehend stories at all. Indeed, the relationship between the time course and order of events "in the world" and their representation in narrative time and narrative order has been shown to be rather more variable across cultures than might be expected given claims about narrative universals.[6] But, however these issues are finally resolved, it is apparent that there is a discernible developmental course that characterizes narrative telling and the thought processes that underlie it.[7] More to illustrate it than to attempt any delineation of it, let me mention one in particular. Hickmann has shown that young children have great difficulty, when recounting what happened in a film, in dealing conjunctively with what happened in the action and what the protagonists were thinking or saying.[8] If this is not due simply to an inability to deal with more than a limited amount of information cognitively or linguistically, at any time there may be a genuine initial difficulty either in taking the subjective perspective or in wedding the objective and subjective. Indeed, some work by Beveridge and Dunn[9] suggests that the distinction between what is intended and what is actually done is a difficult one for young children to make – a distinction often, grasped when the young child has a younger sibling who forces her to face the dilemma of reconciling the two. And Olson and Astington's demonstration of the young child's difficulty in grasping the semantics of factive verbs,[10] particularly those dealing with intention, suggests that the linguistic tools for that reconciliation are absent. In any case, these are the kinds of matters that must surely affect the young child's capacity to grasp narrative structures of varying complexity. The distinguished French literary theorist, Greimas, has suggested that tales of deceit, involving a disjunction between action and intention, are among the most primitive of those that wed the subjective and objective.[11] Do young children readily grasp them? Would that we had a tenth of the number of studies on children's conception of deceit that we have on class inclusion or invariance transformation!

* * *

This is hardly the first time that the distinction between the two modes of thought has been noted. A century ago, Dilthey even went so far as to argue that all efforts to codify human knowledge could be divided into *Naturwissenschaften* and the *Geisteswissenschaften*, the sciences of nature and of humanity, the first seeking generality and the second uniqueness, one guided by the methods of science and logic, the other by a search for the meaning of historical and personal events in their full, comprehensible richness.[12] And Rorty, as stated, has raised the issue in the last years in more modern dress.[13] It is curious, however, that psychologists have never looked at the matter more closely. In the main, we have relegated narrative thought to others. Propp, Levi-Strauss, Ricoeur, Greimas, Todorov, Burke, Jakobson, and others have gone a long way in the last half century toward clarifying the structure of narrative with no assist from psychology.[14] And where we have looked at story production, as with Murray's work on the Thematic Apperception Test,[15] it has been to explore the nature of personality and its projection in a story rather than to explore story making and its functions.

By a curious twist of history, the psychology of thought has concentrated on one mode, the paradigmatic, at the expense of the other. Like its parent, philosophy, it has been concerned with the epistemological question: how mind comes to know the world, to represent it, to reach right conclusions about it, to avoid errors, to achieve generality and abstraction. With the advent of cognitive psychology, we redoubled our efforts to understand the information processing that serves these paradigmatic functions, and the problem of representation has become the keystone in the arch – representation that maps the world, a classically epistemological objective. Strategies, heuristics, and modes of categorization have been explored with zeal and with increasingly narrow scope. Even when "storying" has been investigated, it has been in the spirit of abstract story grammars, or of the generic properties of scenarios.

And in our studies of reasoning and inference, when subjects fail to conform to Bayesian rules and ignore known base-rate probabilities in judging the likelihood of single events, as in the rich research of Kahnemann, Slovic, and Tversky,[16] we still treat these departures as "errors in thought," forms of human folly. And, indeed, so they are – given the tasks set by the investigators. Or when subjects fail to process the information contained in instances of a concept presented to them, as in the old Bruner, Goodnow, and Austin studies,[17] why should it be treated as anything other than a fall from rational grace? Yet, as I shall try to show presently, these so-called errors can also be taken as switchovers (even if inappropriate) to quite a different way of thinking, as a search for a narrative rather than logical structure.

I think the curious twist of history that produced this odd posture in psychology is probably located in our longed-for proximity to the natural sciences: it was more important to study how the scientist came to his right conclusions than how Ibsen produced *The Doll's House* or how Macedonian tale-tellers captivated their audiences with their modularly constructed recitals.[18] Piaget, for all his genius, saw the growth of mind as paralleling the growth of science – or vice versa. There is no reasoned way in his system of characterizing the difference between the prattling of the Department gossip and a Homer, a Joyce, or a Hardy. For some reason, the nature and the growth of thought that are necessary for the elaboration of great stories, great histories, great myths – or even ordinary ones – have not seemed very attractive or challenging to most of us. So we have left the job to the literary scholars and linguists, to the folklorists and anthropologists. And they have studied not the process, but the product, the tales rather than the tellers.

* * *

I began with the bold claim that our two modes of thought were natural kinds. En route to backing up that claim, let me first say what I mean by a natural kind. It is *not* an appeal to naturalism in philosophy in the spirit of Morris Cohen and John Dewey.[19] Rather, it is the more modest (and perhaps more serious) claim that under minimal contextual constraint, each type of thought comes spontaneously into existence in the functioning of human beings, can be recognized by common sense without specialized discovery procedure as the one or the other, is remarked upon as missing in those rare instances when absent, and (most important of all) can be shown to be analyzable into constituent operations that derive from the overall process they constitute. The significance of constituent processes lies in the role they play in narrative construction and paradigmatic reasoning respectively. Even though stories may require for their believability conformity to some of the same rules used in a logical argument (for example, the rule of simple contradiction), the two forms do not do so for the same reason or in the same way. Contradiction affects believability in narrative differently from the way it negates a logical proof. There is no way that contradiction can be made defensible in a logical proof, but modern novelists and playwrights use it and exploit it by special means as in the plays of Pirandello where, for example, characters both exist and do not exist. Without the use of appropriate literary means, however, a play or novel containing contradiction would seem unbelievable.

* * *

So let us examine some of the constituents or components that go into the construction of paradigmatic and narrative thought. Two features distinguish the modes' uses of language and interpretations of action. The first and obvious matter to be examined is, of course, language. Jakobson has distinguished two axes in terms of which language use is organized: a vertical axis of selection, and a horizontal axis of combination.[20] The first has to do with the possible substitution of lexical and other meaning units for each other, a substitution that (within limits) is meaning-preserving: boy, immature male, lad, and so on. But what about substituting phrases or other larger expressions for each other? Here the matter becomes more telltale in differentiating the two modes. Is "I should have been a pair of ragged claws scuttling across floors of silent seas" captured by the expression, "I am depressed?" Is this kind of asymmetry similar to what happens when we substitute the expression, "the biggest city in North America" for "the harbor at the mouth of the Hudson?" One pair easily preserves reference; the other does not, and it is not enough simply to invoke metaphor as the reason.

The horizontal axis of combination derives from the generative design feature of human grammar, its capacity to substitute varied elements within grammatical frames:

He has a secret
He has a bicycle
He has a burning ambition
He has a bee in his bonnet

The distinction is familiar in psychology as the paradigmatic and syntagmatic, used for distinguishing word associations of the kinds "banana: fruit" versus "banana: El Salvador," showing the latter having been found to occur earlier in children and therefore thought to be more primitive. But let us take this with a grain of salt, for it must surely be absurd to assume that two words that can fit into a sentence (the syntagmatic) are more primitively joined than two that bear a relation of synonymy, antinomy, hyponymy, or hyperonymy. They are simply different and testify only to the fact that classification systems develop later than sententiality as a basis for relating words.

The two modes of thinking, for their expression and (I wish to argue) for their cognitive realization, must obviously use the two forms of linguistic organization, one for word selection, the vertical, and the other for sentential combination, the horizontal. But each uses a different criterion. Vertical organization is given two very different functions in the narrative and paradigmatic modes. The narrative mode operates vertically with a view toward maximizing sense at the expense of definite reference, to use Frege's distinction;[21] or to put it more loosely, sacrifices denotation to connotation. It is for this reason that the metaphoric richness of a story or a line of poetry is as important as the events to which it refers and, why, for example, a story cannot be reduced to a set of atomic propositions derived from its particular set of statements. The paradigmatic mode emphasizes reference at the expense of sense. It aspires to the astringent goal of singular, definite, referring expressions with severe restrictions on alternative senses. It is this that makes it possible to ban ambiguity. Its aim is formal description employing terms whose status within a hierarchical system of terms is evident. The sense of any particular term derives from its position within a system of terms. Keil's description of hierarchical semantic trees,[22] as Susan Carey has shown,[23] characterizes paradigmatic usage only, and then only at its most formal reach.

As for the horizontal axis of combination, the criteria guiding usage in the two modes are again radically different. Some years ago, I tried to characterize three bases for the formation of concepts or categories: affective (I would now say "factive"), functional, and formal. We can illustrate the factive by "kind of people I like to spend my spare time with," and the functional by "elements that can be characterized as between atomic weight 6.0 and 6.7 in the Mendeleev Table." The narrative mode concentrates on the construction of sentences that are factive and functional and on their relation, the paradigmatic on the functional and formal and their relation. A simpler way of saying it is that stories are about events in the real world, the functional, and the reactions of people to them, the factive; theories are about events in the real world, the functional, and abstractions that capture some more structured aspect of them that gives them order, the formal. Good narrative is full of human factivity – wanting, opining, decrying – and the writing of scientists and logicians is sparse in this respect.

* * *

This brings us to a second distinguishing feature for the two modes: the two ways in which action can be interpreted. One is in terms of the working out of human intentions in a real or possible world; the other is through the operations of causes, structural requiredness, reasoned correlation.

Arguments (if I may use that term for what is produced in the paradigmatic mode) and stories, if they are to emphasize respectively *cause* and *intention*, require forms of language (or symbol use) that are markedly different. Both, to be sure, must adhere to syntactical requirements, though the poetic extensions of narrative may use certain forms of tense and aspect marking and styles of semigrammaticality not found in descriptive prose. Where real differences begin to be apparent is in the forms of meaning employed by the two modes. One view of meaning, the verificationist theory, is that the meaning of a word or expression is the set of true propositions that can be stated in respect to it. Recall that meaning encompasses two features: reference and sense, what a term or expression "stands for" in some world, and how it relates to other words or expressions. Verificationist meaning places high emphasis on reference. But there are also ideas of meaning that are based on *use*, ideas that stem mainly from Wittgenstein.[24] Use-based meaning relates to the context in which an expression is used and, crucially, to the intention of the speaker in making a particular utterance in a particular context.

Use-based meanings, in addition to referring (however ambiguously they may do so), must, because of the need to match context and to fulfill speaker intentions, fulfill conditions on their performance, to use the jargon. Utterances must be right for the context and convey intention well enough to assure a hearer's uptake of the locution and of its illocutionary force. This implies immediately that there are conventions that govern speaking or, more precisely, communicating by language. Here we are dealing with the domain – real as life, and as murky – of pragmatics. And before we return to our central issue, let me sketch out a few pragmatic devices that must concern us. One is speech acts; a second, conversational implicatures; the third, the "triggering" of presuppositions by the use of certain linguistic devices.

As John Austin first noted,[25] meaningful utterances cannot be captured in the two categories of analytic and empirical propositions: analytic ones like "Man is an animal" or empirical ones like "Most men can speak." The greater part of human talk is made up of warnings, encouragements, greetings, promises, expressions of want, and the like, involving a performative: an act that can be carried out by speaking alone, say, by the act of promising. Or as John Searle put it, speech consists of locutions (what is said) and a conventionally governed illocutionary force (what is intended), uptake of which by an interlocutor depends upon his sharing the convention.[26] And so the famous, "Would you be so kind as to pass the salt?" is not a question about the limits of the hearer's compassion, but a request taking account of the hearer's nonobliged status. Grice has extended and refined this analysis by adding the notion of implicature.[27] Not only are there conventions governing speech acts (felicity conditions on their utterance to be fulfilled, like preparation, essentiality and sincerity), but there is also a highly general Conversational Principle (CP) in operation. This CP contains maxims concerning the quantity to be said, the quality and relevance of the utterance, its sincerity, and so forth. These maxims provide a guide to banality: be brief, perspicuous, as truthful as possible, relevant. Their existence, Grice argues, provides us, by opportunities for patterned violation, with the means for meaning far more than we say, or meaning something quite different from what we say, as in:

> Where's Jack?
> Well, I saw a yellow VW out front of Susan's.

In short, violation of maxims (in this case, perspicuousness and relevance) is intended to recruit presuppositions about what is going on in the ongoing narrative. Which brings us to the third issue, presupposition.

Presupposition is an ancient and complex topic in logic and linguistics, and deserves closer study by psychologists. A presupposition, formally defined, is an implied proposition whose force remains invariant whether the explicit proposition in which it is imbedded is true or false, the classic folk example of which is, of course:

Do you still beat your wife?

This is obviously not the occasion to discuss the logic of presuppositions that remain invariant across negation. Fortunately that has been done brilliantly by Karttunen and Peters[28] and by Gazdar[29] whose penetrating discussion of presuppositional triggers, filters, plugs, and holes is richly suggestive for the psychologist. All of these matters relate to what are called heritage expressions, the manner in which a presupposition is built up over discourse in order to project itself into later statements. Triggers are forms of expression that have the force of projection, and four simple examples will serve to illustrate their manner of operating.

As trigger:

Definite descriptions:	*John saw/didn't see the chimera.*
	There exists a chimera.
Factive verbs:	*John realized/didn't realize he was broke.*
	John was broke.
Implicative verbs:	*John managed/didn't manage to open the door.*
	John tried to open the door.
Iteratives:	*You can't get buggy whips anymore.*
	You used to be able to get buggy whips.

And there are many other triggers. I think it is plain (though the details are not easy) that triggering presuppositions, like intentionality violating conversational maxims, provides a powerful way of "meaning more than you are saying," or going beyond surface text, or packing the text with meaning.

It will seem on first glance that such maneuvers must depend mightily on the presence of mutual knowledge between speaker and hearer: that S knows that H knows and that K knows that H knows that S knows, *ad infinitum*, but this turns out to be far too strict a constraint for what may turn out to be a deep psychological reason. As Sperber and Wilson have noted,[30] it is a characteristic of conversation that interlocutors assume that what somebody said makes sense and will, if in doubt about *what* sense, search for or dream up an appropriate context to assign an utterance that will *give* it sense. Example on a London street (after Sperber and Wilson):

Will you buy a raffle ticket for the RNLB Institution?
No thanks, I spend summers near Manchester.
Ah yes, of course.

Now let me return to my point. Narrative discourse, because it is built around the vicissitudes of human intentions being acted out, uses the full range of speech acts as its keyboard: expressives, declaratives, commissaries, and so forth. Paradigmatic discourse narrows increasingly as it develops toward pure expression of analytically and empirically verifiable propositions of the conventional type; that is, it aspires to be as verifactionist in its meanings as it possibly can, or in John Searle's classification,[31] specializes in *representatives*, the only speech acts that commit the speaker to the truth of what he expresses. Paradigmatic discourse, moreover, avoids all conversational implicatures if it can, and when it cannot, it employs only those that have heritage expressions that permit unambiguous unpacking of utterances back to the canonical or maxim-governed forms. In logic and in science you attempt to mean what you say. In narrative, to be successful, you mean more than you say and treat a text or utterance as open to interpretation rather than literally fixed with, so to speak, the "truth in the text."

Or to put it in terms of the theory of presuppositions, the storyteller depends for the power of his exposition on triggering presuppositions: it is the only way in which narrative time is made to be shorter than the events and psychic states that it is narrating. It permits, as well, using different orderings in the story than that which happened in life. Paradigmatic discourse, on the other hand, eschews or blocks the triggering of presuppositions or renders them as transparent as possible. It substitutes entailments in place of presuppositions – an entailment being an implied proposition that is rendered false if the explicit proposition in which it is embedded is negated.

Stories, to achieve the condensation and the tropes that render them something other than the mere recountal of events, depend upon establishing a high level of sharable presupposition; they rest upon what Joseph Campbell many years ago called a "mythologically instructed community" who will know how to assign appropriate presuppositional interpretations to what is being said.[32] Indeed, as some literary theorists have argued,[33] the birth of literary tropes and other devices depends upon the invention of violations of the banality prescribed by standard conversational maxims, such violations as irony, hyperbole, synecdoche, and the rest. These violations become possible only when discourse is freed from the exclusive demands of verification.

I have couched much of the foregoing discussion in terms of *language* in which paradigmatic and narrative thought is expressed, but I do not intend that *expression* should be the basis for their distinctness. Rather, the point I would make is that each of the two modes of thought each *requires* for its realization both internally in cognition and externally in speech different uses of language. And as one becomes socialized in a, communicative sense, the cognitive modes further differentiate in the sense that the rules of the medium of expression dictate increasingly the compositional rules of thought that find expression in different media. Or, to paraphrase McLuhan's famous catch phrase: the medium compels the message, which then compels the generative thought form for composing it.[34]

* * *

Let me bring the discussion to a close by sampling some of the implications of what has been said for research on the thought processes. Perhaps the best way to do so is to illustrate with research now in progress that demonstrates the one-sidedness of which I initially complained. I prefer to start with some research of my own where I am freer to be savage. Take concept attainment of the kind reported in Bruner, Goodnow, and Austin's *A Study of Thinking*.[35] Forgiveably, perhaps, those authors were out to demonstrate that inference is a product of how we process information in various strategic ways – of using information about instances to construct paradigmatic categories governed by certain rules of combining attributes. The instances these authors presented were, in the main, picture cards of geometric figures in different numbers, with different colors, and with differing numbers of borders. Fortunately, some of the experiments involved "narratable" material: picture cards of adults and children in day dress or nightdress, giving or withholding gifts, and so forth. With the narratable material the authors report (rather wistfully) that the efficiency in information utilization dropped, that subjects hung on to their hypotheses, even when they were contradicted by negative instances, and were somehow less rational all round. There is a hint that subjects were doing something else besides processing information for categorical inference, but the authors did not deign to find out *what* they were doing. Now, more than twenty-five years later, I *have* found out. To put it in Nelson Goodman's expression, they were involved in a different kind of world making, ignoring instruction from the experimenter about how the instances were composed of attributes of different values, and so forth. One of our subjects (my collaborator in this research is Alison McClure) was, for example, operating on the hypothesis that the category might be "a parent and child in a good relationship." As cards were presented to her, she was busily involved in trying to figure out what the experimenter might have had in mind by a good relationship, and if an instance that seemed to negate her hypothesis came along, she would continue to rebuild the kinds of "stories" that might count as "good." Each instance was an occasion for expanding or modifying the story, involving agents, actions, goals, scenes, and instruments in the manner of Kenneth Burke's pentad.[36] In the end, she came out with a rather interesting if cockeyed story – her version of a world in which the instances could live, including such matters as "misunderstandings," "doing things for the good of the child," and so forth. On paradigmatic grounds, she committed errors galore, required staggeringly redundant input, and so on down the list of paradigmatic sins. But her story was an interesting and believable one. She was, after all, a therapist concerned with the family dilemma. If her protocol had been analyzed by Paul Ricoeur or Greimas[37] or by Roy Schafer or Donald Spence,[38] all of them would have commented upon the narrative rationality of the "fiction" she was creating.

Or take the old experiment of Solomon Asch's on trait names, how *intelligent* changes meaning when paired with *cold* or with *warm*.[39] It is a brilliant, trail-blazing study that served Asch well in illustrating the Gestalt-theoretic manner in which an overall impression alters the meaning of the component parts. Henri Zukier and I have been redoing the study, using a wide variety of trait lists, varying in their surface compatibility. Give your subjects an initial opportunity to create a general superordinate impression by inclusion of some compatible traits, like *spiritual, introverted, religious* (yielding such descriptions as "saintly kind of person") and then add *practical* and *money-minded*, and narrative organization takes over: "He's saintly alright, but he's only trying to earn a living in a cut-throat business," or "Yes, of course, he's probably one of those Amish or Mennonite farmers who's great within his own group, but drives a very hard bargain outside." Again the Burke pentad, and now the matter of intentions and consciousness about what the contexts might be and how the person acts in each. The language of subjects changes – factive and implicative verbs increase, modal auxiliaries enter indicating stance, the telltale "just-even-only" constructions enter ("He's only trying to earn a living"), the presuppositional load increases dramatically, intention and awareness come in, the account becomes firmly situated in time and in space and in context.

Or take the equally trail-blazing studies of Kahnemann and Tversky.[40] They have shown that strategies for making inferences about individual events, given base-rate information about the probabilities that govern outcome in classes of similar events, do not follow standard Bayesian models. Recall, you tell your subjects that you are presenting them sketches chosen at random from sketches of a hundred people, seventy of whom became salesmen, thirty librarians. Now read them a sketch about somebody who is "shy and withdrawn .... a meek and tidy soul, ... need for order and structure and a passion for detail ...." In spite of the 70–30 base-rate, subjects will say, "Librarian" – though if the information in the sketch is indifferent, they *will* go the Bayesian way. Which way they go, Henri Zukier assures me on the basis of his research, depends upon their orientation: whether it is scientific and propositionally oriented, or "clinical" and geared to particulars.[41] The scientific produces Bayesianism, the clinical, an account far more based on a narrative world one can construct for the particular case. They conclude, "The results are consistent with the proposition that different judgmental contexts may activate different representations of the problem, and different judgmental objectives, which require different inferential strategies." And again I would argue that the two strategies are not only different but are drawn from two fundamentally different modes of putting together knowledge.

Let me in conclusion comment upon a remark made earlier in passing, to the effect that outcomes produced by the two modes of thought could neither contradict nor corroborate the other. It is a very radical claim, and also very easily misunderstood. Let me say, at the outset, that it is possible to do a logical analysis of a story – or as an undergraduate once told me, Hamlet was not very cost-effective and needed three deaths to get his culprit. Conversely, you can tell good stories about scientific discoveries – Pasteur, Einstein, the Curies, even Freud have all sat for their narrative portraits. My economist friend, Robert Heilbroner, recently said to me, "When an economic theory fails to work easily, we begin telling stories about the Japanese imports or the slowness of the Zuric 'snake'." Yet, when the Japanese imports get included as parameters within the theory, the story does not go away: it can still be told, still judged for its verisimilitude – like the causes of war, the reasons for the decline of the Labor Party in Britain, or the Empire in Rome. Moreover, a story can be shown to be false, and still have a compelling believability about it. For stories per se are not proved false, only some of their component propositions. What I must reiterate is that narrative is a form and the narrative thinking that brings it into being a process that, in the end, preclude verification as the basis for their "reality" or "meaning." And by the same token, logical science and the paradigmatic thinking that supports it rest upon an eventual verification and logical proof that prevail regardless of their counterintuitiveness, their lack of dramatic verisimilitude. Perhaps this is the only sense in which the adage, "Truth is stranger than fiction," is true. Each is a version of the world, and to ask which depicts the real world is to ask a question that even modern metaphysicians believe to be undecidable.

Notes

This paper was given as an Invited Address, Division I, American Psychological Association, Toronto, August 25, 1984.

1 Richard Rorty, *Philosophy and the Mirror of Nature* (Princeton, NJ: Princeton University Press, 1979).
2 Nelson Goodman, *Of Minds and Other Matters* (Cambridge, MA: Harvard University Press, 1984).
3 Nelson Goodman, *Ways of World Making* (Indianapolis and Cambridge: Hackett Publishing Co., 1978); idem, *Of Minds and Other Matters.*
4 Karl Popper, *The Logic of Scientific Discovery* (New York: Harper and Row, 1968).
5 Victor Turner, *From Ritual to Theater: The Human Seriousness of Play* (New York: Performing Arts Journal Publications, 1982); Tzvetan Todorov, *The Poetics of Prose* (Ithaca, NY: Cornell University Press, 1977).
6 Nelson Goodman, "Twisted Tales: Or, Story, Study, Symphony," in *On Narrative,* ed. W. J. T. Mitchell (Chicago, IL: University of Chicago Press, 1981).
7 Brian Sutton-Smith, *The Folkstories of Children* (Philadelphia, PA: University of Pennsylvania Press, 1981).

8 Maya Hickman, "The Implication of Discourse Skills in Vygotsky's Developmental Theory," in *Culture, Communication, and Cognition: Vygotskian Perspectives*, ed. James V. Wertsch (New York: Academic Press, 1983).

9 Michael Beveridge and Judy Dunn, "Communication and the Development of Reflective Thinking" (Paper presented at the Annual Conference of the Developmental Section of the British Psychological Society, University of Edinburgh, 1980).

10 David Olson and Janet Astington, personal communication, 1984.

11 A. J. Greimas and J. Courtes, "The Cognitive Dimension of Narrative Discourse," *New Literary History* 7 (Spring 1976): 433–47.

12 Wilhelm Dilthey, *Pattern and Meaning in History: Thoughts on History and Society*, edited and introduced by Hans P. Rickman (New York: Harper, 1962). For a briefer account, see Hans P. Rickman's essay on Dilthey in the *Encyclopedia of Philosophy* (New York: McMillan, 1967).

13 Rorty, *Philosophy and the Mirror of Nature*.

14 Vladimir Propp, *Morphology of the Folk Tale* (Austin, TX: Texas University Press, 1968); Claude Levi-Strauss, *Structural Anthropology* (New York: Basic Books, 1963); Paul Ricoeur, *Hermeneutics and the Human Sciences* (Cambridge: Cambridge University Press, 1981); Greimas and Courtes, "The Cognitive Dimension of Narrative Discourse"; Todorov, *The Poetics of Prose*; Kenneth Burke, *A Grammar of Motives* (New York: Prentice-Hall, 1945); Roman Jakobson, "Linguistics and Poetics," in *Style in Language*, ed. Thomas A. Sebeok (Cambridge, MA: MIT Press, 1960).

15 Henry A. Murray, *Explorations in Personality* (Oxford: Oxford University Press, 1938).

16 See, for example, Daniel Kahnemann, Paul Slovic, and Amos Tversky, *Judgment under Uncertainty: Heuristics and Biases* (Cambridge: Cambridge University Press, 1982).

17 Jerome Bruner, Jacqueline Goodnow, and George Austin, *A Study of Thinking* (New York: John Wiley and Sons, 1956).

18 Albert Bates Lord, *Singer of Tales* (Cambridge, MA: Harvard University Press, 1960).

19 Morris Cohen, *Reason and Nature: An Essay on the Meaning of Scientific Method* (New York: Harcourt Brace, 1931); John Dewey, *Experience and Nature*, 2nd edn (Chicago, IL and London: Open Court Publishing Co., 1925).

20 Jakobson, "Linguistics and Poetics."

21 Gottlob Frege, "On Sense and Reference," in *Translations from the Philosophical Writings of Gottlob Frege*, ed. Peter T. Geach and Max Black (Oxford: Blackwell, 1952).

22 Frank C. Keil, *Semantic and Conceptual Development: An Ontological Perspective* (Cambridge, MA: Harvard University Press, 1979).

23 Susan Carey, "The Child as Word Learner," in *Linguistic Theory and Psychological Reality*, eds Morris Halle, Joan Bresnan, and George A. Miller (Cambridge, MA: MIT Press, 1978).

24 Ludwig Wittgenstein, *Philosophical Investigations* (Oxford: Blackwell, 1953).

25 John Austin, *How to Do Things with Words* (Oxford: Oxford University Press, 1962).

26 John R. Searle, *Speech Acts: An Essay in the Philosophy of Language* (Cambridge: Cambridge University Press, 1969).

27 H. P. Grice, "Logic and Conversation," in *Syntax and Semantics*, vol. 3. *Speech Acts*, ed. Peter Cole and Jerry L. Morgan (New York: Academic Press, 1975).

28 Lauri Karttunen and R. S. Peters, "Requiem for Presupposition," in *Proceedings* of the Third Annual Meeting of the Berkeley Linguistics Society (1977), pp. 360–71.

29 Gerald Gazdar, *Pragmatics: Implicature, Presupposition, and Logical Form* (New York: Academic Press, 1979).

30 Dan Sperber and Deirdre Wilson, "Mutual Knowledge and Relevance in Theories of Comprehension," in *Mutual Knowledge*, ed. N. V. Smith (London and New York: Academic Press, 1982).

31 John R. Searle, *Experience and Meaning: Studies in the Theory of Speech Acts* (Cambridge: Cambridge University Press, 1979).

32 Joseph Campbell, *The Hero with a Thousand Faces* (New York: Meridien Books, 1956).

33 See, for example, S. Fish, "Normal Circumstances, Literal Language, Direct Speech Acts, the Ordinary, the Obvious. What Goes on Without Saying, and Other Special Cases," in *Interpretative Social Science: A Reader*, ed. Paul Rabinow and William M. Sullivan (Berkeley, CA: University of California Press, 1979).

34 Marshall McLuhan, *Understanding Media* (New York: McGraw-Hill, 1964).
35 Bruner, Goodnow, and Austin, *A Study of Thinking*.
36 Burke, *A Grammar of Motives*.
37 Ricouer, *Hermeneutics and the Human Sciences*; Greimas and Courtes, "The Cognitive Dimension of Narrative Discourse."
38 Roy Schafer, "Narration in the Psychoanalytic Dialogue," in *On Narrative*, ed. W. J. T. Mitchell (Chicago, IL: University of Chicago Press); Donald Spence, *Narrative Truth and Historical Truth* (New York: W. W. Norton, 1982).
39 Solomon E. Asch, "Forming Impressions of Personality," *Journal of Abnormal Social Psychology* 41 (1946): 258–90.
40 Daniel Kahnemann and Amos Tversky, "On the Psychology of Prediction," *Psychological Review* 80 (July 1973): 237–51.
41 Henry Zukter, personal communication.

CHAPTER 11

LIFE AS NARRATIVE

Originally published as *Discurso de Investidura doctor "honoris causa"* (1987), Madrid: Madrid University

I would like to try out an idea that may not be quite ready, indeed may not be quite possible. But I have no doubt it is worth a try. It has to do with the nature of thought and with one of its uses. It has been traditional to treat thought, so to speak, as an instrument of reason. Good thought is right reason, and its efficacy is measured against the laws of logic or induction. Indeed, in its most recent computational form, it is a view of thought that has sped some of its enthusiasts to the belief that all thought is reducible to machine computability.

But logical thought is not the only or even the most ubiquitous mode of thought. For the last several years, I have been looking at another kind of thought,[1] one that is quite different in form from reasoning: the form of thought that goes into the constructing not of logical or inductive arguments but of stories or narratives. What I want to do now is to extend these ideas about narrative to the analysis of the stories we tell about our lives: our "autobiographies."

Philosophically speaking, the approach I shall take to narrative is a constructivist one – a view that takes as its central premise that "world making" is the principal function of mind, whether in the sciences or in the arts. But the moment one applies a constructivist view of narrative to the self-narrative, to the autobiography, one is faced with dilemmas. Take, for example, the constructivist view that "stories" do not "happen" in the real world but, rather, are constructed in people's heads. Or as Henry James once put it, stories happen to people who know how to tell them. Does that mean that our autobiographies are constructed, that they had better be viewed not as a record of what happened (which is in any case a nonexistent record) but rather as a continuing interpretation and reinterpretation of our experience? Just as the philosopher Nelson Goodman argues that physics or painting or history are "ways of worldmaking,"[2] so autobiography (formal or informal) should be viewed as a set of procedures for "life making." And just as it is worthwhile examining in minute detail how physics or history go about their world making, might we not be well advised to explore in equal detail what we do when we construct ourselves autobiographically? Even if the exercise should produce some obdurate dilemmas, it might nonetheless cast some light on what we might mean by such expressions as "a life."

Culture and autobiography

Let me begin by sketching out the general shape of the argument that I wish to explore. The first thesis is this: We seem to have no other way of describing "lived time" save in the form of a narrative. Which is not to say that there are not other temporal forms that can be imposed on the experience of time, but none of them succeeds in capturing the sense of *lived* time: not clock or calendrical time forms, not serial or cyclical orders, not any of these. It is a thesis that will be familiar to many of you, for it has been most recently and powerfully argued by Paul Ricoeur.[3] Even if we set down *annales* in the bare form of events,[4] they will be seen to be events chosen with a view to their place in an implicit narrative.

My second thesis is that the mimesis between life so-called and narrative is a two-way affair: that is to say, just as art imitates life in Aristotle's sense, so, in Oscar Wilde's, life imitates art. Narrative imitates life, life imitates narrative. "Life" in this sense is the same kind of construction of the human imagination as "a narrative" is. It is constructed by human beings through active ratiocination, by the same kind of ratiocination through which we construct narratives. When somebody tells you his life – and that is principally what we shall be talking about – it is always a cognitive achievement rather than a through-the-clear-crystal recital of something univocally given. In the end, it is a narrative achievement. There is no such thing psychologically as "life itself." At very least, it is a selective achievement of memory recall; beyond that, recounting one's life is an interpretive feat. Philosophically speaking, it is hard to imagine being a naive realist about "life itself."

The story of one's own life is, of course, a privileged but troubled narrative in the sense that it is reflexive: the narrator and the central figure in the narrative are the same. This reflexivity creates dilemmas. The critic Paul de Man speaks of the "defacement" imposed by turning around on oneself to create, as he puts it, "a monument."[5] Another critic comments on the autobiographical narrator's irresistible error in accounting for his acts in terms of intentions when, in fact, they might have been quite otherwise determined. In any case, the reflexivity of self-narrative poses problems of a deep and serious order – problems beyond those of verification, beyond the issue of indeterminacy (that the very telling of the self-story distorts what we have in mind to tell), beyond "rationalization." The whole enterprise seems a most shaky one, and some critics, like Louis Renza, even think it is impossible, "an endless prelude."[6]

Yet for all the shakiness of the form, it is perfectly plain that not just any autobiography will do – either for its teller or for his listener, for that matter. One imposes criteria of rightness on the self-report of a life just as one imposes them on the account of a football game or the report of an event in nature. And they are by no means all external criteria as to whether, for example, one did or did not visit Santander in 1956. Besides, it may have been Salamanca in 1953 and by certain criteria of narrative or of psychological adequacy even be "right" if untrue. There are also internal criteria relating to how one felt or what one intended, and these are just as demanding, even if they are not subject to verification. Otherwise, we would not be able to say that certain self-narratives are "shallow" and others "deep." One criterion, of course, is whether a life story "covers" the events of a life. But what is coverage? Are not omissions also important? And we have all read or heard painfully detailed autobiographies of which it can be said that the whole is drastically less than the sum of the parts. They lack interpretation or "meaning," we say. As Peter Winch reminded us a long time ago, it is not so evident in the human sciences or human affairs how to specify criteria by which to judge the rightness of any theory or model, especially a folk theory like an account of "my life."[7] All verificationist criteria turn slippery, and we surely cannot judge rightness by narrative adequacy alone. A rousing tale of a life is not necessarily a "right" account.

All of which creates special problems, as we shall see, and makes autobiographical accounts (even the ones we tell ourselves) notably unstable. On the other hand, this very instability makes life stories highly susceptible to cultural, interpersonal, and linguistic influences. This susceptibility to influence may, in fact, be the reason why "talking cures," religious instruction, and other interventions in a life may often have such profound effects in changing a person's life narrative.

Given their constructed nature and their dependence upon the cultural conventions and language usage, life narratives obviously reflect the prevailing theories about "possible lives" that are part of one's culture. Indeed, one important way of characterizing a culture is by the narrative models it makes available for describing the course of a life. And the tool kit of any culture is replete not only with a stock of canonical life narratives (heroes, Marthas, tricksters, etc.), but with combinable formal constituents from which its members can construct their own life narratives: canonical stances and circumstances, as it were.

But the issue I wish to address is not just about the "telling" of life narratives. The heart of my argument is this: eventually the culturally shaped cognitive and linguistic processes that guide the self-telling of life narratives achieve the power to structure perceptual experience, to organize memory, to segment and purpose-build the very "events" of a life. In the end, we *become* the autobiographical narratives by which we "tell about" our lives. And given the cultural shaping to which I referred, we also become variants of the culture's canonical forms. I cannot imagine a more important psychological research project than one that addresses itself to the "development of autobiography" – how our way of telling about ourselves changes, and how these accounts come to take control of our ways of life. Yet I know of not a single comprehensive study on this subject.

How a culture transmits itself in this way is an anthropological topic and need not concern us directly. Yet a general remark is in order. I want to address the question of how self-narratives as a *literary* form, as autobiography, might have developed. For the issue may throw some light on how more modest, less formulated modes of self-telling have emerged as well. Autobiography, we are told, is a recent and a not very widely distributed literary genre. As the French historian Georges Gusdorf remarks, it is

> limited in time and space; it has not always existed nor does it exist everywhere.... [Its] conscious awareness of the singularity of each individual life is the late product of a specific civilization.... Autobiography becomes possible only under certain metaphysical preconditions.... The man who takes the trouble to tell of himself knows that the present differs from the past and that it will not be repeated in the future.[8]

Gusdorf sees the birth of literary autobiography as issuing from the mixed and unstable marriage between Christian and classical thought in the Middle Ages, further inflamed by the doubts kindled in the Copernican revolution. Doubtless the Reformation also added fuel to the passion for written self-revelation.

While the act of *writing* autobiography is new under the sun – like writing itself – the self-told life narrative is, by all accounts, ancient and universal. People anywhere can tell you some intelligible account of their lives. What varies is the cultural and linguistic perspective or narrative *form* in which it is formulated and expressed. And that too will be found to spring from historical circumstances as these have been incorporated in the culture and language of a people. I suspect that it will be as important to study *historical* developments in forms of self-telling as it is to study their ontogenesis. I have used the expression "forms of self-telling," for I believe it is form rather than content that matters. We must be clear, then, about what we mean by narrative form. Vladimir Propp's classic analysis of folktales reveals, for example, that the *form* of a folktale may remain unchanged even though its content changes.[9] So too self-told life narratives may reveal a common formal structure across a wide variety of content. So let us get to the heart of the matter: to the forms of self-narrative or, indeed, of narrative generally, of which self-narrative is a special case.

Forms of self-narrative

Let me start my account with the Russian formalists, who distinguished three aspects of story: *fabula, sjuzet,* and *forma* – roughly theme, discourse, and genre. The first two (*fabula* and *sjuzet*) have been described by modern literary theorists as, respectively, the *timeless* and the *sequenced* aspects of story. The timeless *fabula* is the mythic, the transcendent plight that a story is about: human jealousy, authority, and obedience, thwarted ambition, and those other plights that lay claim to human universality. The *sjuzet* then incorporates or realizes the timeless *fabula* not only in the form of a plot but also in an unwinding net of language. Frank Kermode says that the joining of *fabula* and *sjuzet* in story is like the blending of timeless mystery and current scandal.[10] The ancient dilemmas of envy, loyalty, jealousy are woven into the acts of Iago, Othello, Desdemona, and Everyman with a fierce particularity and localness that, in Joyce's words, yield an "epiphany of the ordinary." This particularity of time, place, person, and event is also reflected in the mode of the telling, in the discourse properties of the *sjuzet*.

To achieve such epiphanous and unique ordinariness, we are required, as Roman Jakobson used to tell his Russian poets, to "make the ordinary strange."[11] And that must depend not upon plot alone but upon language. For language constructs what it narrates, not only semantically but also pragmatically and stylistically.

One word about the third aspect of narrative – *forma* or genre, an ancient subject dating from Aristotle's *Poetics*. How shall we understand it? Romance, farce, tragedy, *Bildungsroman*, black comedy, adventure story, fairy tale, wonder tale, etc. That might do. A genre is plainly a type (in the linguist's sense) of which there are near endless tokens, and in that sense it may be viewed as a set of grammars for generating different kinds of story plots. But it cannot be that alone. For genre also commits one to use language in a certain way: lyric, say, is conventionally written in the first person/present tense, epic is third person/past tense, etc. One question we shall simply pass over for the moment: Are genres mere literary conventions, or (like Jung's alleged archetypes) are they built into the human genome, or are they an invariant set of plights in the human condition to which we all react in some necessary way? For our present purposes, it does not matter.

We may ask then of any self-told life what is its *fabula* (or gist, or moral, or leit-motiv); how is it converted into an extended tale and through what uses of language; and into what genre is it fitted. That is a start, but it does not get us very far.

There is widespread agreement that stories are about the vicissitudes of human intention and that, to paraphrase Kenneth Burke's classic, *The Grammar of Motives*, story structure is composed minimally of the pentad of an Agent, an Action, a Goal, a Setting, an Instrument – and Trouble.[12] Trouble is what drives the drama, and it is generated by a mismatch between two or more of the five constituents of Burke's pentad: for example, Nora's Goals do not match either the

Setting in which she lives nor the Instruments available to her in Ibsen's *A Doll's House*. The late Victor Turner, a gifted anthropologist who studied Western theater as carefully as he studied the Ndembu in West Africa, locates this "trouble" in the breaching of cultural legitimacy: an initial canonical state is breached, redress is attempted which, if it fails, leads to crisis; crisis, if unresolved, leads eventually to a new legitimate order.[13] The crisis, the role of agents in redress, the making of the new legitimacy – these are the cultural constituents of which the variety of drama is constructed in life as in literature. That is to say, Burke's dramatistic troubles are, for Turner, individual embodiments of deeper cultural crises.

We had better get on to a closer characterization of Agents in stories, since our interest is in self-told life narratives. Narrative studies began with the analysis of myth and folktale. And it is indeed the case that, in these genres, the plot even more than motive drives the Agent. You will find little about the doubts, desires, or other intentional states of either Beowulf or Grendel, nor do you get a clear sense from recorded myth about how Perseus decided to get involved with the Gorgon. Even Oedipus is not so much driven by motives as by plight. As Vladimir Propp put it, the *dramatis personae* of the classical folktale fulfill a function in the plot but do not drive it. But that is only one version of character: Agent as carrier of destiny, whether divine or secular.

As literary forms have developed, they have moved steadily toward an empowerment and subjective enrichment of the Agent protagonist. The most revealing single analysis of this transformation is, I think, to be found in an essay by Amelie Rorty, in which she traces the shape of agency in narrative from the folktale *figure* "who is neither formed by nor owns experience," to *persons* defined by roles and responsibilities in a society for which they get rights in return (as, say, in Jane Austen's novels), to *selves* who must compete for their roles in order to earn their rights (as in Trollope), and finally to *individuals* who transcend and resist society and must create or "rip off" their rights (as, say, in Beckett).[14] These, you will see, are characterizations of the forms of relationship between an intention-driven actor and the settings in which he must act to achieve his goals.

Another word, then, about Agents. Narrative, even at its most primitive, is played out on a dual landscape, to use Greimas's celebrated expression.[15] There is a landscape of *action* on which events unfold. Grendel wreaks destruction on the drinking hall and upon its celebrating warriors in *Beowulf*. But there is a second landscape, a landscape of consciousness, the inner worlds of the protagonists involved in the action. It is the difference between Oedipus taking Jocasta to wife before and after he learns from the messenger that she is his mother. This duality of landscape, Greimas tells us, is an essential ingredient of narrative and accounts in some measure for the ubiquitousness of deceit in tales throughout history. In the modern novel – in contrast to the classic myth or the folktale – there is a more explicit treatment of the landscape of consciousness itself. Agents do not merely deceive; they hope, are doubting and confused, wonder about appearance and reality. Modern literature (perhaps like modern science) becomes more epistemological, less ontological. The omniscient narrator (like the prerelativity "observer") disappears, and with him so does hard-core reality.

As narrative has become "modernized," so too has its language changed. Since, say, Conrad, Proust, Hardy, and Henry James, the language of the novel has accommodated to the perspectivalism and subjectivism that replaced the omniscient narrator. In another place, I have used the term "subjunctivizing" to characterize this shift from expository to perspectival narrative language, a shift from emphasis on actuality to the evocation of possibility marked by the greater use of unpackable presuppositions, of subjunctive discourse, of Gricean conversational implicatures and the like. In the end, the reality of the omniscient narrator disappears into the subjective worlds of the story's protagonists.[16] Linguistically and in spirit as well, the modern novel may be as profound (and perhaps out of the same cradle) as the invention of modern physics.

One last point, for I have lingered too long introducing my subject. Jean-Paul Sartre remarks in his autobiography, "a man is always a teller of stories, he lives surrounded by his own stories and those of other people, he sees everything that happens to him *in terms of* these stories and he tries to live his life as if he were recounting it."[17] His point is a telling one: life stories must mesh, so to speak, within a community of life stories; tellers and listeners must share some "deep structure" about the nature of a "life," for if the rules of life-telling are altogether arbitrary, tellers and listeners will surely be alienated by a failure to grasp what the other is saying or what he thinks the other is hearing. Indeed, such alienation does happen cross-generationally, often with baleful effects. Later, we shall return to the issue of "life-story meshing" in a more concrete way.

Four self-narratives

Let me turn now to the business of how a psychologist goes about studying issues of the kind that we have been discussing. Along with my colleagues Susan Weisser and Carol Staszewski, I have been engaged in a curious study. While it is far from done (whatever that may mean), I would like to tell you enough about it to make what I have been saying a little more concrete.

We were interested in how people tell the stories of their lives and, perhaps simplemindedly, we asked them to do so – telling them to keep it to about half an hour, even if it were an impossible task. We told them that we were not interested in judging them or curing them but that we were very interested in how people saw their lives. After they were done – and most had little trouble in sticking to the time limits or, for that matter, in filling up the time – we asked questions for another half hour or so, questions designed to get a better picture of how their stories had been put together. Had we followed a different procedure, we doubtless would have obtained different accounts. Indeed, had we asked them to tell us their lives in two minutes, perhaps we would have obtained something more like a *fabula* than a *sjuzet*. But such variations will get their innings later. Many people have now sat for their portraits, ranging in age from ten to seventy, and their stories yield rich texts. But I want to talk of only four of them now: a family – a father, a mother, and their grown son and grown daughter, each of their accounts collected independently. There are two more grown children in the family, a son and daughter, both of whom have also told their stories, but four are enough to handle as a start.

We have chosen a family as our target because it constitutes a miniature culture, and provides an opportunity to explore how life stories are made to mesh with each other in Sartre's sense. Beyond that, of course, the individual autobiographies provide us the opportunity to explore the issues of form and structure to which I have already alluded.

If you should now ask how we propose to test whether these four lives "imitated" the narratives each person told, your question would be proper enough, though a bit impatient. The position I have avowed, indeed, leaves entirely moot what could be meant by "lives" altogether, beyond what is contained in the narrative. We shall not even be able to check, as Professor Neisser was able to do in his studies of autobiographical memory,[18] whether particular memories were veridical or distorted in some characteristic way. But our aim is different. We are asking, rather, whether there is in each account a set of selective narrative rules that lead the narrator to structure experience in a particular way, structure it in a manner that gives form to the content and the continuity of the life. And we are interested, as well, in how the family itself formulates certain common rules for doing these things. I hope this will be less abstract as we proceed.

Our family is headed by George Goodhertz, a hard-working heating contractor in his early sixties, a self-made man of moral principles, converted to Catholicism in childhood and mindful of his obligations, though not devout. Though plainly intelligent and well informed, he never finished high school: "had to go to work". His father was, by Mr Goodhertz's sparse characterization, "a drinker" and a poor provider. Mr Goodhertz is neither. Mrs Goodhertz, Rose, is a housewife of immediate Italian descent: family oriented, imbedded in the urban neighborhood where she has lived for nearly thirty years; connected with old friends who still live nearby. Her father was, in her words, "of the old school" – arrogant, a drinker, a poor provider, and unfaithful to her mother. In the opening paragraph of her autobiography she says, "I would have preferred a better childhood, a happier one, but with God's influence, I prayed hard enough for a good husband, and she [*sic*] answered me."

Daughter Debby, in her mid-twenties, is (in her own words) "still unmarried." She graduated a few years ago from a local college that she never liked much and now studies acting. Outgoing, she enjoys friends, old and new, but is determined not to get "stuck" in the old neighborhood with the old friends of her past and their old attitudes. Yet she is not ambitious, but caught, rather, between ideals of local kindliness and of broader adventure, the latter more in the existential form of a desire for experience than by any wish to achieve. She lives at home – in Brooklyn with her parents in the old neighborhood. Her thirty-year-old brother, Carl, who is about to finish his doctorate in neurophysiology at one of the solid, if not distinguished Boston-area universities, is aware of how far beyond family expectations his studies have taken him, but is neither deferential nor aggressive about his leap in status. Like his sister Debby, he remains attached to and in easy contact with his parents though he lives on his own even when he is in New York working at a local university laboratory. At school Carl always felt "special" and different – both in the Catholic high school and then in the Catholic college he attended. The graduate school he chose is secular, and a complete break with his past. He is ambitious to get ahead, but he is not one to take the conventional "up" stairway. Both in his own eyes and, indeed, by conventional standards, he is a bit eccentric and a risk taker. Where his sister Debby (and his mother) welcomes intimacy and closeness, Carl (like his father) keeps people more at arm's length. Experience for its own sake is not his thing. He is as concerned as his sister about not being "tied down."

And that, I now want to assure you, is the end of the omniscient auctorial voice. For our task now is to sample the texts, the narratives of these four lives – father's, mother's, son's, and daughter's – to see not what they are *about* but how the narrators *construct* themselves. Their texts are all we have – though we may seem to have, so to speak, the hermeneutical advantage of four narratives that spring from a common landscape. But as you will see, the advantage that it yields is in narrative power and possibility, not in the ontology of verification. For one view of the world cannot confirm another, though, in Clifford Geertz's evocative phrase, it can "thicken" it.

Let me begin the analysis with Kenneth Burke's pentad, his skeleton of dramatism, and particularly with the setting or Scene of these life stories. Most psychological theories of personality, alas, have no place for place. They would not do well with Stephen Daedalus in Joyce's *Portrait of the Artist as a Young Man*, for he is inexplicable without the Dublin that he carries in his head. In these four life narratives too, place is crucial and it shapes and constrains the stories that are told or, indeed, that could be told. Place is not simply a piece of geography, an established Italian neighborhood in Brooklyn, though it helps to know its "culture" too. It is an intricate construct, whose language dominates the thought of our four narrators. For each, its central axis is "home," which is placed in sharp contrast to what they all refer to as "the real world." They were, by all their own accounts, a "close" family, and their language seals that closeness.

Consider the psychic geography. For each of our narrators, "home" is a place that is inside, private, forgiving, intimate, predictably safe. "The real world" is outside, demanding, anonymous, open, unpredictable, and consequently danger- ous. But home and real world are also contrastive in another way, explicitly for the two children, implicitly and covertly for the parents: home is to be "cooped up," restricted by duties and bored; real world is excitement and opportunity. Early on, the mother says of the children, "We spoiled them for the real world," and the father speaks of "getting them ready for the real world." The son speaks of its hypocrisies that need to be confronted and overcome to achieve one's goals. It is a worthwhile but treacherous battlefield. The daughter idealizes it for the new expe- rience to be harvested there. Each, in their way, creates a different ontological landscape out of "the real world" to give it an appropriate force as the Scene in the narratives they are constructing.

One thing that is striking about all four narratives is the extent to which the spatial distinction home-real world concentrates all four of them on spatial and locative terms in their autobiographical accounts. Take Carl for instance, his account is laden with spatial metaphors: *in/out, here/there, coming from/going to, place/special place.* The movement forward in his story is not so much temporal as spatial: a sequential outward movement from home to neighborhood to Catholic school to the library alone to college to the Catholic peace movement to graduate school and then triumphantly back to New York. In his *Bildungsroman* of a life story, the challenge is to find a place, the right place, and then a special place in each of these concentric outgoings. For Carl, you get involved *in* things, or you feel "*out* of place." You "go to" Boston or to a course or a lab, and fellow students "come from" prestigious schools. Or "I started gaining a fairly special place in the Department," and later "I ended up getting a fairly privileged place in the Department." The "special places" *allow, permit, make possible.* "After about six months I really started settling in and enjoying the program and enjoying the opportunities it gave me." And later, about the students who get a special place, "The faculty are committed to shielding their graduate students from negative repercussions of failure."

Two things are both surprising and revealing about Carl's language. One is the extent to which his sentences take self as object, and the other is the high frequency of the passive voice. With respect to the latter, some 11 percent of his sentences are in the passive voice, which is surprisingly high for such an action-oriented text. But they both are of a piece and tell something interesting about his world making. Recall the importance for Carl of "place" and particularly of the "special place." Whenever he recounts something connected with these places, the places "happen" and then he acts accordingly. His sentences then begin with either a passive or with self-as-object, and then move to the active voice. At a particular colloquium where he knew his stuff, "It allowed me to deal with the faculty on an equal footing."

Or of his debating team experience, "It taught me how to handle myself." Occasions in these "special places" are seen as if they had homelike privileges: allowing and permitting and teaching. It is as if Carl manages the "real world" by colonizing it with "special places" that provide some of the privileges of home.

With Debby, thirty-seven of the first hundred sentences in her life narrative contain spatial metaphors or locatives. The principal clusters are about her place in the family (the *gap* or *span* in ages); the life layout ("the house I was brought home to is the house I live in now"; or "I traveled, my relatives are all over the country"; or "I've been coming to the city by myself ever since I was fourteen"); the coming-back theme ("everybody except me has gone out and come back at one time or another").

So much for Scene, at least for the moment. Come now to the agentive, to Burke's Actor. Rorty's typology turns out to be enormously useful, for in all four self-portraits the tale moves from Actor as figure, figure becoming a person, person becoming a self, self becoming an individual. Well into her fifties, even Mrs Goodhertz has finally taken a job for pay, albeit working as secretary for her husband's heating-contracting business, motivated by the desire for some independence and the wish not to get "stuck" raising her eldest daughter's child. She remarks that it is "her" job and that she now "works." The transformation of her language as she runs through the chronology of her life is striking. When speaking of her childhood, self is often an object in such sentences as: "everything was thrown at us." But finally, by the time she takes her first job as a young woman, "I decided to take things in my own hands." Throughout her account, she "owns her own experience," to use Rorty's phrase. More than eight in ten of her sentences contain a stative verb, a verb dealing with thinking, feeling, intending, believing, praying. (This contrasts with five in ten for her more action-oriented husband.) One is easily deceived, reading Mrs Goodhertz's self-portrait, into thinking that she is accepting of fate, perhaps passive. Instead, she believes in fate, but she also believes that fate can be nudged by her own efforts. And we rather suspect that the style is cultivated. For a closer analysis of her language reveals a very high "subjectivity level" as carried in those stative verbs.

We must return again to Scene, or perhaps to what might better be called mise-en-scène. Both the elder Goodhertzes – unlike their children – construct their lives as if they constituted two sides of a deep divide. That divide is marked by an escape from childhood, an old life, indeed, an old *secret* life of suffering and shame as figures in unbearably capricious family settings. Personhood is on the other side of the divide. Mrs Goodhertz gets to the other side, to personhood, by "praying for the right husband" and getting him, of which more in a moment. Mr Goodhertz crosses the divide by work, hard work, and by the grace of "the owner [who] took me under his wing." To him, achieving mastery of your work and, as we shall see, helping others help themselves are the two dominant ideals. For her, it is somewhat more complex. The linguistic vehicle is the "*but...*" construction. She uses it repeatedly, and in several telltale ways, the most crucial being to distinguish what *is* from what *might have been*, as in talking about teenage drug taking, "....but I am blessed *my* kids didn't start in on it," or "I would have been stricter, but they turned out with less problems than others." The construction is her reminder of what *might* have been and, at the same time, a string on her finger to remind her that she is the agent who produces the better event on the other side of the... *but....* Her courtship and marriage are a case in point. Yes, she was waiting for God to bring the right man, *but* in fact she decided the moment her eyes fell on Mr Goodhertz that *he* was the man and knew not an instant's remorse in throwing over her then fiance.

Their secret childhoods provide a unique source of consciousness for the elder Goodhertzes. It is a concealed secret that they share and that provides the contrast to what they have established as the organizing concept of "home." Mrs Goodhertz's knowledge of her macho father as a bad provider, a drinker, and a philanderer is secret knowledge, quickly and hintingly told in her narrative in a way that brooked no probing. It was there only to let us know why she prayed for a good husband and a better life for her children. Mr Goodhertz goes into even less detail. But note the two following quotations, both about hopes for the children, each said independently of the other. Mr Goodhertz: "I wanted to give them all the things I didn't get as a kid." And Mrs Goodhertz: "To a point, I think, we try not to make our children have too much of what we had."

So Debby and Carl start on the other side of the divide. Each of them tells a tale that is animated by a contrast between a kindly but inert, entrenched, or "given" world and a "new" one that is their own. Carl is a young Werther. His tale begins with the episode when, as an aspiring young football player, he and his teammates are told by the coach to knock out the opposing team's star quarterback. He keeps his own counsel, quits football, and starts on his own road. For Debby the tale is more like the young Stephen Hero in the discarded early version of *Portrait*. She exposes herself to experience as it may come, "trying" in the sense of "trying on" rather than of striving. Her involvement in acting is in the spirit of trying on new roles. Of life she says, "I don't like doing one thing, ...the same thing all my life,...shoved into a house and cooped up with four kids all day." If Carl's autobiography is a *Bildungsroman*, Debby's is an existential novel. His account is linear, from start to end, but it is replete with what literary linguists call *prolepsis*. That is to say, it is full of those odd flash-forwards that implicate the present for the future, like "if I had known then what I know now" and "learning to debate would stand me in good stead later." His narrative is progressive and sequential: the story tracks "real time." It "accounts" for things, and things are mentioned because *they* account for things. Privileged opportunities "happen to" him, as we have seen, and he turns them into ventures.

The exception to this pattern is the dilemma of moral issues – as with the coach's murderous instructions or his becoming a conscientious objector in the Vietnam war, inspired by the Berrigans. Then his language (and his thought) becomes subjunctive rather than instrumental, playing on possibilities and inwardness. In this respect, he is his father's son, for Mr Goodhertz too is principally oriented to action (recall that half his sentences contain nonstative verbs) save when he encounters issues he defines as matters of morality. Don't condemn, he would say, "you never know the whole story." And in the same spirit, Mr Goodhertz's self-portrait is laced with literally dozens of instances of the intransitive verb *to seem*, as if he were forever mindful of a feather edge separating appearance from reality. When Carl decided he would become a conscientious objector against the Vietnam draft, his father stood by him on grounds that Carl's convictions, honestly arrived at, were worthy of respect even though he did not agree with them. Carl unwittingly even describes his intellectual quest in the same instrumental terms that his father uses in describing his ducting work. Both emphasize skills and "know-how," both reject received ways of doing things. Theirs is "instrumental" language and thought, as well suited to talking about heat ducting as to Carl's strikingly procedural approach to visual physiology. The father confesses to having missed intimacy in his life. So, probably, will Carl one day. Their instrumental language leaves little room for it in their discourse.

Debby's highly stative language is specialized for the reception of experience and for exploring the affect that it creates. It is richly adjectival, and the adjectives cluster around inner states. Her own acts are almost elided from her account. The past exists in its own right rather than as a guide to the present or future. In recounting the present there are vivid analeptic flashbacks – as in an unbid memory of an injured chicken on the Long Island Expressway, the traffic too thick for rescue. Like so many of her images, this one was dense with plight and affect. It evoked her tenderness for helpless animals, she told us, then veering off to that topic. And so her order of telling is dominated not by real time sequences but by a going back and forth between what happens and what she feels and believes, and what she felt and believed. In this, and in her heavy use of stative verbs, she is her mother's daughter – and, I suspect, both are locked in the same gender language. Finally, in Debby's self-story "themes and variations" are as recursive as her brother's is progressive, and hers is as lacking in efforts to give causes as his are replete with causative expressions.

Recipes for structuring experience

You will ask whether the narrative forms and the language that goes with them in our four subjects are not simply expressions of their inner states, ways of talk that are required by the nature of those internal states. Perhaps so. But I have been proposing a more radical hypothesis than that. I believe that the ways of telling and the ways of conceptualizing that go with them become so habitual that they finally become recipes for structuring experience itself, for laying down routes into memory, for not only guiding the life narrative up to the present but directing it into the future. I have argued that a life as led is inseparable from a life as told – or more bluntly, a life is not "how it was" but how it is interpreted and reinterpreted, told and retold: Freud's *psychic reality*. Certain basic formal properties of the life narrative do not change easily. Our excursion into experimental autobiography suggests that these formal structures may get laid down early in the discourse of family life and persist stubbornly in spite of changed conditions. Just as Georges Gusdorf argued that a special, historically conditioned, metaphysical condition was needed to bring autobiography into existence as a literary form, so perhaps a metaphysical change is required to alter the narratives that we have settled upon as "being" our lives. The fish will, indeed, be the last to discover water – unless he gets a metaphysical assist.

My life as a student of mind has taught me one incontrovertible lesson. Mind is never free of precommitment. There is no innocent eye, nor is there one that penetrates aboriginal reality. There are instead hypotheses, versions, expected scenarios. Our precommitment about the nature of a life is that it is a story, some narrative however incoherently put together. Perhaps we can say one other thing: any story one may tell about anything is better understood by considering other possible ways in which it can be told. That must surely be as true of the life stories we tell as of any others. In that case, we have come full round to the ancient homily that the only life worth living is the well-examined one. But it puts a different meaning on the homily. If we can learn how people put their narratives together when they tell stories from life, considering as well how they *might* have proceeded, we might then have contributed something new to that great ideal. Even if, with respect to life and narrative, we discover, as in Yeats's line, that we cannot tell the dancer from the dance, that may be good enough.

Notes

1 For example, J. S. Bruner, *Actual Minds, Possible Worlds* (Cambridge: Harvard University Press, 1986).
2 Nelson Goodman, *Ways of Worldmaking* (Indianapolis: Hackett, 1978).
3 Paul Ricoeur, *Time and Narrative* (Chicago, IL: University of Chicago Press, 1984).
4 See Hayden White, "The Value of Narrativity in the Representation of Reality," in W. J. T. Mitchell, ed., *On Narrative* (Chicago, IL: University of Chicago Press, 1984).
5 Paul de Man, *The Rhetoric of Romanticism* (New York: Columbia University Press, 1984), p. 84.
6 Louis Renza, "The Veto of the Imagination: A Theory of Autobiography," in James Olney, ed., *Autobiography: Essays Theoretical and Critical* (Princeton, NJ: Princeton University Press, 1980).
7 Peter Winch, *The Idea of a Social Science* (London: Routledge and Kegan Paul, 1958).
8 Georges Gusdorf, "Conditions and Limits of Autobiography," in Olney, *Autobiography*.
9 Vladimir Propp, *The Morphology of the Folktale* (Austin, TX: University of Texas Press, 1968).
10 Frank Kermode, "Secrets and Narrative Sequence," in Mitchell, *On Narrative*.
11 See J. S. Bruner, "In praise of a teacher–friend," in *A Tribute to Roman Jakobson* (Berlin: Walter de Gruyter, 1983).
12 Kenneth Burke, *The Grammar of Motives* (New York: Prentice-Hall, 1945).
13 Victor Turner, *From Ritual to Theater* (New York: Performing Arts Journal Publications, 1982).
14 Amelie Rorty, "A Literary Postscript: Characters, Persons, Selves, Individuals," in A. O. Rorty, ed., *The Identity of Persons* (Berkeley, CA: University of California Press, 1976).
15 A. Greimas and J. Courtes, "The Cognitive Dimension of Narrative Discourse," *New Literary History* 7 (Spring 1976).
16 For those of you interested in this type of linguistic analysis, I refer you to Tzvetan Todorov's *The Poetics of Prose* (Ithaca, NY: Cornell University Press, 1977) and to my own recent volume, *Actual Minds, Possible Worlds*.
17 Jean-Paul Sartre, *The Words* (New York: Braziller, 1964).
18 Ulric Neisser, "Autobiographical Memory," unpublished manuscript, Emory University, 1987.

CHAPTER 12

THE MEANING OF EDUCATIONAL REFORM

National Association of Montessori Teachers Journal (Special Edition: Schools of Thought: Pathways to Educational Reform) (1991), 16, 29–40, Education Commission of the States

I am very honored to be here today to talk to you about what went on in the trenches and in the marbled halls of the state houses and in the White House during the curriculum reform movement of the late 1960s. I want to relate this to what we can expect during the nineties. A great many people with very lively curiosity and real modesty were involved in curriculum reform in the 1960s, and their ideas on how to teach and what to teach were not only elegant, but struck at the heart of what it means not to know and how we enable someone to know and to move on from there. I want to review some of the beliefs that I think inspired the generation of curriculum reformers because I think the notion was that by getting hold of the curriculum, we got hold of the lever that could move the whole system. It was a naive notion with more than a grain of truth to it, but as we learned, grains of truth need a fertile environment in which to work. I think what that group knew, and I include myself as a member of the group, was that science, literature, and history did not exist externally in nature, but were essentially instruments of the mind. We also knew that it was crucial to make knowledge your own – to turn it into usable tools, not just a lot of inert junk in your head. All that teachers can do for the learner in the process of forming tools in their heads is to help them along their voyage through the use of curriculum.

We have learned that there is no such thing as *the* curriculum, there is only *a* curriculum: it is very specific to a particular situation and to a particular student, and it will vary. For, in effect, it's an animated conversation on a topic that we can never really fully define any more than we can set limits on an animated conversation. Curriculum is a three-way conversation between a learner, someone who is somewhat more expert in an area of study, and a body of knowledge that is difficult to define but that exists in the culture. We need it at every level – to learn what history is, or what arithmetic is, and we need it just as much for advanced study.

I learned of an interesting finding; the only decent predictor of whether or not someone would win a Nobel Prize in science is whether or not that person had worked in the laboratory of a Nobel Prize-winning scientist. It is not because that person has any special pull, because Nobel Prize-winning scientists notoriously have no pull; rather, it's because somehow proximity to these eminent scientific thinkers causes a person to be party to certain ways of thinking – through conversation, jokes, subject matter, materials, etc.

Do you remember Bob Karplus? He created a mathematics curriculum that consisted of nothing more complicated, at the outset, than having kids bounce balls back and forth. He would film this activity and play the film forward and backward to see whether his students could see the difference. Then he would raise the question of symmetry in nature and in physics. Is there a time arrow in certain activities? Can it be conceived of symmetrically? He started a dialogue where students entered into something that might be called distributive intelligence. It's not just their own, it is part of an amplifying culture that brought things into being. They were like those young scientists who had the great good fortune of working in some physics laureate's lab so that they could learn to think and talk in a useful way. So teachers are trying to pass insights on, although they are not really passing them on. They start a conversation and try to instantiate insights in that conversation.

I want to say a word about how the atmosphere that was premised on the idea of enabling a learner is created through the use of powerful prosthetic devices that are called "subjects." Geography is a prosthetic device. It isn't about nature; it's about how you think about the natural environment, just as history is a way of thinking about the past. It isn't the past. Physics isn't about nature, it's a way of thinking about nature. Bear that in mind because I'll come back to it. I want to compare that to the atmosphere that exists now. The main objective in the 1960s was to help those who were face-to-face with kids to start that dialogue and to give them materials that would stimulate it. I can't resist the opportunity to contrast that notion with what's going on now in the Governor's Assessment Reform. I have no objection in principle to creating better measuring instruments in order to find out how well our students are doing in science, in mathematics, in literature, in reading, or whatever. For that matter, I don't object in principle to the assessment of how well our teachers are doing at their jobs, though I think we have to be a lot more subtle about how we go about that. If we think that the poor performance of our educational establishment is due principally to a failure in teacher evaluation or in student assessment, then such a reform movement would be appropriate enough. Do you really think that the problem is that we haven't assessed students and teachers well enough? A recent government report talks about our state governors who proclaimed that by the turn of the century, or whenever the latest date is, we were going to turn things around and be the top in the world in science and mathematics. What in the world does that mean? Just what is to be turned around exactly – assessment procedures and standards? Is that what we're after? If it is just that, then we'll succeed only in fueling our own internal indignation about how little geography our students know, how badly they read, how sorely lacking they are in mathematical skills, how deficient they are in understanding what science is all about, or perhaps worse yet, how wonderful it is that our skills have not declined further. Surely it's a curiously indirect route to improving matters, indirect in the sense that indignation just might conceivably get us to do something further about how we actually conduct our schools and the process of education itself and how it relates to the kids' lives. It might conceivably lead to a different message on public lips about financial support for schools and schooling. Schools are surely as important as the savings and loan industry that we propose to bail out for $300 to $500 billion.

Let me ask now why we are so obsessed with teaching the young science and mathematics. I know the answer, of course: it is to make our country more competitive on world markets. Why, for example, has our fetish on improving our record in the sciences and mathematics lead us to neglect our efforts to teach students about the politics, sociology, and economics of the revolutionary world changes that we're living through and to which we will have to adjust ourselves if we are to survive as a great political and moral force in the world? Why is it, for example, that people risked their lives in Tiananmen Square in Peking, in East

Berlin, Prague, Bucharest, Vilnius, or in the desert? I'm not against providing the nation with mathematically and scientifically literate workers so we can out-compete the Japanese or the new Europe in world markets, but I want to make it absolutely plain that that's not the sort of aim that inspires either students or teachers to learn and care. We forget, at our peril, that the great leap forward in eastern Europe, and soon, hopefully, in South Africa, and the Republic of China, was led not so much by mathematicians and scientists, although they were there too, as by playwrights, poets, philosophers, and even music teachers. Karl Marx and Nelson Mandela had human wisdom and philosophical depth. Thomas Jefferson could not have had his vision without standing on the philosophical shoulders of John Locke and the learned men of the French Enlightenment. We cannot assume that we're going to move forward just by technical proficiency. Surely we need standards and resources to make our schools work well in solving the myriad tasks that they face in improving literacy. But technical resources and standards alone will not work. We need a surer sense of what to teach to whom, and how to go about teaching it in such a way that those who are taught will be more effective, less alienated, and better human beings.

The nation's teachers have been struggling to carry out this daunting task these last two decades, and under the circumstances have been doing it with much courage and skill and against enormous odds. We in the universities and in the scientific and cultural institutions have been giving them precious little help. I am not proud to admit that some of the most strident recent criticism of education has come from such self-appointed guardians of the culture as Alan Bloom, who longs bitterly for an imaginary past while immured in his ivory tower at the University of Chicago. Teachers and schools did not create the conditions that made American education so difficult. They did not create an underclass, nor could they have undermined the research and development mission of competitive American industry anywhere as effectively as the greedy takeover system of the 1980s fueled by junk bonds that were also undermining the self-sufficiency of corporations. It was not teachers or schools who let the money churners and real estate speculators create the disgraceful conditions of homelessness on one side and of consumerism on the other that now afflict our economy and our sense of purpose. Nor did they create the drug problem that Washington now proposes to resolve, not by capping the flow of drugs into the country or destroying the drug cartels, but ironically enough, by giving over the prevention task to the schools. This is madness! What we need is a reform movement with a better sense of where we are going, with deeper convictions about what kind of people we want to be. Then we can mount the kind of community effort that can truly address the future of our educational process using all the resources of intellect and compassion that we can muster, whatever the price. If we can achieve a resounding military victory in the Persian Gulf, how about putting this kind of energy to work to improve our schools? All the assessment standards in the world will not make our multicultural, threatened society come alive again as a competitor in the world's markets or as a nation worth living in and living for. I can do no better than to cite the conclusion of Ernie Boyer's wonderful 87th Annual Report from the Carnegie Commission of the Advancement of Teaching in which he says, speaking of current reform:

> We are troubled that the nation's teachers remain so skeptical. Why is it that teachers, of all people, are demoralized and largely unimpressed by the reform actions taken thus far? The reform movement has been driven largely by legislative and administrative intervention. The push has been concerned more

with regulation than with renewal. Reforms typically have focused on graduation requirements, student achievement, teacher preparation, and testing and
monitoring activities. But in all these matters, as important as they are, teachers largely are uninvolved. Indeed the most disturbing finding in our study is
this: over half the teachers surveyed believe that overall morale within the profession has substantially declined since 1983 [this is 1988 that he's talking
about]. What is urgently needed [he goes on to conclude] in the next phase of
school reform, is a deep commitment to make teachers partners in renewal at
all levels. This challenge now is to move beyond regulations, focus on renewal,
and make teachers full participants [and I would add, leaders] in the process.

I realize that when we talk about reform – renewal, in the new sense – there are
two aspects of the problem. There is a specific aspect of how to teach – what we
can do by way of teaching that I want to talk about, but I can't quite come to that
until I talk about the deep shortcoming that characterized the earlier curriculum
reform movement. I'm aware of how deep and complex the whole problem of pedagogy and curriculum is, and I know that it is not a problem that besets just the
middle class or the dispossessed, or whomever. I find that there exists in this country a strong wish at all levels to recapture a sense of meaning that is above and
beyond the matter of learning history, mathematics, or science. Kids ask, "What
does it mean to be educated?" "What does it mean to go to school?" There is
something deep in the system that questions what school is all about. "Why am I
going to school?" "Am I learning anything here that will make a difference in the
rest of life, aside from the fact that it's a set of hoops that will allow me to get into
the next academic level"? Our country has been breeding a new kind of middle
class. It no longer owns its own wealth. Very few indeed have the kind of wealth,
particularly with the tax system of the last ten years, that enables power to be
inherited in the form of wealth. The best that parents can do is to finance their
children's education so that the children will be qualified for jobs that permit them
to remain "middle class." So education has become a weapon of middle-class survival. The reality is that parents no longer have any money to leave as inheritance.
The only way for them to privilege their children is to give them an education. So
it has become fashionable not only to resist parental pressure but to resist the
schools. These kids, I'm talking about age 10 to age 17, often say that school is like
being on a treadmill, qualifying for something later. It lacks "meaning," they say.
There is some feeling that they would like to be in a community of meaning rather
than a community of "earning qualifications."

I think it is crucial for there to be a national debate about what we mean now
about education. I don't mean to sound like Shirley Williams who was Minister of
Education in Britain when I was resident there, but she had a point when she called
for a national debate on education. She wanted to talk about its aims, what it was
doing, to put it up for discussion, and take it into the schools where teachers and
kids could talk about it too because there is a feeling of falsehood about such a
debate without them – which is quite justified.

My second general suggestion has to do with quite another facet of the problem. I have up to now been talking about the largely suburban, middle-class population. Now I want to talk about the deeper problem of the alienated within our
society, about our dread capacity to create alienation within our culture. We are a
society that will never really have a very broad consensus again. We achieved a
fairly limited consensus through Supreme Court decisions in the 1960s and 1970s.
But there is still no broad consensus about the need for sharing, for caring, and for

communal responsibility. I want to raise this crucial question now, for it lies heavily on my conscience. I testified in *Brown vs. Board of Education* and again in the *Delaware case*.

I am concerned that we are so desperately discouraged by the fact that we always concentrate on how we fail whenever we approach the problem of the alienated and the poor in our culture. All we can cite as success is the fact that a black middle class has moved out of the black ghetto and is now doing fine. We then revert to the problems of the remaining ghettos – which are real enough. We completely forget about the fact that since the days of *Brown vs. Board of Education* there is not only an emergent black middle class, but that the Chief of Staff of the United States Army is black and brilliant, and that New York proudly has David Dinkins as mayor. In some of the residual black ghettos, such as Harlem, however, death by homicide is the greatest risk one faces between the ages of sixteen and thirty, and the next greatest danger of being removed from society is going to jail. We keep talking about the latter as a "hopeless" situation, forgetting that by exerting effort and exerting care we have been able to achieve the former. We have somehow let ourselves be discouraged into the passivity of those years of Reagan know-nothingness. But we cannot allow ourselves to become resigned to failure. We must not allow ourselves to fall into the hardened despair that I've seen among the Palestinians or in Northern Ireland. We need to show ourselves again that we can do the extraordinary things that are required by a state of crisis – if we will handle it as such, as a *crisis*. Our denial of our current crisis cannot be allowed to go on, and it cannot be handled only by the schools. We must face our crisis of domestic neglect soon, and we must do so from the top, from the middle, and from the bottom. I hope that the President, who I think is a man of good will, will be encouraged by his success in bringing off a military-logistical miracle to try his hand at bringing this one off too. We are not going to solve the problem of educational reform alone by addressing it only at the school level. It is part of a much broader problem. That problem is nothing less than the issue of the distribution of opportunity, respect, and wealth in America.

Now what can we say of our schools? What things can we do *within* the school to bring back our educational self-respect? Let me take a step back so we can all see where we're coming from.

A very long time ago I proposed something which was called a spiral curriculum. The idea was that when teaching or learning a subject, you start with an intuitive account that is well within the reach of the student, then circle back later in a more powerful, more generative, more structured way to understand it more deeply with however many recyclings the learner needs in order to master the topic and turn it into an instrument of the mind, a way of thinking. It was a notion that grew out of a more fundamental view of epistemology, about how minds get to know. I stated this view almost in the form of a philosophical proverb: Any subject could be taught to any child at any age in some form that was honest. Another way of saying the same thing is that readiness is not only born but made. You make readiness. The general proposition rests on the still deeper truth that a domain of knowledge can be constructed simply or complexly, abstractly or concretely. The kid who understands the intuitive rule of the lever and can apply it to the playground see-saw is getting within reach of knowing the meaning of quadratic functions. He now has a grasp of one instantiation of an idea that makes teaching him about quadratics a cinch. I'm saying this because we have done it. Give me a balance beam with hooks placed at equal distances along it, some weights that you can hang on the hooks of the balance beam to make it balance, and I will show you.[1] A ten-year-old I was working with once said to me, "This gadget knows all about arithmetic." That gave me pause, and I tried to convince him that it was he who knew arithmetic, not the balance beam. He listened politely, but I don't think I succeeded; maybe that will come later along the curriculum spiral. Anyway, he had learned a meaning of expressions like $x^2 + 5x + 6$ and why they balance – mean the same – as ones like $(x + 2)(x + 3)$.

The research of the last three decades on the growth of reasoning in children has in the main confirmed the rightness of the notion of the spiral curriculum in spite of the fact that we now know about something called domain specificity. It is not true now nor was it ever true that learning Latin improves your reasoning. Subject matters have to be demonstrably within reach of each other to improve each other. There isn't infinite transfer. On the other hand, there is probably more than we know, and we can build up a kind of general confidence that problems are solvable. That has a huge transfer affect. The kid says, "Now how would we do that?" using kind of a royal "we." A good intuitive, practical grasp of the domain at one stage of development leads to better, earlier, and deeper thinking in the next stage when the child meets new problems. We do not wait for readiness to happen. We foster it by making sure they are good at some intuitive domain before we start off on the next one.

However, it's interesting that we don't always do it. It is appalling how poorly history, for example, is taught at most schools and at most universities. Teachers need to give students an idea that there are models for how events happened historically, even if we give them a sort of Toynbeyan model, to the effect that there is challenge and response, or the kind of Paul Kennedy model of what happens to wealthy nations. The particular model doesn't matter, just so it is clear and coherent so that kids can say, "Pretty smart, but it doesn't work." We need models that can be given some basic sense even though they are rejected later. One way to do it is by placing emphasis upon what is story-like about the model. For what we grasp better than anything else are stories, and it is easy for children (or adults) to take them apart, retell them, and analyze what's wrong with them.

Let me give you some examples. Five year olds are delighted with the story of the tortoise and the hare. You can go easily from there to the joke-story that is embodied in "Zeno's Paradox" – which deals with always being halfway from wherever you are going, so how do you ever get there? I asked my five-year-old grandson, "Do you think it's true?" He said, "Oh yeah, but it's silly!" He's absolutely right, but he's now thinking about a very important axiom in the theory of numbers, and he'll never be the same. The heart of the matter is that by telling these stories, children learn how to solve a problem. How do you get out of Zeno's paradox? How does the turtle get where he is going? It is a splendid mental jungle gym for developing thought.

The most natural and earliest way in which we organize our experience and our knowledge is by use of narrative. It may be that the beginnings, the transitions, the full grasps of ideas in a spiral curriculum depend upon embodying those ideas initially into a story or narrative form in order to carry the kid across an area where he is not quite grasping the abstraction. The story form is the first one grasped by kids, and is the one with which they all seem most comfortable. So what is this thing called story, or narrative? Fortunately there's been a very lively decade or so of research on this question from a variety of sources – from linguistics, literary theory, psychology, philosophy, mathematics. I'll begin with some very obvious points about narrative, then we'll relate them a little bit to curriculum. The curriculum I've chosen to relate them to is science, because it seems the most unlikely.

A narrative is a sequence of events. It is discourse, and the first rule for discourse is that there is a prime reason for telling it rather than remaining silent. This is a very deep truth and so obvious that we tend to forget it. Narrative is justified or warranted by virtue of a sequence of events that is in violation of something that we think of as being ordinary or canonical. There has to be something unexpected that gets resolved. That's the point. Why can't that turtle get there if he has to keep going another half? I have heard kids say there has to be something wrong with that arithmetic. That's a good response because there is something deeply wrong with the arithmetic, but there is also something interesting about it. For example, you start with this notion of there being a sequence of things that is told that violates an expectancy, and there is something that creates a crisis, and you either have a redress or you have a new crisis state that stays on as the new canonical condition.

It is easy to use narrative in the study of history, although it isn't used enough. If you said that on Christmas Day in the Great Hall of the Vatican, in the year 800, Pope Leo III put the crown of the Emperor of the Holy Roman Empire on the head of Charlemagne in the presence of all the assembled nobles, some kid has got to say, "What's so great about that?" The fact of the matter is, the moment they ask that kind of question, we're really in business. Who is this Leo III? What kind of a power broker was he? The answer is, a very powerful one. Why? What was he going to get out of it? We soon begin to see the balance-of-power idea of politics and we have some very interesting conversations beginning to emerge. What were those nobles thinking as Charlemagne had the crown placed upon his head? Why not them? What did they think "Europe" meant?

I take an example from my ten-year residence in the 1970s in England. Start some twelve year olds with the marvelous image in the Great Hall of the Vatican on Christmas Day in the year 800 with all the assembled notables and Leo III. They leap quickly from there to the new Europe to be born on July 1, 1992. Given the public rhetoric, it is easy to see a whole millennium as "leading up" to the new Europe. But wait. What happened in between? How come there were so many wars along the way? The students immediately become first-class history critics as they search for the narratives of discord and explore the bases of national selfishness. They become history book critics very easily, but I think we are afraid to let our young have such powers of criticism. We worry about the young becoming too interpretive – perhaps in literature, but not in history. It is unsettling, yet it is crucial if we are to raise a generation with any critical acumen to combat the public relations imagery that seems to pacify our curiosity and protests.

Now let me return to science. It too has its narrative dramas, beautiful solutions to intractable problems. Let me illustrate. Isaac Newton bought a crystal prism on a visit to the Sturbridge Fair. He noticed that when white light from the sun shone through it, it broke into all the familiar component colors of the spectrum, the rainbow. He came to the very counter intuitive, though low elementary conclusion, that white light must be composed of the mixture of all colored light. And this in turn led to the even more bizarre idea of complementary colors – that for every color there is another color that when mixed with it spectrally produces *no* color – i.e., white light. So, for example, red and green is a complementary pair, and yellow and blue is a complementary pair, and so on. So where else does the principle of the cancellation of opposites hold? Pushing ideas to their limit is surely one of the great dramas of the mind. I have no reason to believe that we should wait until graduate school to enjoy this pleasure.

A group of us recently published a book called *Narratives From the Crib*, in which we studied the lively monologues of a little girl, Emmy by name, who liked to talk aloud in bed before she went to sleep.[2] The mother of the child recorded the conversations between her 16th and 32nd months, and we worked for about two years on the recordings. They were absolutely fantastic! Emmy had just been introduced into the rough and tumble world of nursery schools where boys sometimes hit and shove, etc. She talked autobiographically about her troubles, but she also talked about intellectual puzzles – like how come some busses are blue and others yellow. And she would try out her hypotheses aloud – some days there are one kind, some days another, or some in one direction, some in another. She was trying to make a story that made sense – not so different from what every scientist does. Let me give you some examples.

Every historian of science knows that you must lean on any metaphor or story or plot you can get hold of to help you develop your theoretical model. Niels Bohr once confessed how he arrived at the idea of complementarity in physics. Complementarity is the very deep principle that you cannot specify both the position and the velocity of a particle simultaneously, and therefore you can't put them into the same equation. Where did he get this idea? It had struck him first as a moral dilemma. His young son, who is now a very distinguished physicist, had stolen a trinket from the local notions shop in Copenhagen and some days later, stricken with guilt feelings and remorse, had confessed the theft to his father. As Bohr put it, he himself was deeply touched by this moral act of contrition, but was also mindful that his son had committed an act of wrongdoing. But, he said, he was struck by the fact that he could not think of his son *at the same time* both in the light of love and in the light of justice. They were two different ways of thinking. This led him to think that certain states of mind were like the two aspects of his view of his son. Then he realized that this was like those rabbit-pirate pictures or the vase profile pictures where you have a reversible perspective. You either see them one way or the other way but not both ways at the same time. And then, some days later, he came to the realization that the idea that the position of a particle is stationary and in a particular place, and at the same time moving with a velocity, with no position at all, is impossible to think about simultaneously. It's a wonderful story, and it gives you some feeling about what complementarity is. It also gives a beautiful sense of science as an activity of mind rather than as a "description" of nature. Science creates a workable model of nature. It is a tribute to man's mind, and I suspect that more emphasis on science-making as a mental activity would help people understand that point. That requires storytelling and it also involves taking part in science-making one's self, even if at a simple, interactive level.

I have one final story for you. The Queen of England is notorious for her dislike of small talk. A dear friend of mine, Sir Alan Bullock, was Chairman of the Board of the Tate Gallery in London, of which the Queen was the Royal Patroness. He had to act as the Queen's host at the annual dinner. He was very worried about what he would be able to talk with her about. Alan Bullock is a mighty historian, and was then vice chancellor of Oxford University. He hit on the perfect idea. He asked, "Mam, when did the royal family decide to become respectable?" – an absolutely first class question. She answered, "Well, that's a really intriguing question. It was during Victoria's reign when it was realized that the middle class had become central to Britain's prosperity and stability, and at that particular point there was no place for raffish princes." He had found a way of opening up the idea that even royal tradition is an invention. We invent. If we give back the sense of invention to people as human agents, it seems to me that we give back human empowerment. Don't forget the middle lesson, which is namely that human empowerment has to be real, and that it can't be pie in the sky. That is at the heart of my concern. Thank you.

Notes

1   For a demonstration of this little mathematical game and its power, see my book, *Toward a Theory of Instruction*, Cambridge: Harvard University Press, 1966.
2   Katherine Nelson (ed.). Cambridge: Harvard University Press, 1989.

CHAPTER 13

SCIENCE EDUCATION AND TEACHERS

A Karplus Lecture

Journal of Science Education and Technology (1992), 1: 5–12, New York: Plenum Publishing Corporation

I am greatly honored to give the Karplus Lecture this year. Bob Karplus was a key figure in the curriculum reform movement of the late 1960s and 1970s, and the two of us fought in the trenches side by side in those distant days. I was greatly saddened by his death earlier this year, which occurred while I was teaching in his home state at UCLA. He was a lovely man altogether – full of lively curiosity and deep modesty. And his ideas about how to teach science were not only elegant but also from the heart. He knew what it felt like "not to know," what it was like to be a "beginner." As a matter of temperament and principle, *he* knew that not knowing was the chronic condition not only of a student but also of a real scientist. That is what made him a true teacher, a truly courteous teacher.

What he knew was that science is not something that exists out there in nature, but that it is a tool in the mind of the knower – teacher and student alike. Getting to know something is an adventure in how to account for a great many things that you encounter in as simple and elegant a way as possible. And there are lots of ways of getting to that point, lots of different ways. And you don't really ever get there unless you do it, as a learner, on your own terms. You get there on your own terms. All you can do for a learner enroute to their forming a view of their own view is to aid and abet them on their own voyage. The means for aiding and abetting a learner is sometimes called a "curriculum," and what we have learned is that there is no such thing as *the* curriculum. For in effect, a curriculum is like an animated conversation on a topic that can never be fully defined, although one can set limits upon it. I call it an "animated" conversation not only because it is always lively if it is honest, but also because one uses animation in the broader sense – props, pictures, texts, films, and even "demonstrations." Conversation plus show-and-tell plus brooding on it all on one's own.

Bob Karplus' film on the "reversibility" of physical phenomena was a lovely example of a prop. Rather than answering a question, it opens one – the great meta-question of whether you can describe something in nature without specifying the frame of reference or position from which you view it. "Obvious" distinctions like up-down, right-left, moving-stationary suddenly become nonobvious – as they are in physics. Never mind that the film makes everybody think (which in itself is a glorious pedagogical outcome, as we all well know), but it also livens the conversation. Well, the two are not so very different: thinking comes very close to being an internal conversation, and conversation can't be much good unless in some degree you are thinking aloud in the midst of it. That is what these days has come to be called, after the great Bakhtin, the "dialogic imagination." And we shall have more to say about it presently.

I can't resist the opportunity, before getting into my subject, to contrast the spirit of the "curriculum reform" movement in which Bob Karplus was so deeply involved with the present wave of school reform – what for lack of a better expression I shall call "assessment reform," or perhaps I should call it "Governors' reform."

I have no objection in principle to creating better measuring instruments in order to find out how well our students are doing in science, in mathematics, in literature, in reading, in whatever. Or, for that matter, I don't even object in principle to assessments of how our teachers are doing their jobs. If you think that the poor performance of our educational establishment is due principally to a failure in teacher evaluation or in student assessment, then such a reform movement would be appropriate enough. Our State Governors in solemn conclave proclaim that by the turn of the century, or whenever, we will "turn things around and be tops in the world in science and mathematics." And just what is it that is to be turned around? Assessment procedures and "standards"? If only that, then we will succeed only in fueling our internal indignation about how little geography our students know, how badly they read, how sorely lacking they are in mathematical skills, how deficient they are in understanding what science is about. Surely, that is a curiously indirect route to improving matters, indirect in the sense that indignation just *might* conceivably lead us to do something further about how we conduct our schools and the process of education generally. It might even, conceivably, lead to a different message on public lips about financial support for schools and schooling. Schools are surely as important as the savings and load industry that we propose to "bail out" with a three hundred billion dollar handout. It might even lead us to question why, for example, we have made such an exclusive fetish about improving our record in science and mathematics rather than, say, concentrating our effort as well on teaching our students about the politics and economics of the revolutionary world changes through which we are living, or about why human nature risks its neck in the interest of freedom in Tiananman Square in Peking, or in East Berlin, in Prague, in Bucharest, in Vilnius. I am not against providing the nation with scientifically and mathematically literate workers so that we can outcompete the Japanese or the new Europe in world markets – as if that aim alone could ever inspire either teachers or students. We forget at our peril that the great leap forward in Eastern Europe and soon, hopefully, in South Africa and in the Republic of China was led so much by mathematicians and scientists (although they were there too) but by playwrights, poets, philosophers, and even music teachers. What marks a Nelson Mandela or a Vaclav Havel is human wisdom and philosophical depth. And so too was it with Thomas Jefferson; nor could he have had the vision but for standing on the philosophical shoulders of John Locke and the learned men of the French Enlightenment.

Surely we need standards and resources to make our schools work well in solving the myriad tasks they face. But resources and standards alone will not work. We need a surer sense of what to teach to whom and how to go about teaching it in such a way that it will make those taught more effective, less alienated, and better human beings. The nation's teachers have been struggling to carry out this daunting task and, under the circumstances, have been doing it with courage and skill against enormous odds. And we in the universities and in scientific and cultural institutions have been giving them precious little help. I am not proud to admit that much of the most strident recent criticism has come from such self-appointed guardians of the culture as Alan Bloom, who longs bitterly for an imaginary past while immured in his ivory tower. Teachers and schools, let it be said, did not create the conditions that have made American education so difficult. They did not create an underclass. Nor could they have undermined the research and development mission of competitive American industry anywhere as effectively as the greedy takeover tycoons of the 1980s, fueled by junk bonds. Nor did they, like the money-churners and real-estate speculators, create the disgraceful condition of homelessness on one side and of consumerism on the other, both now afflicting our economy and our sense of purpose. Nor the drug problem which Washington now proposes to solve not by capping the flow of drugs into the country or by destroying our home-grown drug cartels but, ironically enough, by giving over the prevention task to the schools.

What we need is a reform movement with a better sense of where we are going, with deeper convictions about what kind of people we want to be. Then, we can mount the kind of community effort that can truly address the future of our educational process – an effort in which all of the resources of intellect and compassion that we can muster, whatever the price, are placed at the disposal of the schools. That is what Robert Karplus stood for in the domain of science – that human beings would be the richer for understanding the physical universe. He did his part by trying to help teachers do their task better. All the standards in the world will like a helping hand, achieve the goal of making our multicultural, our threatened society come alive again, not alive just as a competitor in the world's markets, but as a nation worth living in and living for. I can do no better than to cite the conclusion of Ernest Boyer's 87th Annual Report from the Carnegie Commission for the Advancement of Teaching. He says, speaking of current reforms:

> We are troubled that the nation's teachers remain so skeptical. Why is it that teachers, of all people, are demoralized and largely unimpressed by the reform actions taken [thus far]?...The reform movement has been driven largely by legislative and administrative intervention. The push has been concerned more with regulation than with renewal. Reforms typically have focussed on graduation requirements, student achievement, teacher preparation and testing, and monitoring activities. But in all these matters, important as they are, teachers have been largely uninvolved....Indeed, the most disturbing finding in our study is this: Over half the teachers [surveyed] believe that, overall, morale within the profession has substantially declined since 1983....What is urgently needed – in the next phase of school reform – is a deep commitment to make teachers partners in renewal at all levels....The challenge now is to move beyond regulations, focus on renewal, and make teachers full participants in the process.

Now let me turn to the task at hand – narrative as a mode of thinking, as a structure for organizing our knowledge, and as a vehicle in the process of education, particularly in science education. In order to do so, I must take a step back to consider some fundamentals, and you will bear with me if I do so autobiographically.

A long time ago, I proposed the idea of a "spiral curriculum," the idea that in teaching a subject one begins with an "intuitive" account that was well within the reach of a student, and then circle back later to a more formal or highly structured account, until, with however many more recyclings were necessary, the learner had mastered the topic or subject in its full generative power. In fact, it was a notion that grew out of a more fundamental, more obvious view of epistemology. I had stated this more basic view in the form, almost, of a philosophical proverb, to the effect that "Any subject could be taught to any child at any age in some form that was honest."

Another way of saying the same thing might be to say, "Readiness is not only born but made." The general proposition rests on the still deeper truth that any domain of knowledge can be constructed at varying levels of abstractness or complexity. That is to say, domains of knowledge are *made* not *found*: they can be constructed simply or complexly, abstractly or concretely. And it can easily be demonstrated within certain interesting limits that a so-called "higher level" way of characterizing a domain of knowledge encompasses, replaces, and renders more powerful and precise a "lower level" characterization. That is to say, the intuitive statement "the further out a weight is from the fulcrum of a lever, the more force it will exert," is contained, as it were, in the more powerful and precise Archimedean rules about how levers operate. And Archimedes, in turn, is replaced and contained by the rules of levers as described by quadratic equations. The kid who understands the intuitive rule of the lever and applies it to the playground seesaw is well on his or her way to becoming Archimedean, just as Archimedes was on his way toward that Renaissance algebraist who recognized that expressions in the form $(x^2 + 4x + 4)$ could be equated to multiplicative pairs in the form $(x + 2)(x + 2)$ which in turn could be reexpressed as $(x + 4)(x + 1)$, etc. All of which could tell you some canny ways of placing weights on a beam so that they would balance. A ten-year-old once said to me, having discovered how all of this mathematical abstraction can guide one to making a beam balance, "This gadget knows all about algebra." I tried to dissuade him, to convince him that it was *he* who knew the algebra, not the balance beam. But I doubt I succeeded. That might come later up the curriculum spiral, perhaps in graduate school or perhaps, with the luck of some good teaching, in the very next grade.

Let me say that the research of the last three decades on the growth of reasoning in children has, in the main, confirmed the rightness of the spiral curriculum, although it has also provided us with some cautions. There are stages of development that constrain how fast and how far a child can leap ahead into abstraction. Piaget's views are always to be taken seriously in this regard, but they too must be taken with caution. The child's mind does not move to the higher levels of abstraction like the tide coming in. Development depends also, as Margaret Donaldson, for example, has so beautifully demonstrated, upon the child's practical grasp of the context or situation in which he or she has to reason. A good intuitive, practical grasp of a domain at one stage of development leads to better, earlier, and deeper thinking in the next stage when the child meets challenging new problems in that domain. As teachers, you do not wait for readiness to happen; you foster it by deepening the child's powers at the stage where you find him or her now.

I am fully aware of the fact that what I am telling you is old hat to working teachers. They have grasped all of this intuitively ever since Socrates in the *Meno* set forth the first version of the idea by illustrating how that slave boy could, starting from innocence, quickly grasp the main ideas of plane geometry. But it helps (as with our example) to push our understanding to another level. I still get a lot of mail from teachers; years back it used to average ten a week. Most of it was to cheer me on for going public with what every teacher already knew. But there was also a steady trickle of doubting Thomases who dared me to try to teach the calculus or Mendeleev's periodic table in nursery school. Well, five-year-olds are delighted with the story of the tortoise and the hare. And you can go easily on from there to the joke-story that is embodied in Zeno's paradox – there's still halfway to go, wherever you are, so how do you ever get there. Invariably, given the superiority of intuition, young kids think Zeno's paradox is "silly." But it bothers them. Have you ever heard a six-year-old tell a friend about Zeno's paradox? They do it like a shaggy dog story (which it is, of course). And that now brings me to the heart of the matter – narrative.

Let me say a little about stories and narratives generally. For it is very likely the case that the most natural and earliest way in which we organize our experience and our knowledge is in terms of the narrative form. And it may very well be that the beginnings, the transitions, and the full grasp of ideas in a spiral curriculum depend upon embodying those ideas into a story or narrative form. So what is a narrative? Fortunately, we are aided by a decade of lively research on this problem, and form a variety of sources – linguistics, literary theory, psychology, philosophy, even mathematics.

Begin with some terribly obvious points. A narrative is a sequence of events. The sequence carries the meaning: contrast "The king died, the Queen cried" with its reversed mate, "The Queen cried, the King died." But not every sequence of events is worth recounting. Narrative is discourse, and the prime rule of discourse is that there be a reason for it that distinguishes it from silence. Narrative is justified or warranted by virtue of the sequence of events it recounts being a violation of canonicality: it recounts something unexpected, or something that one's auditor has reason to be in doubt about, or whatever. The "point" of the narrative is to resolve the unexpected, to settle the auditor's doubt, or in some manner to restore or explicate the "imbalance" that prompted the telling of the story in the first place. A story, then, has two sides to it: a sequence of events, and an implied evaluation of the events recounted.

What is particularly interesting about a story as a structure is the two-way street that it travels between its parts and the whole. The events recounted in a story take their meaning from the story as a whole. But the story as a whole is something that is constructed from its parts. This part-whole tail-chasing bears the formidable name, "hermeneutic circle" and it is what causes stories to be subject to interpretation, not to explanation. You cannot explain a story, all you can do is give it variant interpretations. You can *explain* falling bodies by reference to a theory of gravity. But you can only *interpret* what might have happened to Sir Isaac Newton when the legendary apple fell on his head in the orchard. So we say that scientific theories or logical proofs are judged by means of verification or test, or more accurately, by their verifiability or testability, but stories are judged, rather, on the basis of their verisimilitude or "lifelikeness." Indeed, one of the reasons why it is so difficult to establish whether a story is "true" or not is precisely because there is a sense in which a story can be true to life without being true of life. For those who have concerned themselves with such arcane matters as the theory of meaning, this means that stories can make sense but have no reference. It is much harder to construct "fictional science," not to be confused with science fiction, simply because it is immediately caught up in issues of verifiability with respect to a specifiable possible world. And that, after all, is what *real* science is about.

Science uses as its apparatus of exposition such means as logic, mathematics, or whatever helps it achieve consistency, explicitness, and testability. One of its favored weapons is the hypothesis which, if well formed, will be "frangible" – easily found to be false. However derivationally deep any scientific theory may be, its use should lead to the formulation of falsifiable hypotheses, as Karl Popper would say. But you can falsify an awful lot of hypotheses, historians of science make clear, without bringing down the theory from which they have been derived.

Which has suggested to many in recent years that grand theories in science are perhaps more storylike than we had expected, a matter we shall have to revisit presently.

A few other preliminaries and we can get back to the main task. Stories, notably, are about human agents rather than about the world of nature – unless the world of nature is conceived "animistically" as human like. What marks human agents is that their acts are not produced by such physical "forces" as gravity, but by intentional states: desires, beliefs, knowledge, intentions, commitments. It is intrinsically difficult to "explain" why it is that human agents, impelled by intentional states, do as they do or react to each other as they do – particularly in the unexpected or noncanonical situations that constitute stories. This reinforces the requirement of interpretation in understanding stories. As does one other thing. Stories are the product of narrators, and narrators have points of view, even if a narrator claims to be an "eyewitness to the events." Now this is also the case where science is concerned, although the language of science, cloaked in the rhetoric of objectivity, makes every effort to conceal that view save when it is concerned with the "foundations" of its field. The famous "paradigm shifts" that occur during scientific revolutions reflect this cover-up situation, since they betray the fact that the so-called data of science are constructed observations that are designed with a point of view in mind. Light is neither corpuscular nor wavelike; waves and corpuscles are in the theory, in the mind of the theory makers and holders. The observations they devise are designed to determine how well nature fits these pieces of "fictional science."

Now, it has been a curious habit of Western thought since the Greeks to assume that the world is rational and that true knowledge about that world will always take the form of logical or scientific propositions that will be amenable to explanation. Theories, made up of such propositions, it was thought until quite recently, would be found to be true or false by virtue of whether they corresponded to that world. Nowadays we quite properly ask how it is that we can ever know what *the* world is actually like, save by the odd process of constructing theories and making observations once in a while to check how our theories are hanging together – not how the world is hanging together, but our theories. The more advanced a science becomes, the more dependent it becomes upon the speculative models it constructs, and the more "indirect" its measurements of the world become. My physicist friends are fond of the remark that physics is 95% speculation and 5% observation. And they are very attached to the expression "physical intuition" as something that "real" physicists have: they are not *just* tied to observation and measurement, but know how to get around in the theory even without them.

Constructing "speculative models" at the highest levels of science is, of course, highly constrained by the mathematical languages in which advanced theories are formulated. They are so formulated, of course, so that we may be as explicit as possible. Through explicitness, logical contradictions can be avoided. But the mathematics has another function: a well formed mathematics is also a carefully derived logical system, and it is the full derivational power of the mathematics that the scientist is out to exploit. After all, the object of a mathematized theory in physics is not just description, but generativeness. So, for example, if the algebra of quadratic functions describes what might be happening in the domain of levers and balance beams, then the application of such *general* algebraic rules as the associative, distributive, and commutative laws should (with luck) lead to previously unimagined predictions about levers, fulcra, balance beams, etc. When that happens, it is science heaven and a time for prizes.

But as every historian of science in the last hundred years has pointed out, scientists use all sorts of aids and intuitions and stories and metaphors to help them in the quest of getting their speculative model to fit "nature" (or getting "nature" to fit their model by redefining what counts as "nature"). They will use any metaphor or any suggestive figure or fable or foible that may luckily come to hand. Niels Bohr once confessed how he had arrived at the idea of complementarity in physics – illustrated, for example, by the principle that you cannot specify both the position and the velocity of a particle simultaneously and therefore you cannot include them in the same set of equations. The general idea had first struck him as a moral dilemma. His son had stolen a trinket from the local notions shop but, some days later, stricken with guilt, he had confessed the theft to his father. As Bohr put it, he was greatly touched by this moral act of contrition, but was also mindful of his son's wrongdoing. "But I was struck by the fact that I could not think of my son at the same moment both in the light of love and in the light of justice." This led him to think that certain states of mind were like the two aspects of one of those trick figure-ground pictures where you can see either the duck or the rabbit, the vase or the profiles, but not both at the same time. And then some days later, as if the idea were blossoming, it occurred to him that you could not consider the position of a particle as stationary in a particular position and at the same time as moving with a velocity in no particular position at all. The mathematics was easy to fix. It was grasping the right narrative that took the hard work.

To come directly to the point, let me propose that we characteristically convert our efforts at scientific understanding into the form of narratives or, say, "narrative heuristics." "We" includes both scientists and the pupils who inhabit the classrooms in which we teach. This consists of turning the events we are exploring into narrative form, better to high-light what is canonical and expected in our way of looking at them, so that we can more easily discern what is fishy and offbase and what, therefore, needs to be explicated. Here are some examples, some from the frontier, some from the classroom. A physics colleague lamented to me some years ago on a squash court that what was wrong with contemporary physical theory was that it conceived of most events as entirely in the extremely short-term nanosecond range, which made no sense since the physical world went on forever. So, he asked, what kind of "story" could you tell about an enduring universe? I jokingly suggested to him that he should invent a kind of hypothetical physical glue, a substance that went on and on in time – call it, say, glueterium. "Brilliant, brilliant," he said, for reasons still unclear to me. Several years later he told me that it had been a turning point in his thinking, glueterium. Or let me take one from a classroom. The topic was "atomicity," the smallest thing of which other things might be made, which is as old a topic as you can get. The discussion grew lively when it reached the point where it got on to "cutting up" matter into smaller and smaller pieces until, as one of them put it, "they've got to be invisible." Why invisible? somebody asked. "Because the air is made of atoms," which produced a general pause. A kid took advantage of the pause to ask, "Does everything have to be made of the same atoms?" "Well, so how could the same atoms make stones and water both?" "Let's have different kinds of atoms then – hard ones and soft ones and wet ones." "No, that's crazy: let's have them all the same, and they can make up into different shapes like Leggo or something." "And what happens when you split an atom?" "Then the whole thing goes Boom!" Echoes of the early Greek philosophers: not Thales but Empedocles prevailed.

What happens when the discussion takes that turn? Well, to put it as bluntly as possible, the focus of attention shifts, as it were, from an exclusive concern with "nature-as-out-there" to a concern with the *search* for nature – how we *construct* our model of nature. It is that shift that turns the discussion from dead science to live science *making*. And once we do that, we are enabled to invoke criteria like conceivability, verisimilitude, and the other criteria of good stories. Gerald Holton, the distinguished historian of science and a keen observer of the scientific *process*, comments that scientists from earliest times have relied on just such narrativizing to help them, using the metaphors, myths, and fables along the way – snakes that swallow their own tails, how to lift the world, how to leave traces that can be followed back, and so on, and so on.

Let me put it in somewhat different language. The process of science making is narrative. It consists of spinning hypotheses about nature, testing them, correcting the hypotheses, and getting one's head straight. Enroute to producing testable hypotheses, we play with ideas, try to create anomalies, try to find neat puzzle forms that we can apply to intractable troubles so that they can be turned into soluble problems, figure out neat tricks for getting around morasses, and so on. The history of science, as James Bryant Conant tried to show us, can be dramatically recounted as a set of almost heroic narratives in problem solving. His critics liked to point out that the historical case histories that he and his colleagues had prepared, while very interesting, were not science but the history of science. And I am not proposing that we should now substitute the history of science for science itself. What I *am* proposing, rather, is that our instruction in science from the start to the finish be mindful of the lively processes of science making, rather than being an account only of "finished science" as represented in the textbook, in the handbook, and in the standard and often deadly "demonstration experiment."

I know perfectly well that good science teachers (and there are many, though there can never be enough of them) in fact do just what I have been proposing: place the emphasis on live science making rather than upon the achieved remains of, so to say already accomplished science. But in the spirit of Bob Karplus, I want to make a few suggestions about how we in the scientific community can help each other. For I believe that there is what you might call a "soft technology" of good teaching that would be an enormous help in the classroom, a soft technology that would place the emphasis back on the process of science problem solving rather than upon finished science and "the answers." Let me end this talk with a few examples and maybe even a principle or two.

The first suggestion might even qualify as one of those principles. It says: "The art of raising challenging questions is easily as important as the art of giving clear answers." And I would have to add, "The art of cultivating such questions, of keeping good questions alive, is as important as either of those." Good questions are ones that pose dilemmas, subvert obvious or canonical "truths," force incongruities upon our attention that require attention. Curiously enough, much of the best support material produced by the science projects of the curriculum reform movement of the 1960s was of this order. Let me mention a couple of them, both of them produced by the Physical Science Study Committee. One was a "frictionless puck," a squat can of dried ice with a hole in its bottom, such that thawed CO_2 seeped through, causing the puck to float frictionlessly atop its cushion of gas on a pane of window glass. On that surface, under those conditions, bodies set in motion seemed virtually to stay in motion just as counterintuitively as required by Newtonian laws of motion. It's only a neat little hardware store trick, but it leads to endless questions about the "ideal conditions" required of general physical laws, how you figure out ideal conditions, what you might mean by such things as "perfect vacuums" and "frictionless planes," and so on. It gets a narrative conversation going in much the same way as Sir Alan Bullock got a conversation going a few years ago with the Queen of England on the occasion when she as Royal Patroness was to come to the annual dinner of the Museum. Sir Alan, as Chairman of the Board, was her host. He is a mighty historian and was then Vice Chancellor of the University of Oxford. Queen Elizabeth is notorious for her dislike of small talk, so Sir Alan decided he would find a question that would be deeply nontrivial while not being politically too controversial. He hit on the perfect one. "Ma'am," he asked, "when did the Royal Family decide to become respectable." "Well," she said, "it was during Victoria's reign when it was realized that the middle class had become central to Britain's prosperity and stability." And the conversation went on for the better part of an hour. The parallel? Well, able historian that he was, Sir Alan realized that the "Royal image" was a construction, a stipulation, an ideal condition for a theory of royalty. The moral of the story: always look an "ideal condition" in the mouth if you want to find out how the world works.

The other demonstration was a ceiling-hung pendulum with a large can of finely ground dirt at its terminus, with a tiny hole in the middle of the can's bottom and with wrapping paper spread on the floor beneath it. The only thing remarkable about this gadget is that it left a trail of its movements – trajectory length, damping effects, Lissajous figures for its eccentric excursions, the lot. There must be some kind of rule that says that the object of instrumentation is to make it possible to observe what before could not be observed because they were too small or weak, too big and ubiquitous, too fleeting or not fleeting enough, whatever. I think the idea had originally been hit upon by Frank Oppenheimer at the Exploratorium in San Francisco. It is perfect for exploring an unknown world of forces and symmetries: you can dream up and do experiments fifteen an hour. I have seen a group of twelve-year-olds at a summer session in Cambridge learn more fundamentals in an afternoon than I did with dear Mr Doyle in an entire term.

The recording pendulum has a lesson that goes with it, which runs something like this. "If one picture is worth a thousand words, then one well-wrought guess is worth a thousand pictures." A well-wrought guess, of course, is usually and rather grandly called "a hypothesis." What is important about a hypothesis (or a well-wrought guess) is that it derives from something you already know, something generic that allows you to go beyond what you already know. That "something generic" is what I used to call the "structure" of a subject, the knowledge that permitted you to go beyond the particulars you had already encountered. The structure is, so to speak, in the head. Being able to "go beyond the imagination" given to "figure things out" is one of the untarnishable joys of life. One of the great triumphs of learning (and of teaching) is to get things organized in your head in a way that permits you to know more than you "ought" to. And this takes reflection, brooding about what it is that you know. The enemy of reflection is the breakneck pace – the thousand pictures.

In some deep sense, just as Mise van der Rohe said of architecture, we can say of learning, and in particular science learning, that "less is more." And that again has a narrative tang to it. The story is how can you get the most out of the least. And the denouement is learning to think with what you've already got hold of. I believe that this truism lies at the heart of every good curriculum, every good lesson plan, every learning-and-teaching encounter. So when it comes time for the bureaucrats to set their standards and to make up their tests for monitoring how we are doing, they will adopt this one as their primary standard. They will have to construct better tests than the ones we have now. And when the time has come again for us to help each other in devising or constructing curricula in science curricula, I hope this ideal will shine over the effort.

One last word and I am done. I have said nothing about computers, which seems strange in this day and age. I really have nothing to say about them, aside from the fact that I love them and my life would be much more tedious without them. They can be a boon to scientific consciousness and, besides, they have reintroduced the servant in an era when the sages all said we would forevermore be servantless. Best of all, we can construct programs that can "simulate" what we might with great cost and effort do in our heads or on paper, and, in so doing, making us aware of what it is that we must still do ourselves in our own heads. My father used to tell a story about the Chinese delegate to the London Naval Disarmament talks in London in 1921. At the weekend, his British opposite number invited him to his country place, where he witnessed a ding-dong set of tennis between the British diplomat and his eldest son. At the end of the game, the British diplomat asked his Chinese colleague if there were any questions he'd like to ask about the game. "Yes," he replied, "it was very interesting, but I do not understand why you do not get your servants to play it for you." Well, remember that science is like that too.

CHAPTER 14

FOLK PEDAGOGY

The Culture of Education (1996), Cambridge: Blackwells

Thoughtful people have been forever troubled by the enigma of applying theoretical knowledge to practical problems. Applying psychological theory to educational practice is no exception to the rule, not much less puzzling than applying science to medicine. Aristotle comments (rather touchingly) in the *Nichomachean Ethics* (Book V, 1137a): "It is an easy matter to know the effects of honey, wine, hellebore, cautery, and cutting. But to know how, for whom, and when we should apply these as remedies is no less an undertaking than being a physician." Even with scientific advances, the physician's problem is not much easier today than it was in the times of hellebore and cautery: "how, for whom, and when" still loom as problems. The challenge is always to *situate* our knowledge in the living context that poses the "presenting problem," to borrow a bit of medical jargon. And that living context, where education is concerned, is the schoolroom – the schoolroom situated in a broader culture.

That is where, at least in advanced cultures, teachers and pupils come together to effect that crucial but mysterious interchange that we so glibly call "education." Obvious though it may seem, we would do better to concentrate in what follows on "learning and teaching in the setting of school" rather than, as psychologists sometimes do, generalizing from learning in a rat maze, from the nonsense-syllable learning of sophomores incarcerated in a laboratory cubicle, or from the performance of an AI computer simulation at Carnegie-Mellon. Keep before you a busy classroom of nine-year-olds, say, with a hard-working teacher, and ask what kind of theoretical knowledge would help them. A genetic theory that assures them that people differ? Well, perhaps, but not much. Do you work harder with the not-so-bright or ignore them? What about an associationist theory that tells you that nonsense syllables are associated with each other through frequency, recency, contiguity, and similarity effects? Would you want to design a curriculum on knowledge about how nonsense syllables are learned? Well, perhaps a little – where things are a little nonsense-like anyway, such as the names of elements in the periodic table: cerium, lithium, gold, lead...

There is one "presenting problem" that is always with us in dealing with teaching and learning, one that is so pervasive, so constant, so much part of the fabric of living, that we often fail to notice it, fail even to discover it – much as in the proverb "the fish will be the last to discover water." It is the issue of how human beings achieve a meeting of minds, expressed by teachers usually as "how do I reach the children?" or by children as "what's she trying to get at?" This is the classic problem of Other Minds, as it was originally called in philosophy, and its relevance to education has mostly been overlooked until very recently. In the last decade it has become a topic of passionate interest and intense research among psychologists, particularly those interested in development. It is what this chapter is about – the application of this new work to the process of education.

To a degree almost entirely overlooked by anti-subjective behaviorists in the past, our interactions with others are deeply affected by our everyday intuitive theories about how other minds work. These theories, rarely made explicit, are omnipresent but have only recently been subjected to intense study. Such lay theories are now referred to professionally by the rather condescending name of "folk psychology." Folk psychologies reflect certain "wired-in" human tendencies (like seeing people normally as operating under their own control), but they also reflect some deeply ingrained cultural beliefs about "the mind." Not only is folk psychology preoccupied with how the mind works here and now, it is also equipped with notions about how the child's mind learns and even what makes it grow. Just as we are steered in ordinary interaction by our folk psychology, so we are steered in the activity of helping children learn about the world by notions of *folk pedagogy*. Watch any mother, any teacher, even any babysitter with a child and you'll be struck by how much of what they do is steered by notions of "what children's minds are like and how to help them learn," even though they may not be able to verbalize their pedagogical principles.

From this work on folk psychology and folk pedagogy has grown a new, perhaps even a revolutionary insight. It is this: in theorizing about the practice of education in the classroom (or any other setting, for that matter), you had better take into account the folk theories that those engaged in teaching and learning already have. For any innovations that you, as a "proper" pedagogical theorist, may wish to introduce will have to compete with, replace, or otherwise modify the folk theories that already guide both teachers and pupils. For example, if you as a pedagogical theorist are convinced that the best learning occurs when the teacher helps lead the pupil to discover generalizations on her own, you are likely to run into an established cultural belief that a teacher is an authority who is supposed to *tell* the child what the general case is, while the child should be occupying herself with memorizing the particulars. And if you study how most classrooms are conducted, you will often find that most of the teacher's questions to pupils are about particulars that can be answered in a few words or even by "yes" or "no." So your introduction of an innovation in teaching will necessarily involve changing the folk psychological and folk pedagogical theories of teachers – and, to a surprising extent, of pupils as well.

Teaching, in a word, is inevitably based on notions about the nature of the learner's mind. Beliefs and assumptions about teaching, whether in a school or in any other context, are a direct reflection of the beliefs and assumptions the teacher holds about the learner. (Later, we will consider the other side of this coin: how learning is affected by the child's notion of the teacher's mind-set, as when girls come to believe that teachers expect them not to come up with unconventional answers.) Of course, like most deep truths, this one is already well known. Teachers have always tried to adjust their teaching to the backgrounds, abilities, styles, and interests of the children they teach. This is important, but it is not quite what we are after. Our purpose, rather, is to explore more general ways in which learners" minds are conventionally thought about, and the pedagogic practices that follow from these ways of thinking about mind. Nor will we stop there, for we also want to offer some reflections on "consciousness raising" in this setting: what can be accomplished by getting teachers (and students) to think *explicitly* about their folk psychological assumptions, in order to bring them out of the shadows of tacit knowledge.

One way of presenting the general matter of folk psychology and folk pedagogy most starkly is by contrasting our own human species with non-human primates. In our species, children show an astonishingly strong "predisposition to culture"; they are sensitive to and eager to adopt the folkways they see around them. They show a striking interest in the activity of their parents and peers and with no prompting at all try to imitate what they observe. As for adults, as Kruger and Tomasello insist,[1] there is a uniquely human "pedagogic disposition" to exploit this tendency, for adults to demonstrate correct performance for the benefit of the learner. One finds these matching tendencies in different forms in all human societies. But note that these imitative and demonstrational dispositions seem scarcely to exist at all in our nearest primate kin, the chimpanzees. Not only do adult chimpanzees not "teach" their young by demonstrating correct performance, the young for their part seem not to imitate the actions of adults either, at least if we use a sufficiently stringent definition of imitation. If by imitation one means the ability to observe not just the goal achieved but also the means to that achievement, there is little evidence of imitation in chimpanzees raised in the wild[2] and, even more conspicuously, little attempt at teaching. It is very revealing, however, that when a young chimpanzee is raised "as if" he were a human child, and exposed to the ways of humans, he begins to show more imitative dispositions.[3] The evidence on "demonstrational" dispositions in adult chimpanzees is much less clear, but such dispositions may also be there in a rudimentary form.[4]

Tomasello, Ratner, and Kruger have suggested that because non-human primates do not naturally attribute beliefs and knowledge to others, they probably do not recognize their presence in themselves.[5] We humans show, tell, or teach someone something only because we first recognize that they don't know, or that what they believe is false. The failure of non-human primates to ascribe ignorance or false beliefs to their young may, therefore, explain the absence of pedagogic efforts, for it is only when these states are recognized that we try to correct the deficiency by demonstration, explanation, or discussion. Even the most humanly "enculturated" chimpanzees show little, if any, of the attribution that leads to instructional activity.

Research on lesser primates shows the same picture. On the basis of their observations of the behavior of vervet monkeys in the wild,[6] Cheney and Seyfarth were led to conclude: "While monkeys may use abstract concepts and have motives, beliefs, and desires, they…seem unable to attribute mental states to others: they lack a 'theory of mind.'" Work on other species of monkeys reveals similar findings.[7] The general point is clear: assumptions about the mind of the learner underlie attempts at teaching. No ascription of ignorance, no effort to teach.

But to say only that human beings understand other minds and try to teach the incompetent is to overlook the varied ways in which teaching occurs in different cultures. The variety is stunning.[8] We need to know much more about this diversity if we are to appreciate the relation between folk psychology and folk pedagogy in different cultural settings.

Understanding this relationship becomes particularly urgent in addressing issues of educational reform. For once we recognize that a teacher's conception of a learner shapes the instruction he or she employs, then equipping teachers (or parents) with the best available theory of the child's mind becomes crucial. And in the process of doing that, we also need to provide teachers with some insight about their own folk theories that guide their teaching.

Folk pedagogies, for example, reflect a variety of assumptions about children: they may be seen as willful and needing correction; as innocent and to be protected from a vulgar society; as needing skills to be developed only through practice; as empty vessels to be filled with knowledge that only adults can provide; as egocentric and in need of socialization. Folk beliefs of this kind, whether expressed by laypeople or by "experts," badly want some "deconstructing" if their implications are to be appreciated. For whether these views are "right" or not, their impact on teaching activities can be enormous.

A culturally oriented cognitive psychology does not dismiss folk psychology as mere superstition, something only for the anthropological connoisseur of quaint folkways. I have long argued that explaining what children *do* is not enough;[9] the new agenda is to determine what they *think* they are doing and what their reasons are for doing it. Like new work on children's theories of mind,[10] a cultural approach emphasizes that the child only gradually comes to appreciate that she is acting not directly *on* "the world" but on beliefs she holds *about* that world. This crucial shift from naive realism to an understanding of the role of beliefs, occurring in the early school years, is probably never complete. But once it starts, there is often a corresponding shift in what teachers can do to help children. With the shift, for example, children can take on more responsibilities for their own learning and thinking.[11] They can begin to "think about their thinking" as well as about "the world." It is not surprising, then, that achievement testers have become increasingly concerned not just with what children *know* but with how they think they came by their knowledge.[12] It is as Howard Gardner puts it in *The Unschooled Mind:* "We must place ourselves inside the heads of our students and try to understand as far as possible the sources and strengths of their conceptions."[13]

Stated boldly, the emerging thesis is that educational practices in classrooms are premised on a set of folk beliefs about learners' minds, some of which may have worked advertently toward or inadvertently against the child's own welfare. They need to be made explicit and to be reexamined. Different approaches to learning and different forms of instruction – from imitation, to instruction, to discovery, to collaboration – reflect differing beliefs and assumptions about the learner – from actor, to knower, to private experiencer, to collaborative thinker.[14] What higher primates lack and humans continue to evolve is a set of beliefs about the mind. These beliefs, in turn, alter beliefs about the sources and communicability of thought and action. Advances in how we go about understanding children's minds are, then, a prerequisite to any improvement in pedagogy.

Obviously, all this involves much more than learners' minds. Young learners are people in families and communities, struggling to reconcile their desires, beliefs, and goals with the world around them. Our concern may be principally cognitive, relating to the acquisition and uses of knowledge, but we do not mean to restrict our focus to the so-called "rational" mind. Egan reminds us that "Apollo without Dionysus may indeed be a well-informed, good citizen, but he's a dull fellow. He may even be "cultured," in the sense one often gets from traditionalist writings in education....But without Dionysus he will never make and remake a culture."[15] Although our discussion of folk psychology and folk pedagogy has emphasized "teaching and learning" in the conventional sense, we could as easily have emphasized other aspects of the human spirit, ones equally important for educational practice, like folk conceptions of desire, intention, meaning, or even "mastery." But even the notion of "knowledge" is not as peacefully Apollonian as all that.

Consider for example the issue of what knowledge is, where it comes from, how we come by it. These are also matters that have deep cultural roots. To begin with, take the distinction between knowing something concretely and in particular and knowing it as an exemplar of some general rule. Arithmetic addition and multiplication provide a stunning example. Somebody, say, has just learned a concrete arithmetic fact. What does it mean to grasp a "fact" of multiplication, and how does that differ from the idea that multiplication is simply repeated addition, something you already "know"? Well, for one thing, it means that you can *derive* the unknown from the known. That is a pretty heady notion about knowledge, one that might even delight the action-minded Dionysus.

In some much deeper sense, grasping something abstractly is a start toward appreciating that seemingly complicated knowledge can often be derivationally reduced to simpler forms of knowledge that you already possess. The Ellery Queen mystery stories used to include a note inserted on a crucial page in the text telling the reader that he or she now had all the knowledge necessary to solve the crime. Suppose one announced in class after the children had learned multiplication that they now had enough knowledge to understand something called "logarithms," special kinds of numbers that simply bore the names "1," "2," "3," "4," and "5," and that they ought to be able to figure out what these logarithm names "mean" from three examples, each example being a series that bore those names. The first series is 2, 4, 8, 16, 32; the second series 3, 9, 27, 81, 243, and the third series 1, 10, 100, 1,000, 10,000, 100,000. The numbers in each series correspond to the logarithmic names 1, 2, 3, 4, and 5. But how can 8 be called "3," and so too 27 and 1,000? Not only do children "discover" (or invent) the idea of an *exponent* or *power*, but they also discover/invent the idea of exponents to some *base*: that 2 to the third power is 8, that 3 to the third power is 27, and that 10 to the third power is 1,000. Once children (say around age ten) have gone through that experience, their conception of mathematical knowledge as "derivational" will be forever altered: they will grasp that once you know addition and know that addition can be repeated different numbers of times to make multiplication, you already know what logarithms are. All you need to determine is the "base."

Or if that is too "mathematical," you can try getting children to act out Little Red Riding Hood, first as a class drama with everybody having a part, then by actors chosen to represent the main characters to an audience, and finally as a story to be told or read by a storyteller to a group. How do they differ? The moment some child informs you that in the first instance there are only actors and no audience, but in the second there are both, the class will be off and running into a discussion of "drama" to match Victor Turner for excitement.[16] As with the previous example, you will have led children to recognize that they know far more than they thought they ever knew, but that they have to "think about it" to know what they know. And that, after all, was what the Renaissance and the Age of Reason were all about! But to teach and learn that way means that you have adopted a new theory of mind.

Or take the issue of where you get knowledge, an equally profound matter. Children usually begin by assuming that the teacher has the knowledge and passes it on to the class. Under appropriate conditions, they soon learn that others in the class might have knowledge too, and that it can be shared. (Of course they know this from the start, but only about such matters as where things are to be found.) In this second phase, knowledge exists in the group – but inertly in the group. What about group discussion as a way of *creating* knowledge rather than merely finding who has what knowledge?[17] And there is even one step beyond that, one of the most profound aspects of human knowledge. If nobody in the group "knows" the answer, where do you go to "find things out?" This is the leap into culture as a warehouse, a toolhouse, or whatever. There are things known by each individual (more than each realizes); more still is known by the group or is discoverable by discussion within the group; and much more still is stored somewhere else – in the "culture," say, in the heads of more knowledgeable people, in directories, books, maps, and so forth. Virtually by definition, nobody in a culture knows all there is to know about it. So what do we do when we get stuck? And what are the problems we run into in getting the knowledge we need? Start answering that question and you are on the high road toward understanding what a culture is. In no time at all, some kid will begin to recognize that knowledge is power, or that it is a form of wealth, or that it is a safety net.

So let us consider more closely, then, some alternative conceptions about the minds of learners commonly held by educational theorists, teachers, and ultimately by children themselves. For these are what may determine the educational practices that take place in classrooms in different cultural contexts.

Models of mind and models of pedagogy

There are four dominant models of learners' minds that have held sway in our times. Each emphasizes different educational goals. These models are not only conceptions of mind that determine how we teach and "educate," but are also conceptions about the relations between minds and cultures. Rethinking educational psychology requires that we examine each of these alternative conceptions of human development and reevaluate their implications for learning and teaching.

1 Seeing children as imitative learners: the acquisition of "know-how." When an adult demonstrates or models a successful or skilled action to a child, that demonstration is implicitly based on the adult's belief that (a) the child does not know how to do x, and (b) the child can learn how to do x by being *shown*. The act of modeling also presupposes that (c) the child wants to do x; and (d) that she may, in fact, be trying to do x. To learn by imitation the child must recognize the goals pursued by the adult, the means used to achieve those goals, and the fact that the demonstrated action will successfully get her to the goal. By the time children are two years of age, they are capable, unlike chimpanzees raised in the wild, of imitating the act in question. Adults, recognizing children's proclivity for imitation, usually turn their own demonstrative actions into *performances*, acting in a way to demonstrate more vividly just what is involved in "doing it right." In effect, they provide "noiseless exemplars,"[18] of the act, preternaturally clear examples of the desired action.[19]

Such modeling is the basis of apprenticeship, leading the novice into the skilled ways of the expert. The expert seeks to transmit a skill he has acquired through repeated practice to a novice who, in his turn, must then practice the modeled act in order to succeed. There is little distinction in such an exchange between procedural knowledge (knowing how) and propositional knowledge (knowing that). An underlying assumption is that the less skilled can be taught by showing, and that they have the ability to learn through imitation. Another assumption in this process is that modeling and imitating make possible the accumulation of culturally relevant knowledge, even the transmission of culture[20] from one generation to the next.

But using imitation as the vehicle for teaching entails an additional assumption about human competence as well: that it consists of talents, skills, and abilities, rather than knowledge and understanding. Competence on the imitative view comes only through practice. It is a view that precludes teaching about logarithms or drama in the way described earlier. Knowledge "just grows as habits" and is linked neither to theory nor to negotiation or argument. Indeed, we even label cultures that rely heavily upon an imitative folk psychology and folk pedagogy as "traditional." But more technically advanced cultures also rely heavily upon such implicit imitative theories – for example, on apprenticeships for transmitting sophisticated skills. Becoming a scientist or a poet requires more than "knowing the theory"[21] or knowing the rules of iambic pentameter. It is Aristotle and the physician all over again.

So what do we know about demonstration and apprenticeship? Not much, but more than one might suspect. For example, simply demonstrating "how to" and providing practice at doing so is known not to be enough. Studies of expertise demonstrate that just learning how to perform skillfully does not get one to the same level of flexible skill as when one learns by a combination of practice and conceptual explanation – much as a really skillful pianist needs more than clever hands, but needs as well to know something about the theory of harmony, about solfège, about melodic structure. So if a simple theory of imitative learning suits a "traditional" society (and it usually turns out on close inspection that there is more to it than that),[22] it certainly does not suit a more advanced one. Which leads us to the next set of assumptions about human minds.

2 Seeing children as learning from didactic exposure: the acquisition of propositional knowledge. Didactic teaching usually is based on the notion that pupils should be presented with facts, principles, and rules of action which are to be learned, remembered, and then applied. To teach this way is to assume that the learner "does not know that *p*," that he or she is ignorant or innocent of certain facts, rules, or principles that can be conveyed by telling. What is to be learned by the pupil is conceived as "in" the minds of teachers as well as in books, maps, art, computer databases, or wherever. Knowledge is simply to be "looked up" or "listened to." It is an explicit canon or corpus – a representation of the what-is-known. Procedural knowledge, knowing how to, is assumed to follow automatically from knowing certain propositions about facts, theories, and the like: "the square of the hypotenuse of a right triangle is equal to the squares of the other two sides."

In this teaching scenario, abilities are no longer conceived as knowing how to *do* something skillfully, but rather as the ability to acquire new knowledge by the aid of certain "mental abilities": verbal, spatial, numerical, interpersonal, or what-ever. This is probably the most widely adhered to line of folk pedagogy in practice today – whether in history, social studies, literature, geography, or even science and mathematics. Its principal appeal is that it purports to offer a clear specification of just what it is that is to be learned and, equally questionable, that it suggests standards for assessing its achievement. More than any other theory of folk pedagogy, it has spawned objective testing in all its myriad guises. To determine whether a student has "learned" the capital of Albania, all one need do is offer him a multiple choice of Tirana, Milano, Smyrna, and Samarkand.

But damning the didactic assumption is too much like beating a dead horse. For plainly there are contexts where knowledge can usefully be treated as "objective" and given – like knowing the different writs under which a case can be brought under English common law, or knowing that the Fugitive Slave Law became an American statute in 1793, or that the Lisbon earthquake destroyed that city in 1755. The world is indeed full of facts. But facts are not of much use when offered by the hatful – either by teacher to student in class, or in the reverse direction as name dropping in an "objective" exam. We shall return to this point later in considering our fourth perspective.

What we must concentrate upon here is the conception of the child's mind that the didactic view imposes on teaching – its folk pedagogy. In effect, this view presumes that the learner's mind is a tabula rasa, a blank slate. Knowledge put into the mind is taken as cumulative, with later knowledge building upon priorly existing knowledge. More important is this view's assumption that the child's mind is passive, a receptacle waiting to be filled. Active interpretation or construal does not enter the picture. The didactic bias views the child from the outside, from a third-person perspective, rather than trying to "enter her thoughts." It is blankly one-way: teaching is not a mutual dialogue, but a telling by one to the other. In such a regimen, if the child fails to perform adequately, her shortcomings can be explained by her lack of "mental abilities" or her low IQ and the educational establishment goes scot-free.

It is precisely the effort to achieve a first-person perspective, to reconstruct the child's point of view, that marks the third folk pedagogy, to which we turn now.

3   Seeing children as thinkers: the development of intersubjective interchange. The new wave of research on "other minds" described earlier is the latest manifestation of a more general modern effort to recognize the child's perspective in the process of learning. The teacher, on this view, is concerned with understanding what the child thinks and how she arrives at what she believes. Children, like adults, are seen as constructing a *model* of the world to aid them in construing their experience. Pedagogy is to help the child understand better, more powerfully, less one-sidedly. Understanding is fostered through discussion and collaboration, with the child encouraged to express her own views better to achieve some meeting of minds with others who may have other views.

Such a pedagogy of mutuality presumes that all human minds are capable of holding beliefs and ideas which, through discussion and interaction, can be moved toward some shared frame of reference. Both child and adult have points of view, and each is encouraged to recognize the other's, though they may not agree. They must come to recognize that differing views may be based on recognizable reasons and that these reasons provide the basis for adjudicating rival beliefs. Sometimes you are "wrong," sometimes others are – that depends on how well reasoned the views are. Sometimes opposing views are both right – or both wrong. The child is *not* merely ignorant or an empty vessel, but somebody able to reason, to make sense, both on her own and through discourse with others. The child no less than the adult is seen as capable of thinking about her own thinking, and of correcting her ideas and notions through reflection – by "going meta," as it is sometimes called. The child, in a word, is seen as an epistemologist as well as a learner.

No less than the adult, the child is thought of as holding more or less coherent "theories" not only about the world but about her own mind and how it works. These naive theories are brought into congruence with those of parents and teachers not through imitation, not through didactic instruction, but by discourse, collaboration, and negotiation. Knowledge is what is shared within discourse,[23] within a "textual" community.[24] Truths are the product of evidence, argument, and construction rather than of authority, textual or pedagogic. This model of education is mutualist and dialectical, more concerned with interpretation and understanding than with the achievement of factual knowledge or skilled performance.

It is not simply that this mutualist view is "child-centered" (a not very meaningful term at best), but it is much less patronizing toward the child's mind.

It attempts to build an exchange of understanding between the teacher and the child: to find in the intuitions of the child the roots of systematic knowledge, as Dewey urged.

Four lines of recent research have enriched this perspective on teaching and learning. While they are all closely related, they are worth distinguishing. The first has to do with how children develop their ability to "read other minds," to get to know what others are thinking or feeling. It usually gets labeled as research on *intersubjectivity*. Intersubjectivity begins with infant's and mother's pleasure in eye-to-eye contact in the opening weeks of life, moves quickly into the two of them sharing joint attention on common objects, and culminates a first preschool phase with the child and a caretaker achieving a meeting of minds by an early exchange of words – an achievement that is never finished.[25]

The second line of research involves the child's grasp of another's "intentional states" – his beliefs, promises, intentions, desires, in a word his *theories of mind*, as this research is often referred to. It is a program of inquiry into how children acquire their notions about how others come to hold or relinquish various mental states. It is particularly concerned, as well, with the child's sorting of people's beliefs and opinions as being true or right versus being false and wrong, and in the process, this research has found out many intriguing things about the young child's ideas about "false beliefs."[26]

The third line is the study of *metacognition* – what children think about learning and remembering and thinking (especially their own), and how "thinking about" one's own cognitive operations affects one's own mental procedures. The first important contribution to this work, a study by Ann Brown, illustrated how remembering strategies were profoundly changed by the child turning her inner eye on how she herself proceeded in attempting to commit something to memory.[27]

Studies in *collaborative learning* and problem solving constitute the fourth line of new research, which focuses on how children explicate and revise their beliefs in discourse.[28] It has flourished not only in America but also in Sweden, where much recent pedagogical research has been given over to studying how children understand and how they manage their own learning.[29]

What all this research has in common is an effort to understand how children themselves organize their own learning, remembering, guessing, and thinking. Unlike older psychological theories, bent on imposing "scientific" models on children's cognitive activities, this work explores the child's own framework to understand better how he comes to the views that finally prove most useful to him. The child's *own* folk psychology (and its growth) becomes the object of study. And, of course, such research provides the teacher with a far deeper and less condescending sense of what she will encounter in the teaching-learning situation.

Some say that the weakness of this approach is that it tolerates an unacceptable degree of relativity in what is taken as "knowledge." Surely more is required to justify beliefs than merely sharing them with others. That "more" is the machinery of justification for one's beliefs, the canons of scientific and philosophical reasoning. Knowledge, after all, is *justified* belief. One must be pragmatist enough in one's views about the nature of knowledge to recognize the importance of such criticism. It is a foolish "postmodernism" that accepts that all knowledge can be justified simply by finding or forming an "interpretive community" that agrees. Nor need we be so old guard as to insist that knowledge is only knowledge when it is "true" in a way that precludes all competing claims. "True history," without regard to the perspective from which it was written, is at best a mischievous joke and at worst a bid for political hegemony. Claims about "truth" must always be justified.

They must be justified by appeal to reasons that, in the logician's stricter sense, resist disproof and disbelief. Reasons of this kind obviously include appeals to evidence that defy falsifiability. But falsifiability is rarely a "yes-no" matter, for there are often variant interpretations that are compatible with available evidence – if not all of the evidence, then enough of it to be convincing.

There is no reason a priori why the third approach to teaching and learning should not be compatible with this more pragmatic epistemology. It is a very different conception of knowledge from the second perspective, where knowledge was taken to be fixed and independent of the knower's perspective. For the very nature of the knowledge enterprise has changed in our times. Hacking points out, for example, that prior to the seventeenth century an unbridgeable gap was thought to exist between knowledge and opinion, the former objective, the latter subjective.[30] What modernism sponsors is a healthy skepticism about the absoluteness of that gap. We are considering here not "analytic" knowledge – as in logic and mathematics – where the rule of contradiction has a privileged position (that something cannot be both A and not-A). But even at the analytic level the view we are discussing casts a skeptical eye at the premature imposition of formal, logical forms on bodies of empirical knowledge outside the "hard" natural sciences.

In the light of all this, it is surely possible to take one step further in conceiving folk pedagogy – a step that, like the others we have considered, rests on epistemological considerations. At issue is how subjectively held beliefs are turned into viable theories about the world and its facts. How are beliefs turned into hypotheses that hold not because of the faith we place in them but because they stand up in the public marketplace of evidence, interpretation, and agreement with extant knowledge? Hypotheses cannot simply be "sponsored." They must be openly tested. "Today is Tuesday" turns into a conventional fact not by virtue of its being "true" but through conformity with conventions for naming the days of the week. It achieves intersubjectivity by virtue of convention and thereby becomes a "fact" independent of individual beliefs. This is the basis of Popper's well-known defense of "objective knowledge"[31] and of Nagel's view of what he calls "the view from nowhere."[32]

Issues of this order are precisely the ones that this third perspective most admirably and directly deals with. We now turn to the fourth and last of the perspectives on folk pedagogy.

4 *Children as knowledgeable: the management of "objective" knowledge.* Too exclusive a focus on beliefs and "intentional states" and on their negotiation in discourse risks overestimating the importance of social exchange in constructing knowledge. That emphasis can lead us to underestimate the importance of knowledge accumulated in the past. For cultures preserve past reliable knowledge much as the common law preserves a record of how past communal conflicts were adjudicated. In both instances there is an effort to achieve a workable consistency, to shun arbitrariness, to find "general principles." Neither culture nor law is open to abrupt reconstrual. Reconstrual is typically undertaken (to use the legal expression) with "restraint." Past knowledge and reliable practice are not taken lightly. Science is no different: it too resists being stampeded into "scientific revolutions," profligately throwing out old paradigms.[33]

Now to pedagogy. Early on, children encounter the hoary distinction between what is known by "us" (friends, parents, teachers, and so on) and what in some larger sense is simply "known." In these post-positivist, perhaps "post-modern" times, we recognize all too well that the "known" is neither God-given truth nor, as it were, written irrevocably in the Book of Nature. Knowledge in this dispensation is always putatively revisable. But revisability is not to be confused with free-for-all relativism, the view that since *no* theory is the ultimate truth, *all* theories, like all people, are equal. We surely recognize the distinction between Popper's "World Two" of personally held beliefs, hunches, and opinions and his "World Three" of justified knowledge. But what makes the latter "objective" is not that it constitutes some positivist's free-standing, aboriginal reality, but rather that it has stood up to sustained scrutiny and been tested by the best available evidence. All knowledge has a history.

The fourth perspective holds that teaching should help children grasp the distinction between personal knowledge, on the one side, and "what is taken to be known" by the culture, on the other. But they must not only grasp this distinction, but also understand its basis, as it were, in the history of knowledge. How can we incorporate such a perspective in our pedagogy? Stated another way, what have children gained when they begin to distinguish what is known canonically from what they know personally and idiosyncratically?

Janet Astington offers an interesting twist on this classic problem.[34] She finds that when children begin to understand how evidence is used to check beliefs, they often see the process as akin to forming a belief about a belief: "I now have reason to believe that this belief is true (or false, as the case may be)." "Reasons for believing" a hypothesis are not the same order of thing as the belief embodied in the hypothesis itself, and if the former work out well, then the latter graduates from being a belief (or hypothesis) to becoming something more robust – a proved theory or even a body of fact.

And by the same intuition, one can as easily come to see one's personal ideas or beliefs as relating (or not relating) to "what is known" or what is generally believed to have stood the test of time. In this way, we come to view personal conjecture against the background of what has come to be shared with the historical past. Those presently engaged in the pursuit of knowledge become sharers of conjectures with those long dead. But one can go a step further and ask how past conjecture settled into something more solid over the years. You can share Archimedes with seesaw partners on the playground, and know how he came to hold his view. But what about your interpretation of Kate in *Taming of the Shrew* as being like the class tomboy? That couldn't be what Shakespeare had in mind: he didn't "know about" her in that sense. So was there something else like that in his day? There is something appealing and, indeed, enspiriting about facing off one's own version of "knowledge" with the foibles of the archivally famous in our past. Imagine an inner-city high school class – it was a real one, mostly San Antonio Latinos – staging *Oedipus Rex*. They "knew" things about incest that Sophocles may never have dreamt of. It was plain to their gifted teacher/director that they were not in the least intimidated by the DWEM (Dead White European Male) who had written the play some two millennia ago. Yet they were true to the play's spirit.

So the fourth perspective holds that there is something special about "talking" to authors, now dead but still alive in their ancient texts – so long as the objective of the encounter is not worship but discourse and interpretation, "going meta" on thoughts about the past. Try several trios of teenagers, each staging a play about the astonishingly brief account in Genesis where Abraham at God's instruction takes Isaac, his only son, to sacrifice him to God on Mount Moriah. There is a famous set of "versions" of the Abraham story in Kierkegaard's *Fear and Trembling*; try that on them too. Or try out some teenagers on a dozen different reproductions of Annunciation paintings in which the Angel announces to the Virgin that she is to be Queen of Heaven. Ask them what they judge, from the various pictures, might be going through Mary's mind – in a painting where Mary looks like a haughty Renaissance princess, in another where she resembles a humble Martha, in yet another where she looks quite a brazen young lady. It is striking how quickly teenagers leap across the gulf that separates Popper's subjective World Two from his "objective" World Three. The teacher, with class exercises like these, helps the child reach beyond his own impressions to join a past world that would otherwise be remote and beyond him as a knower.[35]

Real schooling

Real schooling, of course, is never confined to one model of the learner or one model of teaching. Most day-to-day education in schools is designed to cultivate skills and abilities, to impart a knowledge of facts and theories, and to cultivate understanding of the beliefs and intentions of those nearby and far away. Any choice of pedagogical practice implies a conception of the learner and may, in time, be adopted by him or her as the appropriate way of thinking about the learning process. For a choice of pedagogy inevitably communicates a conception of the learning process and the learner. Pedagogy is never innocent. It is a medium that carries its own message.

Summary: rethinking minds, cultures, and education

We can conceive of the four views of teaching-and-learning just set forth as being ordered on two dimensions. The first is an "inside-outside" dimension: call it the *internalist-externalist* dimension. Externalist theories emphasize what adults can do for children from outside to foster learning – the bulk of traditional educational psychology. Internalist theories focus on what the child can do, what the child thinks he or she is doing, and how learning can be premised on those intentional states.

The second dimension describes the degree of intersubjectivity or "common understanding" assumed to be required between the pedagogical theorist and the subjects to whom his theories relate. Let us call this the *intersubjective-objectivist* dimension. Objectivist theories regard children as an entomologist might regard a colony of ants or an elephant-trainer an elephant; there is no presumption that the subjects should see themselves in the same terms that the theorist does. Intersubjective theorists, on the other hand, apply the same theories to themselves as they do to their clients. Hence, they seek to create psychological theories that are as useful for the children in organizing their learning and managing their lives as they are for the adults that work with them.

Internalist theories tend to be intersubjective in emphasis. That is to say, if one is concerned with what the child is up to mentally, one is likely to be concerned with formulating a theory of teaching-and-learning that one can share with him or her in order to facilitate the child's efforts. But this is not necessarily so. Much Western cultural anthropology, for example, is internalist and very concerned with "how natives think." But anthropologists' theories are, as it were, not for the "natives" but for their colleagues back home.[36] It is usually assumed, however, tacitly, that the natives are "different" or that they simply would not understand. And, indeed, some psychoanalytically oriented theories of early childhood pedagogy are of this same order – not to be shared with the child. Such theories are much occupied with the child's internal states, but like the native, the child is "different." The adult – theorist or teacher – becomes like an omniscient narrator in nineteenth-century novels: he knows perfectly what is going on in the minds of the novel's protagonist, even though the protagonist herself may not know.

Modern pedagogy is moving increasingly to the view that the child should be aware of her own thought processes, and that it is crucial for the pedagogical theorist and teacher alike to help her to become more metacognitive – to be as aware of how she goes about her learning and thinking as she is about the subject matter she is studying. Achieving skill and accumulating knowledge are not enough. The learner can be helped to achieve full mastery by reflecting as well upon how she is going about her job and how her approach can be improved. Equipping her with a good theory of mind – or a theory of mental functioning – is one part of helping her to do so.

In the end, then, the four perspectives on pedagogy are best thought of as parts of a broader continent, their significance to be understood in the light of their partialness. Nobody can sensibly propose that skills and cultivated abilities are unimportant. Nor can they argue that the accumulation of factual knowledge is trivial. No sensible critic would ever claim that children should not become aware that knowledge is dependent upon perspective and that we share and negotiate our perspectives in the knowledge-seeking process. And it would take a bigot to deny that we become the richer for recognizing the link between reliable knowledge from the past and what we learn in the present. What is needed is that the four perspectives be fused into some congruent unity, recognized as parts of a common continent. Older views of mind and how mind can be cultivated need to be shorn of their narrow exclusionism, and newer views need to be modulated to recognize that while skills and facts never exist *out* of context, they are no less important *in* context.

Modern advances in the study of human development have begun providing us with a new and steadier base upon which a more integrated theory of teaching-and-learning can be erected. And it was with these advances that this chapter was principally concerned – with the child as an active, intentional being; with knowledge as "man-made" rather than simply there; with how our knowledge about the world and about each other gets constructed and negotiated with others, both contemporaries and those long departed. In the chapters following, we will explore these advances and their implications still further.

Notes

1 A. C. Kruger and M. Tomasello, "Cultural Learning and Learning Culture," in David R. Olson, J. L. Franklin, and Nancy Torrance, eds, *Handbook of Education and Human Development* (Oxford: Blackwell, 1996).

2 M. Tomasello, A. C. Kruger, and H. Ratner, "Cultural Learning," *Behavioral and Brain Sciences*, 16(3) (1993): 495–511.

3 E. S. Savage-Rumbaugh, J. Murphy, R. A. Sevcik, K. E. Brakke, S. L. Williams, and D. L. Rumbaugh, "Language Comprehension in Ape and Child," *Monographs of the Society for Research in Child Development*, 58 (3–4, Serial No. 233) (1993).

4 R. S. Fouts, D. H. Fouts, and D. Schoenfeld, "Sign Language Conversational Interaction between Chimpanzees," *Sign Language Studies*, 42 (1984): 1–12; J. Goodall, *The Chimpanzees of Gombe: Patterns of Behavior* (Cambridge, MA: Harvard University Press, 1986).

5 Tomasello, Kruger, and Ratner, "Cultural Learning."

6 D. L. Cheney and R. M. Seyfarth, *How Monkeys See the World* (Chicago, IL: University of Chicago Press, 1990).

7 E. Visalberghi and D. M. Fragaszy, "Do Monkeys Ape?" in S. Parker and K. Gibson, eds, *"Language" and Intelligence in Monkeys and Apes: Comparative Developmental Perspectives* (Cambridge: Cambridge University Press, 1991).

8 B. Rogoff, J. Mistry, A. Goncu, and C. Mosier, "Guided Participation in Cultural Activity by Toddlers and Caregivers," *Monographs of the Society for Research in Child Development*, 58 (8, Serial No. 236) (1993).
9 J. Bruner, *Acts of Meaning* (Cambridge, MA: Harvard University Press, 1990).
10 J. Astington, P. Harris, and D. Olson, eds, *Developing Theories of Mind* (Cambridge: Cambridge University Press, 1988).
11 C. Bereiter and M. Scardamaglia, *Surpassing Ourselves: An Inquiry into the Nature and Implications of Expertise* (Chicago, IL: Open Court, 1993).
12 A. L. Brown and J. C. Campione, "Communities of Learning and Thinking, Or a Context by Any Other Name," in Deanna Kuhn, ed., *Developmental Perspectives on Teaching and Learning Thinking Skills, Contributions in Human Development*, 21 (Basel: Krager, 1990), pp. 108–126.
13 H. Gardner, *The Unschooled Mind* (New York: Basic Books, 1991), p. 253.
14 Tomasello, Kruger, and Ratner, "Cultural Learning."
15 K. Egan, *Primary Understanding* (New York: Routledge, 1988), p. 45.
16 V. Turner, *From Ritual to Theater: The Human Seriousness of Play* (New York: Performing Arts Journal Publications, 1982).
17 Brown and Campione, "Communities of Learning and Thinking."
18 See J. S. Bruner, J. J. Goodnow, and G. A. Austin, *A Study of Thinking* (New York: Wiley, 1956).
19 See also J. S. Bruner and D. R. Olson, "Learning through Experience and Learning through Media," in G. Gerbner, L. P. Gross, and W. Melody, eds, *Communications Technology and Social Policy: Understanding the New "Cultural Revolution"* (New York: Wiley, 1973).
20 Tomasello, Kruger, and Ratner, "Cultural Learning."
21 B. Latour and S. Woolgar, *Laboratory Life: The Social Construction of Scientific Facts* (Princeton, NJ: Princeton University Press, 1986).
22 See T. Gladwin, *East Is a Big Bird* (Cambridge, MA: Harvard University Press, 1970).
23 C. F. Feldman, "Oral Metalanguage," in D. R. Olson and N. Torrance, eds, *Literacy and Orality* (Cambridge: Cambridge University Press, 1991), pp. 47–65.
24 B. Stock, *The Implications of Literacy* (Princeton, NJ: Princeton University Press, 1983).
25 See J. Bruner, "From Joint Attention to the Meeting of Minds," in C. Moore and F. Dunham, eds, *Joint Attention: Its Origin and Role in Development* (New York: Academic Press, 1995).
26 See J. Astington, *The Child's Discovery of the Mind* (Cambridge, MA: Harvard University Press, 1993) for a summary of this work.
27 A. Brown, "The Development of Memory: Knowing, Knowing about Knowing, and Knowing How to Know," in H. W. Reese, ed., *Advances in Child Development and Behavior*, vol. 10 (New York: Academic Press, 1975).
28 C. Bereiter and M. Scardamaglia, *Surpassing Ourselves: An Inquiry into the Nature and Implications of Expertise*; M. Scardamaglia, C. Bereiter, C. Brett, P. J. Burtis, C. Calhoun, and N. Smith Lea, "Educational Applications of a Networked Communal Database," *Interactive Learning Environments*, 2(1) (1992): 45–71; Ann L. Brown and Joseph C. Campione, "Communities of Learning and Thinking, Or a Context by any Other Name," in Deanna Kuhn, ed., *Developmental Perspectives on Teaching and Learning Thinking Skills, Contributions in Human Development*, 21 (Basel: Krager, 1990), pp. 108–126; Roy D. Pea, "Seeing What We Build Together: Distributed Multimedia Learning Environments for Transformative Communications," *The Journal of the Learning Sciences*, 3(3) (1994): 219–225.
29 See, for example, Ingrid Pramling, *Learning to Learn: A Study of Swedish Preschool Children* (New York: Springer-Verlag, 1990).
30 I. Hacking, *The Emergence of Probability: A Philosophical Study of Early Ideas about Probability, Induction, and Statistical Inference* (Cambridge: Cambridge University Press, 1975).
31 K. Popper, *Objective Knowledge: An Evolutionary Approach* (Oxford: Oxford University Press, 1972).
32 T. Nagel, *The View from Nowhere* (New York: Oxford University Press, 1986).
33 T. Kuhn, *The Structure of Scientific Revolutions* (Chicago, IL: University of Chicago Press, 1962).

34 Personal communication.
35 M. Donaldson, *Human Minds: An Exploration* (London: Allen Lane, Penguin Press, 1992).
36 For a particularly thoughtful account of the Western orientation of anthropological writing, see Clifford Geertz, *Works and Lives: The Anthropologist as Author* (Stanford, CA: Stanford University Press, 1988).

CHAPTER 15

WHAT ARE WE LEARNING ABOUT LEARNING IN SCHOOLS?

B. S. Kogan (ed.), *Common Schools, Uncommon Futures: A Working Consensus for School Renewal* (1997), New York: Teachers College Press

My purpose in this chapter is to provide a working map of what we know about learning, particularly about the kind of learning that occurs or *should* occur in schools, and whether, altogether, our knowledge of these matters can guide us in improving the conduct and quality of education and, eventually, the quality of our lives. These are deep matters, and very troubling ones as well, for we are living in revolutionary times whose uncertainties push us either toward retrogressive despair or progressive euphoria, neither of which is a useful stance in times of swift change. Alas, the collision of the two extremes leads to a good deal of overheated rhetoric.

Antinomies of a revolutionary time

Like most revolutionary times, ours is caught up in contradictions, indeed, in genuine antinomies: reasoned pairs of large truths, which, though both may be true, nonetheless contradict each other. Antinomies, though real enough, provide fruitful grounds for confusion. So let me begin by briefly setting out three of the most baffling of these antinomies. They provide us with themes upon which to play out variations later – variations because antinomies do not permit of logical but only of pragmatic resolution. As Niels Bohr liked to remark, the opposite of little truths are false; the opposite of big ones may also be true. So let us dive right in.

The first antinomy is this: On the one hand, it is unquestionably the function of education to enable people to operate at their fullest potential by equipping them with the tools and the sense of opportunity to use their wits, skills, and passions to the full. That the practice of this truism is always faulted probably inheres in the other horn of the antinomy, which goes somewhat as follows: The function of education is to reproduce the culture that supports it. It should not only reproduce it but also further its economic, political, and cultural aims. For example, the educational system of an industrial society should produce a willing and compliant labor force to keep it going: unskilled and semiskilled workers, clerical workers, middle managers, risk-sensitive entrepreneurs – all of whom are convinced that such an industrial society constitutes the right, valid, and only way of living.

Can schooling be construed both as the agency of individual realization and as a reproductive technique for maintaining or furthering a culture? Here the answer is 'not quite yes' – an inevitably flawed 'not quite yes,' for the unfettered ideal of individual realization through education inevitably risks cultural and social unpredictability and, even further, the disruption of legitimate order. The second horn, education as cultural reproduction, risks stagnation, hegemony, and conventionalism, even if it holds out the promise of reducing uncertainty. Finding a way within this antinomic pair does not come easily, particularly not in times of rapid change. Indeed, it could never have come easily at any time. But if one does not face it, one risks failing both ideals.

The second antinomy reflects two contrastive views about the nature and uses of mind, again both meritorious. One side proclaims that learning is, as it were, inside the head, intrapsychic. Solo learners must, in the end, rely on their own intelligence and their own motivation to benefit from what school has to offer. Education provides the means for strengthening and enabling our mental powers for dealing with the 'real world.' In this view, education raises everybody's level of functioning, the more so the greater their inherent endowment or energy; but please do not equate these with IQ. It is more complicated than that.

The contrastive view to the solo learner in this second antinomy is that all mental activity is 'situated' in and supported by a more or a less enabling social setting. We are not just an isolated mind with skills added. How well the student does in mastering and using skills, knowledge, and ways of thinking will depend upon how favoring or enabling a cultural context the teacher creates for the learner. Favoring contexts – opportunities for cultural interaction – matter at every level, and even determine whether or not one's underlying capacities become actualized. Favoring contexts are principally and inevitably interpersonal: collaborative settings involving joint enterprises with peers, parents, and teachers. It is through such collaboration that the developing child gains access to the resources and technology of the culture. But even more benefits accrue from interaction, for there is now good reason to believe that it is through joining in collaborative effort that one forms a self and comes to a sense of one's own agency (Meltzoff and Gopnik 1993, 335–366).

The risks (and the benefits) inherent in pushing either side of this antinomy to the exclusion of the other are so critical that their discussion is better postponed until we can look at them in context, which we will do shortly. Otherwise, we might get stuck in the nature–nurture controversy, for the 'inside-out/outside-in' antinomy is too easily converted into Herrnstein–Murray rhetoric (Herrnstein and Murray 1994).

The third and final antinomy is one that is too rarely made explicit in educational debate. It is about how the meanings of everyday experience are to be construed and by whom. That sounds remotely abstract – until you encounter it face-to-face. Let me outline it bluntly and with some needed exaggeration. One side of the antinomy holds that human experience, 'local knowledge' as it were, is legitimate in its own right; it cannot be reduced to some 'higher,' more authoritative universalistic construal (Geertz 1995). All efforts to impose more authoritative meanings upon local experience are suspect as hegemonic, serving the ends of power and domination, whether so intended or not. This, of course, is a caricature of the kind of antifoundationalism sometimes referred to as 'postmodernism' (Derrida 1978). It is not only an epistemological stance but also a political one. The claim of nonreductiveness and untranslatability often appears in radical feminism, in radical ethnic and anti-imperialist movements, and even in critical legal studies. In education, it undoubtedly fueled the 'deschooling' movement and its kin. But even in its extreme versions, it cannot be dismissed out of hand. It expresses something deep about the dilemmas of living in contemporary bureaucratized society.

The contrastive side of this third antinomy – the search for an authoritatively universal voice – is also likely to get puffed by self-righteousness. But ignore for a moment the pomposity of the self-appointed spokespersons for undisputable universal truths, for there is a compelling claim on this side, too. It inheres in the deep integrity, for good or evil, with which any culture's way of life expresses its historically rooted aspirations for grace, order, well-being, and justice. Human plights, though they may always express themselves locally in time, place, and circumstance and be linked uniquely to the local context, are nonetheless universally rooted in history. While history may be an interpretation of the past, it is not an arbitrary interpretation. To ignore a culture's best historical efforts to cope with its encounters with the universal human condition on the grounds that such efforts fail to capture the political immediacy of the local here-and-now or that they undermine identification with a more local ethnic, gender, or class history is to risk parochialism. Cultural pluralism does not have to prove its virtue by ignoring or vilifying the integrity (and the inevitable transition pains) of its host culture. For all that experience and knowledge may be local and particular, it is still part of a larger continent (Geertz 1995).

Those are the three antinomies: the idiosyncratic/conventional, the individual inside-out/cultural outside-in, and the particular/universal. Without keeping them in mind, it would be impossible to evaluate what we have learned about school learning, for they help keep the issues in balance. There is only one way to have both sides of the three antinomies. As I shall argue now, that way is to take seriously the individual as both an expression of and as an agent of human culture. And this must begin with teachers and pupils in the setting of the school. Let me turn to this now.

Head Start as a microcosm

I begin with Head Start, a revealing microcosm. Though it had many incipient precursors, all rather ideological and utopian, it is unique for having been fueled or ignited by a series of scientific discoveries about the nature of early development. Like most important facts about the human condition, these were quickly converted from facts to metaphors. First, the bare facts insofar as one can strip them down. Animals reared in impoverished environments were later found to be deficient when tested on standard learning and problem-solving tasks (Hunt 1961). Not only that, but their brains seemed to be underdeveloped as well, if I may be permitted to condense a great many, very complicated particulars (Calvin 1983) into an overly simple summary. Some of these findings, by the way, were literally inadvertent by-products of other concerns, as when white rats were reared in 'germ-free' environments to see whether they would develop normal antibodies. They did not; but more interesting still, the germ-free environments, being mighty pallid places, made the rats raised in them exceptionally backward in their learning activities in comparison with their more friskily and unhygienically raised litter-mates (Calvin 1983).

From these meager beginnings, the so-called deprivation hypothesis was born. But education was not an issue; neglected newborns in respirators were the first source of alarm (Ribble 1944). Very soon afterward, however, new research began appearing showing that kids from poverty backgrounds fell progressively further behind once they started school (Bloom 1964 and 1976). This work alerted a much wider community to the possibility that the lack of a 'good start' might lock a kid into later failure. The deprivation hypothesis had found a human locus. Though it was an exceedingly crude formulation, it had the moral force behind it of saying that poor kids were being deprived of a key growth vitamin or some vital immunization shot. That was a powerful start.

Soon after, a spate of direct, controlled studies of real (rather than retrospective) infants began in earnest: their perception, memory, attention, imitation, and action. Such work had been rare. Why it began at just that time and with that much vigor I will leave for historians to decide (Mussen 1970, ch. 5–7). Had there been an implicit taboo on studying little babies in laboratories – a collision between the ethics of tenderness and the cool detachment of research? Or was it just the transistor recording with its miniaturizing possibilities that made it possible to let babies suck pictures into focus or to control what came into view by a slight head turn or flick of the leg (Kalnins and Bruner 1973; Papousek 1979)? Imagine the excitement of finding that the older the infant, the more complicated the checkerboard the infant chose to look at (Salapatek 1975), or that an infant's eye movements were not that different from an adult's when scanning familiar figures (Mackworth and Bruner 1970).

Not surprisingly, these findings quickly caught the public's imagination, and even the august *Times* of London carried a series of articles in praise of the new work. The equally august British historian Lord Bullock was soon quoted to the effect that we were entering a new era in our conception of humans. Infants, it turned out, were much smarter, much more cognitively proactive rather than reactive, much more attentive to the immediate social world around them, and so on than had previously been suspected. And they emphatically did *not* inhabit a world of buzzing, blooming confusion; they were after stability from the start. At least this suggested what the deprivation might be all about.

The burden of these studies pointed to something more active than gross sensorimotor deprivation. One kind of 'deprivation' was social or interactive. Infants sought out and were rewarded by interaction with others; they went out of their way to establish joint attention with others by following their line of vision to discover what they were looking at; infants sought and were calmed by eye-to-eye contact with their caregivers, and so on (Scaife and Bruner 1975; Stechler and Latz 1966). Withholding these opportunities, it was shown by the few studies that undertook to do so (for infancy researchers hate tormenting their subjects), distressed and upset the infants. So the first thing was human interaction. The second thing infants needed was self-initiated activity. In a nutshell, what infants *did* to their mundane environments seemed to have more lasting effects on them than what the environment did to *them*. And what, in fact, they did in their visual search and awkward groping was far more systematic and varied than had been suspected – at least by researchers (Meltzoff and Gopnik 1993, 335–366).

Out of these considerations grew a rather weird and ethnocentric notion of 'cultural deprivation.' 'Culture' somehow got equated with an idealized middle-class version of childrearing in which mother and child interacted with each other in an attuned way, and in which the child was given ample opportunity to initiate things within this interaction. Being deprived of this idealized opportunity was translated as 'cultural deprivation.' There were soon new projects to teach mothers in poverty how to talk more and play more with their infants and how to hand over agency to the child. These projects produced real results. Head Start's curriculum rapidly moved in that same direction. However, one should note something ominous: 'Cultural deprivation' as a term had the effect of blaming the victim – or at least the victim's mother (Cole and Bruner 1971). Since in America, the mothers in question were predominantly black or Hispanic, the implication was that these cultures were at fault, rather than poverty or its despair.

All this was taking place in the decade after *Brown v. Board of Education* (1954), when affirmative action programs were still new and highly disputable.

Head Start was seen as the other side of the coin of affirmative action. It was seen as dedicated to stopping the culture from reproducing itself yet again, particularly its system of racial discrimination that had assured a supply of cheap, unskilled, exploitable labor. Besides, we did not need that kind of labor any more. It looked as if a new consciousness had come to replace the old culture-reproducing inertia.

But never underrate the power of antinomies. By the early 1970s, research began 'proving' that IQ gains from Head Start disappeared within a few years. Ghetto children seemed unable to sustain the gains they made from the initial Head Start boost once they got further into school. There were Jensens and Herrnsteins around to reassert the old inside-out view: Poor kids, particularly black kids, just did not have the endowment – the IQ – to benefit from Head Start (Herrnstein 1982; Jensen 1969). This was not unwelcome music to political tax-cutters playing to an increasingly squeezed middle class who, in any case, had fled to the suburbs to put big cities, high taxes, and poverty problems behind them. So big cities lost not only their manufacturing industries but also their middle class and grew poorer and poorer. Head Start did not disappear, but neither did it grow as much as it might have. Ironically, when the 25-year results on Head Start began coming in, even by itself it had made an astonishing difference. Kids who had been through it were, by comparison to 'controls,' more likely to stay longer and do better in school, to get and to hold jobs longer, to stay out of jail, to commit fewer crimes, and the rest. In fact, it 'paid.' The cost per pupil, even in fancier Head Start programs, far offset economic losses from unemployment, cost of imprisonment, and welfare payments, even leaving aside the moral issues involved (Abt Associates 1979; Barnett 1993; Clarke-Stewart 1982; Schweinhart and Weikart 1980; Zigler and Valentine 1979).

Plainly, Head Start is not a magic bullet, but not because it is not always up to standard; that is easily fixed. It is not enough because, on its own, merely as a starting subculture for young kids, it cannot counteract the social alienation of poor black and Hispanic kids and their mothers, or their mothers and fathers where the family is intact. There is too much in the society working against it. School after Head Start is rarely geared to getting inner-city kids to see schoolwork as a viable option for getting out of poverty. After all, even when one holds IQ constant, the percentage of black youth who are unemployed is twice as high as the rate for the IQ-matched whites. So, as drug peddling and turf wars increase as one of the few viable lines of activity for blacks, homicide becomes the chief threat to life among black inner-city kids, and prison a residence for more than a third of them at some point between ages 16 and 25.

Nevertheless, what we have learned about learning in all this discouraging morass is anything but trivial. It is this, and let nobody overlook it: Even under the least favorable conditions – psychologically, fiscally, educationally – we still succeed in giving some children a sense of their own possibilities. We do it by getting them, and sometimes their parents, to collaborate in an enabling community. My own view is that experiments such as Head Start give kids, and perhaps their mothers, a sense of a possible way through a poverty culture even when it seems to them to be blindly reproducing itself. But its key idea needs to be extended upward to older kids as well.

Let me describe what I mean through a case history, using a school that picks up ghetto kids at around 10 or 11 years of age. Some of them had the benefit of Head Start; most did not. This is a school that is part of the Oakland school system, and it is part of a program financed by both federal and foundation funding, although the greater part of the costs are met by Oakland. It vividly illustrates what we have come to recognize as crucial for enabling children not just to build their skills but also to develop an effective sense of participating in an enabling community.

The project is directed by Ann Brown of the School of Education at the University of California at Berkeley, and it is now becoming the hub of a consortium of schools spread all around the country (Brown 1994; Brown and Palincsar 1989, 393–449). It easily achieves the usual: raising reading levels, raising test scores, and all the other standard end-result things that school reform is supposed to do. Much more to the point, however, is the kind of collaborative school culture it creates for its participating students and teachers alike.

The Oakland project follows a very few but very powerful principles. The first is that it is a learning community, a collaborative community. This means everybody is learning, everybody is helping in the teaching, and everybody is sharing the labor; they are into it as a group. When I was visiting, the class was involved in studying the *Exxon Valdez* oil spill in Alaska, its causes and consequences, and what it could tell us about how to manage an environment. The kids were *not* at the receiving end of an educational transmission belt, nor were the teachers at the sending end. They were all in the business of *constructing* knowledge. Answers were not in books or teachers' heads. They were something you had to construct, and constructing was the real business. The kinds of questions you asked mattered. So did your guesses. Hunches could be checked against information and others' opinions. But you could also reason out answers, either by yourself or with somebody else. That is number two on the list of fundamentals: *knowledge is made, not found*. There are lots of places to get information – these kids had access to some Apple II computers plus the usual dictionaries, clippings, and so on – but knowledge is made from organizing and discussing these things.

How you organize things – for example, how you put things into the computer's memory or, for that matter, into your own – makes a great deal of difference in what you come to know from it when you use it later. So it is very important to discuss how you are going about organizing things, 'you' individually or 'you' working in pairs or small groups, or 'you' at the Apple II. So there is a lot of encouragement, as we say these days, for 'going meta' on what you are doing. That is the third fundamental. Indeed, one teaching assistant served as class ethnographer, and her feedback to the teachers and students about how they did that week was discussed with real reflectiveness the week I was there.

If students have 'hot ideas' during class – like one kid who thought about getting oil off birds by using peanut butter as an 'oil blotter' – they are encouraged to present them either to the class or to the small group they are working with. Children learn how to receive these ideas respectfully. Even if the idea is a little wacky, somebody may come up with a better version. That peanut butter idea led to an interesting discussion of what makes a 'blotter.' And everybody gets a turn at teaching what they have learned, even the hangers-back. They very quickly learn a practical version of 'no man is an island entire unto himself.' The deep lesson, of course, is that thinking and learning are functions of discourse, no matter what your endowment. These kids are enormously stimulating to talk to. Or to use that dreary banality, they are way above average. What?

It is really old stuff. We have known for years now that if you treat people, kids included, as bright, responsible, and part of the group, they will grow into it – some better than others, obviously. Even old people in nursing homes, if treated as responsible members of the community, live longer, get sick less often, and keep their mental powers brisker and longer. I can assure you at firsthand that a good part of the success of Kanzi, that chimpanzee who is mastering language so remarkably at the Yerkes Lab, is that he is being treated by that group of researchers as if, well, he were nearly human. Korean immigrants in America score

15 points higher in IQ than Korean immigrants in Japan, where they are detested, segregated, and treated as if 'inferior.' We desperately need to have a closer look at what we mean by an 'enabling' culture, particularly the enabling culture of a school (Stevenson and Stigler 1992).

Perhaps the successful school cultures – the Oaklands and good Head Starts and many others – are only countercultures for raising consciousness. That would be a real boon, if the little counterculture of a good school produced reflections about other possible worlds. I think there is more to it than that, however. I spoke to some people at the Ministry of Education in Norway who had been involved in a new program to reduce school bullying in that compassionate country. Just raising the topic had had an electric effect on the kids. It obviously had been in the closet waiting for a passport into open discussion, but consciousness raising was not enough. It needed some way of finding its way into the routines of mundane daily actions. It was the very same lesson that Vivian Paley learned in her stunning study of nursery school kids excluding other kids from their little cliques – her wonderfully titled *You Can't Say You Can't Play* (Paley 1992).

The heart of the matter seems to be praxis: how one conducts life in ordinary, everyday, expectable, banal cultural settings. School, too, is ordinary cultural praxis. It is so crucial to the idea of how a culture enables mind that I want to pause over it for a moment. Let me discuss it in the unusual language of a distinguished friend of mine, the French social theorist Pierre Bourdieu (1991). Praxis takes place in any and all settings that provide a 'market in distinctions,' to use his terms. A market in distinctions is anywhere where one 'trades' some form of capital – economic, cultural, or symbolic – in return for some culturally bestowed distinction: profit, approval, identity, respect, collegial support, favors, or recognition. These markets in distinction are ubiquitous: They are in conversation, on the trading floor of the stock exchange, in politics, in school, and around the dinner table. They are ubiquitous, too, in the collaborative exchanges of a classroom. Growing up, and throughout life, we develop mental and bodily orientations toward the world that guide us in the markets where we trade our capital for distinctions – particularly our capital in the form of knowledge, beliefs, values, services, allegiances, and the like. It provides the unremarkable stuff of daily life, and it forms our characters and predispositions. In a word, we act our way into thinking more readily than we think our way into acting.

Building a collaborative culture

It is now time we returned to our three antinomies for a coda. Should education reproduce the culture, or should it enrich and cultivate human potential? The standard double-talk is that, of course, it should do both as best it can. But if we leave it unexamined at that, we have a recipe for mindlessness. I suppose we could do better than that by thinking it through further. So when we proclaim that we will be first in science, math, and languages by the end of the decade to compete in world markets, we ought also (if we are true to the ideal of developing human potential as well) proclaim that when we get there, we will reward everyone by redistributing the wealth, by creating a new GI Bill, or whatever. This might assure the poor and the alienated that working hard in school will not just make the rich richer and the poor poorer. Perhaps if the rules of the game would stay still, and change would stop its tumultuous course, we could approach our compromises in that way. The idiosyncratic would simply provide entry into the reproductively conventional.

I doubt whether we are willing enough, united enough, or courageous enough to face up to the revolution we are living through. If we were, would there really be an issue about *reproducing* the culture? The real issue is trying to get some sense of what we are changing into. I think that we have little better sense of where the culture is moving than did the French in 1789. Was it any better understood by activist Jacobins than by Girondists or the hold-back peasants of the Vendée or the crusty gentry of the ancien régime? Even America's demographic changes are too mind-boggling to grasp firmly. For example, there was a larger proportion of parents who had achieved high school educations in 1980 than there was of parents with grade school educations a half-century before – more than eight in ten. We do not even live where we used to. At the turn of the century, nearly half of America's families lived on farms, with all hands pitching in. That proportion had dropped to less than 5% by 1980. And the number of siblings in the median American family had dropped to less than two per family in 1993, down from nearly four in 1920. Perhaps the swiftest change of all was that the number of children with mothers at work outside the home rose from one in ten in 1940 to six in ten in 1990. In that same short period, the divorce rate increased tenfold – from roughly two per thousand marriages to about twenty-one per thousand. In consequence, during that same period, the percentage of kids living in mother-only households swelled three-fold from 6.7% to 20%. Indeed, the number of kids born into 'Ozzie and Harriet' families – as a recent Russell Sage Foundation report (Hernandez 1993) calls families in a first marriage with father working and mother at home – dropped to about a quarter of live births. This is *smaller* than the proportion of our children born into families living at or below the official poverty level, which amounts today to nearly a third. Immigrant and black children, as has traditionally been the case, fare far worse on all the indices linked with economic well-being.

We seem to be creating two population streams, each with a different culture: the highly urban and increasingly disorganized poor, mostly black or recent immigrant; and the suburban/small-city, mostly white or recent immigrant-descended middle class. While the representation of blacks in this middle class has increased, it is still notably in the minority. Obviously there are other smaller groupings as well, posing problems of their own: the rural poor; isolated and dwindling small-town dwellers; the emerging professional, highly educated upper-middle class, whose chief legacy to their children is an up-scale education rather than inherited wealth; and so on. Let me concentrate on the two main streams: the urban poor and the suburbanized middle class. Nobody planned it that way. Nobody planned it *any* way. And grand aspirations about training up a competitive labor force for the next generation do not touch the intimate issue of how we conduct our schools either in our increasingly poor and disorganized cities or in our lawn-manicured, increasingly self-contained, yet uneasy suburbs. What I am left with is the conviction that the ambitious Charlottesville science–math–language goals set forth in 1989[1] will get their due attention because of the sheer economic vitality of this nation, but that in the process we may lose the sense of community and civility and collaboration that constitutes American grace.

So let me turn back to the issue of school as a collaborative culture, a medium for community rather than a repository of skills for converting inner endowment to real-world savvy (our second antinomy). The difficulty with that isolated solo approach in such times as ours is that competitive skill pickup cannot be counted on. Inner-city poor kids are too apt to believe the skill endowment game is a con game, and suburban kids are too apt to find it boring. On the basis of what we have learned about human learning – that it is best when it is participatory, proactive, communal, collaborative, and given over to constructing meanings rather than receiving them – we would do better to renew our schools along these lines even if only to meet the Charlottesville goals better (National Education Goals Panel, 1991).

There are deeper reasons why we need something like the Oakland/Ann Brown model to cope with the third antinomy, the particular-universalistic one. We know that, given the appropriate collaborative community, children come quickly and easily to taking particulars as tropes or metaphors of something more general circulating in the group. They learn, too, how to negotiate these matters with others. This is surely one wise way to grow in and benefit from revolutionary times. But there are many ways to proceed. Oakland is only one among many. Building to the strengths and interests expressed in different forms of intelligence, along Howard Gardner's (1983) lines, is another. Ted Sizer's Coalition of Essential Schools, financed by the Annenberg Foundation, has its virtues. There is never just one formula for so deep and pervasive a problem. There are even bad errors with good motives from which we can learn. Teaching black history to black children by the old and stunted methods of history teaching in the interest of creating ethnic pride is probably no more successful than teaching pride in America by teaching about George Washington and Parson Weems's apple tree.

What I do know on the basis of the centrality of interpersonal interaction in human development is that whatever the innovation, it cannot get off the ground without an adult actively present – where school is concerned, a teacher willing and prepared to give aid, comfort, scaffolding, and cultural cohesion. You cannot carry on with just the good intentions of governors meeting in Charlottesville; you cannot do it with a bank of the best-programmed computers; and you cannot do it with the best-intended ideology, be it inspired by multiculturalism and bilingual education, by feminist pride, or by scornfully creating lists of great books written by 'dead white males' (like Dante, Locke, and Melville!). Learning in its full complexity involves the creation and negotiation of meaning with others in a culture, and the agent, or the vicar, of that process is a teacher. You cannot teacher-proof a curriculum any more than you can parent-proof a family. So I believe we must begin our refreshment and renewal of American schooling with a new and radical reconsideration of how we recruit, educate, and help our teachers in achieving the kinds of goals I have been discussing. I am not talking about 'teacher training' on the cheap, but the formation and enablement of teachers. This is a serious undertaking. Remember that it was a dedicated teacher corps that finally created the French Republic nearly a century after the Revolution (Judge 1994).

There is a deep puzzle in what I am saying. In the years since *A Nation at Risk* was published (National Commission on Excellence in Education 1983), when our national debate on education became a 'public' media event, we have virtually closed our eyes to the nature, uses, and role of teaching. We have sourly damned the teaching profession as unqualified and concentrated on raising their licensing qualifications. Teaching has been treated as a necessary evil; would that we had computers that could do it. In the process, we have probably alienated our most important ally in renewal: the teacher.

There is nobody in America today who knows better the temper of the American teacher than Ernest Boyer. He conducted a study of their views in the five years following the 1983 publication of *A Nation at Risk*. This is what he reported in his 1988 Annual Report of the Carnegie Endowment for the Advancement of Teaching:

> We are troubled that the nation's teachers remain so skeptical. Why is it that teachers, of all people, are demoralized and largely unimpressed by the reform

actions taken [thus far]? . . . The reform movement has been driven largely by legislative and administrative intervention. The push has been concerned more with regulation than renewal. Reforms typically have focused on graduation requirements, student achievement, teacher preparation and testing, and monitoring activities. But in all these matters, important as they are, teachers have been largely uninvolved. . . . Indeed, the most disturbing finding in our study is this: Over half the teachers [surveyed] believe that, overall, morale within the profession has substantially declined since 1983. . . . What is urgently needed – in the next phase of school reform – is a deep commitment to make teachers partners in renewal at all levels. . . . The challenge now is to move beyond regulations, focus on renewal, and make teachers full participants in the process.

(Boyer 1988, 13–21)

Let us remember the picture I drew of the American family earlier in this essay – whether in the inner city or the rimming suburbs. It can be condensed into one focal image. Children, through a variety of circumstances, have been put on increasingly short rations where *live* interaction with grown-ups is concerned. Working mothers, absent fathers, television isolation, and the rest leave kids peculiarly cut off from a sense of how you enter and cope with the adult world. I am not proposing that schools and teachers stand in for the family. My proposal is more radical than that. Teachers can create the sense of a collaborative culture as no other group in our society can. There are teachers around the country who are doing it now. We must bring them back into the discussion, into the shaping of both ends and means. Everything we know about school learning tells us that teachers are not messengers carrying the word, but a crucial ingredient of the message itself.

Notes

I am grateful to the Spencer Foundation for their grant in support of the work reported in these pages.

1   The Charlottesville goals are a set of six national goals to be met by the year 2000. They were formulated and agreed upon by the President and the nation's governors in Charlottesville, Virginia, in September 1989. At the same meeting, the National Education Goals Panel was set up to establish means of assessment for measuring progress and reporting results. The panel consists of six governors, four members of Congress, and four members of the administration. The six goals are as follows: By the year 2000, all American children will start school ready to learn; the high school graduation rate will increase to at least 90%; American students will leave grades 4, 8, and 12 demonstrating competency in challenging subject matter, such as history, math, science, and geography; American students will be first in the world of science and math achievement; every adult American will be literate and possess the knowledge and skills necessary to compete in a global economy and exercise the rights and responsibilities of citizenship; and every school in the United States will be free of drugs and violence and offer a disciplined environment conducive to learning.

References

Abt Associates. 1979. *Final report of the national day care study.* Vols. 1–5. Cambridge, MA: Abt Books, and Washington, DC: Day Care Division, Administration for Children, Youth and Families (DHHS).

Barnett, W. S. 1993. Benefit-cost analysis of preschool education: Findings from a 25-year follow-up. *American Journal of Orthopsychiatry* 63(4): 500–508.

Bloom, B. S. 1964. *Stability and change in human characteristics*. New York: Wiley.

Bloom, B. S. 1976. *Human characteristics and school learning*. Chicago, IL: University of Chicago Press.

Bourdieu, P. 1991. *Language and symbolic power*. Cambridge, MA: Harvard University Press.

Boyer, E. 1988. *Report of the President*. In *The Carnegie Foundation for the Advancement of Teaching: The eighty-third annual report*. Princeton, NJ: The Carnegie Foundation for the Advancement of Teaching.

Brown, A. L. 1994. The Advancement of Learning. *Educational Researcher* 23(8): 4–12.

Brown, A. L., and A. S. Palincsar. 1989. Guided, cooperative learning and individual knowledge acquisition. In *Knowing, learning, and instruction: Essays in honor of Robert Glaser*, ed. L. B. Resnick. Hillsdale, NJ: Erlbaum.

Brown v. Board of Education of Topeka, Kansas, 347 US 483 (1954).

Calvin, W. H. 1983. From nervous cells to hominid brains. In Calvin, *The throwing madonna: Essays on the brain*. New York; McGraw-Hill.

Clarke-Stewart, A. 1982. *Day care*. Cambridge, MA: Harvard University Press.

Cole, M., and J. S. Bruner. 1971. Cultural differences and inferences about psychological processes. *American Psychologist* 26(10): 867–876.

Derrida, J. 1978. *Writing and difference*. Chicago, IL: University of Chicago Press.

Gardner, H. 1983. *Frames of mind: The theory of multiple intelligences*. New York: Basic Books.

Geertz, C. 1995. *After the fact: Two countries, four decades, one anthropologist*. Cambridge, MA: Harvard University Press.

Hernandez, D. J. 1993. *America's children: Resources from family, government, and the economy*. New York: Russell Sage Foundation.

Herrnstein, R. J. 1982. IQ testing and the media. *The Atlantic Monthly*, August, 250(2): 68–74.

Herrnstein, R. J., and C. Murray. 1994. *The bell curve: Intelligence and class structure in American life*. New York: Free Press.

Hunt, J. M. 1961. *Intelligence and experience*. New York: Ronald Press.

Jensen, A. R. 1969. How much can we boost IQ and scholastic achievement? *Harvard Educational Review*, Winter, 39(1): 1–123.

Judge, H. G. 1994. *The university and the teachers: France, the United States, England*. Wallingford, England: Triangle Books.

Kalnins, I., and J. S. Bruner. 1973. The coordination of visual observation and instrumental behavior in early infancy. *Perception* 2: 307–314.

Mackworth, N. H., and J. S. Bruner. 1970. How adults and children search and recognize pictures. *Human Development* 13(3): 149–177.

Meltzoff, A. N., and A. Gopnik. 1993. The role of imitation in understanding persons and developing a theory of mind. In *Understanding other minds: Perspectives from autism*, ed. S. Baron-Cohen, H. Tager-Flusberg, and D. J. Cohen. Oxford: Oxford University Press.

Mussen, P. H., ed. 1970. *Carmichael's manual of child psychology*. 3rd edn. New York: Wiley.

National Commission on Excellence in Education. 1983. *A nation at risk: The imperative for educational reform*. Washington, DC: US Department of Education.

National Education Goals Panel. 1991. *The national education goals report: Building a nation of learners*. Washington, DC: US Government Printing Office.

Paley, V. G. 1992. *You can't say you can't play*. Cambridge, MA: Harvard University Press.

Papousek, H. 1979. From adaptive responses to social cognition: The learning view of development. In *Psychological development from infancy: Image to intention*, ed. M. H. Bornstein and W. Kessen. Hillsdale, NJ: Erlbaum.

Ribble, M. A. 1944. Infantile experience in relation to personality development. In *Personality and the behavior disorders: A handbook based on experimental and clinical research*, ed. J. M. Hunt. New York: Ronald Press.

Salapatek, P. 1975. Pattern perception in early infancy. In *Infant perception: From sensation to cognition*, ed. L. B. Cohen and P. Salapatek. Vol. 1. New York: Academic Press.

Scaife, M., and J. S. Bruner. 1975. The capacity for joint visual attention in the infant. *Nature* 253: 265–266.

Schweinhart, L. J., and D. P. Weikart. 1980. *Young children grow up: The effects of the Perry preschool program on youths through age 15.* Monographs of the High/Scope Educational Research Foundation, no. 7. Ypsilanti, MI: High/Scope Press.

Stechler, G., and E. Latz. 1966. Some observations on attention and arousal in the human infant. *Journal of the American Academy of Child Psychiatry* 5: 517–525.

Stevenson, H. W., and J. W. Stigler. 1992. *The learning gap: Why our schools are failing and what we can learn from Japanese and Chinese education.* New York: Summit.

Zigler, E., and J. Valentine, eds. 1979. *Project Head Start: A legacy of the war on poverty.* New York: Free Press.

CHAPTER 16

CELEBRATING DIVERGENCE
Piaget and Vygotsky[1]

Human Development (1997), 10: 1–23, Basel: S. Karger

Abstract

Contrasting Piaget's emphasis on the invariant logic of growth with Vygotsky's emphasis upon the centrality of culturally patterned dialogue in the enablement of growth, one is led to conclude that their two approaches were incommensurate. This incommensurateness may expresss a deep and possibly irreconcilable difference between two ways of knowing: one seeking to "explain" and the other to "interpret" human growth and the human condition. We are blessed to have had such gifted exponents of the two views at the very start of our discipline, for their divergence has alerted us to the deeper puzzles posed by research in human development.

First, let me say explicitly what all of us must have been thinking implicitly while contemplating this double centennial. What great good fortune for us, we students of human development, to have had two such giants, Jean Piaget and Lev Vygotsky, inspiring our quest. And it is not just their *intellectual* power that we celebrate, but their greatness of spirit and courage, their willingness to stand up to and to admit the baffling complexities of their subject – the growing mind. They taught us not to oversimplify. For them, mind was never "nothing but". They bequeathed us a heritage free of reductionism – one truly to be treasured (Figure 16.1).

But today our task is not only to celebrate the past but to anticipate the future. Before turning to that task, however, let me say just a word more about resistance to oversimplification. Science demystifies not by ignoring mysteries, but by facing up to them. The unique mystery of mind is its privacy, its inherent subjectivity.[2] But for all its privacy, mind nonetheless generates a product that is public. It generates worldly, useful knowledge, though that knowledge is constructed and never directly apprehended in the objectivist's sense. If this is so for our knowledge of the natural world, it is even more strikingly so for our knowledge of the social world and, in spite of introspection, even for our knowledge about ourselves. What is unique about us as a species is that we not only adapt to the natural and social worlds through appropriate actions, but we also create theories and stories to help us *understand* and even *explain* the world and our actions in it. And we have cared enough about these theories and stories to have burned each other at the stake or even to have gone to war over them.

Piaget and Vygotsky dedicated their lives to the study of how human beings grow to construct and exchange theories about the world and about each other. Each proposed an epistemology that recognized the essentially developmental nature of such theory building. Both were as full of awe at the cognitive constructions of the growing child as they were at the insights of a Pythagoras, a Pascal,

Figure 16.1 Poster from the conference honoring the centennial of Piaget's and Vygotsky's births where the author gave this keynote address. Copyright Society for Sociocultural Research.

a Tolstoy. Their respect for the growing mind changed the study of human development, indeed the intellectual climate of our times.

Yet, these two great men, for all their ample spirit, were, as we all know, profoundly different in outlook. Piaget's genius was to recognize the fundamental role of logic-like operations in human mental activity. Vygotsky's was to recognize that individual human intellectual power depended upon our capacity to appropriate human culture and history as tools of mind. If Piaget sensitized us to the analytic powers of the INRC Four Group and the Sixteen Binary Propositions in explicating the powers of mind, Vygotsky (1962) woke us to the meaning of Francis Bacon's dictum: "Nec manus, nisi intellectus, sibi permissus, multum valent: instrumentis et auxilibus res perficitur."[3] ["Left to themselves, neither hand nor mind alone amounts to much; they are perfected by the instruments and aids that they employ."]

Piaget's perspective

Such a difference, with one thinker emphasizing the role of inner, autochthonous logical processes, and the other the shaping role of culture, inevitably led to sharp divergences in their approaches to mental growth. I want now to explore these differences with a view to speculating upon whether their views are compatible at some deeper level, whether they are incommensurate though complementary; or even, indeed, whether their conceptions of the growth of mind are simply incompatible. Let us not fret about the outcome of our inquiry. Recall Niels Bohr's maxim, "The opposites of great truths may also be true; it is only the opposites of small truths that are false."

Mind, Piaget argues, can be described by (or is?[4]) an organized group of logical operations that mediate between the world, eo ipso, and our knowledge of that world. Since the world cannot be known directly but only by the mediation of these logical operations, our knowledge then is a *construction* to be tested further against ongoing action in the world. Mind's logical operations, which have their start in the internalization of action, constitute a logical calculus whose scope and power grows through decentration from immediate action. Like any logical calculus, the operators in the Piagetian mental calculus generate putatively contradiction-free constructions of the world that can be tested through their success in action, but also by their power to provide understanding. For Piaget, knowledge of the world is made, not found.

Mental growth consists in the child "moving" from simpler to more complex systems of logical operations, the process being effected by the transformation and internalization of action into thought. Once action has become internalized into thought and becomes decentered and reversible, the stage is set for the growth of formal operations in which thought itself becomes its own object and can, accordingly, be translated into conscious propositions. Concrete operational thought requires understanding of the identity of an object across transformations in its appearance or in the actions we perform upon it. Formal operations presuppose a capacity to redescribe thought in the form of propositions, the precondition for which is, in some sense, being able to know what one knows. In both cases, it has always been unclear whether consciousness is a precondition for or a concomitant of taking a cognitive step upward to a higher level. Indeed, the function of consciousness in growth has always seemed to me to be an unsettled issue in Piaget's theory.

Nor, more generally, was it ever plain, despite the pages devoted to the subject, what propelled the child's growing mind from one stage of logical operations to the next higher one. Was it *prise de conscience*, the recognition of contradiction, decentration, failure of praxis, or what? What *has* always been abundantly clear, however, was that mental growth followed an invariant course, whatever propelled it or whatever the *aliment* upon which the growing mind was nourished. So invariant was this course, indeed, that the very history of human thought had itself followed it – this was Piaget's genetic epistemological challenge to the historians of science and knowledge.

In most general terms, what was said to *impel* growth along this invariant course was *disequilibration*, a process created by the relation between two component processes. Encounters with the world were either fitted into – *assimilated* to – previously existing mental structures, or existing structures were changed to *accommodate* them. At one extreme, for example, there is the assimilation of play; at the other, the uncomprehending accommodation of imitation. Neither alone supports adequate praxis nor achieves understanding. But the interplay or conflict of assimilation and accommodation leads to cognitive growth – whether by provoking decentration, consciousness, or whatever. It would not be unfair to say that the dynamics of disequilibration have never been clear.

In consequence of this lack of clarity, the *causes* of growth in Piagetian theory seem chronically under-specified, though the *invariant direction* of that growth seemed clear enough. The theory, in consequence, has become more a *theory of the direction of growth* than of *the causes of growth*. But Piaget's decision to concentrate upon the necessary *direction* of mental growth rather than upon its contingent *causes* was daring, brilliant – and characteristic. For historically, efforts to study growth's causes had come virtually to a dead end. Piaget's new emphasis miraculously broke the thrall of old-line associationisms and learning theories that dated back to Aristotle, and that had been regularly renewed in more recent times by empirical philosophers from Hobbes and Locke onward. Such theories were too subject to the contingencies of encounter to satisfy Piaget's need; all failed to deal with the inherent *systematicity* of mental growth by putting the systematicity in the world rather than in the growth of mind itself. It was the latter that posed Piaget's *problematik*. Never mind that disequilibration and decentration were plagued by underdetermination. At least they kept intact his more general view of growth as *systematic* rather than as driven helter-skelter by the contingencies of association and reinforcement. Never mind his views led to endless problems with *décalage* – why systematic growth in one domain of knowledge does not always generalize to others; the "décalage issue" may yet lead us to a better understanding of what constitutes *domains of knowledge* (Hirschfeld and Gelman, 1994).

So much for the bare foundations of Piaget's theory. Obviously, I have oversimplified shamelessly. But before moving on, let me note one puzzling gap in his theory. It concerns *intersubjectivity*: how we manage to know each other's minds, know them well enough to aid each other in constructing our worlds through negotiation, instruction, enculturation, and so on. Even the well known work of Doise and Mugny (1979) saw the role of "others" in Piagetian tasks as, so to speak, compelling decentration by proposing different solutions. Others helped not as collaborators or fellow members of a culture, but as challenging a reigning solution by proposing a different one – a component process in the experimental or "nomothetic" method that led to cognitive growth.

To make this clear, I must explain how Piaget described his task as a developmental psychologist. In his densely packed Unesco book on the human sciences (Piaget, 1974a), he characterizes knowledge achievement as divisible into four "methodological domains." The first was the nomothetic, guided by decentered (i.e., objectified) analytic experimentation. This included his own version of development psychology, and its domain was the development of nomothetic understanding in the young. A second domain was historical, "the purpose of which is to reconstitute and interpret the unfolding of all manifestations of social life across time" (Piaget, 1974a, p. 28). The third domain was the "legal sciences" which explore norms or "duties" (*sollen*) without regard to their causes. And finally there is the fourth, the philosophical, whose aim is to coordinate all forms of knowledge into a "concept of the world."

To repeat what I said, I think Piaget, as a self-styled nomothetic scientist, saw his task as studying the growth of nomothetic knowledge construction in the child. And even in that domain, his views betray a striking methodological, anticultural individualism. His neglect of intersubjectivity (and culture altogether) was not so much inadvertent, I think, as principled and self-imposed.

Piaget's choice of formal logic as a model of human mental operations also distanced him from the historical cultural domain, where interpretive cognition prevails. It obviously led him to neglect any mental operations not subsumable in a well-formed logical calculus – notably those *hermeneutic* operations involved in "reconstituting and interpreting" the social world. Some critics, like Stephen Toulmin (1978), even accused him of believing that children could simply reinvent the culture. Yet, on the other hand, Piaget's early work on moral development reveals a sensitivity to the growing child's *reinterpretation* of extant cultural norms, even if he shows little interest in interpretation as a mental process in its own right. So the gap in Piagetian theory includes intersubjectivity and the forms of culture that rest on its operations – matters to which we will revert later.

Vygotsky's perspective

Now to Vygotsky. Extracting the foundations of his theory is not easy, for his was not a hypothetico-deductive style, whether for lack of time (he began his systematic study of psychology at 28, and after much official harassment, died of tuberculosis before 40), or perhaps because his early literary formation inclined him more toward intuitive *aperçus* than propositional derivation. But I think far more important than either of those was Vygotsky's form of revolutionary political activism, which I will come to presently. So be it.

While for Vygotsky, as for Piaget, mind mediates between the external world and individual experience, Vygotsky never conceived of mind as expressing a logical calculus. Mind, rather, comprised process for endowing experience with *meaning*. Meaning making, in Vygotsky's view of the matter, requires not only language but a grasp of the cultural context in which *language is used*. Mental development consists in mastering higher order, culturally embodied symbolic structures, each of which may incorporate or even displace what existed before, as with algebra absorbing and replacing arithmetic. These higher order systems are cultural products. As instruments of mind, they do not mature exclusively through endogenous principles of growth. They are not only appropriated from the tool kit of the culture and its language, but depend upon continued social interaction. Consequently, the most central question for Vygotsky is how a culture's symbolic tools manage through social interaction to get from "outside" into our "inside" repertory of thought.

Indeed, "internalization," though never fully explicated by Vygotsky, is perhaps the major deus ex machina in his system. But unlike learning by association, internalization also implied systematicity for him: e.g., once internalization occurs, "....he child does not have to restructure separately all of his earlier concepts, which indeed would be a Sisyphean labor. Once a new structure has been incorporated into his thinking...it gradually spreads to the older concepts *as they are drawn into the intellectual operations of the higher type*" (Vygotsky, 1962, p. ix, italics added). But "being drawn into" such operations also relies upon social exchange, suggesting that some of the systematicity of growth resides in the systematic nature of discourse and culture itself.

For Vygotsky, mental life first expresses itself in interaction with others. The results of such interactions then become internalized and enter the stream of thought. Since social interaction is principally constituted and mediated by speech, what gets internalized into the child's stream of thought are the meanings and forms generated in verbal exchange which themselves are products of the broader cultural-historical system. Thus equipped, mind not only expresses the culture but, by virtue of the generative powers of these systems, like language, it is able to be "free" or to go beyond being a mere slave of the prevailing cultural order – a liberationist view to which we'll return in a moment.

The generative powers of language-in-mind, Vygotsky tells us, depend upon consciousness. But for him (as for Piaget) its modus operandi was never well developed. Vygotsky's views about consciousness obviously had deep political implications in those times, a kind of Marxist ideological hot potato, for his views provoked an official "battle of consciousness" that went on for years, even after his death (Cole and Scribner, 1974; Joravsky, 1989). But we need to consider one more matter before we can clarify what might have been meant.

That matter is the Zone of Proximal Development (ZPD), so central to Vygotskian theory. To put it simply, the ZPD is the gap between what one can do on one's own, unassisted, and what one can do with hints and aids from a knowledgeable other. The ZPD is where pedagogy and intersubjectivity enter the Vygotskian picture. But how does pedagogy work? Through shielding a learner from distraction, by forefronting crucial features of a problem, by sequencing the steps to understanding, by promoting negotiation, or by some other form of "scaffolding" the task at hand (Brown and Campione, 1990; Bruner *et al.*, 1977; Tharp and Gallimore, 1988; Tomasello *et al.*, 1993; Wood *et al.*, 1976)? How does the helper/tutor know what the learner needs? Here, intersubjectivity enters – alas, more implied than explicated. Most important, however, the ZPD poses specific questions as to how culture gets internalized by the mediation of others (Shore, 1996). As Tomasello *et al.* (1993) point out, the very transmission of culture depends upon (a) some principled concordance between a learner's capabilities and what the culture has on offer; (b) some person in the culture, a tutor, who can sense what a learner needs and delivers it, and (c) some shared agreement about how such an inter-subjective arrangement is supposed to work canonically in *this particular culture*, as in Rogoff *et al.*'s (1993) recent comparative study of Salt Lake City middle-class 5 year olds and their mothers in contrast to their counterparts in a Guatemalan Mayan Indian town. To put it bluntly, the ZPD recognizes that *Homo* is the only species that uses teaching in any systematic way and asks what it takes for somebody to teach or be taught by another.

So, if Piaget was preoccupied with the invariant order of mental development, Vygotsky was on his part preoccupied with how others provide the cultural patterning that makes the process of development possible. But please note that neither was blind to the other alternative – as with Vygotsky's belief that mental development moved from mastery of concrete particulars to higher mastery of the abstract, or in Piaget's belief that progress to the propositional stage required cultural support (Piaget and Inhelder, 1958).

How relate these two great systematists to each other? Certainly not by ignoring their profound differences. For even their "founding missions" were incommensurate. Piaget grew up on the edges of Neuchatelois Protestant theology, where, as we know from Vidal's (1994) study, he began with a passion to "naturalize" or secularize religious views about the unity of creation. His passion for systematicity expressed itself even in his boyhood studies of mollusks. In early adulthood, his passion for systemic order recentered itself in the epistemic domain and in how the growing mind achieved a connected, systematic world view.

Vygotsky, by contrast, grew up in a world of revolution, a world of excited promise. His Russia and Piaget's Switzerland could not have been further apart. Nor could Vygotsky's skeptical, rather Jewish, literary irony, be further removed from Piaget's more Protestant and intellectually stoic single-mindedness. Even Vygotsky's Marxism had a subjectivist, interpretive feel – more like Gramsci, say, than like the doctrinaire Russian nomenklatura of his day. Like Gramsci, he believed that culture shaped mind for hegemonic ends, and that a change in the cultural order could liberate consciousness from hegemonic bonds (Gramsci, 1995). For him, *nature* was there to be used and transformed by *culture*. "Culture," he says in an early paper, "does not produce anything apart from that which is given by nature. But it transforms nature to suit the ends of man" (Vygotsky, 1929, p. 418), and this transformation is effected by the child "mastering...the habits and forms of cultural behavior, the cultural methods of reasoning" (Vygotsky, 1929, p. 415).

I cannot stress enough the liberationist quality of Vygotsky's Marxism. But it was not that unusual in his day. Many Russian literary intellectuals saw Marxism as a lever for prying the Russian mind from its Procrustean bed of "orientalism" and Orthodoxy, its feudal patriarchalism (Joravsky, 1989). Indeed, Luria's (1976) renowned study on the impact of collectivist farming, inspired by Vygotsky, was typical of this liberationist optimism. Even Lenin's Minister of Culture, the charismatic and later discredited Lunacharsky, urged Russian poets and painters to liberate the Russian people with the "Shock of the New" (Hughes, 1991). Vygotsky himself, in *Language and Thought*, even likens Marxism to earlier "scientific" revolutions that freed man from superstitions about nature.

What better instrument than the ZPD for assuring that promise of almost limitless growth? It served equally well as activist doctrine and scientific theory. We had it in us naturally to move ahead, given the right social arrangements and opportunities. Perhaps Piaget's invariant order of growth served a dual function for him as well, joining his earlier metaphysical-religious convictions with his later scientific ones. Each was surely a child of his time and place.

Fruitful incommensurability

But looking ahead, we all know that any overall theory of mental development (assuming there will ever be such) needs to account *both* for why mental development is so often steadfastly invariant, so resistant to inspired pedagogy, so limited in transfer, and, as well, for why mental development sometimes leaps swiftly, brilliantly, opportunistically, even dizzyingly. So should we try to combine Piaget and Vygotsky into a common system in the hope of explaining both extremes of this astonishing human variability? I think that would be naive. The justifiable pedagogical optimism of cultural revolutionaries is *not* just the sunny side of the equally justified stoicism of principled pedagogical "realism." The two perspectives grow from different world views that generate different pedagogical strategies, different research paradigms, perhaps even different epistemologies, at least for a while. Better each go their own way. Let the Dionysian partisan activists specialize in finding the levers of change – e.g., how collaborative learning environments empower learners, what scaffolding helps learners over what seemed before to be "innate" constraints. But also let the Apollonian realists explore "natural" constraints and seek out the regularities they impose on development, wherever found in whatever culture. The counterpoint of the two is surely what creates excitement and invention. I think history bears me out. My dear friend, Thomas Kuhn, was not alone in celebrating the energizing counterpoint of conflicting paradigms. It suffices that each side know what the other is up to, to form an "epistemic loyal opposition" for each other.

But there is a deeper reason for scorning facile reconciliation. The two perspectives under discussion may represent two incommensurate approaches to development. One is concerned with knowledge in the light of its universal or inherent *validity* and *verifiability*; the other with knowledge as local, context bound, particular (Smith, 1995, p. 9). In classic terms, one studies thought in its nomothetic and explanatory manifestation, the other in its idiographic and interpretive expression. Niels Bohr's maxim again: the opposite of great truths may also be true?

Let me, finally, explore this possibility – that the two approaches constitute two principled, incommensurate ways by which human beings make sense of the world – by *proof* and universal logical necessity, and by *interpretive* reconstruction of relevant circumstances. The first, the nomothetic, aims to convert intuitions and hunches about recurrent regularities into causal statements by the use of logical and empirical test procedures. Its outcome eventually takes the form of robust scientific theories, preferably framed in logico-mathematical terms. But certain domains of knowledge seem not to be amenable to such standard nomothetic science, particularly domains in which human beings are transactionally involved, reacting to each other in anticipation of how the other might react to their reaction as in daily life and in history.

To comprehend such circumstances, we characteristically use another way of making sense. Its objective seems less to prove or verify than to construct a meaningful *narrative*, or story. If verificational sense making seems better to fit the world of nature, the narrative mode seems a better fit to the world of human social interaction. Rather than testing our intuitions about the causal or logical basis of experienced regularities as in the nomothetic mode, we seek in the second mode to explicate experience by converting it into a narrative structure. *Causal necessity* in the first mode is matched by a sense of *narrative necessity* in the second. But narrative necessity, unlike logical or inductive proof, does not yield unique or preclusive descriptions: there can be several equally compelling stories about the same set of "events." And since these "events," so-called, can and usually do include the indeterminable intentional states of people involved in the story, they may never be subject to total confirmation. It was a positivist tenet that narratives could be neatly divided into the true and the fictional. But that innocent binary has fared poorly in our times. True stories are as shaped by narrative necessities as fictional ones. Even in the writing of history, you cannot conceal an underlying narrative by recounting the story in presumably testable, nomothetic "covering laws" drawn from "scientific sociology" (Danto, 1985; Hempel, 1965). For narratives, in their very nature, create the shape of the events you must deal with, make them their "functions" (Propp, 1968).

We know now that narratives construct a social world that, in Durkheim's (1915) terms, has exteriority and constraint. They are constitutive of the realities they depict. Stories not only generate social realities, but become hardened into institutional structures that then perpetuate and enforce them – as with legal codes enforced by police powers. For narratives inevitably presuppose norms and legitimacy, as when (in the law) certain stories with certain outcomes are taken to be matters of "state interest." But all narratives, not only "law narratives" recount how a norm or standard was breached or might be breached, how that breach created a condition requiring redress. Plots, episodes, and characters, moreover, are virtually always tokens of more general types, local tokens that fit a more universal genre, even making them translatable from one culture to another. This suggests that the so-called necessity of narrative is more universal than sometimes thought, though different from the logical necessity of formal proof. Whether this narrative necessity is, as it were, something inherent in the human condition or in mind itself, whether it is inherent in the universal structure of language, whether it grows out of human prehistory – none of this is clear, though all have come to be better understood in recent decades.

Following von Wright (1971), we say that the method of proof yields *explanation* with its attendant benefits of predictability, easy falsifiability, and replicability. The method of narrative authentication yields *understanding* after the fact, and rests upon interpretation. We know now that the two are not antithetic to each other, that explaining and interpreting have different developmental trajectories, have different social uses, and must be studied by quite different methods. We have also come to understand, as already noted, that they cannot be reduced one to the other, nor is it clear whether they derive from some deeper set of common principles. All that we can say is that causal explanations can often be reframed in narrative terms, just as stories can be reformulated as sets of testable propositions concerning causation or contingency. In such reframings, however, the structure of the initial account is destroyed, though the initial and transformed versions may be recognized (perhaps mistakenly) as "referring" to the "same" events. The two modes of knowing, while distinctive and irreducible, bear an anomalous relation to each other that still defies full epistemological analysis (Bruner, 1985, 1990, 1993, 1995, 1996a,b).

Piaget was principally (though not entirely) preoccupied with the ontogenesis of *causal explanation* and its *logical and empirical justification.* This was even the focus of his masterful studies of moral development, a topic that does not ordinarily lend itself to such an approach. Vygotsky, on the other hand, was principally (though not entirely) concerned with the ontogenesis of *interpretation* and *understanding.* Piaget devised methods of inquiry and a theory appropriate to analyzing how children explain and how they justify their explanations – and did it brilliantly. The price he paid, of course, was the usual price one pays for ignoring context, transactional dynamics, background knowledge, and cultural variation. To grasp how somebody interprets or understands something, which was Vygotsky's concern, requires that we take into account their cultural and linguistic background and the context in which they find themselves both "in the small," in the sense of a particular communicative situation, and "in the large" of a patterned cultural system. Vygotsky's emphasis, accordingly, was on situated meanings and on situated meaning-making, which inevitably generates a cultural-historical approach. The two approaches, in consequence, diverged increasingly as they matured – perhaps, some would say, to a stage of incommensurability.

I think, and I hope you agree, that we are enormously fortunate to have had two such rich theoretical accounts as an inheritance from our mentors, even if they prove to be incommensurate. Just as depth perception requires a disparity between two views of a scene, so in the human sciences the same may be true: depth demands disparity. So I conclude this excursion into the thought of these two great developmental psychologists with a salute to their profound difference. To have had either of them as a guide would have been a gift. To have had them both is stronger stuff, and even though it may at times seem overwhelming, we are the better for it.

Notes

1   A keynote address delivered in Geneva on 15 September 1996 at a joint meeting of the "Growing Mind Conference" in honor of the centennial of Jean Piaget's birth, and the "Vygotsky-Piaget Conference" of the IInd Congress of Socio-Cultural Research, honoring both Lev Vygotsky's and Piaget's centennial.
2   Both Piaget and Vygotsky were very explicit on this point. See Piaget (1974a, pp. 28ff); Bruner's (1987) preface to volume one of Vygotsky's collected works; and also Joravsky (1989, p. 262ff).
3   Piaget's view of the roles of tools and technology in shaping the growing mind, strikingly different from the Baconian one, is discussed in his *Prise de conscience* (1974b); and in his *Réussir et comprendre* (1974c). The very first paragraph of the Preface of the latter volume implicitly casts the Baconian idea into doubt by a citation from one of its latter-day critics (cf. *Réussir et comprendre*, p. v.)
4   Piaget has always been ambiguous about whether logical structures and operations were evidenced *in* the child's repertory of acts or whether, rather, they characterized Piaget's

form of a theory of the child's mind. The "existence" of such structures *in* the child's mind requires corroboration by reference to specific behaviors that instantiate *all* the specific properties entailed by the structure. That task was never undertaken by Piaget and, indeed, it is dubious whether such a claim could ever be corroborated, as Feldman and Toulmin (1976) point out, given what is entailed by the idea of logical structure. Certainly, recent research on children's "theories of mind" do not corroborate claims about "Genevan" formal logical structures in the mind of the child. Moreover, it is as philosophically implausible to claim that there can be *one and only one* mental structure operative in anybody's mind as to claim there is one and only one "mathematical" structure that accounts for nature. The first and still the most cogent critique of the Piagetian position that a "logically structured" set of operations exists "in the mind" rather than in the theorist's account of mind is to be found in Feldman and Toulmin (1976).

References

Brown, A. L. & Campione, J. C. (1990). Communities of learning and thinking, or a context by any other name. In D. Kuhn (Ed.), *Developmental perspectives on teaching and learning thinking skills (Vol. 21, Contributions in human development)*. Basel: Karger.

Bruner, J. S. (1985). Narrative and paradigmatic modes of thought. In E. Eisner (Ed.), *Learning and teaching the ways of knowing* (84th Yearbook of the National Society for the Study of Education). Chicago, IL: University of Chicago Press.

Bruner, J. (1987). Prologue to the English edition. In R. W. Rieber & A. S. Carton (Eds), *The collected works of L. S. Vygotsky, Vol. 1*. New York: Plenum Publishing.

Bruner, J. (1990). *Acts of meaning*. Cambridge, MA: Harvard University Press.

Bruner, J. (1993). Explaining and interpreting: Two ways of using mind. In G. Harman (Ed.), *Conceptions of the human mind: Essays in honor of George A. Miller*. Hillsdale, NJ: Lawrence Erlbaum Associates.

Bruner, J. (1995). The Astington-Olson Complaint: A Comment. *Human Development. 38*, 203–213.

Bruner, J. (1996a). *The culture of education*. Cambridge, MA: Harvard University Press.

Bruner, J. (1996b). Meyerson aujourd'hui: Quelques réflexions sur la psychologie culturelle. In F. Parot (Ed.), *Essays in honor of I. Meyerson*. Paris: Presses Universitaires de France.

Bruner, J. S., Caudill, E., & Ninio, A. (1997). Language and experience. In R. S. Peters (Ed.), *John Dewey reconsidered* (The John Dewey Lectures, University of London, 1975). London: Routledge & Kegan Paul.

Cole, M. & Scribner, S. (1974). *Culture and thought: A psychological introduction*. New York: Wiley.

Danto, A. (1985). *Narration and knowledge*. New York: Columbia University Press.

Doise, W. & Mugny, G. (1979). Individual and collective conflicts of centration in cognitive development. *European Journal of Social Psychology, 9*, 105–109.

Durkheim, E. (1915). *The elementary forms of the religious life*. London: MacMillan.

Feldman, C. F. & Toulmin, S. (1976). Logic and the theory of mind. In J. K. Cole (Ed.), *Nebraska Symposium on Motivation 1975*. Lincoln: University of Nebraska Press.

Gramsci, A. (1975). *Letters from prison* (L. Lawner, Trans.). London: Jonathan Cape.

Hempel, C. G. (1965). The function of general laws in history. In C. G. Hempel (Ed.), *Aspects of scientific explanation: And other essays in the philosophy of science*. New York: Free Press.

Hirschfeld, L. A. & Gelman, S. A. (Eds) (1994). *Mapping the mind: Domain specificity in cognition and culture*. Cambridge, UK: Cambridge University Press.

Hughes, R. (1991). *The shock of the new* (Rev. edn). New York: Knopf.

Joravsky, D. (1989). *Russian psychology: A critical history*. New York: Basil Blackwell.

Luria, A. R. (1976). *Cognitive development: Its cultural and social foundations*. Cambridge, MA: Harvard University Press.

Piaget, J. (1974a). *The place of the sciences of man in the system of sciences*. New York: Harper & Row.

Piaget, J. (1974b). *Prise de conscience*. Paris: Presses Universitaires.

Piaget, J. (1974c). Réussir et comprendre. Paris: Presses Universitaires.

Piaget, J. & Inhelder, B. (1958). *The growth of logical thinking from childhood to adolescence: An essay on the construction of formal operational structures* (A. Parsons & S. Milgram, Trans.). New York: Basic Books.

Propp, V. (1968). *Morphology of the folktale* (2nd edn). Austin, TX: University of Texas Press.

Rogoff, B., Mistry, J., Göncü, A., & Mosier, C. (1993). Guided participation in cultural activity by toddlers and caregivers. *Monographs of the Society for Research in Child Development*, Serial No. 236, 58(8).

Shore, B. (1996). *Culture in mind*. New York: Oxford University Press.

Smith, L. (1995). Preface. In J. Piaget (Ed.), *Sociological studies*. London: Routledge.

Tharp, R. G. & Gallimore, R. (1988). *Rousing minds to life: Teaching, learning, and schooling in social context*. Cambridge, UK: Cambridge University Press.

Tomasello, M., Kruger, A. C., & Ratner, H. H. (1993). Cultural learning. *Behavioral and Brain Sciences, 16*(3), 495–552.

Toulmin, S. (September 28, 1978). The Mozart of psychology. *New York Review of Books, 25*(14), 51–57.

Vidal, F. (1994). *Piaget before Piaget*. Cambridge, MA: Harvard University Press.

Vygotsky, L. (1929). The problem of the cultural development of the child. *Journal of Genetic Psychology, 36*, 415–434.

Vygotsky, L. (1962). *Thought and language*. Cambridge, MA: MIT Press.

Wood, D., Bruner, J. S., & Ross, G. (1976). The role of tutoring in problem solving. *Journal of Child Psychology and Psychiatry, 17*, 89–100.

von Wright, G. H. (1971). *Explanation and understanding*. Ithaca, NY: Cornell University Press.

CHAPTER 17

INFANCY AND CULTURE
A story

S. Chaiklin, M. Hedegaard, and U. Jensen (eds), *Activity Theory and Social Practice* (1999), Denmark: Aarhus University Press

I

Never mind the long, long history of ideas about infancy. Philippe Ariès (1962) has told us enough to make us fully aware that *any* story we tell about human infancy grows as much out of ideological convictions and cultural beliefs as out of observation – whether, for example, it is original sin to be redeemed as in the Christian version of infancy, or innate rationality, that is destined to be saved from superstition as in the Enlightenment, or primary process to be saved by the reality principle as in Freudian theory. What I have to say will, doubtless, also have to be examined for ideological presuppositions – submitted to close scrutiny, to use a severe term from Anglo-Saxon jurisprudence. And that is as it should be, even though I will cite buckets of experimental evidence to make my points! So here goes: the story of early infancy that has grown over the last couple of decades – or at least my version of it and, as such, inevitably a reflection of our contemporary cultural scene of which I am an inevitable part. For how can anybody escape that!

II

I shall give my account, tell my story of infancy in terms of crucial research landmarks. And the opening chapter begins with the research of Bill Kessen (1965) and his group working on infant attention: infants deploying their attention *selectively* and under their own control, not just as push-me-pull-you creatures of the environment. The prototypical experiment is an actual one by Kessen (1963), showing that the older the infants, the more often and the longer they choose to look at more informationally pregnant, asymmetric or irregular checkerboard patterns. What *this study* found was that human information processing capacity not only increases with age, which is old hat, but that infants *select* pieces of the world to attend to that fit their capacity limits and then work within those limits. In a word, human beings dislike dull banality from the start, but they also dislike the confusion of overload as well and from the start work avoid both. Now, in those distant days of the 1960s, this finding was, so say, so *proactively* agentive, so downright *cognitive* as to upset the applecart about infancy as a "blooming buzzing confusion" with which we'd been saddled by our forebears. I was so bowled over, indeed, that I hopped right on the train to New Haven to have a look! Could it be that young infants were like *other* human beings! Not altogether so, obviously, but though so to make us rethink our view of the passive infant.

Then came the discovery that infants were capable not only of monitoring their own attention, but quite capable as well of acting instrumentally to *alter* the stimulus world around them to make it fit their attentional requirements. All they needed was the means. Hanus Papousek (1961) duly demonstrated just that. His young infants easily mastered the trick of turning their heads twice in a row to one side in order to cause exciting jazzy lights to flash over their cribs for a few seconds. Only operant conditioning? But what kind of a reinforcer is a jazzy light bank? Infants, it turned out, were interested in a little visual excitement, and quickly got skilled in knowing how to get it – and possibly to control it or use it to their advantage. Hmmm.

Aren't cultural Zeitgeists curious! Just about that time, studies by Krech and Rosenzweig (Rosenzweig, 1966) began demonstrating that young rats raised in a Luna Park environment that was full of engaging sensorimotor temptations grew up much smarter than their litter mates raised in duller settings. Sure enough, for Gig Levine (Levine & Alpert, 1959), intending to raise animals germ-free and stress-free to see if that affected their later immune reactions, found that animals raised in dull aseptic peacefulness grew up much stupider (and more disease prone at that) than their *louche*, communally cage-dwelling littermate controls. Hmmm, again.

We all began having second thoughts about the older folk psychology's claims about passive infants in a world of "blooming, buzzing confusion." How had such an idea ever got started? If young kids started life passively in a self-made, feature-less *Ganzfeld* of nothingness, how did they ever get out of it? How do you ever get something from nothing? Logic dictates *ihil ex nihilo*. A baby has got to have enough structure to provide some working standard of clarity if she's to attend selectively to the world. Without it, she'd be lost. Babies simply could not be without some conception of structure, simplicity, order.

That thought led my then research assistant, Ilse Kalnins, and I to devise in experiment that, we thought, would put the matter to the test (Kalnins & Bruner, 1973). It did not take much. We devised a pacifier nipple, sucking on which would generate an electrical current by compressing a four-legged strain gauge, the more sucking, the more current. God bless piezo-electricity! The current could then be used to control various features of the world – in this case, to control the focus of a picture of a motherly, smiling woman's face projected on a screen at the infant's eye level. In one condition, sucking on the nipple brought the motherly face from out of focus into focus, the picture drifting out of focus when the baby stopped sucking. In the other condition, an in-focus picture was driven out of focus by sucking, the picture moving automatically back into focus when sucking stopped. The long and short of it was that babies sucked briskly to produce a clear picture, but would desist from sucking when it caused the picture to blur (and desisting is not easy when you're a six-month-old performing for a mad psychologist in a clean-smelling, unfamiliar room). So much for blooming buzzing confusion! (I recall a visiting New Delhi pediatrician who was observing one of our subjects through a one-way screen. "That's impossible," she said on emerging, "a baby's world is a buzzing blooming confusion.") *Sic transit gloria mundi.*

By now, of course, we are well into the 1960s, into America's New Frontier under the restless President Johnson, into Head Start and into newspaper articles about the unique place of infancy and early childhood in shaping life – like one in a series of three written by John Davies in *The Times of London* on changing views of human nature. He singled out the "new idea of competence in infancy" as among the most revolutionary. I mention this here to remind you that where the original nature of humankind is concerned, knowledge and culture quickly begin walking hand in hand. Something deep was happening in Western culture (of which more later), and research was changing with it – whether leading it or following it, we cannot know.

The next chapter in the story takes a fascinating turn: it is about *intersub-jectivity*, how we read each others' minds and when and how this process starts. It's a topic that began engaging us as a result of new efforts to understand the blight of child-hood autism, but it quickly grew to encompass matters as diverse as the evolution of higher primates and the very nature of human enculturation. I and my gang of irrepressible graduate students and postdocs at Oxford were up to our ears in it – Alison Gopnik, the two Andys, Meltzoff and Whiten, Alan Leslie, Mike Scaife, Paul Harris, George Butterworth, to mention only some of their boisterous num-ber. And if we ever tired of the subject, there was always Colwyn Trevarthen on a quick visit from Edinburgh to get us back into it. We spent hours debating about it, convinced that culture-using human beings could not possibly have entered a culture unless they were able to "read the minds" of those around them.

The experiment that served as the trope was one that Mike Scaife and I (Scaife & Bruner, 1975) did: infants, we soon discovered, follow an adult's line of regard in search of what the adult is attending to. Yes, they are interested in the world, but *particularly* interested in those aspects of the world that are shared with others. In the twinkling of an eye, the old philosophical problem of Other Minds got trans-ferred (to be parochial Oxford) from Merton Street to South Parks Road, from the philosopher's study to the psychologist's lab – and soon it was to go beyond there. Within a decade, a thriving cottage industry of baby labs took it over and "theories of mind" became the great growth stock of developmental research.[1]

The emphasis had shifted from the competent *solo* infant mastering the natural world virtually on her own to a concern with how infants (and all of us!) ever come to understand each other's minds sufficiently well to live in a human culture. And it is still shifting in that direction. In some ways, this was not altogether a new concern. The post-World War II *culture-and-personality* craze moved in this direc-tion. But it was so enchanted and enslaved by the previous primary-process dogma regarding infancy that it quandered its attention on bowel training, weaning rituals, and never got round to the intersubjectivity issue.

Cognitive research on autism reopened the gate, the wedge study surely being Alan Leslie's (1991) on the symptomatic absence of pretend play in young autists. Why were autistic children so deficient in pretending? His powerful claim was that autism so seriously destroyed an infant's or child's grasp of other minds, that it was impossible for sufferers even to *pretend* to be an Other. This work was followed by a flood of research elaborating the many particulars of his claim (see Baron-Cohen, Tager-Flusberg, & Cohen, 1993; Happe, 1994; and Sigman & Capps, 1997, for a sampling of this fascinating literature).

The work on "theory of mind," as it soon came to be called, had an impact far beyond the pathogenesis of autism. It reawakened speculation in many less specialized fields, particularly in primatology where there had already been some challenging exploratory work on the subject – by Chance and Jolly (1970), by Menzel (1974), by Premack and Woodruff (1978). Take as an example Menzel's (1974) early work, showing that young primates in a one-acre field anticipated the line of *travel* of one of their number known by them to know where food had been hidden in the field. They did it by monitoring the know-it-all's *gaze* direction and anticipating where he might be going. Or take the work on the use of *deliberate deceit* in primate social interaction (Byrne & Whiten, 1991): How could higher primates *deliberately* deceive a conspecific unless they had some notion of other minds?

But the real explosion surely began with Sue Savage-Rumbaugh's study on the *enculturation* of the now famous young bonobo, Kanzi (Savage-Rumbaugh *et al.*, 1993). To make a long and incomplete story short and much too conclusive, what has been found is that Kanzi had not only mastered Von Glasersfeld's "chip" language (which extended his communicative range enormously) but, equally to the point, he had been brought by his human handlers to a new level of appreciation of their "intentional states:" their intentions, desires, expectations, beliefs. Kanzi had, in the *gemütlich* human intersubjectivity of the Georgia State Language Center, taken a giant step toward *enculturation*. To get a creature to that state, in a word, requires "treating somebody like a human in a human setting," which means treating them as if they had mental states and as if they knew that *you* had mental states you expected *them* to understand, to paraphrase the letter I received from Michael Tomasello (personal communication, 1992) in the midst of this work. It also means appreciating that intentional states mediate what we *do*. To be enculturated, to put it grandly, means to come to share the folk psychology of your culture.

And that places some odd and seemingly incidental observations in a new light, like, for example, Meltzoff and Gopnik's (1993) report that new parents take especial delight in "discovering" that their young babies, in their words "have minds, just like us." Whether they do or they don't at the outset, parents seem to know intuitively just the right thing to do to get them there, to promote enculturation. And believe me, there are plenty of data that should convince you that you'd better act as if your baby has something in mind! For, if you act otherwise, say by staying "poker faced" in response to your young baby's changing expressions (which itself is difficult to do), you will quickly produce tears and distress, as Stechler and Latz (1966) showed many years ago. Even Kanzi eventually got frustrated by his "natural-raised" sister's lack of intersubjective responsiveness – just like a "real kid" (Savage-Rumbaugh *et al.*, 1993). For let us not forget that Kanzi shares enough of the humanoid genome to make him more than a little sensitive to our human way of enculturation – but *only* if he has been exposed to distinctively human upbringing.

Now to the final but incomplete chapter of our story. We humans seem geared from the start to deal with each others' intentions, at least to be enormously sensitive to them in their various guises. Positivist philosophers, like Dan Dennett (1991), may be embarassed by human intentional states, deep-freezing them as an "intentional stance," but eighteen-month-olds are not the least so. I refer again to a Meltzoff (1995) finding. Infants imitate the *intended* behavior of an Other and not its surface properties. In brief, if the outcome of an adult's act is thwarted or blocked, infants of eighteen months will imitate it *as if it had been carried through right to its goal*. Human infants do easily and naturally (and to the delight of their careers) what Kanzi does stumblingly, and only if he has the luck of being advised by that gang of very human and dedicated graduate students and postdocs at the Georgia State Language Lab.

Now in a fundamental way, culture requires a sensitivity not simply to that others do, but what they *intend* to do, not to what they say but what they *mean* – how they intend their utterance to be taken. It is crucial, then, at the start infants be sensitive to intention and intentionality.[2] If they were not, they could not find their way into the complex network of monical mutual expectancies that characterizes human culture. Or, at last, that is how it seems to us from our contemporary perspective on how the world works.

III

That is the gist of the story I want to tell – still very much infinished, but definitely getting there. Our cultural historian friends *love* it of course. In it, they see the "discovery" of the informationally active, socially interactive infant mind as reflecting our departure from the Industrial Age with its machine models, and they also see in it our entry into the new Information Age where cognition, symbol use, and social networking are crucial. No doubt they're right and perhaps that's why it's so easy to tell the story in French! Je veux dire, tout simplement, que telle l'histoire soit presque irrésistible. Et surement, c'est vrai dans un certain sens. Le bebé passive et sans aucun esprit actif a devenu demodé dans le climat culturel d'aujourd'hui. Mais...

But I suspect there's another moral to the story too. I suspect that when one enters into a new revolutionary period, as we surely have, a sure sign is that we look afresh at what we mean by the original nature of man and how that nature expresses itself from the start. Infancy research has become (yet again) the new arena for battling out *the* classic and enduring issues of the changing culture – human agency, the nature of interdependence, the limits of responsibility, the scope of human meaning making, the interaction of genes and the environment. So it was in the seed-days of Soviet communisms – the battles over consciousness, reflection, language. But one scarcely needs modern examples to make the point. But so it has always been. Think of the elaborate eschatology of Christianity about Man's original sin, or recall Marcel Mauss on the functions of *rites de passage* in primitive societies.

No surprise, then, that there is something uniquely consciousness-raising and even politically compelling about reflection and research on immaturity and its potentials. It seems able to move mountains, even political ones. I still can't believe what happened when Urie Bronfenbrenner and I first proposed Head Start to the White House Office of Economic Opportunity. "Impossible, hadn't we ever read the Constitution on who controls schools?" Today it is political suicide for a Congressman to suggest cutting it back.

How does psychology enter the ideological issues that are constantly being generated by the dialectical nature of all cultures?[3] I do not mean pop or partisan psychology, but honest-to-god, hardworking psychology of the kind we do and of the kind I've been talking about. Does it just naturally arise out of what we in the West like to call "scientific curiosity" so that it just happens to be there, as it were, right in the nick of time? I deeply doubt that. Scientific curiosity does not just feed on itself. It lives as well on background presuppositions, inevitably religious-metaphysical in origin, about the nature of nature and the nature of man. At the heart of every coherent system of cultural beliefs, there lies a conception of man, of his perfectibility and weakness and what conditions limit or promote these. Living in a culture predisposes us to search for and even to find *empirical* confirmations of these deep beliefs. We just get clever in how we design our studies and set up our experiments, *clever* not dishonest. But culture, as I have argued elsewhere, is not a mould into which thought is poured. It is a dialectic between the canonical expectable and the imaginatively possible. The Fugitive Slave Law of 1793, for all the cruelty it spawned in antebellum America, also spawned the imaginative possibilities of Harriet Beecher Stowe's *Uncle Tom's Cabin*. Monarchical devotion to the canonical Divine Rights of Kings bred John Locke's *Treatise on Government* – and eventually the United States Constitution.

And so it is with honest psychology. Of course, given the authoritarian structure of the family, the newborn is passive. But as the culture changes, and with it the family, there are other ways of conceiving of infancy as well. Indeed, there even arises a temptation to look at infancy again. And see what happened?

So, just as great novels and great philosophical formulations can change a culture, often more swiftly than we think, so can new and powerful insights into the humanly human possible change our views what society is and what it could be. That is the dialectic of culture, and that is why cultural growth is sometimes saltatory rather than glacial in speed. We can never be quite sure about how delicately balanced are those two elements in a culture: the canonical, the expected, the normative, on the one hand, and imagined possible worlds on the other. And I am not the least daunted, let me note, that the story of early infancy that I've just told you partakes of an imagined possible world – despite all the *t* tests and *p* values at greater than 0.001.

What I am arguing is almost too self-evident to be contestable. Psychology is *not* outside of or *au dela de la culture*. It is a part of it. In that deep sense, it both reflects the culture and changes it. It is neither honest nor even coy to claim that all that drives us is The Truth. For the opposites of great truths, as that prescient Danish thinker Niels Bohr taught us, are often also true. Psychologists, like everybody else, are participants in their culture. We tell our stories *salve veritatis*, but *veritas* is rarely singular or, rather, never for long. For psychology too grows out of the life and the conditions of the culture. So, despite our *t* tests, we are in the midst of it – just like the historians who shape the past in order to presage the future or to justify the present, and just like all those other scholars who explore the possibilities inherent in being human.

So please take my story for what it is. Hear it both as real psychology and as a voice in the dialectic of culture.

Notes

1 For a thoughtful overview of this outpouring at mid-voyage, see Feldman (1992). Among the major books on the subject are several "overview" volumes, ranging from Astington's (1993) book on the then state of the art, through Perner (1991) to Wellman (1990).
2 I shall leave out of the discussion the issue of *intentionality* – what things and signs are intended to *stand for*. For a discussion of this broader issue see Bruner (1998).
3 For a fuller discussion of the "dialectic of culture" and its capacity to generate ideological conflict, see Amsterdam and Bruner (2000).

References

Amsterdam, A. G. & Bruner, J. (2000). *Minding the Law*. Cambridge, MA: Harvard University Press.

Ariés P. (1962). *Centuries of childhood: A social history of family life*. New York: Knopf.

Astington, J. (1993). *The child's discovery of the mind*. Cambridge, MA: Harvard University Press.

Baron-Cohen, S., Tager-Flusberg, H., & Cohen, D. J. (Eds) (1993). *Understanding other minds: Perspectives from autism*. New York: Oxford University Press.

Bruner, J. (1998). Rouies to reference, *Pragmatics and Cognition*, 6 (1–2), 209–227.

Byrne, R. W. & Whiten, A. (1991). Computation and mindreading in primate tactical deception. In A. Whiten (Ed.), *Natural theories of mind: Evolution, development, and simulation of everyday mindreading* (pp. 127–141). Oxford, England: Blackwell.

Chance, M. R. A. & Jolly, C. J. (1970). *Social groups of monkeys, apes, and men*. New York: Dutton

Dennett, D. C. (1991). *Consciousness explained*. Boston, MA: Little-Brown.

Feldman, C. (1992). The new theory of theory of mind. *Human Development*, 35, 107–117.

Happé, F. (1994). *Autism: An introduction to psychological theory*. London: University College Press.

Kalnins, I. & Bruner, J. (1973). The coordination of visual observation and instrumental behavior in early infancy. *Perception*, 2, 307–314.

Kessen, W. (1963). Research on the psychological development of infants: An overview, *Merrill-Palmer Quarterly, 9*, 83–94.

Kessen, W. (1965). *The child*. New York: Wiley.

Leslie, A. (1991). The theory of mind impairment in autism: evidence for a modular mechanism of development. In A. Whiten (Ed.), *Natural theories of mind: Evolution, development, and simulation of everyday mindreading* (pp. 63–78). Oxford, England: Blackwell.

Levine, S. & Alpert, M. (1959). Differential maturation of the central nervous system. *Archives of General Psychiatry, 1*, 403–405.

Meltzoff, A. N. (1995). Understanding the intentions of others: Reenactment of intended acts by 18-month-old children. *Developmental Psychology, 31*, 938–950.

Meltzoff, A. N. & Gopnik, A. (1993). The role of imitation in understanding persons and developing a theory of mind. In S. Baron-Cohen, H. Tager-Flusberg, & D. J. Cohen (Eds.), *Understanding other minds: Perspectives from autism* (pp. 335–366). New York: Oxford University Press.

Menzel, E. (1974). A group of young chimpanzees in a one-acre field. In M. Schrier & F. Stolnitz (Eds). *Behavior of non-human primates* (Vol. 5, pp. 83–153). New York: Academic Press.

Papousek, H. (1961). Conditioned head rotation reflexes in infants in the first months of life. *Acta Pædiatrica, 50*, 565–576.

Perner, J. (1991). *Understanding the representational mind*. Cambridge, MA: MIT Press.

Premack, D. & Woodruff, G. (1978). Does the chimpanzee have a theory of mind? *Brain and Behavioral Sciences, 1*, 515–526.

Rosenzweig, M. R. (1966). Environmental complexity, cerebral change, and behavior. *American Psychologist, 21*, 321–332.

Savage-Rumbaugh, E. S., Murphy, J., Sevcik, R. A., Brakke, K. E., Williams, S. L., & Rumbaugh, D. L. (1993). Language comprehension in ape and child. *Monographs of the Society for Research in Child Development, 58* (3–4, Serial No. 233).

Scaife, M. & Bruner, J. S. (1975). The capacity for joint visual attention in the infant. *Nature, 253*, 265–266.

Sigman, M. & Capps, L. (1997). *Children with autism: A developmental perspective*. Cambridge, MA: Harvard University Press.

Stechler, G. & Latz, E. (1966). Some observations on attention and arousal in the human infant. *Journal of the American Academy of Child Psychiatry, 5*, 517–525.

Wellman, H. (1990). *The child's theory of mind*. Cambridge, MA: MIT Press.

CHAPTER 18

SOME REFLECTIONS ON EDUCATION RESEARCH

E. Langemann and L. Shulman (eds), *Issues in Educational Research: Problems and Possibilities* (1999), San Francisco, CA: Jossey Bass

Education research as an empirical enterprise should have been quite unproblematic. Its progress might well have been expected to parallel what happened in other forms of "engineering," where theoretical knowledge is applied to practical problems – like biology applied to medicine or physics to bridge building. But its history, since its beginnings in the latter part of the nineteenth century, has been anything but. It does not seem to have succeeded in the usual way of establishing practices that eventually came to be taken for granted, like vaccination or pasteurization. If education research has established any taken-for-granted practice, it is the measurement of individual differences, whether in mental accomplishment or mental ability. But even this achievement was limited. Although the *reliability* of mental measurement has not been seriously questioned, its *validity* has been: you can give the test again and get the same scores, or show that the odd and even items yield comparable scores, but what do the scores *mean*?

Reservations about validity are telling, for they amount to saying, perhaps unjustly, that education research has "succeeded" by generating methods that may be pragmatically useful but lack theoretical depth – low-grade engineering at best. This shallowness was exemplified, for example, by the early school survey movement (Casswell, 1929), whose essential program was to measure, say, the "efficiency" of schools in teaching such subjects as spelling by doing census-like inquiries into the spelling performance of schoolchildren, with little if any concern for the theoretical niceties involved, say, in language acquisition. This has led critics to contend, perhaps unjustly, that education research has mainly been involved in redescribing culturally canonical common sense in more statistically reliable, pragmatically useful ways – "intelligence" as IQ, or musical aptitude as a score on the Seashore scale. The pragmatic utility of such procedures comes from their predicting fairly well how children will do in school or in their music classes, without shedding much light on the nature of intelligence or of musical talent as such.

Such seemingly rigorous redescriptions of canonical common sense, critics further claim, and again perhaps unjustly, often misinterpreted what they were intended to redescribe, with unfortunate results. Sometimes these misinterpretations are simply in the interest of seeming to be "scientific" – like arguing that test reliability is an "operational definition" of validity, as in the silly claim that "intelligence is what intelligence tests measure." But sometimes (if only inadvertently), such claims lead to grievous (if implicit) political and ideological consequences – as when the claim is made that IQ is "constant" over age and experience, a finding achieved by systematically eliminating test items from IQ tests that are known to change with "experience" and exposure to a culture's tool kit. In consequence, a short generation later, immigration quotas disfavoring Southern and Eastern European immigrants are justified by reference to their scoring norms on the Army's General Classification Test! (For a general account of the issues surrounding IQ, see Gould, 1981, and what is in effect a rejoinder to it, Herrnstein and Murray, 1994.)

It is not surprising, then, that test-based education research is condemned not only for its theoretical shallowness but for its political-ideological insensitivity. The charge has been that it is more often guided by short-term policy considerations (like classifying recruits in World War I) than by long-term aspirations to "improve the educational system" or "realize human potential."

So despite its modest achievements, the findings of education research have frequently fueled bitter controversies – ideological and political ones at that. One expects of such research that it might shed light not only on the nature of mind but on how to cultivate its powers and sensibilities. And the critic's claim is that education research became so enamored of its own self-made image as a "rigorous science" that it opted for a dispositional theory of mind that left little room for questions about how its powers and sensibilities are cultivated – as with its mantras about the so-called constancy and heritability of the IQ. In so doing, it left itself open to attacks on even its principal methodological premise. Is mental ability, whether specialized or general, really amenable to measurement by standardized tests employing uniform criteria? What of cultural diversity? Do abilities always express themselves in the same way? Do different cultural settings require the same kinds of sensibility? And besides, given that these questions are at all contestable, who finally sets the "official" uniformity standards for assessing mental abilities? While these are, as it were, all technical questions, they are ideological ones as well. And in the eyes of many critics, the education research community has been notoriously blind about the lethal mix with which it is dealing. Nor is there much sympathy for the usual sociology-of-science excuse that, after all, education research was only trying to find a place for itself above the salt at the scientific banquet table (Lagemann, 1997).

So its start and its first round have not been very auspicious – certainly unlike the opening histories of other engineering enterprises, like medicine or civil engineering.

What is different about education research?

I would like to stand back a little from all this early contentiousness and consider whether there are deeper and more endemic reasons that education research is not like those other forms of engineering that make progress by applying principles from the natural sciences to practical problems. It seems to me that there have been several obstacles to progress in education research that are inherent in the enterprise.

Perhaps the most important is that its objectives – the cultivation of mind, the betterment of life, or whatever else – are in principle culturally contestable issues that inevitably become ideological or political issues not readily resolved by scientific research alone. There is always disagreement about what "being educated" entails – what skills and sensibilities, what stock of knowledge and beliefs, what values constitute the educated person (Bruner, 1996).

A second inherent difficulty is that education research relies on general principles drawn from the human sciences. And these principles, it is said, are "not up to the job." They are "immature" (according to one view) or inherently different from the "prediction-and-control" pattern of the natural sciences (according to another).

And finally there is the troubling question raised by the topic of this book. What kind of research can be useful in setting education's aims or, more broadly, in guiding educational policy? Education is a public undertaking, and the policies that guide it, although ultimately aimed at individuals, are designed for institutions. Can education research properly address itself to these institutional questions, given its tradition of individualism as both a field of scholarship and a methodology?

I am concerned with all three of these broad problems. But I have intentionally avoided treating them separately, for they are highly interconnected.

Coping with the difference

Consider first the charge that education research must rely on principles drawn from the human sciences that are not "up to the job" of engineering. The conventional way of characterizing this shortcoming is by invoking the immaturity of the human sciences. But to accept the charge of "immaturity" at face value may obscure an even more important matter – a difference in kind between the human and the natural sciences that makes education research an entirely different form of "engineering" from those based on the natural sciences.

Indeed, the human sciences seem to become even more different from the natural sciences as they mature – with more emphasis on understanding and less on explanation in Georg von Wright's (1971) sense. This same trend seems characteristic of education research as well. As it develops, the less it seems to resemble standard research in the interest of guarding public health or building better bridges, even granting that there are some surface similarities. One can argue, for example, that the discovery of the power of literacy is analogous to the discovery of radar or an anticholera vaccine (see Olson, 1996).

So what is the difference between, say, wiping out an epidemic or building a good bridge and deciding how best to educate a new generation?

The answer is surely plain. Deciding how to educate a new generation not only lacks the a priori singularity of purpose of, say, protecting their health; indeed, it even involves making decisions about what constitutes "good education." It is banal to say so, but death, even its prevention, is not a controversial issue: whether to end a cholera plague is not a contestable matter. It is self-evident. Death is inherently undesirable, and it is a secondary matter whether it is "understood" scientifically or, as in some indigenous societies, it is thought that witchcraft is part of its epidemiology (Evans-Pritchard, 1937). Disease and death, whatever else they may be, are facts of nature.

Education is of quite a different order. Its aims are culturally constituted – generated within a culture. "Educating" somebody is drastically different from keeping the person alive or preventing death. There was nothing "naturally" desirable, for example, about teaching young ladies in antebellum Virginia to speak and read French. It was simply taken as a sign of cultivation among Virginia's gentry. The only consequence for failing to become cultivated in this way might be exclusion from the higher reaches of plantation social life. So how did a mastery of French become a trope for "being cultivated" in that society?

Doubtless, all societies everywhere have some sort of criterion for distinguishing "cultivated" from "uncultivated" people, and one can even make up an evolutionary

Just-So story about why that should be. But the particular criterion chosen to stand for being cultivated seems, if not arbitrary, then at least rooted in tradition rather than in nature. And who knows how French speaking gained its symbolic power! Was it the Enlightenment, the reflected charms of French court life, an instinctive alignment with England's classic antagonist – what?

Doubtless, too, all cultures recognize, promote, and even reward "cultivatedness," whatever form it may take. It stands for behaving in a fashion acceptable to those who matter in the broader sodality – one's reference group. Its "value" is symbolic, deriving not from laws of nature but from some cultural consensus, from some canonical pattern that emerged after long, often fitful maturing. In consequence, "cultivatedness" takes many forms in different cultures – modes of thought and expression, even ways of dress that are taken by other members of the culture as "signs" of somebody participating in the maintenance of the culture. In that sense, cultivatedness is a conservative virtue.

But to survive, a culture must also look to the future. For although we educate young people to honor the culture's traditions of sensibility or cultivatedness – its past – we also seek to equip them with "flexibility" and "resilience." We even rewrite the past and its canonicities with a view to relating it to our hopes or fears about the future – as in Anglo-American common law, where precedents are meant to guide rather than to determine judicial decisions. And so, for example, we tinker with history curricula to update our traditions better to fit them to the present – and presumably the future. Even the sciences and mathematics do not escape such tinkering. The "new" mathematics, for example, was dismissed as faddish when first proposed. The argument against it was that you could not balance your bank account in the "new math" – a bit like arguing that you cannot pave a road in plane geometry. The covert message was, of course, that education (including mathematics) should have a practical aim, a latter-day twist on the "cultivatedness" theme (or a counter-twist on it). So when the information revolution finally spewed computers into the consumer market, the "new" mathematics ceased being faddish and yesterday's "nerd" might now be a Bill Gates in the making. Characteristically, we are uneasy about balancing the past and the future, almost Hamlet-like – keen for "world history" curricula yet banning foreign books from the school library. Perhaps it is in the nature of culturally constituted aims, including educational aims, that this be so. Human cultures, in negotiating their normative standards, typically establish a dialectic between the canonically expectable and the imaginatively possible – the canonical embodied in such coercive institutions as the law, public education, and other "standard operating procedures"; the imaginatively possible in theater, literature, and "cultural criticism," as we have come to call it. (For a fuller discussion of this view of "cultural dialectic," see Amsterdam and Bruner, 2000; they exemplify this dialectic process by reference to common law practices.)

To revert to my earlier point about the difference between the constituted nature of educational goals in contrast to the stark nonnegotiability of medical goals, one other point needs to be made. There is a sense in which one's very position – one's social class and status – depends on how conventionally well educated one is. For "being educated" itself becomes a mark of social class and status, or being educated at certain prestigious institutions, whether The Ivy, Oxbridge, or *les grands écoles*. Access to education, then, provides entry into the power structure of a society and the criteria by which one gains access become ever more contentious – as if a multiplier had been inserted into the contestability equation.

Or, to put it in Pierre Bourdieu's (1977) terms, a society's ways of distributing status-endowing symbolic resources to its members is a major factor in determining one's "market" position within the society. It is this fact that makes education such an intensely political issue and that makes it so difficult to maintain a balance between the traditional and the innovative. Stakeholders in the status quo panic at the possibility of lost status; aspirants for new status become enlivened by a "revolution of rising expectations." And the "education wars" heat up into political battles. It is all too familiar.

Which brings us back to the political climate in which education research must operate. It is all well and good to determine, say, that one way of teaching reading is better than another – a finding surely worth its salt. But though a technical discovery, it leaves untouched such surrounding political issues as who shall be taught to read in what language in which school with teachers of what qualifications. These turn out to be cultural-political as well as cognitive-intellectual issues. Witness, for example, the recent battle over Black English.

But return now to the human sciences and the manner in which they differ from the natural sciences. In response to such issues as those we have been discussing, they have taken a much more interpretative stance. (For discussion of the nature and role of interpretation in the human sciences, see Bruner, 1991, 1996.) And although that stance is still an unsettled one, it already has led to important changes, not only within its constituent disciplines (like psychology, sociology, anthropology, even linguistics) where one finds a new emphasis on constructivism and pragmatism, but in educational research itself. There are now lively disciplines like educational anthropology, educational sociology, and even educational political science. Their objective is to examine more directly the cultural dialectic by which a society expresses its values through its educational practices. It takes for granted that educational aims are culturally constituted, rather than given or neutrally natural. These new developments (well represented in this book) do not by any means bar education research from using the scientific method or the reasoning of population statistics. They simply underline the importance of recognizing that education as such is guided by contestable cultural norms and that, for example, although there are biological constraints on educability, they do not speak for themselves. It may be a "scientific fact," for example, that the children of the better educated get the best education. But it is also a fact that it does not justify itself on the ground, for example, that these children are "naturally" brighter. Perhaps the culture's Golden Apple should go to those educational institutions that can do best for children whose parents never went to college. After all, we need to be sensitive to the dangers of creating an inherited meritocracy.

Education research, if it is to be effective in the broader society, must extend its concern, as it is now doing, beyond the classroom and beyond pedagogy narrowly defined. It needs also to participate in the task of discerning the consequences of such culturally constituted ends as a society prescribes for its education system. Education research, under the circumstances, becomes a cultural science, however much it may rely on methods developed in the natural sciences.

Research for goal setting

I want to turn now to how (or whether) research may be used to help set our educational aims or goals. The first question is whether research ever determines the aims of any enterprise. Research traditionally is about how: how to achieve ends arrived at by conviction or faith. But that surely is not the whole story, for research can also establish an existence theorem – that is, it can establish what is possible. And, indeed, education research has been, and continues to be, involved in such research. Many of the chapters in this book report just such "existence theorem" research projects – all of which is not to say that just because some educational objective can, contrary to common belief, be achieved it is, *eo ipso*, desirable. But it may be. If a cooperative classroom regimen produces as good or better results than a competitive one, it is worth considering whether we should encourage, even institutionalize systems that foster cooperative learning (Brown and Campione, 1990.

Indeed, it is not just QED existence theorem research that can have such a "renewing" effect on educational aims, but theoretical formulations as well, even when they are only en route to being established (or rejected). I offer as examples the idea of a "spiral curriculum" (Bruner, 1960) based on the notion that a conceptual structure is first grasped intuitively and then only later reformulated in more formal symbolic terms, or the idea that the important thing about a child's answer is not simply whether it is right or wrong but what question the answer is addressing.

But breakthrough theorems are rare, if precious. We also do research to determine whether, once established, our ends have been achieved and, if not, what prevented this. Why aren't first-year high school students mastering algebra, or third graders showing more respect for school property? Indeed, it is from such studies that we often learn what our aims really were. Aims are odd in that way. What makes them so is that "policy" is often an amalgam of what we want to achieve framed in terms of how we want to achieve them. Policy evolves over long periods of time, often given symbolic shape by watershed conflicts along the way, usually in the form of contested measures – some new statute or ordinance opposed, a bond issue that barely squeaked through, a lost school board election. In the process of this contesting, means become (or seem to become) ends. (It has always been my view, for example, that "foreign policy" gets made in cables sent out to American embassies abroad in response to particular problems. It is this truism that led eventually, some say, to creation of a Policy and Planning staff in the US State Department, one of whose chief tasks is to monitor the policy that emerges from this dynamic process.) The grand aims of "policy" easily get lost or obscured by the means chosen to achieve them. Indeed, aims rarely are discussed save cloaked in the limiting rhetoric of local and concrete proposals like bond issues, teachers' pay, charter schools, and the like. Policies, in this sense, accrete rather messily, and they get "taken" over in all their messiness by advocates and activists. New Labour in Britain, for example, wants accountability through a national curriculum and national assessments (taking a leaf from their Conservative forebears), but it also wants teachers to show initiative in their teaching (Broadfoot, 1997) and to feel identified with New Labour! So it is not the least anomalous that they now feel the need for research to discover what this stance has done, what the costs are in educational practice for "capturing the political center." Nor is it surprising that, say, Project Head Start leaders feel the need for research to determine what their professed policies actually led to in practice, in how Head Start *really* operates locally (Lubeck, 1998). The looseness of Head Start's policy directive, ironically enough, is almost a contrast case to the National Curriculum/National Examination rigidity of British education, yet both of them end up in doubt about what praxis their respective policies led to.

We all know full well that the formulation of a policy, while it may signal an intent, can also set self-defeating traps. Richard Daugherty (1995) has recently related the history of the effort of the British Conservative government in 1988 to gain control over local educational authorities by introducing the National Curriculum and National Assessment. By 1994 the Ministry of Education had had to make so many compromises that it was itself confused about its policy. But what it had accomplished (research was to show) was that it had turned teachers and politicians into enemies – hardly intended! Reviewing Daugherty's masterful if rather depressing account, Patricia Broadfoot (1997, p. 404), a particularly shrewd and knowledgeable observer of the British scene, concludes that the thing that was missing in this period of policymaking was not so much substance but "mutual understanding,... mutual respect, and trust." As she puts it in effect, you cannot simply formulate a policy to control and monitor an education system by curriculum and assessment requirements, when that system had before been so "free" that its only "requirement" had been that there be a weekly hour of religious instruction, which itself was mandated to be nonpartisan. In fact (and not surprising), teachers and local authorities interpreted the Education Act of 1988 as a sign of distrust on the part of the Conservative government. The issue at hand was one of political-cultural trust with long roots into Britain's class-ridden history. Would purely *education* research have been sufficient in such a setting?

And so it is with education research bearing on education's aims and policy. It cannot be exclusively concerned with classrooms and pedagogy.

I want to offer an American version of what I have just recounted – the 1988 Charlottesville Declaration. The Governors famously proclaimed in Charlottesville that in order to keep America competitive in world markets, we must improve the quality of American education generally, but particularly (and this was taken as virtually self-evident) by improving the teaching of science, mathematics, and literacy. Teachers were not part of the decision process. But this time another kind of anomaly produced the trouble. For within a decade, research studies began showing that the Charlottesville "policy" was based on a misleading oversimplification of the relation between means and ends. Even taking it for granted that one of the aims of education is to maintain or improve one's share of world markets, doing so required far fewer technically trained people and far more middle managers than had been supposed (Carnevale and Rose, 1998). The aim of "science and mathematics for all" was plainly an incomplete and a shortsighted one. At just about the same time, incidentally, it was found that American high school students scored far down in the science-mathematics league standing as revealed by the respected TIMSS (Third International Mathematics and Science Study) testing program – and at a time when the United States was thriving on world markets.

Should these findings lead us to reconsider the "aims" of our education policy? Perhaps. They might even lead us to look at history a little differently. After all, Britain's world power (market share included) was achieved during a period in which an Oxbridge "first" in Classics put one at the head of the competitive pack. A narrower technical degree was hardly despised, but a large number of them was never thought of as crucial to Britain's success.

This is not to say that Charlottesville was "wrong" – only that it was unsubtle in its setting of educational aims. But note again that the matter arising from this is no longer strictly educational. The real question that remains is what it takes to run a highly technical, highly successful economy. And not surprising, that question is now being taken back to the drawing board, so to speak, in order to assess what one should expect from an educational system in support of a nation's struggle for world markets.

But that question immediately poses another one. Even if one were so utilitarian as to entertain the idea that a nation's educational aims should be dictated by struggle for world markets, does it suffice to emphasize technical skill alone, or even managerial skills for that matter? Can we maintain a democracy on such a narrow base? What of maintaining a sense of participation in the democratic process or, indeed, of cultivating a proper skepticism about the exclusive place of economic and corporate ends in designing educational policies? Is not the dignity and worth of the common man proclaimed in our democratic Constitution also a crucial end to be sought? After all, was not John Locke's radical doctrine of empiricism, emphasizing each man and woman's ability and right to decide things on their own, as much an educational as a political doctrine? In thinking about educational policy, we do well to remember that Locke's words were being heeded not only at Constitution Hall, where the framers were forging a new Constitution, but at Germantown Friends Academy, not far down the road, where the school's masters were framing a new curriculum for the children of the founder generation (Brinton, 1965). And as the times have changed, we have gone on reframing our curricula to meet the changing times in much the same spirit as our courts have gone on reframing their interpretations of our Constitution with that end in mind. Education – and education research – cannot be kept separate from the life of the culture at large.

Further thoughts

And that, in effect, leads me to the one broad conclusion that I must draw from these reflections: education research should never have been conceived as principally dedicated to evaluating the efficacy or impact of "present practices." The major research question that it faces is *not* simply how well our schools and systems of pedagogy teach spelling or mathematics or literacy. Rather, the master question from which the mission of education research is derived is: *What should be taught to whom, and with what pedagogical object in mind?* That master question is threefold: what, to whom, and how? Education research, under such a dispensation, becomes an adjunct of educational planning and design. It becomes design research in the sense that it explores possible ways in which educational objectives can be formulated and carried out in the light of cultural objectives and values in the broad. To put it in a metaphor, the Charlottesville Declaration should have followed a long period of education research into the possible roles of education in American life and in America's place in the world economy.

I commented that the trend in education research was precisely along the lines of the conclusion I have just stated – toward a broader, more general mission. But I want to be clear that I am not proposing a technocratic solution to the effect that education research should establish our education goals as well as help design the methods of achieving them. Rather, the proposal is that modern societies are sufficiently complex so that even the task of setting the goals of education requires careful research as to what may be needed in order to achieve such goals as may be set. Perhaps such prior research would save us from such simplicities as those contained in the Charlottesville Declaration – that to compete in a global economy, what you need is simply more and more training in science and math. Had there been further thought on the matter, perhaps the first conclusion might have been that we needed much better knowledge about the role of education and schooling in shaping the ways of the society. Schools and the education system, we finally realize, are as much a cultural problem as they are a solution to one. Perhaps the new age of education research should begin with a searching study of the costs and benefits of using schooling as our mode of (presumably) bringing the young into the culture.

References

Amsterdam, A. G. and Bruner, J. *Minding the Law*. Cambridge, MA: Harvard University Press, 2000.

Bourdieu, P. *Outline of a Theory of Practice*. New York: Cambridge University Press, 1977.

Brinton, C. *The Anatomy of Revolution*. (Rev. and exp. edn). New York: Random House, 1965.

Broadfoot, P. "Assessment: The English Panacea." *Oxford Review of Education*, 1997, 23(3), 401–405.

Brown, A. and Campione, J. C. "Communities of Learning and Thinking, or a Context by Any Other Name." In D. Kuhn (ed.), *Developmental Perspectives on Teaching and Learning Thinking Skills: Contributions in Human Development, 21* (pp. 108–126). Basel: Karger, 1990.

Bruner, J. *The Process of Education*. Cambridge, MA: Harvard University Press, 1960.

Bruner, J. *Acts of Meaning*. Cambridge, MA: Harvard University Press, 1991.

Bruner, J. *The Culture of Education*. Cambridge, MA: Harvard University Press, 1996.

Carnevale, A. P. and Rose, S. J. *Education for What? The New Office Economy*. Princeton, NJ: Educational Testing Service, 1998.

Casswell, H. L. *City School Surveys: An Interpretation and Analysis*. New York: Bureau of Publications, Teachers College, Columbia University, 1929.

Daugherty, R. *National Curriculum Assessment: A Review of Policy*. Bristol, PA: Falmer Press, 1995.

Evans-Pritchard, E. E. *Witchcraft Among the Azande*. New York: Oxford University Press, 1937.

Gould, S. J. *The Mismeasure of Man*. New York: Norton, 1981.

Herrnstein, R. J. and Murray, C. *The Bell Curve: Intelligence and Class Structure in American Life*. New York: Free Press, 1994.

Lagemann, E. C. "Contested Terrain: A History of Education Research in the United States, 1890–1990." *Educational Researcher*, December 1997, 5–17.

Lubeck, S. *Research on Head Start*. Report to a Spencer Foundation conference on Culture, Human Development, and Education. Cambridge, MA: Harvard Graduate School of Education, Oct. 1998.

Olson, D. *The World in Print*. New York: Cambridge University Press, 1996.

von Wright, G. H. *Explanation and Understanding*. Ithaca, NY: Cornell University Press, 1971.

CHAPTER 19

EDUCATION REFORM
A report card

The Bulletin, Winter 2003, Boston, MA: American Academy of Arts and Sciences

Marshall S. Smith

Two years ago, I ended a seven-year stint as undersecretary of the US Department of Education. Tonight I would like to talk a little bit about quantitative studies – how I thought about them in the government and what I think might be done to improve them. I'll start with some history, going back forty years or so; then I'll talk a little bit about my sense of our progress. I will close with a brief report card on reform, as interpreted through the words of John Adams.

Forty years ago, in the 1960s, various activities in education were influenced by empirical studies. I will not argue that empirical studies drove such developments as the passage of Head Start and Title I. Lots of other things that went on in the sixties – including the civil rights movement and other social movements of those times – were far more important than quantitative studies. Nevertheless, important quantitative studies were carried out, and they were part of the mix. A famous study of the effects of preschools, conducted in Ypsilanti, Michigan, contributed to (and was certainly cited during) the passage of Head Start. Among the researchers who were influential in that era, none exceeded Jerome Bruner. His landmark 1960 book *The Process of Education* was a crucial factor in the generation of a range of educational programs and experiments in the 1960s, including Title I and Head Start. During the early 1960s, I believe, Jerry was also a member of the President's Advisory Panel of Education.

Title I – the federally funded supplemental reading program for at-risk first-graders – changed the nature of evaluation in this country. A new federal provision – a Robert Kennedy amendment – required that every Title I project in the 14,000 local education agencies in the country had to be evaluated. The few words in that provision heightened thinking about evaluation in a major way.

In my own first research experience outside of the university, in the summer of 1965, I was on a team that helped to evaluate the Title I program in Boston. We spent most of that summer arguing about whether we should be measuring only outcomes – only student achievement – or whether we should also be measuring some of the background variables and intervention processes that affected achievement. That argument continues, thirty-five years later. I think we know quite a bit more about it now than we did before, though people on both sides are still as passionate.

Many of you are familiar with James Coleman's report on *Equality of Educational Opportunity*, issued by the government in 1966. The findings of that report and subsequent reports building on Coleman's survey, especially *Racial*

Isolation in the Public Schools, were instrumental in stimulating a large-scale social experiment: the widespread busing of students to achieve racial integration in US public schools. The consequences of that experiment, and of early evaluations of both Head Start and Title I – many of which were slightly negative – began to change a lot of people's thinking about what kinds of investments the country should be making in education, as well as in other areas.

I recall a phone call I got in 1969 or 1970 from Pat Moynihan, then domestic policy adviser for President Nixon. During his first stint at Harvard, from 1966 to 1969, Pat had been influenced by the Coleman report to believe that perhaps education didn't quite have the effect he once thought it had. Also, Head Start evaluations had led him to think that Head Start didn't quite have the intended effect. During the call, I was in my kitchen in Cambridge with two very young children, while he was in his office in the White House.

Pat had been advocating in the government for the negative income tax. He asked me whether I would rather put $1,000 into a family to cover one year of Head Start for one of its children or put $1,000 into that family to buy food, clothing, and shelter by means of a negative income tax. I conveniently ducked the question by saying I'd do both. But the question was an important one because it signaled an orientation toward thinking about what kinds of interventions would have the greatest effect – an orientation that was possible only because there had been empirical studies of at least some of the various domestic interventions.

Later on, in the 1970s, methods were developed for synthesizing the results of quantitative studies. Richard Light and Paul Smith started that off with a little article in the *Harvard Educational Review*. Gene Glass came up with the concept of metaanalysis, which advanced research synthesis dramatically. During the 1970s, we in education began to look at qualitative studies more – and in some ways, qualitative studies began to drive out empirical studies for the next fifteen years.

This was a phenomenon of some importance. We lost some of the momentum around empirical studies, I believe – but at the same time, we gained some real insights into theories of intervention and into the ways and processes of classrooms, schools, and other organizations. So on the one hand, our field drew a sharp distinction between qualitative and quantitative that should never be drawn, in my view. This led to an almost ideological battle in the field of education. But if you look carefully down the middle on this one, you will find that those qualitative studies provided valuable insights that allowed people to begin to piece together the findings of research on how students learn and how teachers teach, and to apply those findings to situations that were more complex. Those insights gained us a great deal.

Then came the 1980s. Many of you will remember the 1983 government report titled *A Nation at Risk*, which relied on international quantitative data to assess education policy. Increasing attention also was focused on national assessments and test scores. Great growth occurred in cognitive science, yielding useful theories on how people learn. The eighties also brought the class-size experiment – a massive randomized field trial that has had an enormous effect on policy over time.

As we moved through the 1990s and into the new millennium, almost every state in the nation adopted a framework of standards-based school reform. The intent of the reforms is to bring resources, policies, and assessments into alignment with standards that specify clear and explicit goals for student learning. The assessments are used for accountability purposes. This is a package that has bipartisan support. It started with strong support by the Clinton administration and is now being supported by the current administration.

An increased emphasis on accountability, reflected in the standards-based reforms, has also influenced other parts of our society. Accountability based on quantitatively measurable outcomes has moved both the government and the private sector to become much more sensitive to the kinds of effects that can be measured. In many areas, including education, that has sometimes led to a narrowing of the kinds of outcomes people worry about which may be a negative byproduct of the policy. We seem to value what we measure, rather than rigorously measure what we value. Consequently, if we assess only things that are easy or inexpensive to measure, we may end up placing value on the wrong things. This happens too often in education. Nonetheless, measures focus people's attention. The emphasis on empirically based accountability has created coherence out of incoherence in many instances, not least in the government.

The positivist belief in the value of empirical and verifiable findings has also increased attention to the empirical evaluation of education policies and practices. This – unfortunately, in my view – has resulted in a rash of dramatic statements about randomized field trials being the "gold standard" of research. This form of rhetoric often implies that other forms of research are inferior, rather than that they provide different kinds of data and different insights. In fact, the fascination with randomized trials seems to have been elevated to an ideological level by some. The National Research Council addresses the issues of different methodologies for different purposes in an elegant new report. On the other hand, the interest in randomized trials may be seen as a counterbalance to an equally ideological perspective of many in the late 1980s and early 1990s who regarded qualitative research as the only path to truth.

The concerns about effectiveness have not only heightened attention to methodological issues; they have also resulted in increased attention to theory. The National Research Council, for instance, has issued some excellent books on theories of learning, including how children learn to read and do mathematics.

Program evaluation has benefited from this. We are beginning to marry good and appropriate methodologies with better theory, and our evaluations are becoming more and more powerful and useful for policy development. Anthony Petrosino's work at the Academy on theory and evaluation is becoming very influential. We better understand the challenges of implementation. We are also seeing improvements in synthesizing the results of prior research. The inception of the Campbell Collaboration in the late 1990s was a formal way of beginning to approach the synthesis problem.

Of course, technology is changing many of the rules right now. It is changing our ways of modeling and our ways of organizing data. It is changing our access to data in dramatic ways. In the humanities and arts areas, the opportunities for new forms of research and analysis are extraordinary. Through technology, we are now able to do things we couldn't even dream of doing before.

At least four of the major events or findings in these areas can be traced back to Fred Mosteller. There are surely many other links with which I am not familiar; I will note just four of his important contributions in areas that I have mentioned. He played a very significant role in interpreting the Coleman report; gave extraordinary legitimacy to the class-size study; fostered strides in synthetic analysis, both as Richard Light's mentor and as a supporter of the Campbell Collaboration; and made major contributions through his work on the National Assessment of Educational Progress in the early days.

In 1957 I took a course with Fred. Ever since, I've carried a Mosteller quote in the back of my mind, and I looked it up the other day in the 1953 edition of the

Handbook of Social Psychology. What I found just goes to show that Fred hasn't changed his beliefs about the importance of carefully planned, theoretically driven research designs. Mosteller and Bush wrote, "In no circumstances do we think that sophisticated analytical devices should replace clean design and careful execution, unless very unusual economic considerations arise." Clear thinking should prevail.

Now, let me ask a rhetorical question: If we know so much about all of this, why don't we have better policy? Other countries appear to have strong linkages between improved knowledge and improvement in their schools. Back in the 1950s, the National Science Foundation developed a set of very exciting and rigorous math and science courses in response to the challenge represented by *Sputnik.* For a good while during the 1960s, lots of schools in the United States adopted those courses, and some actually still use them. In general, though, they began to die out around 1969 or 1970. Yet they were used in other countries for far longer. Materials based on US research are picked up and used by other countries fairly regularly. Yet in the United States, the curriculum materials developed through NSF investments in the 1950s and 1960s lasted only a while, and materials developed in the 1990s have been largely unused – some having been bought and then shelved by publishers that did not want them competing with their own textbooks.

But the publishers are not the only culprits. The governance system can also be part of the problem. In the United States, we have an amazingly complex policy environment. California alone, for example, has seven different state agencies that influence the development and implementation of education policy. The elected state school officer and state governor are both Democrats, but they don't talk to each other, because they're battling over the turf. A variety of other groups out there are also in the fray. California has term limits, so there is almost no legislative memory. And the legislators seem to evaluate the quality of their term on the basis of the amount and number of legislative items passed rather than the effectiveness and coherence of the laws. This is not just a problem in California; state and federal legislators have the same disease. California also has government by public proposition, which means that anybody with a lot of money can put anything they please on the ballot. Consequently, a cacophony of chaotic provisions is placed into law, and that makes effective governance almost impossible.

On the other hand, as I learned during my years with the government, policymakers actually do listen. I was in the Clinton administration for seven years, in a policymaking role, and I don't think there was any major issue where quantitative research didn't enter into the picture. There's no reason to think that it made a telling contribution, but people thought about it, worried about it, and looked at it. In some instances, research – for example, the Tennessee study of class size – really tipped the balance because it changed people's views in the Office of Management and Budget, the president's office, and Congress.

Generally, however, the effect sizes in research studies are small. If effect sizes are small, and if multiple studies are done, we are likely to get a distribution of effects that covers zero and goes into negative territory. As a consequence, anybody who wants to argue any position can base the argument on empirical research.

Let me spend a couple of minutes on a report card on education reform, just to give you some sense of where I think we stand today. I'm not going to relate it back too much to empirical research – just a little bit. It's a complicated picture. We have a set of standards-based reforms now that are in their early adolescence – nine, ten, eleven years old at best. In California, they're only three or four years old. So nationwide, these reforms are going through tremendous growing pains.

Although there are still many debates over the reforms, I believe they have begun to have some effect over time. Math scores on the National Assessment of Educational Progress have risen significantly in the fourth and eighth grades – by over a grade level – in the past six or seven years. That's quite a bit of progress. And that's not just for white students; it's also for African American, Hispanic, and Asian students.

We have individual states that do very well in the international studies. It is a difficult thing for us, as a country, to be compared with Singapore, or even with Holland, or Denmark, or Norway. One might think that Minnesota, for example, would compare more closely with Norway or Sweden than would the entire United States – or that some fairly small, well-off area of the United States might compare more closely with Singapore than would the whole United States. When we do look at places that are well off and compare them with Singapore, our students do pretty well. They don't quite reach the level that the students in Singapore do, but they are competitive. When we look at how Minnesota does, compared with the Scandinavian countries, it actually does very well.

Some states have shown significant gains in many regards over the past few years. Texas, North Carolina, and Connecticut – all states that have pushed these standards-based reforms hard – show good gains in reading and mathematics. As for Massachusetts, we'll see – there's a big debate here. Virginia, Maryland, and other states have shown substantial gains. Nonetheless, we have a long way to go, especially for our least advantaged.

Many think that US education reform is taking us much too far in the direction of testing and assessment. Others think that perhaps we are not pushing hard enough. I was pleased to find support for my own views on the reforms in David McCullough's book *John Adams*, which I read on my plane trip here. I was struck by two quotes from Adams on education because they fit with my assessment of where we stand right now.

Here's one of them, written about 220 years ago: "A memorable change must be made in the system of education, and knowledge must become so general as to raise the lower ranks of society nearer to the higher."

I would venture to say that the lower ranks of society today are almost as low on the education totem pole as they were 220 years ago. We haven't changed that particular phenomenon in our society. We still have people at the bottom, and we can predict who they are, by and large. We know where they live. We know what the problems of their schools are – and we haven't done enough about it. So our reforms haven't done very well on that particular dimension.

The second quote that impressed me was from a letter John Adams wrote to John Quincy Adams at around the same time. John Quincy had just been denied admission to Harvard, despite having demonstrated his extraordinary abilities. He'd been told that he would have to complete several months of tutoring in Greek with the Reverend Shaw in Haverhill in order to go to Harvard.

Apparently, Adams was a bit concerned that John Quincy would study too hard and get too involved in his Greek. He wrote to him, "The smell of the midnight lamp is very unwholesome. Never defraud yourself of sleep, nor your walk. You need not be in a hurry." What was essential, Adams advised, was an inquisitive mind. John Quincy must get to know the most exceptional scholars and question them closely: "Ask them about their tutors, manner of teaching. Observe what books lie on their tables. Ask them about the late War, or fall into questions of Literature, Science, or what will you."

There is a message of caution for us in Adams's prophetic words. We may be losing, in our passion for increasing achievement test scores in mathematics, reading, and science, the breadth of knowledge and understanding that needs to be developed in all students if they are to be productive citizens of our increasingly complex society.

Jerome Bruner

I want to comment first on what I see as some of the deep wisdom in Mike's analyses, emphasizing some things that he didn't have a chance to discuss in detail. Then, after that, I want to offer a slightly different perspective with regard to where we Americans stand internationally in the World Education League. In doing so, I want to use a lesson I learned from Fred Mosteller, who has been my friend and mentor for many, many years, starting back at Princeton in another century. Fred likes to say, "In comparing performance scores, don't just pay attention to the means. Look at the variance too." Well, that's what I want to do: look at variability. I'll turn to that presently.

But let me look first at some of the lessons that Mike set forth in his talk. The first was that there has to be a good fit between what a program for educational improvement is seeking to improve, and how it goes about assessing its results. In assessing a program, to put his point briefly, you can't just use any old standardized test. The assessment test needs to fit the objectives of your attempted intervention. There are no all-purpose assessment procedures that fit all needs. Adequate assessment has to be relevant to the theory behind the intervention program you are evaluating. You can't fly blind – but that, in effect, is what you end up doing if you don't design your assessment to fit the objectives of your intervention.

I remember this classic problem from the early days of the Physical Science Study Committee (PSSC), one of the first curriculum reform efforts of the 1960s, directed by Jerrold Zacharias and Franny Friedman at MIT. A lot of people urged them to evaluate the PSSC curriculum effort with the standardized physics tests available at the time. Zacharias replied boldly, "Hell no, we're not teaching that kind of physics." So PSSC developed new assessment procedures (with the help of the Educational Testing Service) geared to their own instructional objectives and to their own ideas about what it meant to understand physics. It was a real step forward.

Indeed, every educational intervention program has some underlying theory that shapes it, implicitly or explicitly, and the more explicit it is, the better the evaluation will be. Even when the theory is "simply" that small classes get better results than large ones, as in Fred Mosteller's now famously successful Tennessee Study, there is an underlying theory that is not as simple as it seems. If you mindlessly attempt to replicate it, as they did in the state of California, the chaos is unbelievable. First of all, the way in which you set up small classes has to have some mind for who's teaching. Teaching small classes requires skills in communicating.

So, what of California's replication? They didn't have enough teachers available, so they began hiring teachers willy-nilly – and got more than the usual proportion of weak and inexperienced ones. Small classes also require more classrooms, not just corridors or hastily remodeled closets and bathrooms. It's not surprising that "reduced class size" didn't bear fruit in California.

But there's more to it than that. We don't fully know why smaller classes work better, given the right conditions; we haven't thought through the question. Is it that smaller classes lead to a different strategy on the part of the teacher, to different discourse patterns? Do they change the teacher-pupil authority relationship? We need a lot more theory to proceed wisely.

Let me give an example. I have been studying the famous preschools in Reggio Emilia in Italy. Here's a surprising finding: when a teacher asks a child something, she waits for an answer. If the child has some difficulty answering, the teacher typically asks the other children in the class to help little Giovanna or Giuseppe figure out an answer, and a discussion starts. The context changes: knowledge seeking becomes communal. I've seen some astonishing scenes there. I've even started using this approach teaching graduate students. I'm still trying to think through the theory behind it, and even making a little progress. As Mike has been trying to tell us, people need to think about what they have in mind with their interventions. Then they'll be able to evaluate properly.

Now I want to move on to Fred Mosteller's admonition about attending to variance. I'd like to look at it from the point of view of American performance on the tests now being widely used for comparing adult "literacy" in the nineteen most well-off countries in the world, including top-ranking America. These tests, devised by the Office of Economic Cooperation and Development, are thoughtfully designed and carefully translated into the different languages required. There are three subtests: one for ability to recognize prose, as in news stories and the like; another for "document literacy," or the ability to understand order forms, tables, and so on; and a third for "quantitative literacy," or knowing how to perform such tasks as balancing a checkbook and figuring a tip. Let's take a look at some findings from these tests.

First of all, as everybody knows, America doesn't do well on international tests. For example, among those nineteen well-off countries, we're ninth on the prose score, fourteenth on the document score, and thirteenth on quantitative – twelfth among nineteen on the composite score. You'd think, given our riches, we'd do better than that.

But where we undoubtedly lead the world is in variability, or dispersion. American standard deviations on all the tests are just about at the top. For example, on the prose test, we rank first in the size of our standard deviation; on the document test and on the quantitative test, we rank second. We lead the world in the standard deviation of composite scores – the most diverse country in the well-off world.

If you look at the test-score difference between the top tenth percentile and the lowest tenth percentile in each country, again we lead the pack. Our lowest percentile is way, way down; our top tenth is way, way up. America seems to have a gift for fostering maldistribution or inequality. No country in the civilized world can match us in terms of the maldistribution of wealth, the gap between rich and poor. And it seems, too, that none can match the gap we create between our most literate and least literate countrymen. Ours is a diversity of inequality.

What about the history of all this? Are we getting better or worse in literacy, in comparison with other well-to-do nations? We can estimate this by looking at different age groups, and what comes out is not encouraging. Our youngest Americans – ages sixteen to twenty-five – rank fourteenth out of nineteen in the world on the composite literacy score. The age group twenty-six to thirty-five ranks eleventh. With the group that is thirty-six to forty-five years old, we go to fifth place. And the two oldest groups, ages forty-six to fifty-five and fifty-six to sixty-five, are second and third in the world ranking. So either America is falling behind, or the rest of the world is surging ahead, in literacy.

How much of this has to do with immigration? Our native-born Americans ranked tenth out of the seventeen countries on which there were immigration fig-ures. Our foreign-born ranked sixteenth out of those seventeen countries. Our own past history suggests that when immigrants get segregated in caste conditions, as in our inner-city slums, second-generation "immigrants" continue to lag behind or even get pushed down further. So immigration is an issue, alright, though not an enormous one numerically.

I suspect, though, that the ones who are falling furthest behind world standards are poor blacks and poor second-generation Latinos. Yet there is an irony in this decline, for we know from intensive studies that with improved teacher expertise and classroom conditions, these groups can be greatly helped. If we in America are willing to do something about it, plenty can be done. But not much is being done. So our world position remains parlous – not to mention the conditions that such inequalities produce here in the United States.

If we follow Mike's wisdom, we can begin to turn the tide, though we will have to take measures beyond the usual educational ones – for instance, assuring a more equitable distribution of wealth. After all, we know that the sense of helplessness and despair produced by poverty is the worst block against improved school per-formance. On that basis, school reform without concomitant economic reform is simply not sufficient.

So, to return to Mike's message, we should indeed look more deeply and more theoretically at the causes of good and poor school performance, and propose reforms that take into account what it is that makes American society so prone to inequality – what it is that puts us in top position for variability in national literacy.

CHAPTER 20

A SHORT HISTORY OF PSYCHOLOGICAL THEORIES OF LEARNING

Daedalus, Winter 2004, American Academy of Arts and Sciences

Learning remains an elusive topic, despite the endless research lavished on it. And what we mean by it, of course, is shaped by how we choose to study it. Concentrate on how children master their native language and you arrive at a very different conception of learning than had you researched how undergraduates memorize nonsense syllables. Does learning to finger a Bach cello sonata tap the same learning processes as learning to trace your way through a finger maze? Is all learning alike, reducible to a common set of principles?

Two learning tasks are said to be alike if mastering one makes mastering the other easier – the so-called transfer criterion. But what is transferred? Is it responses? Rules? Or do we simply learn how to learn, as when with enough practice we become exam-wise or tax-form-wise? How do we learn the lay of the land? How do we learn to concentrate our attention?

And then there are questions about differences in how learning occurs. Do all species learn in the same way and do the bright and the dull go about it in like manner? And what about external inducements, rewards, and punishments? Are all learning situations comparable?

I used to give the star performers of the experiments I'd just completed to my young daughter. These rats seemed to develop a more open curiosity under her magnanimous care. What, indeed, does domestication do to an animal's approach to learning? Were those insights achieved by Wolfgang Koehler's pampered chimpanzees – their figuring out how to rake in an out-of-reach banana by putting two sticks together, for instance – simply the result of the leisurely tutelage they received on that German island of Tenerife?[1] It used to be said, only half jokingly, that Yale stimulus-response-reinforcement learning theory was different from more cognitive California theory because Clark Hull in New Haven taught his graduate students that rats "should get on with it," while Edward Tolman counseled his at Berkeley that rats need time enough to pause at the choice points in a maze.

And finally, do we learn for learning's sake, or must we be extrinsically motivated to do so? Assuming the latter, the Yerkes-Dodson law tells us that too much or too little motivation reduces learning. I checked that out once myself and got a surprise. I found that very hungry and just moderately hungry rats learned to find their way through a succession of pairs of doors. The correct path through was marked redundantly in two ways: follow a left-right-left-right path, or just choose the darker door at each choice point. The hungry rats learned only one of the two cues; the moderately hungry rats learned both. The less hungry rats had a more open curiosity – like my daughter's pets.

Given all this, it is natural enough that scientists would want somehow to simplify what we mean by "studying learning." And, of course, the standard way of doing that is to agree on some paradigm that would make it possible to compare results. That is exactly what happened at the very start of learning research. But, as often happens, rival paradigms came into existence and, alas, this research soon became a war of would-be paradigms. Indeed, the learning theory wars that resulted came to dominate the psychological research scene from the latter nineteenth century until a decade after World War II, with various "schools" devising clever experiments to demonstrate how well their paradigm worked, or how poorly rival ones fared.

There were two competing paradigms from the start, each with its variants. The principal one, a child of its times, was molecular associationism, a metaphoric extension of the atomism of nineteenth-century physics. (As the quip goes, psychology is forever subject to physics envy.) The atomism of learning theory embodies the notion that learning consists of the association of ideas, memories, sensations, whatever; at its heart is the conception of the associative bond, the linkage that co-occurrence or spatial proximity produces between two sensations or ideas. While associationism is of ancient provenance, it had more recent philosophical adherents as well – not only Aristotle, but Locke, Berkeley, Hume, and pére et fils Mills. Indeed, by the mid-nineteenth century, philosopher-psychologist Johann Friedrich Herbart had proclaimed the associative bond as the keystone of the new psychology.

This paradigm found further, if indirect, support in the newly burgeoning brain physiology of those times. As the nineteenth century entered its last quarter, the older phrenology of the days of Gall and Spurzheim was reformulated in terms of newly discovered cortically localized "centers" in the cerebral cortex, each dedicated to a particular function. Perhaps the most compelling localization study was the one conducted in 1870 by the German physiologists Fritsch and Hitzig. In their study, electrical stimulation of different spots in the medial-lateral cortex produced particular, quite finite motor responses: stimulating one spot produced flexion of a monkey's forearm, another would turn his eyes upward, still another would turn them downward.[2] If the brain were organized in this localized punctate way, psychologists asked, why not the mind as well? One needs to remember that the prevailing philosophical view among those scholars was psychophysical parallelism, which held that mind and brain move along parallel tracks.

Their critics, however, championed another model – that of molar configurationism. This paradigm took as its major premise that mind and brain alike operate as integral systems controlling the functioning of component parts. Like its rival, it too rested its case on brain physiology, for there was already plenty of evidence that overall cortical processes controlled localized centers – the neural "mass action" holism represented by the renowned Pierre Flourens.

The brain's mass action was analogous to the phenomenology of everyday life – that ordinary experience transcends its bits and pieces. The "urban scene," after all, is more than just a collection of taxis, buildings, pedestrians; its properties as a whole shape the elements that make it up. Gestalt psychology was, of course, the most direct expression of this view, and it had much to say about how learning was a matter of overall organization rather than of local associative linkages.

Consider now the rise of the associationist paradigm. That closing quarter of the nineteenth century was a time of many new studies of learning – mostly concerned with the memorization of lists of words or pairs of words to be associated. But it was the nonsense syllable principally that gave associative bonding its scientific flavor. Hermann Ebbinghaus used nonsense syllables in order to rule out past experience and "meaning" in explanations of learning. Ebbinghaus's 1885 *Ueber das Gedaechtnis* is a tedious account of learning lists of nonsense syllables (with Ebbinghaus himself as the subject of most of the experiments). His findings – for example, that nonsense syllables in the middle of the list are more slowly learned than ones at the beginning or end – are easily reproducible.[3]

But the associative bond, even between nonsense syllables, soon came to seem mentalistic, too fragile to suit the scientific taste of the times. So by the turn of the century it was replaced by Pavlov's more scientifically solid "conditioned reflex." Pavlov's paradigm physicalized associationism, turning its content into something more measurable while preserving its associative form intact. All his paradigm required was linking and relinking stimuli and responses: a salivary reflex, once produced by food, was now evoked by a bell signaling the coming of food. Pavlov's Nobel Prize in physiology seemed to clinch the triumph of physicalism. But Pavlov himself was not altogether pleased, as we'll see later.

Now turn to configurationism, which had no shortage of psychologists to support it, dubious as many were of associationism's abstractness and its remoteness from ordinary experience. Configurationism had the support of brain research as well, with the holistic neurology of the indomitable Flourens still very much in vogue. Also in those fin de siècle times there was a rising tide of interest in how language and culture shaped mind, with figures like Emile Durkheim and Max Weber in the neighboring discipline of sociology urging that culture – not just individual encounters with the world of physical nature – also forms mind.

Gestalt theory was the prime exemplar of the configurationist trend in those early years, though it hit its full stride only after World War I. Its credo was that all systems – physical, biological, and mental – have the intrinsic character of controlling the local elements that compose them. Field theory in physics was its model, and its proclaimed maxim was "The whole is greater than the sum of its parts," which the Gestaltists proceeded to confirm with a steady stream of clever studies on human perception. The Koehler chimpanzee studies on Tenerife were intended to make the same point where learning was concerned: There was no way in which those chimpanzees could turn a pair of sticks into a reaching tool by the simple "association" of elements. It took an act of insight to do so, a way of configuring the whole situation.

Koehler had a deep belief in the ubiquitousness of configurationism in all of nature. He launched one of his first major attacks on associationism by arguing the insufficiency of atomism, in a book bearing the forbidding, if telltale title, *Ueber die physische Gestalten im ruhe und im stationaren Zustanden* (On physical configurations at rest and in stationary states). If atomism was insufficient even in physics, Koehler asked, how could it serve as a paradigm for psychology?[4] He applied a phenomenon in visual perception to make an analogy that would drive home his point: When two nearby points of light are briefly flashed one after the other, the eye perceives pure apparent movement, not the light points moving. The whole, then, is indeed different from a sum of its parts.

Now as it happens, Pavlov himself came to advocate a kind of linguistic configurationism. How does the conditioned response square with an ordered phenomenon such as language? Does language change how stimuli are interpreted, how a conditioned stimulus is substituted for an unconditioned one in the case of human beings? Troubled by such issues in his later years, Pavlov proposed a Second Signal System whose stimuli were not raw physical inputs, but language imbedded in codes and categories. Thus linguistic synonymy influenced stimulus substitution in ordinary conditioning.

Some say that Pavlov was driven to his new views by communist ideologues with prematurely Gramscian leanings, but in fact his Second Signal System was quite in keeping with the European tradition of human studies, *Geisteswissenschaft*, rather than with *Naturwissenschaft* – a well-revered tradition among the Russian intelligentsia. Still, structuralism was virtually the hallmark of the lively Russian literary and linguistic scene of Pavlov's day, and the Second Signal System was certainly, to some degree, a response to that scene. I recall flying to Moscow from Paris in the 1960s with the celebrated Russian emigé linguist Roman Jakobson. He laughed when I told him about Pavlov's later turn and about the accusation that he had knuckled under to the *nomenklatura*. "No, no, Jerry, communist ideologues weren't needed, just being Russian was enough. And being a Russian intellectual besides! Not even Pavlov could live with the idea that language makes no difference, that people learn like dogs!"

Small wonder that cultural theorists like Vygotsky and Luria took over after Pavlov and that many of the post-Pavlovian young studied Gestalt psychology at the Institute of Psychology in Berlin in the years after.[5]

The climax of the rivalry between associationism and configurationism came in America in the years before World War I. Nourished by the imposing Edward Lee Thorndike of Teachers College, Columbia University, the associative paradigm had flourished in the United States. Thorndike had been a postdoctoral student at one of the major centers of associationism in Germany. On his return to America (and Teachers College) he popularized practice and repetition as the routes to proficient school learning: practice and repeat as you would were you memorizing nonsense syllables.[6]

But the associationist research program soon changed in America under the influence of Pavlov. J. B. Watson, the founder of American behaviorism, who popularized Pavlov and gave his findings an American twist, by stressing how all learning occurred through stimulus and response. I sometimes wonder whether it was Watson's oversimplifications that eventually drove American associationist learning theorists to their zealous rigor in exploring Pavlov's ideas. It was the energy and determination of their research that made America for half a century the home of later Pavlovianism, a half century dominated by the likes of Walter Hunter, Clark Hull, Edward Guthrie, B. F. Skinner, Kenneth Spence – all distinguished, self-professed stimulus-response learning theorists.

Their forte was the well-designed animal experiment: maze running, discrimination learning, operant conditioning à la Skinner box, and the like – mostly with rats as subjects, but sometimes pigeons, and occasionally monkeys. Undergraduates were used as well, but again, mostly in rote learning experiments – in what was referred to in my graduate student days at Harvard as "dustbowl empiricism." It was in these days that Pavlov's dog became a metaphor for American know-nothing anti-intellectualism.

The burden of the behaviorists' findings, taken collectively, was that repetition of a task, with suitable reinforcement for completing each trial, improved performance. There were subtleties, to be sure – like the deleterious effects of massing trials rather than spacing them, creating interference by setting positive and negative reinforcement in a conflicting relationship, and the like. But the overall outcome of the work, where ordinary everyday learning was concerned, was, I believe, much as I've stated it. I'll return to this matter later.

But, as in Europe earlier, a contrarian configurationism soon came into being. Partly it was influenced by Gestalt theorists, now in America and sparking the opposition, but it had American roots as well, nourished particularly by

Edward Tolman, who was sympathetic to the work of Koehler and was a close friend of Kurt Lewin, a latter-day leader in the Berlin Gestalt group. Tolman's brother Richard, moreover, was a distinguished nuclear physicist and shielded him well from old-fashioned atomistic notions – and, indeed, from physicalistic temptations. Tolman, from the start, was a cognitivist.

Tolman's first major book appeared in 1932 and it quickly gained adherents among the discontented, and there were plenty of them. His students – notably David Krech, but many others as well – also joined the battle against associationism. By World War II, there was virtually open conflict in America between configurationist and associationist learning theorists – the first holding that learning is principally a task of organizing knowledge from the top down, the second insisting that it is accreting it from the bottom up. The configurationists, though still a minority, had been officially well received on the American scene when they fled Hitler's Europe. Koehler was invited to deliver the William James Lectures at Harvard, and Kurt Lewin became virtually a cult figure in social psychology. The displaced members of the old Gestalt group were soon well placed in leading American universities. They made commonsense phenomenology seem commonsense rather than arcane, an achievement given the hold of behaviorist American psychology. Learning began to be understood as grasping things in context, not in bits.

Take Edward Tolman's research as an example. He taught that learning is like mapmaking and that to learn is to organize things in the light of their utility for achieving ends. In "Cognitive Maps in Rats and Men," his still renowned Research Lecture to the Berkeley faculty in 1947, Tolman claimed that trial and error is not so much acting out habits to discover which are effective, but rather a looking back and forth to get the lay of the land in order to construct a solution. That is why he urged his graduate students not to rush their rats through the maze.[7] He believed that our cognitive maps are not mirrors of the happen-stance of our encounters with the world, but a record of our strivings and what has proved relevant to their outcome. His views in this sense were basically pragmatist, perhaps because of his years of exposure as a psychology graduate student to Harvard's pragmatist philosophers, particularly C. I. Lewis, whom he greatly admired. Following Tolman's lead, David Krech went to the extent of proposing that learning is hypothesis driven, not just passive registration. Even rats, Krech tried to show, generate hypotheses.[8]

It's revealing to compare Tolman with the leading, perhaps most radical associationist behaviorist of the same period, B. F. Skinner. Skinner was surely as compelling in defense of operant conditioning as Tolman was of cognitive map theory. His central concept was the operant response – an act not initially under the direct control of some particular feature of the immediate environment. An example of an operant response is provided by a starting pigeon in a Skinner box whose pecking of the button on the box's wall either produces or fails to produce a reinforcement (a grain of seed, say). Any reinforcement increases the likelihood of the operant response occurring again, the level of likelihood depending upon whether the reinforcement always follows the response or does so only sometimes, and whether it does so regularly (periodically) or irregularly (aperiodically). Partial aperiodic reinforcement, for example, evokes a rather more persistent response than one might expect, though Skinner would scoff at interpreting such persistence as hope springing eternal. Learning, in Skinner's austere terms, is under the sole control of schedules of reinforcement: reinforcement can only be positive; punishment does not affect learning. And that is about it. As Skinner would sometimes say, a bit ironically, learning scarcely needs a theory.[9]

Not all behavioral associationists, to be sure, shared Skinner's disdain for theory. Clark Hull at Yale, indeed, elaborated his theory into a highly refined set of axioms about what constitutes positive and negative reinforcement, what makes a conditioned stimulus generalize along a certain gradient, how organisms anticipate reinforcers, and the like – all in rather exquisite and specialized detail. His first books – the 1943 *Principles of Behavior* and the more triumphally titled 1952 *A Behavior System* – bristle with tables and idealized learning curves and with abstract formulae for relating those findings to his central axioms – perhaps a prophetic effort to devise a mathematical model of learning, the preoccupation of computational psychologists a generation later.[10]

The conflicts between Hull and Skinner, and between both of them and Tolman, were the last battles of the learning theory wars. Learning theory in the classic sense died around 1960 – though there are still Skinnerians who stalwartly continue to publish operant findings, mostly for each other. I know of no more Tolmanians or Hullians.[11]

It was the cognitive revolution that brought down learning theory or, perhaps, focused attention elsewhere. After 1960, say, stimulus-response learning theory seemed quaintly stunted, hemmed in by its own self-denial. As for more molar, cognitive learning theories, many of their ideas were restated and absorbed into general cognitive theories such as Newell and Simon's on problem solving, or Bruner, Goodnow, and Austin's on thinking, or Miller, Galanter, and Pribram's on planning.[12] By the latter 1960s, learning was being translated into the concepts of information processing, with no compulsion to elevate one kind of learning over another in terms of its "basic" properties. Certainly, the old wars were over. And so, interestingly, were the old rat labs and their ubiquitous mazes.

As I reflect on the transition period, I think that it was the study of language and particularly of language acquisition that precipitated learning theory's decline. Language use and its acquisition are too out of reach of piecemeal S-R learning: efforts to bring them into the fold soon become absurd, and linguists have mostly dismissed them as such.

The contemporary linguistic assault on associationist learning theory began with Noam Chomsky's gloves-off critical review of Skinner's *Verbal Behavior*.[13] But the mentalist, problem-solving emphasis it introduced has now expanded beyond language as such. One now asks whether cultural codes are learned in some language-like way. Neither psycholinguistics nor cultural psychologists think of learning in the old-fashioned learning-theory way.

I think it would be fair to say that, under this new dispensation, more has been learned during the last three decades about language acquisition than in any prior century – more, indeed, than in all of them combined. And it's well to remember that the flood of research that made this possible was precipitated by the linguist Chomsky, not by a learning theorist.

The turn to language, moreover, has shifted learning-related research away from many of the older, artificial experimental paradigms – mazes, paired-associate word lists, nonsense syllables, and the rest. Let me give an example: the prediction that children must be so early tuned to the structure of their native language that they pick up its phonemic distinctions in parental talk even before they learn to understand or talk the language proper. It is a prediction that grows out of linguistic and developmental theory. And you can test it in context *directly* – by seeing whether childrens' prelinguistic babbling has a higher frequency of native-language phoneme sounds than of foreign ones. And so it does: French babies babble in French, Spanish in Spanish, etc. With such experiments, one tests in context, not in a maze, and knows without extrapolation whether the experiment has any bearing on real learning by real people in real life.

Shall we conclude, then, that three-quarters of a century of warfare between associationist and configurational learning theories taught us little or nothing about the real nature of learning? That would be a mistake.

Both Pavlov's dogs and Koehler's chimpanzees did, in fact, learn, though in different ways and in different circumstances. And we have ample reason to suspect that neither of their approaches can be reduced to the other. In the next turn of things perhaps we will figure out how to put them together. But of one thing at least I am quite convinced. You cannot strip learning of its content, nor study it in a "neutral" context. It is always situated, always related to some ongoing enterprise. Perhaps there is no such thing as "learning in general" – and perhaps that is what we should learn from Pavlov's dogs, Koehler's chimps, and the disputes over learning that they once symbolized.

Notes

1 Wolfgang Koehler, *The Mentality of Apes* (New York: Harcourt Brace, 1926). This was originally published in German in 1917.
2 The classic article was Gustav Fritsch and Eduard Hitzig, "Ueber die elektrische Errigbarkheit des Grosshirns," *Archiv der Anatomie und Physiologie* (1870): 300–332.
3 Ebbinghaus's 1885 classic is available in English only in brief, but representative excerpts may be found in Wayne Dennis, *Readings in the History of Psychology* (New York: Appleton-Century-Crofts, 1948), 304–313. Interestingly enough, Ebbinghaus's original monograph was published in its entirety in English translation in 1913 by Teachers College, Columbia University – very much in keeping with the then dominant emphasis on rote learning in American education. It has long been out of print.
4 For Koehler's philosophical allegiances, see Mary Henle, ed., *The Selected Papers of Wolfgang Koehler* (New York: Liveright, 1971). Perhaps the best and most accessible account of Gestalt psychology's empirical accomplishments (mostly before Hitler's rise to power) is Kurt Koffka, *Principles of Gestalt Psychology* (New York: Harcourt Brace, 1935).
5 Lev Vygotsky, *Thought and Language* (Cambridge, MA: MIT Press, 1962); Aleksandr Romanovich Luria, *The Role of Speech in the Regulation of Normal and Abnormal Behavior* (New York: Liveright, 1961).
6 Edward L. Thorndike's classic is the three-volume *Educational Psychology*, which appeared in 1913–1914.
7 Tolman's most influential book was *Purposive Behavior in Animals and Men* (New York: Century, 1932). His Berkeley lecture was later elaborated in his International Congress address, "Cognitive Maps in Rats and Men." *Psychological Review* 55 (4) (1948): 189–208.
8 Krech's bold study (written under his original name) is I. Krechevsky. " 'Hypothesis' versus 'Chance' in the Presolution Period in Discrimination Learning," *University of California Publications in Psychology* 6 (1932): 27–44.
9 B. F. Skinner, "Are Theories of Learning Necessary?" *Psychological Review* 57 (1950): 193–216.
10 Clark L. Hull, *Principles of Behavior* (New York: Appleton-Century-Crofts, 1942) and *A Behavior System: An Introduction to Behavior Theory Concerning the Individual Organism* (New Haven, CO: Yale University Press, 1952).
11 The most detailed and authoritative volume on the classic learning theories is Ernest R. Hilgard, *Theories of Learning*, 2nd edn (New York: Appleton-Century-Crofts, 1956).
12 Alan Newell and Herbert A. Simon, *Human Problem Solving* (Englewood, NJ: Prentice Hall, 1972); Jerome Bruner, Jacqueline Goodnow, and George A. Austin, *A Study of Thinking* (New York: Wiley, 1956); George A. Miller, Eugene Galanter, and Karl Pribram, *Plans and the Structure of Behavior* (New York: Holt, Rinehart, and Winston, 1960).

13 B. F. Skinner, *Verbal Behavior* (Cambridge, MA: Harvard University Press, 1947). Chomsky's structuralist-mentalist views were first published in his *Syntactic Structures* (The Hague: Mouton, 1957). His frontal attack on Skinner's *Verbal Behavior* (in *Language* 35 [1959]: 26–34) only two years later came as a rather unexpected, though scarcely a conceptual, surprise.

CHAPTER 21

CULTURE, MIND, AND NARRATIVE

Enfance, Written especially for the present volume,
The original article is in French

How does a *culture*, the seeming ordinariness of everyday life around us, manage to *shape* our minds in such a way that we become "typical" Danes or Frenchmen, or for that matter, "typical" professors or bank managers? It is a very ancient question, of course. Yet the answers that have been forthcoming have, in the main, been too general to satisfy. Yes of course, child rearing matters, and yes of course, so do such things as social class. But do such generalities help us understand how people's minds come, somehow, to reflect the puzzling everydayness of life, whatever the culture. That is what I want to concern myself with: culture as it affects our everyday ways of *thinking about* life.

I want to argue that one of the principal ways in which our minds are shaped to daily life is through the stories we tell and listen to – whether truth or fiction. We learn our culture principally through the stories that circulate within its bounds.

So perhaps we should begin by asking what's involved in *learning* a culture. Surely it's not like learning a national anthems, once for all and by heart. Nor do we learn our culture's ways as we learn geometry, everything deriving, theorem-like, from a few underlying generative axioms. And certainly we don't learn its ways as anthropologists do – driven to discover how everything, seemingly, relates systematically to everything else.

Cultures, rather, are clever, makeshift, opportunistic systems, systems of loosely related beliefs and practices that are often in conflict with each other. Indeed, if they are to survive, therefore, cultures must provide their members not only with beliefs and practices, however discordant they may be, but must provide them as well with ways of coming to terms with these discordances, exceptions, contradictions. Western cultures, for example, teach us that we should try selflessly to help each other, but at the same time urge us to look after our own self-interest. To be sure, we have institutions for dealing with such conflicts, like our legal systems and our courts of law, but mostly we manage without recourse to such last-ditch institutions. We seem, indeed, to develop informal means, notable sensitivities for coping with such conflicts without having recourse to lawyers and judges. How do we come by these sensitivities, these informal means?

One of the major ways in which to do so, I shall argue, is through the everyday use of the story form, a medium for depicting *and* for resolving the inevitable clash between the conventionally expected and the seemingly unexpected, even the forbidden. Take not story-telling for granted as idle local chatter. Humble though it may be, we could not get on without it. That is what I want to talk about today.

But could this be, given that stories are so *particular*, so *local*. But let me argue that culture itself, in the words of the gifted anthropologist, Clifford Geertz, is *always local*. Nobody ever lives in the whole of it. Even when we invoke culture-wide generalities to explain our acts, we must justify and live them out on the local scene. To use Pierre Bourdieu's expression, we each shelter ourselves in a restricted *habitus* – as waiters, lawyers, mothers, New Yorkers, fruit-stand operators, prostitutes, professors, or some combination thereof. Yet we manage to get on reasonably well within the culture at large, and with surprising ease – even two Danes, one born and bred in bustling Copenhagen, the other in the quiet rural countryside up around Skagen. Of course, they both speak Danish. But that's surely not enough. So what is it then that creates this cultural commonality; this mutual recognizability?

One crucial feature of it is that people within a culture feel that they "know" each others' minds better than they know the minds of others not in the culture – what in current technical lingo is called *intersubjectivity* – "I know that you know that I know ... " Indeed, such intersubjective sharing is probably a *sine qua non* for the very existence of human cultures. For no species on the face of the Earth save *Homo sapiens* has this gift. It's what makes it possible for us to imitate, instruct, and collaborate with each other, this sense that we know what the other is thinking or feeling. Indeed, this gift may actually depend, and certainly relates to our irresistible tendency to *understand our social world by couching it in narrative terms*. For when we "enter" other Minds, we do so through the instrument of narrative.

Of course, we can't *really* "read" others' minds directly, save perhaps in some primitive empathic way. We do so guided by a virtually innate predisposition to see things in a narrative form. Let me lean on the brilliant literary theorist, Kenneth Burke, to make this clearer.

Stories are based upon an irresistible five-fold or "Pentad" structure. There is an *Agent* who performs some *Action* that has some *Goal* as well as somebody who is its *Recipient*. It all takes place in some local *Setting*. Agent, Action, Goal, Recipient, Setting. These, interestingly, correspond to what philosophers refer to as the universal "arguments of action" – action's underlying universal logic, or as I would put it, its underlying psychological frame. But to make a story requires some discernible *lack of fit* between those elements. An *Agent*'s *Action* is inappropriate to a particular *Setting*. Or the *Action* is ineffective for achieving an intended *Goal*. Or the *Recipient* of the *Action* doesn't belong in this *Setting*. Burke calls this misfit *Trouble*, and for him *Trouble* is the "engine of narrative." *Trouble* is when the ordinary meets the unexpected, which is what life is like much of the time in any culture. It is the narrative form, then, that provides us with the means of framing the surprises and conflicts that can arise in *any* particular culture. And, of course, the actual *content* of the elements of the Pentad will vary from culture to culture, as will the nature of the Trouble created by their discordance.

Claude Levi-Strauss provides us with some useful guidance on this matter. Cultures are sustained, he argues, not so much by a communally shared *Weltanschauung* but, rather, by conventionalized exchange systems, systems for exchanging goods and services, marriage mates, esteem, and information. It is not necessary for everybody within a culture to "know" how the entire system works as a whole. All they need is local knowledge. A culture is made up of and sustained by locally connecting exchange practices.

But given the multiple and often conflicting exchange tasks that any culture must cope with, cultures rarely function smoothly, effortlessly, univocally, plagued as they are by conflicting expectations and irresoluble uncertainties. Who anywhere knows how to deal calmly and concurrently with love, power, and esteem? Living in a culture requires not only knowing what's *conventionally* expected, but having some sense of the unexpected *troubles* that the conventional can produce.

And now at last we can come directly to the *functions* of narrative, and why it is in effect universal. It is precisely narrative's function to instantiate and localize what is conventionally expected in a culture, *and* also to illustrate the troubles and perils that the conventionally expected may produce. I shall argue that story telling – fictional and "real" alike – is every culture's way of alerting it's members to just such vicissitudes.

Not surprising, then, that story telling is culturally universal. Nor is it surprising that the narrative gift comes to us "naturally," perhaps even innately, permitting even children to learn of the possible and its risks early in life. Nobody, indeed, has to be taught to tell or understand stories. Children who cannot, as with severe Asperger's syndrome or autism, are simply unable to enter the culture (Baron-Cohen, 1993).

So what, then, *is* a story? What do we mean by narrative?

A story, any story, starts by presuming the existence of the ordinary and conventional in some world. This is what we call a story's *initial canonical state*, a presumption or recital of some stable ordinariness to which our customary habits of mind are already tuned. Take this story, constructed "from my own experience."

> Some days ago, my wife said we needed some really good butter, for she wanted to make one of her crepe dishes for dinner that evening. I said I'd pick some up at our neighborhood grocer's on my way home from the Law School at the end of the day.

There's the start: ordinary, customary, familiar, local: the *canonical opening*.

But narrative, please note, requires that this ordinariness be upset – the story's *peripeteia*, as it's called:

> But when I got to the grocer's on my way home from work, I found the place (usually bustling) absolutely stock-still, everybody looking as if frozen in place. "What's going on?" I asked Florence, the women who looks after the check-out counter. "There's just been a robbery here, two guys with guns. They emptied my cash register just now, just before you walked in. And they just left through the back door. I'm still shaking all over."

That's the second stage. *Peripeteia* is Aristotle's term in the *Poetics* for violations of the customary or expected, literally "adventure" in classic Greek.

Next in narrative, is the *action*: efforts to undo the peripeteia, to restore or revise the canonical state of things.

> So I said to her, "It's odd, isn't it. A robbery in *this* neighborhood, with Gristede's practically across the street from our NYU Institute of Mathematics. In the nearly twenty years I've lived here, nothing like this has ever happened before. And with our Greenwich Village crime rate way down? What's going on?"

Was I trying to produce a resolution by dismissing the likelihood of another robbery – *resolution* is the fourth component of a story, what brings the story's action to a conclusive end.

Stories may also have a *coda*, a commentary or "lesson," as in an Aesop fable with its "A stitch in time saves nine." That's out of fashion nowadays. Nonetheless, my story has one.

> Florence, the cash-register girl said, "I wonder whether things are changing around here." I said I wondered too and that maybe Gristede's should report the robbery not only to the New York police in our precinct but to the NYU police as well. When I left, though, I realized as I was walking out that I'd completely forgotten to buy the butter! I was embarrassed about going back, lest Florence think my calming talk was bogus.

Very well, then: an initial canon, the peripeteia, the action, the resolution, the implied or explicit coda – the itinerary of a typical story. But while these story segments may be cross-culturally universal, the form they take will reflect the ways of the culture in which they are situated. And indeed, they will inevitably reflect the *perspective of the narrator*, however much the conventions of story telling (at least in the West) try to make stories seem as if they were autochthonous, free standing, "just the facts." Just the facts?

Look at my version of "what happened": a neighborhood store in a university neighborhood across the street from an Institute of Mathematics; and me, the narrator, a self-revealed rather domesticated university professor whose wife is about to prepare a *crepe Suzette*. Florence, the cash-register lady, would have told it from the perspective of a working-class store clerk whose life had been threatened by the loaded gun of somebody out to exploit her unprotected livelihood. She was inside the story's action; I was outside.

But our stories, we say, need to "seem" true in order to be believable – to exhibit *verisimilitude*, as we say. But what makes a story *seem* true is its fit to cultural expectations. Even when it is fiction, far-out fiction. For the function of fiction is to explore the kinship of the possible to the already culturally familiar. And language, with its tropes and metaphors, permit us to do so – to explore the putatively customary and ordinary in an imaginary setting and, at the same time, to see the troubles that bedevil it even in imagination. A culture's fiction is its way of exploring its possible limits – which, of course, exposes the professional story-teller to the wrath of dictators and tyrants. So a culture's stories reflect not only the comforts of conformity, but also its glimmerings of possibility. So stories can be dangerous stuff – and, indeed, are recognized as such by most systems of law that contain such categories, as "slander," "fraud," "defamation of character," and the like.

But narrative *fiction* too is risky, no matter in which culture "make-believe" stories are told. They too must reflect the ordinary conventionalities and the ordinary troubles of a culture, else they are in danger of cultural condemnation. And perhaps it is in recognition of this peril that skilled story tellers fall back on displacement, metaphor, feigned fantasy, and, as we have come to call it, "the art of the novel."

So let me close with a masterful story to illustrate more vividly the metaphoric evasions of great literary stories. And I'll use Joseph Conrad's masterful *The Secret Sharer* as an example.

> The young captain in the tale is on his very first ship's command, perhaps not yet very sure of himself. His ship is anchored off a foreign tropical coast, fully loaded, and ready to return home. Our young captain has decided to depart at dawn the next morning. To assure that his crew gets a good night's sleep, he decides that he alone will stand the night watch at anchor.

That's the canonical opener, familiar enough though far off. Then the peripeteia:

> Walking the deck the young captain notices a boarding ladder has been carelessly left hanging over the ship's side and he goes routinely to pull it up. Whereupon he discovers there is somebody in the water below hanging on to the ladder's foot, a stranger. The young captain bids the stranger come aboard (the stranger's name is Leggatt, we presently learn).
>
> Leggatt, it turns out, had jumped overboard from another ship, the *Sephora*, anchored a kilometer off. He had escaped from its brig where he'd been imprisoned for having killed a shipmate during a storm, perhaps justifiably and inadvertently in the line of duty. The young captain, moved, takes Leggatt to his own quarters to hide him, planning to let him over the side unnoticed when his ship departs at dawn.

And now to the *resolution*.

> When dawn comes, ship's anchor up and sails set, the young captain steers his ship daringly close in on shore better for Leggatt to swim to safety unnoticed. Into the water he goes – a "secret sharer" and "proud swimmer," as the young captain calls out to him. But the early morning breeze is so light and fickle close in on shore that the ship is in danger of losing way and drifting disastrously ashore.
>
> What finally enables the young captain to tell whether his ship is still under way or Leggatt's hat floating motionless in the water. Leggatt, it seems, had forgotten to take it with him when he slipped overboard, but the young captain had thrown it to him hoping it would shield him from the tropic sun. Now, floating motionless in the water, it could reveal whether the ship was moving. Disaster is averted, and the "secret sharer" is ashore.
>
> Resolution!

The coda is left to the reader. Why is Leggatt a *secret* sharer? What's being *shared*? Why *hide* Leggatt? Is it his (possibly) unjust accusation of murder? Why all this on the young captain's *first* command? Why the merciful hat in the water? In a word, with which cultural conventions is Conrad concerned, and against which of its putative troubles is he warning us? I first read "The Secret Sharer" when I was fourteen or so – a great but somewhat disturbing adventure tale, I thought then. I confess I assign it now – along with Sophocles' *Antigone* and Conrad's *Billy Budd* – to advanced law students concerned with the jurisprudence of "fair" punishment. My reason for doing so is that I want them to be more conscious of the ways in which the story form, narrative, can shape their minds to the ways in which the conventional ordinarinesses of culture (legal culture in this instance) are bedeviled by often irreconcilable troubles and ambiguities.

Isn't that why we all read stories, boy and girl, man and woman? That's how we learn a culture's rich particularities.

For the benefit of my more psychological colleagues, I want to offer this short addendum on perspective in narrative – particularly with regard to what is now called the "inward turn" in narrative, usually dated as beginning in mid-nineteenth century with the emergence of the modern novel, but surely present even in Sophocles' *Antigone*.

A story needs a narrator and, as we noted in my "grocery robbery" tale, narrators vary in their perspective. You can tell a story from "outside" or "inside" – concentrating on what presumably "happened" or on what was going on in the minds of the story's protagonists. With respect to the first, there are ready-made conventions that allow the narrator virtually to disappear, to make it seem as though the Agent, Action, Recipient, Goal, Setting, and Trouble were simply *there*, needing only a report from the outside – naive realism, as philosophers would call it. It has deep and ancient roots in ancient mythology and folk tales about which Victor Turner has written brilliantly (xxxx).

Telling stories from the inside usually follows one of two alternative routes. One goes inward by concentrating upon the inherent contradiction in the *events recounted* – like the young captain finding Leggatt at the foot of the ladder, or finally letting him escape ashore though at the risk of losing control of his ship. Or, indeed, the famous hat floating still in the water. Characters act out events, and through their acts we know them, not through exposure of their inner lives. The narrator is presumably telling only what happened.

The alternative route of the inner turn centers on subjectivity itself, recounting the inner states of the protagonists along with such events as are needed to frame these inner states. The inner turn requires a much more percipient, virtually omniscient narrator.

The first inward turn is surely as ancient as Greek drama. The second is a reflection of a changing culture in mid-19th century Europe, a culture of protest against the ordinary that produced not only the modern novel but Sigmund Freud, new theater, and the art of Picasso, Mondrian, and Matisse. But while the changing culture initially provoked the inward turn toward subjectivity in the modern novel, it has been the modern novel that then further fostered the culture's inward turn. Or as the literary joke has it, Dublin produced Joyce, but then Joyce produced Dublin.

A second addendum

My colleague Anthony Amsterdam and I taught a seminar last year on how peoples, ancient and modern, balance the demands of state security on the one hand with individual civil rights on the other. For example, our students read two versions of *Antigone*, a tale of the bitter struggle between King Creon and Antigone, whether her slaughtered brother Polynices, having rebelled against the King, should be given proper burial or left to the crows and dogs in the market-place where he lay. One version was Sophocles' original, the other the daring 1943 version by the Frenchman, Jean Anhouil, produced and performed in Paris during the German occupation. Anhouil's piece is subtly but forcefully slanted toward the abuses of dictatorship. Sophocles' *Antigone* is, well, Sophocles on *la condition humaine*.

The students also read briefs in one of the then pending American "enemy combatant" detention cases, the one of two years ago, *Hamdi v. Rumsfeld*, in which the US Supreme Court finally denied any President the right to imprison an American citizen, to deny him trial, and to hold him indefinitely incommunicado without right to legal counsel – even on charges of his being an "enemy combatant." It was "real life," a case affecting, indeed, the future of democracy in America.

The impact on our students was remarkable! Sophocles and Jean Anouihl provided a sense of possible worlds that, of course, was stunning, complex, tragic. Who indeed has the right to forbid a fellow being the ultimate dignity of burial, and on what grounds? As for the Federal appellate briefs, read after the two *Antigones*: who indeed, and in what kind of state, has the right to imprison even a suspected "enemy combatant" without his having a right to trial? The law briefs in

Hamdi were being read not just as "official documents" (which, of course, they are) but as the narratives that they were. And so too the *Antigones* (to which we returned after *Hamdi*): they were no long "just" plays for the theater, but possible worlds.

In some striking way, great fiction, known to be fiction, and gripping real life drama, known to be real life, came to interpenetrate each other. The students were gripped, but so were we, their presumed teachers. It is not that we brought the culture of ancient Greece or of war-beleaguered France to American university students. That's silly. What we did, rather, is to make them mindful of how the customary and ordinary – the culturally obvious and acceptable – is forever likely to generate troubles and obscurities. It is in the nature of human culture that it be so. What we all do for each other is to keep telling our stories. That is how we live with the ordinary and its setbacks.

A final addendum

I want to end, finally, with a classic Italian folk-tale, a very short one, "Those Stubborn Souls, the Biellese." The people around Biella are famous for their independent-mindedness. The story is about how Biellese culture expressed itself in the mind of a Biellese farmer – and about his subsequent troubles with God, the Creator.

> A farmer was on his way down to Biella one day. The weather was so stormy that it was next to impossible to get over the roads. But the farmer had important business and pushed onward in the face of the driving rain.
>
> He met an old man who said to him, "A good day to you! Where are you going, my good man, in such haste?"
>
> "To Biella," answered the farmer, without slowing down.
>
> "You might at least say, 'God willing'."
>
> The farmer stopped, looked the old man in the eye, and snapped, "God willing, I'm on my way to Biella. But even if God isn't willing, I still have to go there all the same."
>
> Now the old man happened to be the Lord. "In that case you'll go to Biella in seven years," he said. "In the meantime, jump into this swamp and stay there for seven years."
>
> Suddenly the farmer changed into a frog and jumped into the swamp.
>
> Seven years went by. The farmer came out of the swamp, turned back into a man, clapped his hat on his head, and continued on his way to market.
>
> After a short time he met the old man again. "And where are you going, my good man?"
>
> "To Biella."
>
> "You might say, 'God willing.'"
>
> "If God wills it, fine. If not, I know the consequences and can now go into the swamp unassisted." Not for the life of him would he say one word more.

I have been to Biella. They still tell the story. They are still as Biellese as ever.

INDEX